# Secrets of the iPod and iTunes

## Fifth Edition

Christopher Breen

# Secrets of the iPod and iTunes, Fifth Edition

Christopher Breen

TechTV Press is published in association with Peachpit, a division of Pearson Technology Group.

Peachpit
1249 Eighth Street
Berkeley, CA 94710
510/524-2178
800/283-9444
510/524-2221 (fax)
Find us on the World Wide Web at: www.peachpit.com and
www.g4techtv.com

Copyright © 2005 by Christopher Breen

Editor: Nancy Peterson
Production Coordinator: Simmy Cover
Copyeditor: Kathy Simpson
Compositors: Rick Gordon, Emerald Valley Graphics; Deborah Roberti, Espresso Graphics
Indexer: Joy Dean Lee
Cover Design: Aren Howell
Cover Illustration: Alan Clements
Interior Design: Kim Scott

## Notice of Rights

All rights reserved. No part of this book may be reproduced or transmitted in any form by any means, electronic, mechanical, photocopying, recording, or otherwise, without the prior written permission of the publisher. For information on getting permission for reprints and excerpts, contact permissions@peachpit.com.

## Notice of Liability

The information in this book is distributed on an "As Is" basis, without warranty. While every precaution has been taken in the preparation of the book, neither the author nor Peachpit Press, shall have any liability to any person or entity with respect to any loss or damage caused or alleged to be caused directly or indirectly by the instructions contained in this book or by the computer software and hardware products described in it.

## Trademarks

Apple, iPod, iTunes, and Mac are trademarks of Apple Computer, Inc., registered in the U.S. and other countries. Throughout this book, trademarks are used. Rather than put a trademark symbol in every occurrence of a trademarked name, we state that we are using the names in an editorial fashion only and to the benefit of the trademark owner with no intention of infringement of the trademark. No such use, or the use of any trade name is intended to convey endorsement or other affiliation with this book.

ISBN 0-321-30459-4

9 8 7 6 5 4 3 2 1

Printed and bound in the United States of America.

*To my own little iBreen, Addie.*

# Acknowledgments

This book wouldn't be in your hands if not for the hard work and care of the following individuals.

At Peachpit Press: My editor and pal, Nancy Peterson (who, in addition to making sense of my nonsense, laughs at my goat jokes); Cliff Colby (who edited a fair chunk of the first edition and proffered the original idea for an iPod book); Marjorie Baer (who gave the green light for the first edition); Rebecca Ross (who handled the contract negotiations with such aplomb); Nancy Ruenzel (Peachpit's publisher, who signed off on yet another go-round of this book and was good enough to break her iPod and, thus, provide me with another story to tell in Chapter 9); Kathy Simpson (who copyedited all five editions of the book and made some brilliant catches); Simmy Cover (who stepped in to coordinate production of the book); Kim Lombardi (who is a book-promoting machine); Kelly Ryer (iPod pioneer who asked all the right questions); and Rick Gordon for his expertise in laying out the book's pages.

At home: My wife, Claire, who once again kept the other parts of our lives together while I applied nose to grindstone in the basement; and the boys of System 9 for being such groovy cats.

Abroad: Useful Apple folks include Stan Ng, the iPod product manager; and Keri Walker, Queen of Review Units, who not only saw to it that I received the iPod *test units* I needed, but also was very forgiving when, a couple of years ago, I admitted to her that I'd intentionally destroyed one of her beta units. Leo Laporte for helping me shamelessly plug this book on TechTV's now-deceased airwaves. I must also tip my fedora to the many vendors who supplied the swag...er, test units of the products mentioned in these pages: Altec Lansing, Belkin, Dr. Bott, Future Sonics, Griffin Technology, Now Software, Joe Masters (EphPod), Mediafour, Red Chair Software, SiK Inc., Waterfield Designs, Incase, Design Group, and XtremeMac. Sam Braff for coming through in a pinch. My partners in crime at PlaylistMag.com: Dan Frakes, Jason Snell, and Rick LePage. Finally, of course, the designers behind the iPod and iTunes. They just get better and better!

# Table of Contents

Introduction . . . . . . . . . . . . . . . . . . . . . . . . . . . . . . . . . . . . . . . . . . . . . . . . . xi

**Chapter 1**  Contents, Controls, and Interface    1

Contents: Original iPod (including the iPod Special Edition: U2) . . . . 2
    The CD Package . . . . . . . . . . . . . . . . . . . . . . . . . . . . . . . . . . . . . . . . 2
    The Earbuds . . . . . . . . . . . . . . . . . . . . . . . . . . . . . . . . . . . . . . . . . . 5
    The FireWire Cable, USB 2.0 Cable, and Power Adapter . . . . . . . . . . 6
    The iPod Dock . . . . . . . . . . . . . . . . . . . . . . . . . . . . . . . . . . . . . . . . . 8
    The iPod . . . . . . . . . . . . . . . . . . . . . . . . . . . . . . . . . . . . . . . . . . . . . 9
Contents: iPod mini . . . . . . . . . . . . . . . . . . . . . . . . . . . . . . . . . . . . . . 11
    The CD Package . . . . . . . . . . . . . . . . . . . . . . . . . . . . . . . . . . . . . . 11
    The Cables, Adapters, and Earbuds . . . . . . . . . . . . . . . . . . . . . . . . 11
    The Belt Clip . . . . . . . . . . . . . . . . . . . . . . . . . . . . . . . . . . . . . . . . . 12
    What's Missing . . . . . . . . . . . . . . . . . . . . . . . . . . . . . . . . . . . . . . . 12
Contents: iPod Photo . . . . . . . . . . . . . . . . . . . . . . . . . . . . . . . . . . . . . 13
    The A/V Cable . . . . . . . . . . . . . . . . . . . . . . . . . . . . . . . . . . . . . . . . 13
    iPod Photo Dock . . . . . . . . . . . . . . . . . . . . . . . . . . . . . . . . . . . . . . 14
    Carrying Case . . . . . . . . . . . . . . . . . . . . . . . . . . . . . . . . . . . . . . . . 14
    Capacity . . . . . . . . . . . . . . . . . . . . . . . . . . . . . . . . . . . . . . . . . . . . 14
    Skip Protection . . . . . . . . . . . . . . . . . . . . . . . . . . . . . . . . . . . . . . . 15
    Supported Audio Formats . . . . . . . . . . . . . . . . . . . . . . . . . . . . . . . 17
Controls . . . . . . . . . . . . . . . . . . . . . . . . . . . . . . . . . . . . . . . . . . . . . . . 18
    On the Face of It . . . . . . . . . . . . . . . . . . . . . . . . . . . . . . . . . . . . . . 19
    Up Top (Early iPods) . . . . . . . . . . . . . . . . . . . . . . . . . . . . . . . . . . . 25
    Top and Bottom (Dock-connector iPods) . . . . . . . . . . . . . . . . . . . . 26
Interface . . . . . . . . . . . . . . . . . . . . . . . . . . . . . . . . . . . . . . . . . . . . . . 28
    Main Screen . . . . . . . . . . . . . . . . . . . . . . . . . . . . . . . . . . . . . . . . . 28
    Music (Fourth-generation iPods and iPod Photo Only) . . . . . . . . . 29
    Browse (Not Found on Fourth-generation iPods and
        iPod Photo) . . . . . . . . . . . . . . . . . . . . . . . . . . . . . . . . . . . . . . . 34
    Photos (iPod Photo only) . . . . . . . . . . . . . . . . . . . . . . . . . . . . . . . . 38
    Extras . . . . . . . . . . . . . . . . . . . . . . . . . . . . . . . . . . . . . . . . . . . . . . 38
    Settings . . . . . . . . . . . . . . . . . . . . . . . . . . . . . . . . . . . . . . . . . . . . 47
    Shuffle Songs (Fourth-generation iPods and iPod Photo Only) . . . . 55

## Chapter 2  Managing Music with iTunes                57

iTunes, uTunes, We All Croon for iTunes . . . . . . . . . . . . . . . . . . . . . . . . 58
iTunes Requirements . . . . . . . . . . . . . . . . . . . . . . . . . . . . . . . . . . . . . . . 60
Ripping a CD . . . . . . . . . . . . . . . . . . . . . . . . . . . . . . . . . . . . . . . . . . . . . 61
Songs from the Web . . . . . . . . . . . . . . . . . . . . . . . . . . . . . . . . . . . . . . . 68
    Managing File Types . . . . . . . . . . . . . . . . . . . . . . . . . . . . . . . . . . . . 70
    Moving Music into iTunes . . . . . . . . . . . . . . . . . . . . . . . . . . . . . . . 75
Creating and Configuring a Playlist . . . . . . . . . . . . . . . . . . . . . . . . . . . 77
    Standard Playlists . . . . . . . . . . . . . . . . . . . . . . . . . . . . . . . . . . . . . . 77
    Playlist from Selection . . . . . . . . . . . . . . . . . . . . . . . . . . . . . . . . . . 78
    Smart Playlists . . . . . . . . . . . . . . . . . . . . . . . . . . . . . . . . . . . . . . . . 79
Moving Music to the iPod . . . . . . . . . . . . . . . . . . . . . . . . . . . . . . . . . . 87
    The Music Tab . . . . . . . . . . . . . . . . . . . . . . . . . . . . . . . . . . . . . . . . 89
    The General Tab . . . . . . . . . . . . . . . . . . . . . . . . . . . . . . . . . . . . . . 93
Voice Recordings and iTunes . . . . . . . . . . . . . . . . . . . . . . . . . . . . . . . . 96
The Get Info Window . . . . . . . . . . . . . . . . . . . . . . . . . . . . . . . . . . . . . 96
    Sound Check . . . . . . . . . . . . . . . . . . . . . . . . . . . . . . . . . . . . . . . . . 99
Other iTunes Tricks . . . . . . . . . . . . . . . . . . . . . . . . . . . . . . . . . . . . . . 101

## Chapter 3  Picture Perfect: iPod Photo              105

A New iPod or No? . . . . . . . . . . . . . . . . . . . . . . . . . . . . . . . . . . . . . . . 106
    Some of the Same . . . . . . . . . . . . . . . . . . . . . . . . . . . . . . . . . . . . 106
    Expectations vs. Reality . . . . . . . . . . . . . . . . . . . . . . . . . . . . . . . . 106
    It Comes in Colors . . . . . . . . . . . . . . . . . . . . . . . . . . . . . . . . . . . 107
    Television Network . . . . . . . . . . . . . . . . . . . . . . . . . . . . . . . . . . 108
Porting Pictures . . . . . . . . . . . . . . . . . . . . . . . . . . . . . . . . . . . . . . . . . 109
    iTunes Delivers . . . . . . . . . . . . . . . . . . . . . . . . . . . . . . . . . . . . . 109
Viewing Pictures . . . . . . . . . . . . . . . . . . . . . . . . . . . . . . . . . . . . . . . . 115
Slipping into a Slideshow . . . . . . . . . . . . . . . . . . . . . . . . . . . . . . . . . . 117
    Slideshow Settings . . . . . . . . . . . . . . . . . . . . . . . . . . . . . . . . . . . 117
    Projecting Pictures . . . . . . . . . . . . . . . . . . . . . . . . . . . . . . . . . . . 120

## Chapter 4  The iTunes Music Store                  123

The One-stop Shop . . . . . . . . . . . . . . . . . . . . . . . . . . . . . . . . . . . . . . 125
Prepare to Shop . . . . . . . . . . . . . . . . . . . . . . . . . . . . . . . . . . . . . . . . . 128
    What You Need . . . . . . . . . . . . . . . . . . . . . . . . . . . . . . . . . . . . . 128
    Signing On . . . . . . . . . . . . . . . . . . . . . . . . . . . . . . . . . . . . . . . . . 131

Tooling Around ..................................................... 134
    Navigating The Store's Floors ............................. 135
    Audio Appetizers: Previewing Songs ...................... 162
    Learning About New Music ................................ 164
Getting the Goods ................................................. 164
    The Pick-and-pay Method ................................. 164
    The Shopping-cart Method ................................ 167
Playing with Your Purchases ..................................... 170
    Play It ..................................................... 170
    Burn It .................................................... 173
Beyond The Store: Audible.com ................................. 174
    Downloading and Playing Audible.com Files (Macintosh) ..... 175
    Downloading and Playing Audible.com Files (Windows) ...... 176
    Audiobooks and Audible.com Tips ......................... 177
Put It on Your iPod .............................................. 178
    Requirements ............................................. 178
    Moving Music to Your iPod ............................... 179
Troubleshooting The Store ...................................... 181

# Chapter 5  Of iPods and PCs                                    185

Configuring Your PC .............................................. 187
    Making the Connection: Hardware ......................... 188
    Completing the Connection: Software ..................... 190
iPod for Windows Software ...................................... 193
    Installing the iPod Software .............................. 193
Musicmatch Jukebox ............................................. 196
    Musicmatch Jukebox Installation .......................... 197
    The iPod Manager ........................................ 199
    Musicmatch Jukebox Overview ............................ 200
    Ripping a CD ............................................. 202
    Moving Music into Musicmatch Jukebox ................... 203
    Creating and Configuring a Playlist ....................... 205
    Moving Music to the iPod ................................ 207
    Editing Track Tags ........................................ 210
    Other Musicmatch Jukebox Tricks ......................... 212
Software Alternatives ............................................ 214
    XPlay 2 ................................................... 214
    Anapod Explorer .......................................... 223
    EphPod 2 ................................................. 232

## Chapter 6  The Removable Drive            243

FireWire to Go ................................................... 244
    Installing the Mac OS on Your iPod ......................... 247
    Additional Data Storage .................................... 257
The Hidden Revealed: Song Storage on the iPod ................. 260
    Music Sharing: Right or Wrong? ............................. 261
    Moving Music .............................................. 263

## Chapter 7  Making iContact                277

Getting Addressed ............................................. 278
    First on the Block: iPod Organizer .......................... 278
    Viva vCard ................................................. 284
Working with Contacts ........................................ 286
    The Manual Method: Macintosh ............................. 286
    The Manual Method: Windows .............................. 289
    The Automated Method: Macintosh ......................... 293
    The Automated Method: Windows .......................... 302
    Removing Contacts from Your iPod ......................... 309
Beyond Addresses ............................................. 310
    Hacking a .vcf File ......................................... 311
    Entering Data Via an Email Client or Contact Manager ....... 312
    Additional Utilities of Interest .............................. 313
Notes ......................................................... 317
    The Truth about Tags ...................................... 318
    The Missing Links .......................................... 319
    Say It with a Song ......................................... 320
    Locking It Down ........................................... 321
    Notes Tools ................................................ 322

## Chapter 8  Make a Date                    327

Va-va-va-vCal ................................................. 328
    A Little History ............................................ 328
    Anatomy of a vCal File ..................................... 328
Working with Calendars ....................................... 330
    Creating Calendars ......................................... 331
    Manually Transferring Calendars to the iPod ................ 344
    Manually Removing Calendars from the iPod ................ 346
    Automatically Transferring Calendars to the iPod ............ 347

## Chapter 9  Accessories                                         351

   The Clip-on iPod .................................................353
      What to Look For .............................................354
      On the Cases .................................................355
   Adaptive Technology ............................................362
      iPod to Computer ............................................363
      iPod to Home Stereo .........................................363
      iPod to Hard-wired Computer Speakers .......................364
      iPod to Two Headphones ....................................364
      iPod to Car Stereo ...........................................365
   Power to the People .............................................372
      iPod Power Adapter .........................................372
      PocketDock .................................................372
      World Travel Adapter Kit .....................................373
      FireJuice ....................................................374
      Auto Charger ................................................374
      Backup Batteries .............................................377
      HotWire .....................................................378
   The Ears Have It .................................................378
      Earbuds .....................................................379
      Neckband Headphones ......................................380
      Open-air Headphones .......................................381
      Closed Headphones .........................................381
   Miscellanea .....................................................382
      Belkin Voice Recorder and Universal Microphone Adapter ......382
      iTalk ........................................................383
      Media Reader for iPod and Digital Camera Link for iPod
          w/ Dock Connector .......................................385
      iPod Remote ................................................390
      iPod Dock/iPod mini Dock ...................................390
      NaviPod Wireless Remote ....................................391
      Altec Lansing inMotion Speakers .............................392
      JBL On Stage ................................................393
      Bose SoundDock .............................................394
      Tivoli Audio iPAL ............................................395
      FMXtra ......................................................395
      Groove Bag Triplet and Tote Speaker Purses ...................396
      PowerMate ..................................................397
      AirPort Express ..............................................398
      The Personalized iPod .......................................399

## Chapter 10  Troubleshooting Your iPod  401

Problems and Solutions . . . . . . . . . . . . . . . . . . . . . . . . . . . . . . . . . . . . . . . . . . 402
    The Missing iPod . . . . . . . . . . . . . . . . . . . . . . . . . . . . . . . . . . . . . . . . . . 402
    The Confused iPod . . . . . . . . . . . . . . . . . . . . . . . . . . . . . . . . . . . . . . . . 403
    The Really Confused iPod . . . . . . . . . . . . . . . . . . . . . . . . . . . . . . . . . . 412
    The Ultra-really Confused iPod . . . . . . . . . . . . . . . . . . . . . . . . . . . . . 414
    The Far-too-quiet European iPod . . . . . . . . . . . . . . . . . . . . . . . . . . . . 416
    The Broken iPod . . . . . . . . . . . . . . . . . . . . . . . . . . . . . . . . . . . . . . . . . . 417
    The Frozen iPod . . . . . . . . . . . . . . . . . . . . . . . . . . . . . . . . . . . . . . . . . . 418
Inside the First- and Second-generation iPods . . . . . . . . . . . . . . . . . . . 428
    Beneath the Cover . . . . . . . . . . . . . . . . . . . . . . . . . . . . . . . . . . . . . . . . 428
    It's What's Inside That Counts: Disassembling
        the First-generation iPod . . . . . . . . . . . . . . . . . . . . . . . . . . . . . . 430
Opening the Third-generation iPod . . . . . . . . . . . . . . . . . . . . . . . . . . . . . 435
    The Hard Drive . . . . . . . . . . . . . . . . . . . . . . . . . . . . . . . . . . . . . . . . . . . 435
    The Battery . . . . . . . . . . . . . . . . . . . . . . . . . . . . . . . . . . . . . . . . . . . . . . 435
    The Circuit Board . . . . . . . . . . . . . . . . . . . . . . . . . . . . . . . . . . . . . . . . 436
    It's What's Inside That Counts: Disassembling
        the Third-generation iPod . . . . . . . . . . . . . . . . . . . . . . . . . . . . . . 437
Opening the iPod mini . . . . . . . . . . . . . . . . . . . . . . . . . . . . . . . . . . . . . . . . 440
    The Hard Drive . . . . . . . . . . . . . . . . . . . . . . . . . . . . . . . . . . . . . . . . . . . 440
    The Battery . . . . . . . . . . . . . . . . . . . . . . . . . . . . . . . . . . . . . . . . . . . . . . 440
    The Circuit Board . . . . . . . . . . . . . . . . . . . . . . . . . . . . . . . . . . . . . . . . 442
    It's What's Inside That Counts: Disassembling
        the iPod mini . . . . . . . . . . . . . . . . . . . . . . . . . . . . . . . . . . . . . . . . 443
Thank You . . . . . . . . . . . . . . . . . . . . . . . . . . . . . . . . . . . . . . . . . . . . . . . . . . . 449

*Index* . . . . . . . . . . . . . . . . . . . . . . . . . . . . . . . . . . . . . . . . . . . . . . . . . . . . . . . 451

# Introduction

"Secrets? Of the *iPod and iTunes!?* What secrets could such a simple device and intuitive program possibly harbor? To operate the iPod, you push a button, rotate your thumb around a wheel, and it just works, right? To transfer songs from an audio CD to iTunes, you shove a disc in your computer's media drive and press the Import button. Gee, I can hardly wait to read its companion volume, *Secrets of the Hamilton Beach 4-Slice IntelliToast® Toaster!*"

Our focus-group studies indicate that 1 in 14 have this reaction when they pick up a copy of the book you now hold in your hands.

Yet here I am, back with a completely revised fifth edition of this book. What could be so confounding about Apple's diminutive music player and its music-management application that justifies five editions of a book that purports to reveal their hidden depths? Allow me to answer that question by asking a few of my own.

You're not sure whether to purchase an iPod, iPod Photo, or iPod mini. What exactly is the difference between the three, and is it worth paying more money for the iPod Photo?

Your iPod refuses to start up, displaying a folder icon with an exclamation point. How do you fix it?

Your iPod won't hold a charge. Is it broken?

You have an iPod Photo, a digital camera, and a load of photographs. How can you set up your iPod to show those pictures?

You have a Windows iPod that you'd like to use with your Macintosh. Can you?

Your iPod mini holds just 3.7 GB of data, yet your music library exceeds 8 GB. How can you configure iTunes to fit the most (and the best) of your library on your mini?

How do you configure your iPod to boot your Macintosh?

You really like the Party Shuffle playlist you've created in iTunes. How do you move this playlist to your iPod?

You have an iPod sold in Europe, and *man,* is it quiet. Is there anything you can do to increase its volume?

And speaking of volume, the volume of the tunes on your iPod is all over the map—one song loud, the next quiet, the next just right. Is there anything you can do to make volume consistent from one song to the next?

Apple claims that the iPod can play for up to 8, 10, 12, or 15 hours (depending on which model you have), yet yours poops out after playing only Elvis Costello's first four albums. What can you do to increase battery life?

You've purchased an iPod mini, which supposedly holds 4 GB of data, yet yours shows a capacity of 3.7. Where did the other 0.3 GB go?

How can you move contacts and calendar events from your personal information manager to your iPod?

You'd like to suck up to the boss in the hope of sliding into that junior-manager position, and you know that he's addicted to the iTunes Music Store. How do you arrange to give him a gift certificate from The Store?

How would you go about copying songs from your iPod to your computer?

The answers to these questions (and many, many more) are between the covers of this book. Yes, although the iPod and iTunes may be terrifically intuitive creations, they're also far more flexible (and occasionally perplexing) than their mild-mannered interfaces imply. And that, dear 1-in-14 reader, is why I invite you to explore the many secrets of the iPod and iTunes in this fifth edition.

Disregarding the less-obvious features of the iPod for a moment, what makes the iPod, iPod Photo, and iPod mini so worthy of our attention? There are their weight and size, of course; the iPod is 6.2 ounces and less for the newest models, and smaller than a pinochle deck. The iPod Photo is just .06 inches thicker and .2 ounces heavier than the 40 GB fourth-generation iPod. And the iPod mini weighs in at a scant 3.6 ounces and is the size of a business card. Also, the 60 GB iPod Photo holds 15,000 four-minute songs for a continuous playing time of nearly six *weeks* (or *more* if you follow the tips in this book).

But most impressive of all is the feature I alluded to earlier: the simplicity of the devices. Like so many Apple products before them, the iPods are most astonishing for their elegant design and ease of use. There just aren't more beautiful or intuitive music players available today.

Best of all, the iPods have wonders to behold other than just their capability to pump out a thousand or more toe-tapping tunes.

In these pages, I'll reveal all the iPod's wonders—from managing your music collection to projecting your pictures on a television to keeping your contacts and appointments close at hand. You'll learn about the intimate relationship between the i-siblings—iPod and iTunes—and how to make the most of that relationship. You'll take a tour of Apple's iTunes Music Store and see how to gain the greatest benefit from the music you purchase online. We'll explore the iPod Photo's picture powers and learn how to synchronize images between your computer and this tuneful slideshow player. I'll examine the iPod as a storage device for your computer and show you how to dress up your iPod with the latest accessories. And when you're finished with the outside, I'll take you on a tour of the iPod's innards, scrutinizing what makes this machine tick (and what can keep it from ticking) and offering troubleshooting tips for those times when the music and pictures inexplicably stop.

In short, this smallish tome will cover the iPod from stem to stern.

# iPod, Therefore iAm

Before eyeballing the ins and outs of the iPod, it's worth taking a step back and asking, "Why iPod?"

With all the wondrous devices to which Apple might have devoted its legendary creative power, why create yet another music player? To learn the answer to this question, you must look at a technology that has changed the way we use and share digital media: MP3.

# The MP3 Revolution

In 1987, a German company, Fraunhofer IIS-A, began working on a system for creating digital audio files that consumed little storage space while maintaining much of the original file's quality. Among other things, this work was motivated by the fact that one minute of CD-quality stereo music consumed about 10 MB of storage space—storage space that at the time was very costly. The eventual result of this work was something called the MPEG Audio Layer-3 compression standard, now commonly known as MP3.

This standard uses *perceptual coding* techniques to eliminate audio data that the human ear is unlikely to discern. So efficient is MP3 encoding that you can use it to reduce an audio file's size by a factor of 12 yet maintain most of the sound quality of the original file. Thanks to MP3, a four-minute song that normally would devour 40 MB of hard drive space now weighs in at less than 4 MB.

The availability of more-compact and less-expensive storage media—hard drives and media cards—made MP3 an attractive option for use on home computers and, eventually, portable music players. But the fact that such files were easier to store was only one piece of the puzzle. MP3 really came into its own thanks to the widespread dispersal of a seemingly unrelated technology: broadband Internet access.

In the days when much of the world accessed the Internet with sloth-like modems, downloading a 4 MB file could be an all-night affair. When that file could be downloaded in a minute, the idea of moving high-quality audio files across the Internet became an extremely attractive proposition—particularly among college students who had both lightning-fast, school-supplied access to the Internet and a keen interest in music.

Given that MP3 was a growing concern among such a significant portion of the population, manufacturers of audio devices predictably began seeking ways to incorporate MP3 technology into future products.

# Share and Share Alike

Anyone with the faintest interest in technology has heard of the Napster music-sharing service, through which audio files—largely encoded with MP3—were swapped wholesale across the Internet (much to the chagrin of the recording industry). Music-device manufacturers understood that although those who downloaded MP3 files were pleased enough to play back these files on their computers, many would be even more pleased if they could transport and listen to these files on a portable device.

After the courts determined that such devices were indeed legal—that they were not specifically designed as go-between devices that might aid music piracy, but as a final destination for music files—small MP3 players such as the Rio 600 found their way to market. Regrettably, these players stored less than an hour of music without the addition of expensive media storage cards. (And even with these additional storage cards, such players rarely exceeded two hours' playing time.) Moving MP3 files from the computer to the player over the player's slow serial-port or USB connection could take a long time, and the software required to move files from one device to another was hardly intuitive. Navigating from song to song on these things was a tedious affair, requiring you to page through menu after menu on a tiny screen. Finally, these players cost upward of a couple hundred dollars. Although the technology was interesting, only gearheads with more money than sense were likely to replace their inexpensive portable CD players with one of these devices.

Even with these limitations, portable MP3 players still sold in respectable numbers. But just imagine the kind of sales you could generate if you created a portable music player that successfully worked around the storage, transfer-rate, and navigation problems.

Apple smelled an opportunity.

# iPod, Arise!

On October 23, 2001, Apple held a press conference in Cupertino, California, to announce a new product—the first noncomputer product released by Apple since the ill-fated console gaming system, Pippin, and the first such product produced since Apple co-founder Steve Jobs returned to the company. Web-based rumor sites were rife with speculation about the new device. Would it be a revolutionary personal information manager? An advanced console computing system? The ultimate crock pot?

When Mr. Jobs ended the speculation and revealed the iPod at a press conference, some of those in attendance were disappointed initially. "Sure, it stores a ton of music, offers loads of battery life, transfers files in an instant, and is easy to use (and easy on the eyes). But after all the hype, you've called us here to show off an *MP3 player?* And you want *how much* for it!? You must be joking!"

Then Apple did a very smart thing. At the end of the event, each person in attendance was handed an iPod of his or her very own.

Cynics among us might suggest that Apple attempted to curry favor and lessen the shock of the first iPod's $399 price tag by offering members of the press free swag. Far from it. The folks at Apple understood that to truly appreciate the iPod, you had to hold it in your hand, admire its sleek design, swiftly wheel through its menus, and absorb its rich sound.

The tactic worked. Although nearly every review of the iPod mentioned that $399 was a lot of money for a music player, few disputed the notion that similar devices were clunky and crude in comparison.

Despite the price and the fact that it worked best only with the assistance of a Macintosh computer, the iPod became *the* music player to own—so much so, in fact, that Apple sold 125,000 of them in the iPod's first 60 days of existence, and people who had never considered owning a Mac bought one simply so they could use it with the iPod.

## The iPod expands

In March 2002, Apple released a second iPod model that featured a 10 GB hard drive (versus the original's 5 GB drive). Although many people hoped that subsequent iPod models would be less expensive than the original, this second iteration cost $499—$100 more. Lessening the sting was the accompanying iPod Software 1.1 Updater, which made the iPod more functional by including such features as the ability to keep contacts on your iPod, music *scrubbing* (a feature for accurately navigating forward and backward through a song as it plays), on-board equalization (the process of boosting or cutting certain audio frequencies, also known as *EQ*), and the option to shuffle playback by song or album. Apple also announced that when customers ordered from the online Apple Store, both the 5 and 10 GB models could be engraved with two lines of text (27 characters per line, including spaces and punctuation) for an additional $49.

## iPod: The second generation

On October 17, 2002, a new generation of iPods was announced. This group included the $299 5 GB model, the $399 10 GB iPod, and the $499 20 GB unit. In addition to new prices and a higher-capacity model, the features that distinguished this passel of music players were the capability to keep calendar information on the iPod, a new touch-sensitive scroll wheel (previous models included a wheel that turned, whereas the wheel on the new units didn't turn), redesigned earbuds that fit smaller ear canals more comfortably, support for Audible.com content (Mac version only), a FireWire port cover, and inclusion of a wired remote control and carrying case for the 10 and 20 GB models. Apple also welcomed PC users into the iPod fold by issuing models that were compatible with Windows.

## Third time's a charmer

Six months later, Apple unveiled yet another generation of iPods. This group saw the end of the 5 GB model. Instead, Apple maintained the same pricing structure—$299, $399, and $499—for a 10, 15, and 30 GB lineup.

Whereas the October 2002 iPods were an evolutionary release, these third-generation players were a redefinition of the original. The new iPods were sleeker and lighter. They featured a new front-panel design that placed touch-sensitive (and backlit) navigation buttons above the scroll wheel. Gone was the FireWire connector at the top of the iPod. It was replaced by a proprietary connector at the bottom of the unit that supported both FireWire and USB 2.0 connections.

Like the previous iterations, the midrange and high-end models included cases and wired remote controls. These two models also came bundled with a docking station—a plastic stand for the iPod that included a connector for charging the iPod, as well as an audio output jack for connecting the iPod to a home stereo.

These iPods incorporated changes within as well as without. Apple dropped the idea of an iPod for Windows and another for Macintosh; the new iPods worked with either platform right out of the box. The software bundled with the new iPods allowed users to customize menus and play two additional games. And these new devices added support for MPEG-4 music encoding—an audio compression scheme that creates files smaller and better-sounding than MP3 files encoded at the same bit rate.

And on the same day, Apple flung open the doors of its online music shop, the iTunes Music Store, to Macintosh users. Music purchased and downloaded from the iTunes Music Store could be stored and played on the Macintosh, burned to CD, and played on a single variety of portable music player: the iPod.

In early September 2003, Apple upgraded the mid- and high-priced iPods to include higher-capacity hard drives—20 and 40 GB, respectively. Although that upgrade was a nice bump for those who were about to purchase an iPod, the big news didn't come until October 16. On that day, Apple took a couple of giant steps forward.

### Opening the door to Windows

To begin with, Apple introduced a software update that—with the assistance of a couple of add-on devices from Belkin—allows third-generation iPods to record audio through a Belkin microphone inserted into the iPod's Headphone jack and remote connector. This same update supports another long-requested feature—the ability to turn the iPod into a storage center for digital photographs. This is accomplished with the help of a Belkin device—the Media Reader for iPod—that lets you transfer data from supported media cards (CompactFlash and SmartMedia, for example) to a third-generation iPod.

More important, October 16, 2003, elevated Windows iPod users from second-class citizens to members in good standing of the iPod community. On that day, Apple opened the iTunes Music Store to Windows users and also issued a version of iTunes that's compatible with PCs running Windows XP or 2000.

No longer do Windows iPod users have to struggle with the capable but convoluted Musicmatch Jukebox application. Like their Mac-using counterparts, Windows users can now record CDs, purchase music (and more!) online, and transfer their music to the iPod within a single application. 'Pod parity has finally come to Windows users—and judging from the fact that they used the Windows version of iTunes to purchase more than a million songs from the iTunes Music Store in the course of the first three days they had access to The Store, they're thrilled.

# The Impish iPod

As competition in the online music and digital music player industry began to heat up in the waning months of 2003, it became clear that if Apple wanted to maintain its edge, it had to offer a less expensive iPod to compete with flash-memory-based players. It revealed its intention to do so in January 2004, when it announced the $249 iPod mini—a smaller version of the iPod that came in five colors (gold, silver, blue, green, and pink), sported a new control wheel, and carried a 4 GB hard drive. In other regards, the iPod mini offered the same capabilities as the original iPod.

As with the original 5 GB iPod, many people were taken aback by the price of the iPod mini. Few considered $249 to be inexpensive, and if you were going to spend that kind of money, why not pungle up an additional $50 for an iPod with 3.7 times the storage of the mini? (On the day of the iPod mini announcement, Apple bumped up the storage capacity of the $299 iPod to 15 GB.)

Apple countered that while it was happy to sell its customers 15 GB iPods rather than iPod minis, the tinier iPod was intended to compete not with the iPod, but with the flash-memory-based players that cost $50 to $100 less than the iPod mini but offered less storage and fewer features.

## Taking a Hint from Little Brother

When Apple announced the fourth-generation iPod on July 19, 2004, it could have done so by proclaiming that the "maxi-mini" was born, for the fourth-generation iPod is, in some ways, closer in design to the iPod mini than it is to the previous three generations of white iPods. Available in 20 and 40 GB configurations priced at $299 and $399, respectively, the fourth-generation iPod bears the same kind of click-wheel controller used on the mini. And like the mini, it can be charged via USB 2.0.

But the fourth-generation iPod is more than just a bigger mini. Apple mucked with the power management of this model so that it can play up to 12 hours on a single charge. Its menu system differs from that of other models as well—offering a Shuffle Songs command on the main screen so you can easily hear a random selection of the iPod's music without digging through its menus. And this is the first model iPod in a long time that doesn't include a free remote control or case. If you check the specs on the third-generation iPod, you'll see that Apple offers more hard drive capacity for less money on these iPods. To help make this possible, Apple made these accessories optional (though a dock is included with the 40 GB fourth-generation iPod).

## HP and the iPod

On January 8, 2004, HP announced that it was getting into the iPod business in a serious way. Specifically, the company would sell HP-branded iPods. For months after this announcement, many speculated how the HP iPod would differ from the one offered by Apple. Would it come in HP blue? Would the word "Invent" be etched into the back of every player? Would it play Windows .wma files?

As it turns out, no, no, and, no.

On September 15, 2004, HP released its first iPods and they were very nearly the same 20 and 40 GB fourth-generation iPods offered by Apple. The one difference was that the HP logo appeared on the back of these units.

So why would Apple join forces with HP to sell iPods rather than sell them itself? To put iTunes on the desktop of every HP computer sold.

Microsoft launched its MSN Music Service—an online music store that competes with Apple's iTunes Music Store—in early September 2004. Like other Microsoft products such as the company's Web browser, Internet Explorer, the MSN Music Service was bundled with every Windows PC. Having the MSN Music Service a click away rather than a download-and-install-and-click-away (as was the case with iTunes) gave Microsoft's product a big advantage. Apple wanted to lessen some of that advantage by placing iTunes on the desktop of computers made by the number 2 provider of PCs (Dell, being the number 1 provider). HP agreed to it for the chance to sell iPods.

## U2 Ought to Be in Pictures

Tick forward to San Jose's California Theatre on October 26, 2004. The invitation to the press event held that day read "Steve Jobs, Bono and The Edge invite you to attend a special event." And special it was.

The event began with the unveiling of the iPod Photo, the first iPod to feature a color display capable of showing up to 25,000 pictures stored on the iPod. Bearing either a 40 GB or 60 GB hard drive (priced at $499 and $599 respectively), these iPods can be configured to display their pictures on a television with the assistance of an included audio/visual cable or via an S-video cable strung between a television and the iPod's included dock. They also feature greater battery life than previous iPods, letting you play music continuously for over 15 hours on a single battery charge.

And how did U2 figure into all of this? The lads from the Emerald Isle were on hand to help present another iPod model—the iPod Special Edition: U2. Though functionally no different from a 20 GB fourth-generation iPod, this special player is the first "big" iPod to come in colors—specifically a black face with red click wheel. Along with a coupon for $50 off of U2's entire 400+ song catalog from Apple's iTunes Music Store (normally priced at $149), this special iPod also carries the signatures of the four U2 members etched on the back plate.

## The iPod's Future

What's next? More-comprehensive data management? A scheme for storing movies and projecting them on a television? A built-in satellite radio receiver with recording functions? Only Apple can say for sure where the iPod's future lies. But given Apple's inclination for innovation, it's a safe bet that today's iPod is only the beginning.

And what a beginning it's been.

# Contents, Controls, and Interface

1

I've spent enough time in the bricks-and-mortar Apple Stores to know that many of you pick up this book prior to purchasing an iPod in order to determine whether the iPod Photo, the original white iPod, or its smaller sibling, the iPod mini, are all they're cracked up to be. At the risk of giving away this book's plot, I can state without reservation that, yes, they are. But why take my word for it when a careful reading of this chapter will tell you much of what you need to know in order to charge your iPod, work your way around its controls, and make the best use of the extras Apple places in the iPod box?

# Contents: Original iPod (including the iPod Special Edition: U2)

If you can contain your excitement, try to linger over unwrapping the iPod's box. The packaging is as beautifully designed as the iPod itself—from the elegant and understated outer sleeve to the inner box that folds open like a jewelry case.

## The CD Package

After you do remove the box's outer sleeve and open the box, you'll find a small white envelope labeled simply "Enjoy." With the release of the fourth generation of iPods, Apple has significantly bulked up the documentation bundled with the iPod. In this envelope, you'll find a 35-page Getting Started guide that shows you how to start playing music on your new toy, a blue piece of paper that screams "FREE MUSIC for Your iPod" (but which is really a come-on for the iTunes Music Store), a copy of the iPod's warranty, and a software license agreement that covers the software included on the CD. This CD—also tucked inside the "Enjoy" envelope—contains the latest iPod Software Updater for the iPod and iPod mini, tutorials for the iPod mini and regular iPod in PDF format, and PDF user guides for both varieties of iPod. When you view this CD with a Macintosh, you'll find separate installers for iTunes and QuickTime. The installer file for the PC includes both iTunes and QuickTime.

If you're like most people, you may glance at the Getting Started guide and may fire up the tutorial and user guide to peruse the first couple of pages, but will shove the other paperwork out of the way. Because you won't read the fine print, allow me to draw your attention to the most important points in these documents:

- **Learn more.** The Getting Started guide suggests that if you want to learn more about your iPod than what is presented in this guide, you should spin through the CD, visit www.apple.com/ipod, and choose iPod Help from the iTunes Help menu. These suggestions are worth paying attention to. Although the book you hold in your hands is comprehensive, capabilities may have been added to the iPod and iTunes since this book went to print.

- **One-year warranty.** Those of you who own one of the first-generation iPods are undoubtedly about to put down this book and send me a stern letter that begins: "Listen, Mr. Smartypants Writer, my iPod came with a 90-day warranty. Why intentionally deceive your readers?"

  To which I have to answer, "Who, me?" You see, the original iPods *did* ship with a 90-day warranty. After Apple received a significant amount of flak for offering such a skimpy warranty, however, it ever-so-quietly changed the terms of that warranty to one year on all iPods.

  Note, however, that when Apple released the third generation of iPods, it changed the warranty yet again. Yes, your iPod is covered for a period of one year. But if a defect arises after you've owned the thing for 180 days, you must pay a $30 shipping and handling charge for the return of your iPod. "Shipping and handling" may mean nothing more than an Apple Genius making a round trip to the storeroom to fetch a new iPod in exchange for the funky one you brought in. Regardless of the cost per footfall, that's what you agreed to when you opened the iPod box, and therefore, you must pungle up.

  Apple has recently allowed the iPod to be covered by AppleCare— a $59 plan that extends your warranty by an additional year. With this plan you'll get free phone support and repair coverage for up to two years. For more details visit http://store.apple.com/1-800-MY-APPLE/WebObjects/AppleStore?productLearnMore=M9404LL/A. Although I'll cover the matter in greater detail later in the book, I'll mention right at the get-go that if you intend to use your iPod a lot, AppleCare is a sound investment.

- **Permitted uses and restrictions.** By using the iPod and its software, you automatically agree to the software license agreement. When you agree to this thing, you swear that you won't use the software to copy material that you are not legally permitted to reproduce. I'll discuss the ethics of piracy as we proceed, but in the meantime, know that if you use iTunes to copy CDs that you don't own or pack your iPod with music files pirated from the Internet, you are breaking the terms of the agreement and conceivably could be called on the carpet by Apple for doing so.

- **Don't hurt yourself.** The Safety and Cleaning portion of the User's Guide suggests that you avoid performing obviously boneheaded actions with your iPod. Jamming the earbuds into the deepest recesses of your ear canals and cranking the volume could damage your hearing, for example. Operating an automobile while listening to the iPod through the earbuds could make driving less safe. Using the iPod in areas where the temperature exceeds 95 degrees Fahrenheit for long periods could break the iPod (but it likely would break you first). And taking the thing into the bathtub with you isn't such a smooth idea unless running a few thousand volts through your body is your idea of a good time.

- **Don't crack it open.** Apple suggests that you run the risk of electric shock and voiding your warranty by opening your iPod. The company also claims that you will find no user-serviceable parts inside. This is mostly true. Although you're unlikely to shock yourself by opening an iPod that isn't plugged in, these devices are tightly sealed, and when you crack one open, you'll likely leave signs that you've been monkeying about (and sure as shootin', any tech worth his or her salt will deny your warranty claim upon detecting those signs). As you'll learn in the Troubleshooting section of this book, there *are* a couple of user-serviceable parts inside (well, user-serviceable to the extent that they can be replaced or used in another iPod). See Chapter 10 for details.

- Finally, Apple thought it important enough to put the following in all capital letters, so I suppose it bears repeating here:

"THE APPLE SOFTWARE IS NOT INTENDED FOR USE IN THE OPERATION OF NUCLEAR FACILITIES, AIRCRAFT NAVIGATION OR COMMUNICATION SYSTEMS, AIR TRAFFIC CONTROL SYSTEMS, LIFE SUPPORT MACHINES OR OTHER EQUIPMENT IN WHICH THE FAILURE OF THE APPLE SOFTWARE COULD LEAD TO DEATH, PERSONAL INJURY, OR SEVERE PHYSICAL OR ENVIRONMENTAL DAMAGE."

So please, when you assemble the backyard nuclear power plant or air-traffic-control system, use software other than iTunes to monitor your reactor or guide your planes. Your neighbors will thank you for it.

# The Earbuds

Your iPod comes with a set of headphones that you place inside—rather than over—your ears (**Figure 1.1**). This style of headphones is known as *earbuds*. Two foam disks fit over the earbuds. (Apple includes two pairs of these foam disks in the box.) These disks not only grip the inside of the ear—helping keep the earbuds in place—but also make the earbuds more comfortable to wear. The hard plastic surface of the earbuds will begin to hurt after a while. And yes, the disks clearly display detritus picked up inside your ears—thus discouraging others from borrowing your headphones.

**Figure 1.1**
The iPod's earbuds and pads.

Just as you'll find a wide range of foot and head sizes among groups of people, the size of the opening to the ear varies. The earbuds included with the first generation of iPods were a little larger than other earbuds you may have seen. Some people (including your humble author) found these headphones uncomfortable. The latest iPods include smaller earbuds that I find much more comfortable. With the foam disks in place, you shouldn't have trouble keeping the earbuds in place, regardless of how large or small the opening to your ears is. But if you find the earbuds uncomfortable, you can purchase smaller or larger earbuds, or you can opt for a pair of over-the-ear headphones (see Chapter 8).

If the included earbuds do fit you, you may or may not be pleased with their performance. Apple made great efforts to create the finest music player on the planet, and it didn't skimp on the headphones, but sound is subjective, and you may find that other headphones deliver a more pleasing sound to your ears. If you believe you deserve better sound than your Apple earbuds provide, by all means audition other headphones.

The included earbuds use 18mm drivers with Neodymium transducer magnets and offer a frequency range of 20 to 20,000 Hz. If you're like me, you wouldn't know a Neodymium transducer magnet if it walked up and offered to buy you lunch, but you should know that the frequency range of 20 to 20,000 Hz is what's offered by a good home stereo.

## The FireWire Cable, USB 2.0 Cable, and Power Adapter

But wait—there's more. Beneath the "Enjoy" envelope and the cardboard that cradles the iPod, you'll find the iPod's proprietary FireWire and USB 2.0 power and data cables, plus the power adapter. Earlier versions of the iPod box housed a FireWire 6-pin-to-4-pin cable adapter for the benefit of Windows users whose PCs have a 4-pin FireWire port. Now that the iPod supports charging and data transfer via USB 2.0 (and Apple includes a USB 2.0 cable with every iPod), this adapter was deemed to be unnecessary. Reflecting the cohesiveness of the overall design, the FireWire and USB 2.0 cables and power adapter come in white and are stamped with the Apple logo.

The FireWire and USB 2.0 cables included with the latest iPods each carry their namesake connector on one end (a 6-pin FireWire plug on the FireWire cable, a standard rectangular USB connector on the USB cable) and a proprietary connector on the other. Apple had to design a data connector that supported both FireWire and USB 2.0 connections—thus, the proprietary cable. The cable is also thinner than the cables included with the first two generations of iPods. In this case, less is better. A thinner cable puts less stress on the connector at the bottom of the iPod.

The power adapter sports a single FireWire port at the back and features retractable power prongs—a wonderful idea if you don't want whatever you carry the adapter in to be punctured by the prongs. For this reason, Windows users without a FireWire connector (or powered USB 2.0 connector, if they're using a fourth-generation iPod, iPod Photo, or iPod mini) on their PC should retain their FireWire cable for the purpose of charging the iPod.

The power adapter isn't required to charge your iPod. The iPod will charge when it's connected to a Mac or PC outfitted with a 6-pin

FireWire connector or, if you have a fourth-generation iPod, iPod Photo, or iPod mini, a USB 2.0 connector (though the computer has to be on and awake; a sleeping computer won't charge your iPod). But the iPod *is* a portable device, after all, and because it is, you may not have a computer with you when you want to charge it. Simple enough—just string the included FireWire data/power cable between the adapter and the iPod, and wait as long as four hours for the iPod to charge fully. (It will charge to 80 percent of battery capacity in about two hours.)

Note that the power adapter is capable of handling AC input from 100 to 240 volts—meaning that with the proper adapter, you can power the iPod in countries that use the 240-volt standard without having to use a power converter . You may need to replace the adapter's plug with a plug appropriate for the country you're visiting.

To make that possible, the power adapter's plug section can be detached and replaced with one of the plugs available in Apple's $39 World Travel Adapter Kit—a collection of plugs that work in North America, Japan, China, the United Kingdom, Europe, Korea, Australia, and Hong Kong. These plugs also work with the power adapters for Apple's iBook, PowerBook, and AirPort Express.

## Play Time and Battery Life

Apple claims that the fourth-generation iPods can play for 12 hours, the iPod Photo can play music for 15 hours and a slideshow for 5 hours, and the iPod mini can play for more than 8 hours when fully charged. (Previous iPod models could play for 10 hours on a charge.) This is absolutely true—given the proper conditions.

First, make sure that your iPod is running iPod Software 1.2.6 Updater or later. A bug introduced in an earlier version of the iPod software quickly drained the battery. Second, engage the iPod's Hold switch when you're not using it. It's possible to switch the iPod on accidentally, which drains the battery. When the Hold switch is on, the iPod's controls won't work.

Also, operate the iPod in temperatures between 50 and 95 degrees Fahrenheit. In a cooler environment, an iPod may not wake from sleep. To warm it up, hold your iPod in your hand or tuck it into your armpit for a few minutes. (*That* should perk you up on a cold morning.)

*continues on next page*

> **Play Time and Battery Life** *(continued)*
>
> Apple suggests that you'll squeeze the most life out of an iPod charge by playing files that are smaller than 9 MB, keeping your mitts off the Next Track and Previous Track buttons, turning off backlighting, setting the iPod's equalization settings (the controls for boosting or cutting certain audio frequencies—known as *EQ*) to None, and turning off the Sound Check option.
>
> Files larger than 9 MB cause the iPod to access the hard drive more often and use up the iPod's battery charge more quickly. Pushing the Next Track and Previous Track buttons likewise requires the iPod to access the hard drive more often. Slathering EQ on your tunes or evening out the volume between songs with Sound Check apparently taxes the hard drive as well. And the power necessary to light up your iPod's screen is sure to shorten play time.
>
> Also, you'll significantly shorten the original iPod's charge if, while using a voice recorder attachment, you pause a completed recording rather than end it by saving it. When you pause such a recording, the hard drive continues to spin, draining your battery. A stopped recording allows the hard drive to spin down.

## The iPod Dock

At the bottom of the iPod, you'll find the proprietary port that handles power and data connections. Why move this port from the top of the iPod—where it resided for the first two generations of the device—to the bottom? So that you can use a dock, of course.

That diminutive Dock—included with the 40 GB iPod—features an audio Line Out port and data connector on the back and mounts the iPod at a slightly rakish angle (**Figure 1.2**).

**Figure 1.2**
The iPod Dock.

You can put this Dock to work in a couple of ways. The first is to string one of the data/power cables bundled with the iPod between the Dock and your computer. If your iPod is configured to update automatically when you connect it to your computer, synchronizing the iPod with your iTunes or, if you prefer, your Musicmatch Jukebox library is as simple as can be. Just plunk the iPod into the Dock. In next to no time, iTunes (or Musicmatch Jukebox, if you've chosen to use it rather than iTunes on your PC) launches and updates the iPod with any tunes you've placed on your computer. And if the Dock is connected to a powered FireWire or USB 2.0 port, just leave the iPod in the Dock to charge it.

The Dock is also useful for plugging your iPod into your home stereo. Just run an audio cable (in all likelihood, a stereo Y cable that features two RCA plugs on one end and a stereo minijack connector on the other) between the Dock and a spare input on your home stereo receiver. Place your iPod in the Dock, and play it just as you would if you were using it with headphones. To charge the iPod at the same time, attach the included FireWire data/power cable to the back of the Dock, and plug the other end (the end that sports the FireWire connector) into the power adapter.

# The iPod

And, of course, there's the iPod itself.

Now that you own it, you're welcome to remove the iPod from the box, strip away the protective plastic sheeting, and ignore or admire the admonition printed on the plastic: *Don't steal music.*

The first thing you'll likely notice is that the iPod is even more lovely than it appears in the magazine ads and on the Web and TV. The second thing is that it's more solidly built than you probably imagined. The 20 GB fourth-generation iPod, at 4.1 inches tall, 2.4 inches wide, and 0.57 inch thick (the 40 GB model is a bit thicker, at 0.69 inch), has a nice feel in your hand at 5.6 ounces (or 6.2 ounces, if you have the 40 GB model).

It's also easier to smudge than you might have guessed. The ultra-reflective back plate is a visual delight, but the second you touch your iPod, fingerprints and smudges will mar its surface. If smears and smudges bother you, carry a soft eyeglass cleaning cloth, and buff the back whenever the mood strikes.

Not so obvious are what lurks within the iPod and what the device can do. I'll clear up the mystery in the remaining pages of this book.

## Remote Control and Case: Free No More

If you have an older iPod that shipped with Apple's Remote Control and carrying case, you may wonder why I've failed to mention those items here. They've mostly gone the way of the dodo, that's why.

Well, not exactly. The *free* versions of these doodads have performed this very lifelike imitation of the famed flightless bird, unless you've purchased an iPod Photo. In the case of the picture-perfect iPod, the case is still bundled. However, when Apple released the fourth-generation iPod, it offered the 20 and 40 GB models at $100 less than third-generation iPods of the same capacity. To help maintain profits, Apple pulled the remote control and case from the box. But it continues to sell each for $39 a pop.

While there was some griping when people unwrapped the first few new fourth-generation iPods and failed to discover these items, I have to admit that I don't miss them. Although some people find the remote control very handy—it is, after all, a nicely designed piece of gear that allows you to command your iPod without removing it from a pocket or case—not everyone used it. (I, for example, have three of the things sealed in their original wrappers.) And as you'll learn in Chapter 9, I'm not terribly impressed with Apple's case. It's stylish but doesn't offer enough protection to suit me; neither does it allow access to the iPod's front controls.

Frankly, I'm thrilled that Apple saved me a hundred smackers by making these items pay-us-if-you-want-them options.

This book went to press before the iPod Special Edition: U2 went on sale in mid-November 2004, so I haven't had a chance to rummage through its box. My best guess is that the contents of the box vary little from what you get in the fourth-generation iPod's box (after all, it really is nothing more than a 20 GB fourth-generation iPod). Perhaps Apple will change the color of the earbuds and cables to match the U2 iPod's basic black and red click-wheel. The one difference I am aware of is the inclusion of a coupon for $50 off the price of the virtual box set of U2's catalog at the iTunes Music Store. This collection of music includes over 400 U2 tracks and normally sells for $149. With that coupon you can have the tracks for $99.

# Contents: iPod mini

The contents of the original iPod's box and that of the iPod mini are similar enough that I needn't go over the same ground in these next few pages. Rather, I'll take a moment or two to describe the difference between the contents of the two packages.

## The CD Package

The iPod mini's User's Guide is a bit bulkier than the one included with the original iPod. Though not as comprehensive as this book, it's a useful guide for doing the obvious things and performing basic troubleshooting procedures, such as resetting the device.

The CD that accompanies the documentation includes versions of the iPod mini Software Updater, iTunes, and QuickTime for both Macintosh and Windows. Should you lose your documentation, never fear. Copies of the User's Guide can also be found on the disc.

Although the documentation and CD bundled with the mini I purchased a few weeks before writing this edition of the book don't reflect it, Apple should have standardized the documentation and CD that accompany all iPods by the time you read this. Apple's plan seems to be to issue a CD that covers all iPods and a paper User's Guide that outlines the basics of iPodding, leaving the specifics of each model to PDF files on the disc.

 Something not mentioned in Apple's documentation but worth noting is that should you purchase a regular iPod or mini from the Apple Store and return it within 10 days, a 10% restocking fee applies (so yes, you can forget about buying one for the prom and returning it for a full refund the next day).

## The Cables, Adapters, and Earbuds

Like the original, fourth-generation iPod and the iPod Photo, the iPod mini's box contains both a FireWire cable and a USB 2.0 cable. Each cable carries Apple's proprietary data/power connector on one end.

As you might expect, the FireWire cable includes a 6-pin FireWire connector, and the USB 2.0 carries a standard USB 2.0 connector. Regrettably, those Windows users whose PCs sport a 4-pin FireWire connector and lack a USB 2.0 connector will have to seek out a 6-pin-to-4-pin FireWire adapter as one is not included in the box.

The mini's power adapter and earbuds are the same as those that ship with the original iPod.

## The Belt Clip

Apple understands that most people would rather not have their $249 gold, silver, green, blue, or pink investment clatter to the ground. With that in mind, you'll find a spring-loaded, white plastic belt clip in the mini's box (**Figure 1.3**). The U-shaped clip wraps around the side of the mini and holds it securely in place. Unlike Apple's $39 case for the original iPods, this clip offers no protection for the outside of your iPod. For this reason, your second mini-related purchase (after this book) is a case that adequately protects your mini (see Chapter 8 for case recommendations).

**Figure 1.3**
The mini's included belt clip.

## What's Missing

As with the fourth-generation iPod and iPod Photo, you'll find no remote control in the mini's box (and no Dock, either). You can purchase a remote control and Dock separately. Apple's $39 iPod Remote Control works with both the iPod mini and the original iPod (**Figure 1.4**). The fourth-generation iPod and iPod Photo's Dock is too roomy to fit the mini adequately—though I've been able to use a mini with the Dock intended for the third-generation iPod. Apple has designed a Dock specifically for the mini. It, too, sells for $39.

**Figure 1.4**
The now-optional remote control sports Play, Pause, Fast Forward, Rewind, and Volume controls.

## Contents: iPod Photo

The newest additions to the iPod family, both the 40 and 60 GB iPod Photos, come bundled with all the accessories that accompany the fourth-generation iPod's box—FireWire cable, USB 2.0 cable, Apple earbuds, power adapter, documentation, and a CD-ROM disc with software compatible with Windows and the Mac OS—as well as a few extras.

## The A/V Cable

Not only can you view pictures on the iPod Photo's two-inch display, with the proper cable you can see your pictures on a television. This is that proper cable and Apple included it in the box. Measuring just under five feet long (59 inches from tip to tip, if you must know), the cable bears a three-ring mini-plug on one end and three RCA plugs on the other—one for composite video and the other two for the left and right audio channels (**Figure 1.5**).

**Figure 1.5**
The iPod Photo's AV cable with two audio output jacks and a composite video output jack.

To put the cable to best use, you plug the miniplug into the iPod Photo's headphone port and the three RCA plugs into the appropriate jacks on your TV.

## iPod Photo Dock

The iPod Photo Dock differs from any other iPod dock in its inclusion of an S-Video port. As you might suspect, this port is intended for connecting the iPod Photo to an S-Video input—the input on your TV, VCR, or camcorder, for example (**Figure 1.6**). As I'll explain in the chapter devoted to the iPod Photo, S-Video provides a cleaner video signal than what you get from the iPod's headphone (composite video) port. Apple doesn't include an S-Video cable in the iPod Photo's box, although you can purchase one at any electronics store.

You can purchase an additional iPod Photo Dock for $39.

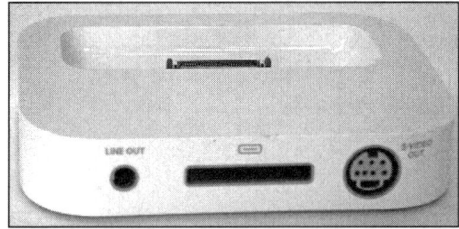

**Figure 1.6**
Unlike previous iPod docks, the iPod Photo Dock sports an S-Video port.

## Carrying Case

Move along, nothing to see here. It's Apple's standard iPod case.

## Capacity

As this book goes to press, Apple offers three iPod models—the iPod mini that houses a 4 GB hard drive, the two white fourth-generation iPod models that include 20 or 40 GB drives, and the iPod Photo that houses either a 40 or 60 GB drive. Rather than fill this chapter with the phrase "Oh, and that includes the iPod Special Edition: U2 too," let's just agree that the U2 iPod is nothing more than a gussied-up 20 GB fourth-generation iPod.

The hard-drive capacity is a bit deceiving. The drives technically hold 4 GB, 20 GB, 40 GB, and 60 GB respectively, but after they're formatted, you'll find that the mini holds 3.7 GB, the 20 GB iPod holds 18.5 GB, the

40 GB fourth-generation and iPod Photo holds 37 GB, and the 60 GB iPod Photo formats to 55.7 GB. The reason for the discrepancy is that Apple and hard-drive manufacturers measure megabytes differently. Drive manufacturers maintain that 1 MB equals 1 million bytes (1,000 × 1,000 bytes). Apple claims that a megabyte is actually 1,048,576 bytes (1,024 × 1,024 bytes). So this difference is really a difference in semantics. The drive manufacturer and Apple agree that a 20 GB drive is a 20 GB drive. It's just that the computer and iPod OS show that such a drive actually holds less information if you use Apple's definition of a megabyte.

Regardless of how megabytes are calculated, you do lose a portion of the hard drive's space. The iPod can't run without the files necessary to make it work, and those files take up some space. Also, when the drive is formatted, a small portion of the hard drive is reserved for internal chores.

Is the possible loss of 0.3, 1.5, 3 , and 4.3 GB something to lose sleep over? Hardly. You have ample room to store music, files, and, in the case of the iPod Photo, additional files as well. The mini, for example, can hold 1,000 four-minute AAC songs encoded at 128 kilobits per second (Kbps)—more than 66 hours of music. The 20 GB model holds 5,000 songs (that's 333.3 hours or almost 14 days of music), the 40 GB iPod and iPod Photo hold more than 10,000 songs (equaling 666.6 hours or nearly enough music to play your iPod nonstop throughout the entire month of February without hearing the same song twice), and the 60 GB iPod Photo houses 15,000 tunes when the player is packed with music, which equals just over 41 days of non-stop rockin.' I'll discuss kilobits and music encoding elsewhere in the book, but for the time being, all you need to know is that this 128 Kbps rate produces files with remarkable sound quality. Many files that you'll find on the Web are encoded at the same rate of 128 Kbps, but in MP3 format. To most people, such MP3 files sound distinctly inferior to their AAC counterparts.

# Skip Protection

All iPods sport a 32 MB DRAM (Dynamic RAM) memory buffer. When the fourth-generation iPod and iPod mini move music from the hard drive to your ears, they load into that buffer about 20 minutes of music (if you're playing an MP3 file encoded at 160 Kbps). The iPod Photo appears to move less music into the buffer in order to also place pictures in memory. After shoveling the music into the buffer, the hard drive spins down, saving wear and tear on both the drive and the iPod's battery.

This scheme also allows up to 25 minutes of skip-free music playback on the fourth-generation iPod and iPod mini and 17 minutes of skip protection on the iPod Photo. Yes, for the time it takes to get a decent cardiovascular workout, you can jump, jive, and wail, listening to your music with nary a glitch. The iPod will skip only when data is being moved off the hard drive and into the buffer.

If you've never owned another disk-based music player, you might not realize how impressive this feature is. Lesser players offer skip protection that's measured in seconds rather than minutes.

## What's the Difference?

The iPod once came in two flavors: one for Macintosh and another for Windows. The current and last generation of iPods work with either computer platform. Are there differences between iPods formatted for the Macintosh and those formatted for Windows?

As the iPod matures, there are fewer differences. They measure up this way:

The software is slightly different. Prior to October 16, 2003, the software was wildly different—Mac users used iTunes and Windows users were given Musicmatch Jukebox. That changed when Apple released a Windows version of iTunes—a program that is nearly identical to the Macintosh version. iTunes 4.6 for Windows and Mac differ in that the version written for Windows can convert .wma audio files—an audio format not compatible with the iPod that was created by Microsoft—to the AAC audio format. The Mac version doesn't include this conversion option.

The way that the iPod's hard drive is formatted is different as well. By default, the iPod's hard drive is formatted as a Mac OS Extended (HFS+) volume—the same kind of formatting that's used by default on the Macintosh. When you plug the iPod into a Windows PC, the iPod's hard drive is formatted as a FAT32 volume—the native formatting scheme for Windows.

> **What's the Difference?** *(continued)*
>
> Windows PCs can't recognize a Mac OS Extended volume natively, so should you plug your Mac iPod into a PC, the PC wouldn't recognize the iPod unless it had the iPod Windows software on it. In the past, the PC would dumbly refuse to deal with the iPod, acting as though the iPod didn't exist. Now, however, if you install the Windows software that accompanies the latest iPods and plug a Mac-formatted iPod or iPod mini into the PC, the PC will prompt you to reformat the iPod for Windows.
>
> As I mentioned earlier, the Mac can recognize FAT32 volumes. If you plug an iPod formatted for Windows into a Mac, the Mac will treat it almost exactly like a Macintosh iPod. You can use iTunes to move music to the iPod, as well as add calendars, contacts, and notes to the device. The only thing you can't do with a Windows original iPod is install a Macintosh operating system on it and then boot from the iPod (as I mention in Chapter 6, the iPod mini won't boot either a Mac or a Windows PC).

## Supported Audio Formats

Although the iPod is usually referred to as an MP3 player, it can actually play music encoded in a few formats. AAC is the most desirable because (as I explained in the introduction) thanks to their relatively small sizes, you can jam a lot of AAC files into the iPod. The iPod supports importing and playback of AAC, MP3, AIFF (Audio Interchange File Format, the kind of files used on audio CDs), WAV files (the Microsoft Windows audio format), and—new to iTunes and the iPod with the release of iTunes 4.5—Apple Lossless Codec. It does not play files encoded in Microsoft's proprietary .wma (Windows Media Player) format—making the iPod incompatible with online music services that sell music in that format.

Because they're not compressed, AIFF and WAV files are of higher quality than AAC and MP3 files. But AAC and MP3 files encoded at 320 Kbps—the maximum resolution allowed for MP3 files on the iPod—sound amazingly good.

The tradeoff is that these files consume 10 MB per minute of stereo music. Using AIFF and WAV files means not only giving up a lot of hard drive space for fewer files (you can fit about 92 four-minute AIFF files on an iPod mini), but also draining the RAM buffer much more quickly. This situation causes the hard drive to kick in more often and the battery to drain more rapidly. Also, because of the file sizes, moving AIFF and WAV songs from your computer to the iPod takes longer than moving the same number of AAC or MP3 files.

Apple now offers a compromise between enormous files that sound great and compressed files that sound darned good. That compromise is its Apple Lossless Codec—a scheme that maintains all of a file's audio fidelity while creating a file a little over half the size of the original.

Loading Apple Lossless Codec or AAC files onto a Windows iPod requires that you use iTunes for Windows or a third-party Windows application such as XPlay, EphPod, or Anapod Explorer, which I discuss at greater length in Chapter 5. The Musicmatch Jukebox software that shipped with iPods before late October 2003 doesn't support AAC files (for either encoding or copying to the iPod).

Fortunately, iTunes for Windows does bring AAC encoding and playback to the PC, as well as AIFF and Apple Lossless Codec compatibility (other formats unsupported by Musicmatch Jukebox). This is reason enough for Windows iPod owners to download iTunes, if it wasn't bundled with their iPods.

# Controls

The iPod has rightly been praised for its ease of use. As with all its products, Apple strove to make the iPod as intuitive as possible, placing a limited number of controls and ports on the device. When Apple designed the business card–sized iPod mini, it had to be even more careful about the placement of its controls than with the original iPod. With such a limited set of controls, of course, some controls have to perform more than one function. In the following pages, I examine just what the controls and ports on the original iPod and iPod mini do.

## On the Face of It

On the front of your iPod (**Figure 1.7**), you'll find a display and set of navigation controls. On the first two generations of iPods, these controls are arrayed around a central scroll wheel and are mechanical—meaning that they move and activate switches underneath the buttons. On the third-generation iPods, these controls are above the scroll wheel and are touch-sensitive; they activate when they come into contact with your flesh but, allegedly, not when a nonfleshy object (such as the case) touches them.

**Figure 1.7**
The fourth-generation iPod's display and navigation controls.

Because the mini's size accurately reflects its name, Apple's designers had to consider carefully the makeup of its display and controls. With a device that measured 2 inches by 3.6 inches, there was no room for frippery. Proving that Apple's designers are among the best in the world, they not only created a display and controls that matched the functionality of the third-generation iPod, but also in many ways surpassed it (**Figure 1.8**).

**Figure 1.8**
The iPod mini's display and navigation controls.

They did so by creating a scroll wheel that incorporates the navigation buttons. Unlike the first two generations of the iPod, on which the buttons are arrayed around the outside of the wheel, these buttons are part of the wheel itself (**Figure 1.9**). Their sensors sit beneath the scroll wheel at the four compass points, and the scroll wheel sits upon a short spindle, allowing it to rock in all directions. To activate one of the buttons, just press the scroll wheel in the direction of that button.

**Figure 1.9**
The fourth-generation iPod's click wheel.

Knowing a good thing when it designs it, Apple dropped the touch-sensitive buttons when it created the fourth-generation iPod and included a slightly larger version of this click wheel.

Because the wheel is designed to rock in only one direction at a time, you can't press two navigation buttons at once to invoke the Reset and Disk Mode commands. Apple thoughtfully changed these commands so that they're activated with the simultaneous press of a navigation button and the Select button. (In Chapter 10, you'll learn how to activate these hidden commands on the original iPod, the iPod Photo, and the iPod mini.)

## The displays

Near the top of the original iPod sits a 2-inch-diagonal, grayscale liquid crystal display with a resolution of 160 by 128 pixels. You can turn on backlighting (switch on a light that makes the display easier to read in low-light situations) by holding down the Menu button. With all iPods using iPod Software 1.3 Updater or later, you can also switch on backlighting by choosing Backlight from the iPod's main menu.

The iPod Photo also sports a 2-inch display, but with an important difference—this one can display up to 65,536 colors at a resolution of 220 by 176 pixels. When lit, the display is brilliantly crisp. When dimmed, it can be easily read outdoors but is less clear indoors where you may have to view it off-axis to see what's on the screen (**Figure 1.10**).

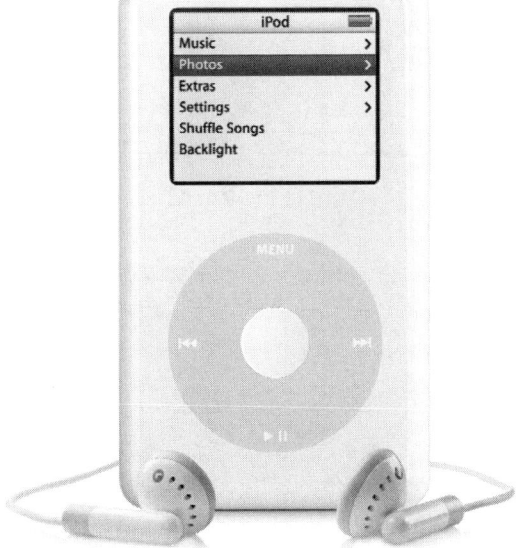

**Figure 1.10**
The front of the iPod Photo looks exactly like a fourth-generation iPod save for its color screen. Photo courtesy of Apple Computer.

Measured diagonally, the mini's backlit display is just under half an inch smaller than that of the original iPod and iPod Photo, yet in nearly all cases, it projects as much text as the other members of the iPod family. It does this by using a different font from the one used on the original iPod. This font (called Espy) was originally used by Apple's Newton hand-held computer. The original iPod uses the Chicago font and displays text in a larger font size. Espy is very easy to read at smaller sizes—the perfect choice for the mini.

## Play/Pause button

If you scan the surface of your iPod, you'll notice that it bears no recognizable On/Off switch. That job is handled by the Play/Pause button—located at the bottom of the iPod control wheel on older iPods, in the third position in the row of buttons on the third-generation iPods, and at the bottom of the click wheel on the iPod mini, the iPod Photo, and fourth-generation iPods. Just press this button to switch the iPod on, and hold it down for about 3 seconds to switch the iPod off.

As its name hints, this button is the one you push to play or pause the highlighted song.

## Previous/Rewind button

This button is located on the far-left side of the wheel on first-, second-, and fourth-generation iPods, the iPod Photo, and the iPod mini. It's the far-left button on the third-generation iPod. Press this button once to go to the previous song in the playlist; hold it down to rewind through a song. When you rewind or fast-forward through a song, you move in small increments at first. As you continue to hold the button down, you move in larger increments.

On the iPod Photo, the Previous/Rewind button also moves you back through a slideshow.

## Next/Fast Forward button

Look to the far right on first-, second-, and fourth-generation iPods, the iPod Photo, and the iPod mini; look to the rightmost button on the third-generation iPod. Press this button once to go to the next song in the playlist; hold it down to fast-forward through a song. When you rewind or fast-forward through a song, you move in small increments at first. As you continue to hold the button down, you move in larger increments.

On the iPod Photo, the Next/Forward button advances you through a slideshow.

## Menu button

Pressing the well-marked Menu button takes you back through the interface the way you came. If you've moved from the main iPod screen to the Browse screen, for example, and you press the Menu button, you'll move back to the main iPod screen. If you've moved from the main iPod screen through the Playlist screen to a particular song within a particular playlist, each time you press the Menu button, you'll move back one screen.

Holding the Menu button down for about 2 seconds turns backlighting on or off.

## Scroll wheel

Inside the ring of buttons on first- and second-generation iPods, below the bevy of buttons on third-generation iPods, and marked with the navigation controls on fourth-generation iPods and iPod minis, is the scroll wheel. On the original 5 and 10 GB iPods, this scroll wheel turned; on later models, it doesn't. Rather, the scroll wheel is stationary and touch-sensitive. Move your thumb across it to "scroll" the wheel.

Moving the wheel (or, in the case of recent iPods, your thumb) clockwise highlights items below the selected item; moving the wheel counter-clockwise highlights items above the selected item. If a window is larger than the display, moving the scroll wheel causes the window to scroll up or down when the first or last item in the list is highlighted.

You also use the scroll wheel to adjust volume and move to a particular location in a song.

The iPod includes a feature that allows you to hear a click as you use the scroll wheel. This wonderful feature provides you aural feedback on how quickly you're spinning the wheel. On iPod models prior to the fourth generation (including the original iPod mini), this sound came from inside the iPod. The fourth-generation iPods include the option to hear the click from within the iPod, through the headphone port, or both.

## Select button

The bull's-eye of all iPods—the center button—selects a menu item. If the Settings menu item is selected, for example, pushing the Select button moves you to the Settings screen, where you can select additional settings.

When you press the Select button while a song is playing and the Play screen is visible, you move to another Play screen, where you can *scrub* (quickly navigate forward and back with the scroll wheel) your song. On third-generation iPods and later (including the iPod mini and iPod Photo), pressing this button twice while a song plays moves you to a rating screen, where you can assign a rating of one to five stars for the song that's playing (**Figure 1.11**).

**Figure 1.11**
Recent iPods allow you to rate songs from one to five stars.

Note that this works differently if you have an iPod Photo, the song you're playing includes album art, and the iTunes' Display Album Artwork on Your iPod option is enabled. Under these conditions, when you press the Select button while a song plays, you're taken to a screen that shows a larger image of the album art. Press Select again and you're taken to the scrub screen. Press Select one more time to see the ratings screen.

# Up Top (Early iPods)

The tops of the first- and second-generation iPods (**Figure 1.12**) carry two ports and one switch. Here's what they do.

**Figure 1.12**

The ports on the second-generation iPod.

## FireWire port

As the name implies, this port is where you plug in your 6-pin FireWire cable. The iPod uses the FireWire cable both for power (power pulled from either an up-and-running-but-not-sleeping computer or the power adapter) and for transferring data between the iPod and a Mac or PC. The second-generation iPod models include a plastic cover that keeps gunk out of the FireWire port. The original iPods lack this cover.

## Headphone jack

When the iPod was first released, a few people were concerned that it bore only a single audio-out port: the Headphone jack. Other, less-capable music players carried two ports: one for headphones and another for line-level output, which is the kind of output that's acceptable to home and car stereos.

It turned out that there was no need for concern. Of course you can plug a set of headphones into the iPod, and yes, you can use any set of headphones as long as it carries a stereo Walkman-style miniplug. But you can also plug the iPod into your stereo. Elsewhere in the book, I'll explain how to do so. For those of you who are interested in such numbers, the iPod has a maximum output power of 60mW rms (30mW per channel) everywhere except in Europe.

No, I'm not kidding. The default output of the iPod exceeds the decibel limit allowed for consumer audio devices in France. European iPods ship with the volume level adjusted in a way that's acceptable to the French government. In the Troubleshooting chapter (Chapter 9), I'll offer hints about ways to skirt this limitation.

### Hold switch

When you push the Hold switch to the left, the front buttons lock. This feature is particularly handy when you don't want the iPod to begin playing when it's bumped in your backpack or pushed in your pocket.

## Top and Bottom (Dock-connector iPods)

Apple has changed the port configuration on recent iPods. They work this way.

### Headphone jack and Hold switch

Today's third- and fourth-generation iPods, the iPod Photo, and iPod mini sport a Headphone jack, a Hold switch, and a Remote Control connector up top (**Figure 1.13**, **Figure 1.14**). The Headphone jack and Hold switch work nearly the same way as they do on the older iPods, providing audio output and disabling the iPod's controls.

**Figure 1.13**
The top of the fourth-generation iPods.

**Figure 1.14**
The port atop the iPod mini.

I say "nearly" because the Headphone jack, in combination with the Remote Control connector on third- and fourth-generation iPods and the iPod Photo, supports not only audio output, but also audio input. With a compatible microphone, you can record low-quality audio (8kHz) on your original iPod. As I write this, there are three devices for doing this: Belkin's $35 iPod Voice Recorder (www.belkin.com), Belkin's $30 iPod Microphone Adapter (which allows you to record with a compatible microphone of your choice), and the $40 iTalk from Griffin Technology (www.griffintechnology.com). Voice recording is not currently supported on the iPod mini.

 The iPod Photo's Headphone jack is different from other iPods in that it's capable of also transmitting composite video (which I'll explain in greater detail in Chapter 3).

## Dock Connector port

The iPod's designers replaced the FireWire port of the old iPods with a proprietary port that handles both power and data chores for the device. This Dock Connector port, on the bottom of the third- and fourth-generation iPods, the iPod Photo, and iPod mini, supports data transfer via both FireWire and USB 2.0 (**Figure 1.15**, **Figure 1.16**).

**Figure 1.15**
The data/power port at the bottom of the iPod.

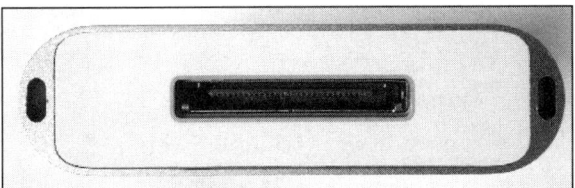

**Figure 1.16**
The data/power port at the bottom of the iPod mini.

# Interface

Considering how easy the iPod is to use, it's hard to believe the number of navigation screens that make up its interface. In the following pages, I scrutinize each screen. Except where indicated, the interface for the original iPod and the mini is exactly the same.

## Main Screen

The main screen (**Figure 1.17**), which displays the word *iPod* at the top, is your gateway to the iPod. In a way, it's akin to the Mac's Finder or Windows' My Computer window—a place to get started.

**Figure 1.17**
The fourth-generation iPod's main screen.

Apple changed the main screen of the iPod with the fourth-generation models. The fourth-generation iPod's main screen contains these commands:

- Music
- Extras
- Settings
- Shuffle Songs
- Backlight
- Now Playing (if a song is playing or paused)

Living up to its name, the iPod Photo includes an additional command in its main screen—Photos—so its main screen reads like this (**Figure 1.18**):

- Music
- Photos
- Extras
- Settings
- Shuffle Songs
- Backlight
- Now Playing (if a song is playing or paused)

**Figure 1.18**
The iPod Photo's main screen.

In the main screen on an iPod mini and an original iPod running iPod Software 1.3 Updater through iPod Software 2.2 Updater (the version of the iPod software current for third-generation iPods as this book goes to press), you can, by default, select the following items:

- Playlists
- Browse
- Extras
- Settings
- Backlight
- Now Playing (if a song is playing or paused)

Earlier versions of the iPod software do not include the Backlight command; instead, they offer an About command. On iPods running iPod Software 1.3 Updater or later, the About command is available in the Settings screen (described later in this chapter). Here's what you'll find within each item.

# Music (Fourth-generation iPods and iPod Photo Only)

As we go to press, this entry appears only on fourth-generation iPods and the iPod Photo (**Figure 1.19**). The Music entry serves an almost identical purpose as earlier iPods' Browse entry. When you choose the Music command and press Select, the resulting Music screen reveals these entries: Playlists, Artists, Albums, Songs, Genres, Composers, and Audiobooks. I explain the purpose of all these entries in the following sections.

**Figure 1.19**
The fourth-generation iPod and iPod Photo's Music screen.

## Playlists

Regardless of which iPod you're using, when you choose Playlists (**Figure 1.20**) and press the Select button, you'll see a screen that contains the playlists you have downloaded to your iPod. These playlists are created and configured in iTunes or another music application, such as the Windows programs Musicmatch Jukebox, EphPod, Anapod Explorer, and XPlay. How you configure them is up to you. You may, for example, want to gather all your jazz favorites in one playlist and put ska in another. Or, if you have an iPod shared by the family, Dad may gather his psychedelic songs of the '60s in his personal playlist, whereas sister Sue creates a playlist full of hip-hop and house music. When I discuss iTunes and other music applications in later chapters, I'll look at additional approaches for putting together playlists.

**Figure 1.20**
The Playlists screen.

You may notice a couple of other playlists that you didn't create: 60's Music, My Top Rated, Recently Played, and Top 25 Most Played, for example. These are Smart Playlists—playlists automatically created by iTunes. As their names hint, these playlists list songs recorded in the '60s, songs that you think are just swell, songs that you've played in the not-too-distant past, and songs that you've played more often than others.

After you select a playlist and press the Select button, the songs within that playlist appear in a scrollable screen (**Figure 1.21**), and the name of the playlist appears at the top of the screen. Just select the song you want to play, and press the Select button. When you do, you'll move to the Now Playing screen (**Figure 1.22**), which can display the number of songs in the playlist, the name of the song playing, the artist, and, on the original iPod, the name of the album from which the song came. On an iPod Photo, you'll also see a picture of the album cover if the song has this information embedded in it and iTunes' Display Album Artwork on Your iPod option is enabled. Because the iPod mini's screen is so small, Apple decided to omit album information from the Now Playing screen on these smaller iPods. (If some of this information didn't appear in iTunes originally, it won't be displayed on your iPod.) Also appearing in this screen are two timer displays: elapsed time and remaining time. The screen contains a graphic thermometer display that gives you a visual representation of how far along you are in the song.

**Figure 1.21**
The songs within a playlist.

**Figure 1.22**
The Play screen.

 Text that runs off the screen in the Song, Artist, and Album screens is treated differently on the iPod Photo than it is on other iPods. The white iPods and the iPod mini place an ellipsis (...) at the end of an entry that exceeds the width of the screen. The iPod Photo will scroll selected text from right to left if it's longer than the screen can accommodate.

You can move one more screen from the Now Playing screen by using the scroll wheel or Select button. If you turn the scroll wheel, you'll move to a screen nearly identical to the Now Playing screen where you can adjust the iPod's volume (**Figure 1.23**). When you stop moving the scroll wheel, you'll be taken back to the Now Playing screen after a couple of seconds. If you press the Select button on any iPod except the iPod Photo while you're in the Now Playing screen, you'll be able to scrub through the song (**Figure 1.24**). (As I explained earlier, the iPod Photo displays an album art screen if a song has such art, you've chosen to enable that album art, and you press the Select button when in the

Now Playing screen.) Like the Now Playing screen, the Scrub screen carries a thermometer display that indicates the playing location with a small diamond. Just push the scroll wheel back or forth to start scrubbing.

**Figure 1.23**
The Play screen's volume control.

**Figure 1.24**
The Play screen's scrub control.

## On-The-Go Dock-connector iPods

Scroll to the bottom of the Playlists screen on a third- or fourth-generation iPod, iPod Photo, or iPod mini, and you'll find an additional playlist that you didn't create: the On-The-Go playlist (**Figure 1.25**). Introduced with iPod Software 2.0 Updater, this playlist is a special one that you create directly on the iPod. It's particularly useful when you need to create a new playlist *right now* and don't have a computer you can plug your iPod into. It works this way:

**1.** Select a song, artist, playlist, or album.

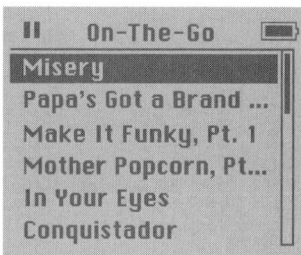

**Figure 1.25**
The On-The-Go menu allows you to create custom playlists directly on the iPod.

2. Hold down the Select button until the selected item flashes a few times.

   This flashing indicates that the item has been added to the On-The-Go playlist.

3. Repeat this procedure for any other songs, artists, playlists, and albums you want to add to the list.

4. When you're ready to play your selections, choose On-The-Go from the Playlists screen, and press the Select button.

   In the resulting On-The-Go screen, you'll see a list of songs you've added to the list in the order in which you added them. (The song, artist, playlist, or album you selected first will appear at the top of the list.)

5. Press Select to begin playing the playlist.

To clear the On-The-Go playlist, scroll to the bottom of the playlist, and select Clear Playlist. In the resulting Clear screen, select Clear Playlist; then press Select.

When you update an iPod mini or a third-generation iPod that's running the iPod Software 2.1 Updater or later, the On-The-Go playlist you created appears in iTunes' Source list as well as in the iPod's Playlist screen—thus ensuring that you don't lose the contents of the playlists you so carefully created on the iPod. Each such playlist is numbered successively: On-The-Go 1, On-The-Go 2, and On-The-Go 3, for example. These playlists are copied back to your iPod, and the On-The-Go entry is cleared.

With the fourth-generation iPod and iPod Photo, Apple expands the On-The-Go playlist's capabilities, allowing you to create multiple On-The-Go playlists on your iPod. To do so, follow these steps:

1. Follow the steps above to create an On-The-Go playlist.

2. Scroll to the On-The-Go entry in the Playlists screen, and press Select.

   The songs you added to your playlists appear in the On-The-Go screen.

**3.** Scroll to the bottom of the On-The-Go screen, select Save Playlist, and press Select.

**4.** In the resulting Save screen, scroll to Save Playlist, and press Select.

Your playlist will be saved as New Playlist 1. Each time you save a new On-The-Go playlist, it will be called New Playlist and assigned a number one greater than the last New Playlist created.

When you synchronize your fourth-generation iPod or iPod Photo with iTunes, your saved On-The-Go playlists will appear successively numbered in iTunes, bearing the name On-The-Go—On-The-Go 1, On-The-Go 2, and (you guessed it) On-The-Go 3, for example. During synchronization, these On-The-Go playlists are copied to your iPod, and the New Playlist entries are removed.

# Browse (Not Found on Fourth-generation iPods and iPod Photo)

The iPod allows you to browse the contents of your portable player in several ways: by Artists, Albums, Songs, Genres, and Composers. When you highlight the Browse selection in the iPod's main window and press the Select button, you'll find all these choices listed in the Browse window. The fourth-generation iPod and iPod Photo don't contain a Browse command. Rather, the Music command serves nearly the same purpose and contains all the entries below. Here's what you'll find for each entry.

## Artists

The Artists screen displays the names of any artists on your iPod (**Figure 1.26**). Choose an artist's name and press Select, and you'll be transported to that artist's screen, where you have the opportunity to play every song on your iPod by that artist or select a particular album by that artist.

**Figure 1.26**
The Artists screen.

You'll also spy the All entry at the top of the Artists screen. Should you choose this entry, you'll be taken to the All Albums screen, where you can select all albums by all artists. The All Albums screen contains an All command of its own. Select this command, and you'll move to the All Songs screen, which lists all songs by all artists on your iPod. (But if a song doesn't have an artist entry, the song won't appear in this screen.)

## Albums

Choose the Albums entry and press Select, and you'll see every album on your iPod (**Figure 1.27**). Choose an album and press the Select button to play the album from beginning to end. The Albums screen also contains an All button, which, when selected, displays all the songs on all the albums on your iPod. (If the song doesn't have an album entry, it won't appear in this screen.)

**Figure 1.27**
The Albums screen.

 An album entry can contain a single song. As long as the album field has been filled in for a particular song within iTunes or another iPod-compatible application (I'll discuss this topic in Chapters 2 and 4), that song will appear in the Albums screen.

## Songs

Choose Songs and press Select, and you'll be presented with a list of all the songs on your iPod (**Figure 1.28**).

**Figure 1.28**
The Songs screen.

## Genres

The iPod has the capability to sort songs by genre: Acoustic, Blues, Reggae, and Techno, for example. If a song has been tagged with a genre entry (see the sidebar "I'll Need to See Some ID" in this section), you can choose it by genre in the Genres screen (**Figure 1.29**).

**Figure 1.29**
The Genres screen.

## Composers

The iPod can also group songs by composers. This feature, added in iPod Software 1.2 Updater, allows you to sort classical music more easily (**Figure 1.30**).

**Figure 1.30**
The Composers screen.

## Audiobooks (fourth-generation iPods and iPod Photo only)

As you'll learn later in the book, the iPod is capable of playing audiobook files purchased from Audible.com and the iTunes Music Store. These audiobooks can be identified by their extension—.aa if you purchased the book from Audible.com, or .m4b if you bought it from the iTunes Music Store. When a fourth-generation iPod or iPod Photo stores one of these specially formatted files, the audiobook's name appears in the iPod's Audiobooks window (which appears when you choose the Audiobooks command in the Music screen and press the Select button). Previous iPods mix audiobooks in with your music files.

 If you have an earlier iPod, you don't have access to the Audiobooks command. However, you can duplicate its functionality by creating a Smart Playlist in iTunes that identifies your audiobooks and places them in a special playlist. Load this playlist onto your iPod, and choose it to listen to your books. I'll provide more specific instructions for creating Smart Playlists in Chapter 2.

### I'll Need to See Some ID

You're undoubtedly wondering how the iPod knows that Bob Marley's "Buffalo Soldier" is reggae and that Paul Hindemith composed *Mathis der Maler*. There's no profound trick to it. The iPod simply looks at each file's *ID3 tags*. ID3 tags are little bits of information that are included with a song's music data, such as title, album, artist, composer, genre, and year the song was recorded.

If someone has taken the time to enter this information (someone like you, for example), the iPod will use it to sort songs by genre, composer, or decade recorded. You can edit a song's ID3 tag in iTunes. In Chapter 2 I'll show you how.

## Photos (iPod Photo only)

Coincidentally enough, the Photo command appears only on the iPod Photo (**Figure 1.31**). Rather than sprinkle tidbits of information about this iPod model here and there, I've devoted an entire chapter to it. For more information on the wonderful places this command takes you, see Chapter 3.

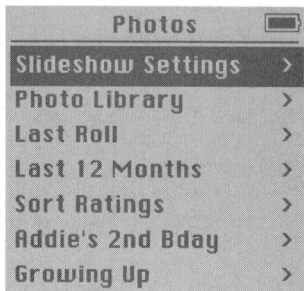

**Figure 1.31**
The iPod Photo's Photos screen.

## Extras

The Extras screen is the means to all the iPod's nonmusical functions—its contacts, calendars, clock, and games. Here's what you'll find for each entry.

### Clock

Yes, the iPod can tell time. Clicking Clock displays the current time and date on all iPods. On third-generation iPods and later, clicking Clock also displays commands for setting the iPod's alarm clock, sleep timer, and date and time (**Figure 1.32**).

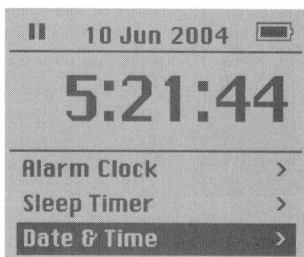

**Figure 1.32**
The Clock screen.

## Alarm Clock

The Alarm Clock screen provides options for turning the alarm on and off, setting the time for the alarm to go off, and specifying the sound the alarm will play (a simple beep or the contents of one of the playlists on your iPod). This function is not available on the first- and second-generation iPods.

If the iPod's alarm clock goes off while you're listening to music with headphones, you're likely to miss the alarm if it's set to beep. Unlike alarms tied to calendar events, the alarm clock issues no visual display—it beeps or plays a playlist; that's it. If you think you'll be listening to music when the alarm is configured to perform its lowly job, choose a playlist as an alarm rather than a beep. When the iPod suddenly changes playlists, you'll know that the alarm has gone off.

## Sleep Timer

To save battery power, the iPod includes a sleep function that powers down your iPod after a certain time has elapsed. The Sleep Timer settings allow you to determine how long an interval of inactivity has to pass before your iPod takes a snooze. The available settings are Off, 15 Minutes, 30 Minutes, 60 Minutes, 90 Minutes, and 120 Minutes. On older iPods, this command is in the Settings screen.

## Date & Time

The Date & Time command is your means for setting the time zone that your iPod inhabits, as well as the current date and time. On older iPods, this command is in the Settings screen.

## Set Time Zone

Click this command, and in the resulting Time Zone screen, choose your time zone—anything between and including Eniwetok to Auckland. This function is not available on first- and second-generation iPods.

### Set Time & Date

Select and click this command to set the iPod's date and time. Use the scroll wheel to change the hour, minutes, AM/PM, date, month, and year values, and use the Forward and Previous buttons to move from value to value. This function is not available on first- and second-generation iPods.

### Time

Use this command to display a 12- or 24-hour clock. This function is not available on first- and second-generation iPods.

### Time in Title

This command allows the iPod to display the time in the iPod's title bar. This function is not available on first- and second-generation iPods.

 On third-generation and later iPods, the Set Time Zone, Set Date & Time, Time, and Time in Title commands are also available in the Date & Time screen that's accessible from the Settings screen.

## Contacts

The capability for the iPod to store and view contacts was introduced in the iPod Software 1.1 Updater. I'll discuss how to create contacts elsewhere in the book. In the meantime, you need to know only that to access your contacts, you choose Contacts in the Extras screen and press the Select button (**Figure 1.33**). Scroll through your list of contacts and press Select again to view the information within a contact. If a contact contains more information than will fit in the display, use the scroll wheel to scroll down the window.

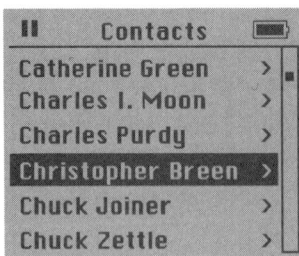

**Figure 1.33**
The Contacts screen.

If you haven't placed any contacts on your iPod, clicking the Contacts command will reveal two entries on the Contacts screen: Instructions and Sample. You can probably guess that selecting Instructions provides you directions on how to move contacts to your iPod. The Sample command shows you what a complete contact looks like.

## Calendar

The capability for the iPod to list your appointments came with version 1.2 of the iPod software. I'll address calendar creation later in the book, so for now, just know that when you click the Calendar entry on a third- or fourth-generation iPod, iPod Photo, or iPod mini, you'll see options for viewing all your calendars in a single calendar window, viewing separate calendars (your work or home calendar, for example) if you've created your calendars on the Mac with Apple's iCal, viewing calendars you've created with applications other than iCal under an "Other" heading, viewing To Do items, and setting an alarm for calendar events.

When you select a calendar, the current month is displayed in a window with the current day highlighted (**Figure 1.34**). If a day has an event attached to it, that day displays a small black rectangle. Use the scroll wheel to move to a different day; scroll forward to look into the future, and scroll back to be transported back in time. To jump to the next or previous month, use the Fast Forward or Rewind buttons, respectively. When you want to see the details of an event, scroll to its day and press the Select button. The details of that event will be displayed in the resulting screen.

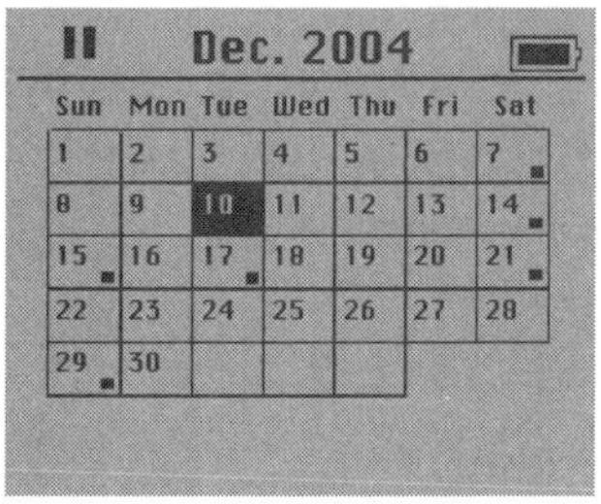

**Figure 1.34**
The Calendar screen.

Older iPods have more limited calendar functions. Although you can view all your calendars, individual calendars created with iCal, or "Other" calendars created by applications other than iCal, you can't view To Do items. On these iPods, you configure calendar alarms in the Settings screen. The three available settings are Off (no alarm is issued), On (a little tinkling sound erupts from the iPod—the iPod itself, not the headphones—and an alarm screen that describes the event is displayed), and Silent (the alarm screen appears without audio accompaniment).

Calendar alarms for the third- and fourth-generation iPod, iPod Photo, and iPod mini appear in the Calendars screen. The three alarm options on these iPods are Off, Beep (the same thing as On for older iPods), and Silent.

## Notes

New with the third-generation iPods was a Notes feature that allows you to store text files (4 KB or smaller, or about 4,096 characters) on your iPod. To add notes to your iPod, mount the iPod on your computer (the iPod must be configured to appear on the Desktop), double-click the iPod to reveal its contents, and drag a text file into the iPod's Notes folder. When you unmount your iPod, you'll find the contents of your text file in the Notes area of the Extras screen. The first- and second-generation iPods don't have this function.

## Photo Import (third- and fourth-generation iPods and iPod Photo only)

One of the recent spiffy additions to the iPod's compendium of features is the capability to store digital photographs on third- and fourth-generation iPods and iPod Photo (this feature is currently not supported on the iPod mini). You can accomplish this with the help of a compatible media transfer unit. (Belkin's $99 Media Reader for iPod is the only such unit as we go to press.) When you plug such a device into a third- or fourth-generation iPod or iPod Photo's data port, the iPod displays a screen indicating that the device is attached. When you insert a media card (such as a SmartMedia card), the iPod tells you how many pictures the card holds and offers you the option to download those pictures to your iPod.

When you've performed this operation once on a third- and fourth-generation iPod, the Photo Import command appears in the Extras area of the iPod (on the iPod Photo this command appears in the Photos screen). To import pictures, highlight this command, press Select, and you're transported to the Photos screen, where you find an Import Photos command, as well as a list of the import sessions you've previously performed (denoted as "rolls" of pictures—Roll #1, for example). You can see the date when the pictures were imported to the iPod, how many photos are in the roll, and how many megabytes the roll consumes by selecting a roll and pressing Select to move to the Roll screen (**Figure 1.35**). You'll also see options for deleting the roll and canceling (which takes you back to the Photos screen). I'll discuss importing photos with a third- and fourth-generation iPod at greater length in the Accessories chapter and deal with the iPod Photo's capabilities in Chapter 3.

**Figure 1.35**
A "roll" of film stored on the iPod.

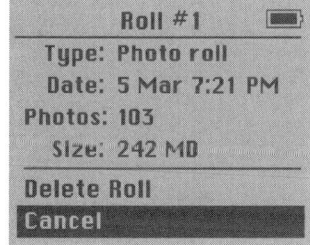

 Belkin offers another photocentric device: the $79 Belkin Digital Camera Link for iPod. It currently works with the third- and fourth-generation iPods and iPod Photo and will download pictures from a digital camera via the camera's USB cable.

## Voice Memos (third- and fourth-generation iPods and iPod Photo only)

Another nifty original iPod addition is the device's ability to record voice memos. When you plug a compatible recording device into the Headphone jack and remote control port, the Voice Memos command appears in the iPod's Extras screen. Currently, only Belkin's Voice Recorder, Universal Microphone Adapter, and Griffin Technology's iTalk devices are compatible with the iPod voice-recording function, and voice memos work only with third- and fourth-generation iPods and the iPod Photo. (This feature is incompatible with the mini.)

Click the Select button, and you're taken to the Voice Memos screen, where you can choose to record a new voice memo or play back memos you've already recorded (**Figure 1.36**). You'll find more information about Voice Memos in the Accessories chapter.

**Figure 1.36**
The Voice Memos screen.

## Games

Once upon a time, the iPod had a single hidden game that you could access only if you held down the Select button for several seconds in a particular screen. With the iPod Updater 1.2, Apple decided to reveal this secret game—a form of the classic Breakout game called Brick (**Figure 1.37**)—by placing the Game command in the Extras screen.

**Figure 1.37**
The Brick game screen.

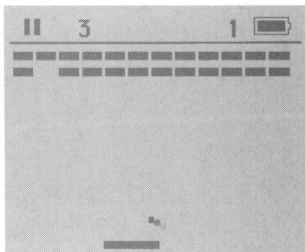

Apple includes three additional games—Music Quiz, Parachute, and Solitaire—with the third- and fourth-generation iPods, iPod Photo, and iPod mini. (Regrettably, the iPod Software 1.3 Updater and later doesn't add these games to older iPods.) When you choose the Games option in the Extras screen of iPods that carry the Dock connector, you'll see listings for Brick, Music Quiz, Parachute, and Solitaire.

To play Brick, just select it and press the Select button. Press Select again to begin the game, and use the scroll wheel to move the paddle.

 Maybe it's just my perception, but it seems that Brick is a harder game on the mini than it is on the original iPod. With the mini's smaller screen, it seems that the wall of bricks is closer to the paddle, making less travel time for the ball and, therefore, a faster game.

Music Quiz—a game that comes with the iPod Software 2.1 Updater and later—is a "needle drop" game. For the benefit of my younger readers who question why in the world anyone would want to drop a needle and what could possibly be so sporting about it, allow me to explain.

The needle I refer to is the one you find on a phonograph. To play the game, you place a phonograph's tone arm at a random location on a spinning phonograph record—usually, in the middle of a song. The point of the game is to try to guess, in the shortest time possible, which song is playing.

The iPod's Music Quiz replicates this gay diversion by playing a random portion of a song stored on your iPod and displaying five titles on the iPod's screen (**Figure 1.38**). Your job is to scroll to the correct title and push the Select button as quickly as your fingers allow. If you fail to perform this function in 10 seconds, you lose. The more swiftly you correctly identify the song, the more points you earn. At the seven-second mark, one of the titles disappears. At five seconds, another vanishes, and so on until just one title remains and your time expires.

**Figure 1.38**
A Music Quiz screen.

Although some may consider this game to be a not-terribly-productive way to drain your iPod's battery, it could have some practical application in a music class. Students enrolled in music history classes are often required to identify a piece of music based on hearing just a snippet. An iPod loaded with the right music could be a helpful study aid.

Parachute, on the other hand, has little practical value (but you may find it more fun than Music Quiz). After you've selected the game, press Select to begin (**Figure 1.39**). Your job is to rotate the cannon (using the scroll wheel) and blast helicopters and parachutists out of the sky. You lose the game when a certain number of parachutists land safely or one lands directly on your cannon emplacement.

**Figure 1.39**
The Parachute game.

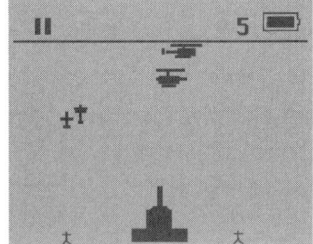

Solitaire is an implementation of the classic Klondike card game (**Figure 1.40**). To play, arrange alternating colors of cards in descending sequence—a sequence that could run jack of hearts, 10 of spades, 9 of diamonds, 8 of clubs, and so on—in the bottom portion of the screen. In the top portion of the window, you arrange cards in an ascending sequence of the same suit—ace, 2, 3, 4, and 5 of hearts, for example. In other words: classic solitaire.

**Figure 1.40**
Yes, those little figures represent numbers and suits.

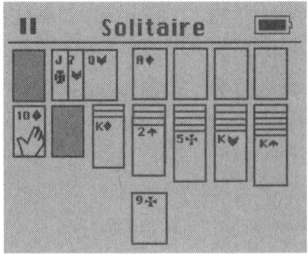

Navigating this game is not completely intuitive. Use the scroll wheel to move the hand pointer to the card you want to move. Press Select to move the selected card to the bottom of the screen. Then move the pointer to where you want to place the card and press Select again. The game tries to be helpful by moving the pointer to the place where you're most likely to place the card.

The other difficulty with Solitaire—at least when played on any iPod other than the iPod Photo—is that the writing on the cards is so tiny; it's nearly impossible to play the game without the iPod's backlight switched on. This is *not* the game you want to play when you're running on battery power.

 You'll still want to play Solitaire with an iPod Photo's backlighting switched on (heck, you'll want to do nearly everything with this iPod's backlighting engaged because it looks so cool), but you'll find the cards much easier to read in color than they are in an older iPod's grayscale.

# Settings

The Settings screen (**Figure 1.41**) is the path to your iPod preferences—including backlight timer and startup-volume settings, EQ selection, and the language the iPod displays. The following sections look at these settings individually.

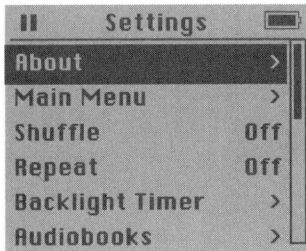

**Figure 1.41**
The Settings screen.

## About

The About screen is where you'll find the name of your iPod (changeable within iTunes and such Windows players as Musicmatch Jukebox and XPlay), the number of songs the iPod currently holds (and, where applicable, the number of photos), the total hard-drive space, the amount of available space, the software version, and your iPod's serial number. If you have the Windows iPod, you'll also see the Format Windows entry. (The Mac version of the iPod doesn't bother to tell you that it's formatted for the Macintosh.)

On iPods running iPod Software 1.2 Updater and earlier, this command is in the iPod's main menu.

## Main Menu

This command was introduced with the third generation of iPods. The Main Menu command offers you a way to customize what you see in the iPod's main screen. Choose Main Menu, and press the Select button. In the resulting screen on the fourth-generation iPod, you can choose to view the following commands: Music, Playlists, Artists, Albums, Songs, Genres, Composers, Audiobooks, Extras, Clock, Contacts, Calendar, Notes, Photo Import, Voice Memos, Games, Shuffle Songs, Backlight, Sleep, and Reset Main Menu (**Figure 1.42**). To enable or disable a command, press the Select button to toggle the command on or off. To return the main menu to its default setting, choose the Reset Main Menu command, press Select, choose Reset in the Reset Menus screen, and press Select again.

**Figure 1.42**
Go to the Main Menu screen to customize the iPod's main menu.

The iPod Photo adds Photos and Photo Import to this list.

The iPod mini and third-generation iPod do not include the Music, Audiobooks, and Shuffle Songs options on their Main Menu screens. This option is not available at all on first- and second-generation iPods.

## Shuffle

Selecting Shuffle and pressing the Select button toggles you through three settings: Off, Songs, and Albums. On iPods made prior to the fourth-generation iPod, when Shuffle is set to Off, the iPod plays the songs in a playlist in the order in which they appear onscreen. The Songs setting plays all the songs within a selected playlist or album in random order. If no album or playlist is selected, the iPod plays all the songs on the iPod in random order. And the Albums setting plays the songs within each album in order but shuffles the order in which the albums are played.

The fourth-generation iPod and iPod Photo shuffle a bit differently. As you'll see in a few pages, the fourth-generation iPod and the iPod Photo's main screens include a Shuffle Songs command. How the Settings screen's Shuffle command is configured has some effect on how this Shuffle Songs command works. See the "Shuffle Songs" section later in this chapter to learn more.

## Repeat

The Repeat setting also offers three options: Off, One, and All. When you choose Off, the iPod won't repeat songs. Choose One, and you'll hear the selected song play repeatedly. Choose All, and all the songs within the selected playlist or album will repeat when the playlist or album has played all the way through. If you haven't selected a playlist or album, all the songs on the iPod will repeat after they've played through.

## Backlight Timer

The iPod's backlight pulls its power from the battery, and when it's left on for very long, you significantly shorten the time you can play your iPod on a single charge. For this reason, Apple includes a backlight timer that automatically switches off backlighting after a certain user-configurable interval. You set that interval by choosing the Backlight Timer setting.

On iPods prior to the iPod Photo, settings available to you are Off, 2 Seconds, 5 Seconds, 10 Seconds, 20 Seconds, and (for those who give not a whit about battery life or who are running the iPod from the power adapter) Always On. The iPod Photo includes one additional setting—15 Seconds.

## Audiobooks (fourth-generation iPods and iPod Photo only)

One of the unique features of the fourth-generation iPod and iPod Photo is their ability to slow down or speed up the playback of audiobooks without changing the pitch of the narrator. When you select Audiobooks in the Settings screen, you're offered three options on the resulting Audiobooks screen: Slower, Normal, and Faster (**Figure 1.43**). The Slower and Faster commands slow down or speed up playback by about 25 percent, respectively.

**Figure 1.43**
With the fourth-generation iPod and iPod Photo, you can slow down or speed up playback of audiobooks.

You're likely thinking that it would take a minor miracle to pull this off without the book's sounding odd. You're right; it would. And so far, Apple has failed to achieve this miracle. When you slow down an audiobook, the resulting audio sounds like it was recorded in a particularly reverberant bathroom; you hear a very short echo after each word. Files that have been speeded up appear to have lost all the spaces between words, making the book sound as though it's being read by an overcaffeinated auctioneer.

## EQ

Ever since the 1.1 software update, you've been able to assign specific *equalization* (EQ) settings to your iPod. And what, exactly, is equalization? It's the process of boosting or cutting certain frequencies in the audio spectrum—making the low frequencies louder and the high frequencies quieter, for example. If you've ever adjusted the bass and treble controls on your home or car stereo, you get the idea.

The iPod now comes with the same EQ settings as iTunes 4. Those settings include:

- Off
- Acoustic
- Bass Booster
- Bass Reducer
- Classical
- Dance
- Deep
- Electronic
- Flat
- Hip Hop
- Jazz
- Latin
- Loudness
- Lounge
- Piano
- Pop
- R & B
- Rock
- Small Speakers
- Spoken Word
- Treble Booster
- Treble Reducer
- Vocal Booster

Although you can listen to each EQ setting to get an idea of what it does, you may find it easier to open iTunes; choose Equalizer from the Window menu; and, in the resulting Equalizer window, choose the various EQ settings from the window's pop-up menu. The equalizer's 10-band sliders will show you which frequencies have been boosted and which have been cut. Any slider that appears above the 0 dB line indicates a frequency that has been boosted. Conversely, sliders that appear below 0 dB have been cut.

I'll look at the equalizer in greater depth when I examine iTunes.

## EQ and the iPod

Apple was kind enough to include a configurable equalizer (EQ) as part of the iPod Software 1.1 Updater and later, but the way that the EQ settings in iTunes and the iPod interact is a little confusing. Allow me to end that confusion.

Macintosh users undoubtedly know that in iTunes 2, 3, and 4, you can assign an EQ setting to songs individually by clicking the song, pressing Command-I, clicking the Options tab, and then choosing an EQ setting from the Equalizer Preset menu. You can do the same thing in the Windows version of iTunes (EQ is not supported by Musicmatch Jukebox, however). When you move songs to your iPod, these EQ settings move right along with them, but you won't be able to use them unless you configure the iPod correctly.

If, for example, you have EQ switched off on the iPod, songs that have an assigned EQ preset won't play with that setting. Instead, your songs will play without the benefit of EQ. If you set the iPod's EQ to Flat, the EQ setting that you preset in iTunes will play on the iPod. If you select one of the other EQ settings on the iPod (Latin or Electronic, for example), songs without EQ presets assigned in iTunes will use the iPod EQ setting. Songs with EQ settings assigned in iTunes will use the iTunes setting.

If you'd like to hear how a particular song sounds on your iPod with a different EQ setting, start playing the song on the iPod, press the Menu button until you return to the Main screen, select Settings, select EQ, and then select one of the EQ settings. The song will immediately take on the EQ setting you've chosen, but this setting won't stick on subsequent playback. If you want to change the song's EQ more permanently, you must do so in iTunes.

## Sound Check

New with the iPod Software 1.2 Updater, Sound Check attempts to maintain a consistent volume among songs. Before Sound Check arrived on the scene, you'd constantly fiddle with the iPod's volume because one song was too loud, the next too quiet, the next quieter still, and the next painfully loud. Sound Check does its best to produce volumes that don't vary so wildly.

To use Sound Check, you must first select the Sound Check option in iTunes 3 or 4 (iTunes 2, the version of iTunes that's compatible with

Mac OS 9, doesn't carry the Sound Check feature), have iTunes 3 or 4 apply Sound Check to the music files on your computer, and then download those Sound Checked files to your iPod.

## Contrast (not available on the iPod Photo)

To change the display's contrast, select the Contrast setting, press Select, and use the scroll wheel to darken or lighten the display.

The iPod Photo doesn't include any controls for changing the brightness, contrast, or color balance of the screen.

## Clicker

This simple On/Off setting on all iPods, save the fourth-generation model, allows you to turn off the click that the iPod makes when you press a button or move your thumb across the scroll wheel.

The fourth-generation iPod and iPod Photo has a more advanced clicker than previous iPods. When you choose Clicker and press the Select button on one of these iPods, you have four options: Off, Speaker, Headphones, and Both. As the names imply, Speaker causes the iPod to emit a clicking sound from within the device, Headphones plays a click sound through the headphone jack, and Both channels the click sound through both the internal speaker element and the headphone jack.

## Date & Time

On the third- and fourth-generation iPods, iPod Photo, and iPod mini, this command is also accessible from the Date & Time command in the Clock screen.

As I said when discussing the Clock command, this command includes options for configuring the time zone, date, and time; displaying a 12- or 24-hour clock; and placing the current time in the iPod's menu bar.

On first- and second-generation iPods, you can use this command to set only the time zone and the current date and time.

## Contacts

The Contacts setting allows you to sort your contacts by last or first name and to display those contacts by last or first name.

## Language

The iPod can display 14 languages: English, Japanese, French, German, Spanish, Italian, Danish, Dutch, Norwegian, Swedish, Finnish, Korean, and Chinese (Traditional and Simplified). In some instances, the iPod can display multiple languages. It's possible to view American titles on an iPod that displays the Japanese language, for example. I'll show you how when I talk about iTunes.

Should someone set your iPod to a language you don't understand (one of my favorite April Fool's jokes, by the way), you can reset it. On iPods prior to the fourth-generation model, choose the fourth command from the top in the Main menu, choose the third menu from the bottom in the next screen, and then select your language in the resulting list. With the fourth-generation iPod, select the third command from the top and then the third command from the bottom on the next screen to access the Language screen. With the iPod Photo, you choose the fourth command from the top and then the third command from the bottom.

## Legal

If you care to view a few copyright notices, feel free to choose the Legal setting and press the Select button.

## Reset All Settings

As the name implies, selecting Reset All Settings, pressing the Select button, and selecting Reset returns the iPod to its default settings. This doesn't mean that your music library will be erased. Rather, this setting turns Shuffle off, Repeat off, Sound Check off, EQ off, Backlight Timer off, Contrast to the middle setting, Alarm on, Sleep Timer off, and Clicker on. Then it transports you to the Language screen, where English is selected by default (though this setup may be different on iPods sold in non-English-speaking countries).

# Shuffle Songs (Fourth-generation iPods and iPod Photo Only)

When Apple's engineers redesigned the menu structure for the fourth-generation iPod, they decided to give iPod owners easy access to a shuffle command. The result of their work is the Shuffle Songs command in the main screen.

One might think that pressing this button simply plays all the material on the iPod in random order. Not exactly. Shuffle Songs changes its behavior based on the Shuffle setting in the iPod's Settings screen. It works this way:

If you press Shuffle Songs when Shuffle is set to Off or to Songs, the iPod will play songs at random. Note that it won't play any files it recognizes as audiobooks.

If you press Shuffle Songs when Shuffle is set to Albums, the iPod picks an album at random and then plays the songs on that album in succession (the order in which they appear on the album). When that album finishes playing, the iPod plays a different album.

Note that if you also switch the Repeat command in the Settings menu to All and press Shuffle Songs, the iPod plays through all the songs on the iPod in the order determined by the Shuffle command and then repeats them in the same order in which they were shuffled originally. For example, if you have three songs on your iPod—A, B, and C—and the iPod shuffles them to be in B, C, A order, when they repeat, they'll repeat as B, C, and A. The iPod won't reshuffle them.

# Managing Music with iTunes

A high-performance automobile is little more than an interesting amalgam of metal and plastic if it's missing tires and fuel. Sure, given the proper slope (and, perhaps, a helpful tailwind), that car is capable of movement, but the resulting journey leaves much to be desired. So, too, the iPod is a less-capable music-making vehicle without Apple's music player/encoder, iTunes. The two—like coffee and cream, dill and pickle, and Fred and Ginger—were simply meant for each other.

This chapter isn't intended to take the place of a full-featured guide to iTunes, such as Peachpit Press' *iTunes 4 for Macintosh and Windows: Visual QuickStart Guide*. But to best understand what makes the iPod's world turn, you must be familiar with how it and iTunes work together to move music (and pictures, in the case of the iPod Photo) on and off your iPod. In the following pages, you'll learn just that.

# iTunes, uTunes, We All Croon for iTunes

Released in January 2001, iTunes was Apple's second "i" application. (The first was the digital video-editing application iMovie.) Like Casady & Greene's SoundJam, iTunes was capable of playing and encoding MP3 files on a Macintosh. It featured a simple interface that allowed users to turn audio CDs into MP3 files easily, drag and drop songs between the Library (a master list of all the songs on your Mac) and user-created playlists, and record (or *burn*) customized audio CDs from within the application.

When Apple unveiled the first iPod, it also took the wraps off iTunes 2: an enhanced version of iTunes that, in addition to providing the means for moving music from the Mac to the iPod, introduced a 10-band graphic equalizer (EQ) with 22 presets, a sound enhancer that brings a livelier sound to tunes played in the application, and the ability to fade tracks played in iTunes into one another. (As we go to press, sound enhancement and fades don't transfer to the iPod.)

To accompany its release of new iPod models in July 2002, Apple issued iTunes 3, a Mac OS X-only version of iTunes that included such enhancements as the Sound Check feature, support for playing back Audible.com spoken-word files, the capability to rate songs, and support for Smart Playlists—playlists you create based on such factors as rating, the number of times you've played a track, and style.

Given Apple's penchant for taking the wraps off a new version of iTunes when it updates the iPod, few were shocked by Apple's tandem announcement of the third-generation iPod and iTunes 4 at a press event in April 2003. This version of iTunes acted as the gateway to Apple's online music emporium, the iTunes Music Store. (See Chapter 4 for everything you need to know about The Store.) It also brought MPEG-4 audio encoding support—in the form of Dolby Laboratories' Advanced Audio Coding (AAC) format—to iTunes. (This format allows you to create smaller, better-sounding audio files than those encoded in MP3 format.) iTunes 4 also let you share music easily on a local network via Apple's OpenTalk (once called Rendezvous) networking technology. Additionally, the program let you burn archives of your music to DVD, as well as add album artwork to your iTunes Library. And DJs undoubtedly thrilled to the fact that iTunes 4 allowed you to categorize tunes by the number of beats played per minute.

What might have come as a greater surprise to Apple-watchers was the company's October 16, 2003, release of iTunes version 4.1—the first version compatible with the Windows operating system. Apple considered this release to be so significant (and out of character) that its ads boldly proclaimed, "Hell Froze Over."

Whether Hades has chilled to that degree is debatable (my understanding is that The Big Freeze must wait until the Chicago Cubs win the World Series), but there's no questioning the significance of this event. It not only opens the doors of the iTunes Music Stores to millions of PC users, but also (finally) brings parity to the Windows iPod.

Before iTunes for Windows, a Windows iPod was a slightly poor relation to its Macintosh cousin. It didn't support the Sound Check feature, let alone browsing by composer, play counts, play dates (a feature that keeps track of recently played songs), or ratings. Because it was clueless about play dates and ratings, it lacked the ability to use Smart Playlists (a feature I'll look at later in this chapter). And quite frankly, the software that was bundled with the Windows iPod—Musicmatch Jukebox—though serviceable, is not as intuitive as iTunes.

But the days when Windows users had to settle for a second-class iPod are over. Thanks to iTunes for Windows, you'll get the same functionality from an iPod whether you run it under the Mac OS or under Windows.

The one-year anniversary of the iTunes Music Store—April 28, 2004—brought yet another update to iTunes. This update improved the iTunes Music Store by offering user-created mixes (called iMixes), music videos you could watch from within iTunes, free weekly song downloads, and charts of some 1,200 radio stations across the United States. This update also allowed those with an iTunes Music Store account to play the music they purchased from The Store on up to five registered computers. (Previously, you could play purchased music on up to three registered computers.) Additionally, Apple reduced the number of copies of a playlist you could burn to a CD from 10 to 7.

And this update included a feature that let those using the Windows version of iTunes convert unprotected Windows Media Audio files (.wma)—files incompatible with iTunes and the iPod—to Apple's AAC format.

Some iPod owners received direct benefit from this update as well. iTunes 4.5 introduced the Apple Lossless Encoder, a scheme that compresses music files to a little over half their original size while maintaining all their original fidelity. Thanks to the Apple Lossless Encoder, audiophiles who were unhappy with the compressed formats compatible with the iPod—MP3 and AAC—no longer had to pack their iPods with AIFF and WAV files to get better sound from their music players. Regrettably, the Apple Lossless Encoder was compatible only with iPods that carried a Dock connector (at that time, third-generation iPods and the iPod mini).

Less than two months later, Apple updated iTunes yet again—to version 4.6. This update was designed largely to support Apple's AirPort Express, a wireless 802.11g hub that supports streaming audio from a wireless-networking-equipped computer to your home stereo. We'll take a long look at AirPort Express in the Accessories chapter.

Coincident with the October 2004 announcement of the iPod Photo and iPod Special Edition: U2, Apple updated iTunes to version 4.7. Along with some bug fixes and performance enhancements, this latest version of iTunes included options necessary for moving pictures onto an iPod Photo, added a command for locating duplicate songs, and rejiggered the Preferences window to include a new iPod tab.

What kind of functionality can you expect from this dynamic duo? Read on, and I'll reveal all.

## iTunes Requirements

To use the latest version of iTunes, Mac users must be running Mac OS X 10.1.5 or later with a 400 MHz PowerPC G3 processor or better. QuickTime 6.2 or later is required to encode files in the AAC format. To copy photos to an iPod Photo, you must be running Mac OS X 10.2.6 or later. If you want to use AirPort Express, you must be running Mac OS X 10.3 or later.

Because Apple abandoned Mac OS 9 long ago, iTunes 3 and 4 work only in Mac OS X. For those who can't or won't move to Mac OS X, Apple still offers its last OS 9-compatible version of iTunes—iTunes 2—for download at http://docs.info.apple.com/article.html?artnum=120073. Mac users who continue to run Mac OS 9 can download music to their Mac OS 9-compatible iPods with iTunes 2 but won't be able to take advantage of the new features in iTunes 3 and 4.

There are some iPods that aren't compatible with Mac OS 9? Indeed so. First- and second-generation iPods are fully compatible with Mac OS 9 and iTunes 2. A third-generation iPod will mount on the Desktop of a Mac running Mac OS 9, but iTunes 2 won't recognize it. Mac OS 9 is wholly stupid when it comes to fourth-generation iPods and the iPod mini—it won't see them in iTunes 2 or even mount them on the Desktop.

Windows users must be running Windows 2000 or XP on a 500 MHz Pentium-class processor or better. QuickTime 6.5.2 or later is required. (QuickTime is included with iTunes for Windows.) If your PC is running an earlier version of Windows (say, Windows 98), you must use Musicmatch Jukebox or another compatible Windows program rather than iTunes to manage music on your iPod (although you can use Red Chair Software's Anapod Explorer with Windows 98SE and Me). I discuss Musicmatch Jukebox and other iPod-friendly applications at length in Chapter 5.

Where necessary, I identify the Macintosh and Windows versions of iTunes by their respective platforms—iTunes 4.7 for Windows, for example—or version number. If a feature works in all versions of iTunes and on both computer platforms, I refer simply to iTunes. The original iTunes for Macintosh (which sports no version number) doesn't support the iPod and, therefore, is not terribly useful for the purposes of this book.

# Ripping a CD

Apple intended the process of converting the music on an audio CD to computer data to be painless, and it is. Here's how to go about it:

   **1.** Launch iTunes.

2. Insert an audio CD into your computer's CD or DVD drive.

By default, iTunes will try to identify the CD you've inserted and log onto the Web to download the CD's song titles—a very handy feature for those who find typing such minutia to be tedious. But if you'd prefer that this didn't happen, choose Preferences (in the iTunes menu in OS X and in the Edit menu in Windows and Mac OS 9.2 and earlier), click the General tab, and uncheck the Connect to Internet When Needed check box (**Figure 2.1**).

**Figure 2.1**
To download song titles from a CD automatically, make sure that the Connect to Internet When Needed option is selected in the iTunes Preferences dialog box.

The CD appears in iTunes' Source list and the titles in the Song list to the right (**Figure 2.2**).

**Figure 2.2**
This album's song titles were downloaded from the Web automatically by iTunes.

3. To convert the audio tracks to a format compatible with your iPod—AAC, MP3, Apple Lossless, AIFF, or WAV—click the Import button (**Figure 2.3**) in the top-right corner of the iTunes window.

(To import only certain songs, choose Select None from the Edit menu and then click the boxes next to the songs you want to import. Click the Import button to import just those selected songs.)

iTunes begins encoding the files.

**Figure 2.3**
Click this button to import CD tracks into iTunes.

 iTunes will import songs via the encoder you've chosen in the Importing section of the iTunes Preferences dialog box (**Figure 2.4**). By default, iTunes 2 and 3 import songs as MP3 files. iTunes 4 imports songs in AAC format. (Encoding files in AAC format is not possible in earlier versions.) iTunes 4.5 and later can also import songs by using the Apple Lossless Encoder. All versions of iTunes can import songs as AIFF and WAV files. For more information on setting importing preferences, see the sidebar "Import Business: File Formats and Bit Rates" in this section.

**Figure 2.4**
iTunes 4's default file-encoding settings.

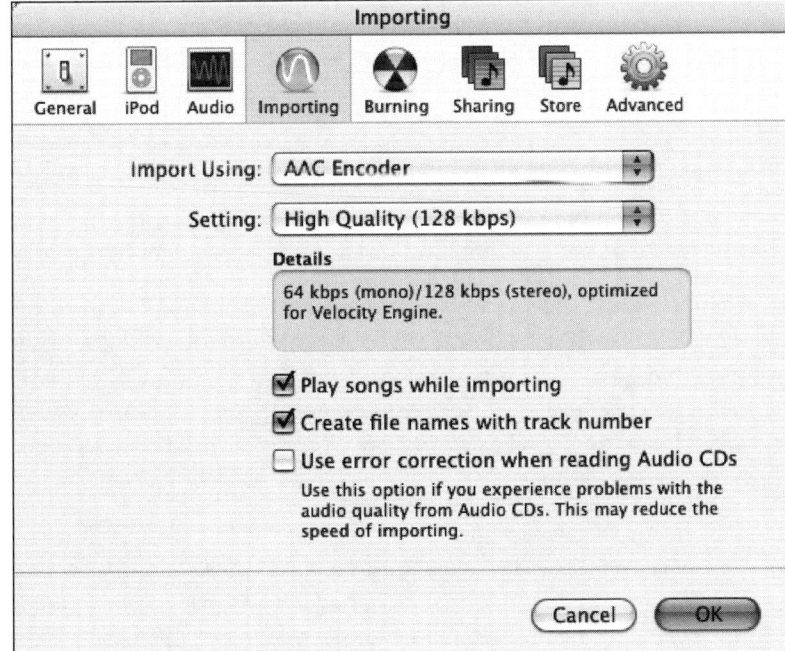

iTunes 4.1 introduced a new option, which remains today, in the Importing section of the Preferences window: Use Error Correction When Reading Audio CDs. If some of your CDs are scratched and tend to skip when you import them, try switching on this option to import a cleaner copy of the music. Note that this option slows the import process, so enable it only for problem CDs.

**4.** Click the Library button.

You'll see the songs you just imported.

**5.** To listen to a song, click its name in the list and then click the Play button or press the spacebar.

## The Unrippable Disc

There's no question that the practice of "sharing" music on the Internet has given the music industry a bad case of the jim-jams. These industry folk seem to believe (quite reasonably) that if people give music away, far fewer dollars will flutter into music-company coffers.

The music industry is attempting to stem the flow of music piracy by several means, including lobbying our elected officials for legislation that gives the music industry broad powers to protect its assets, selling older material at more reasonable prices, selling music on the Web through such sources as the iTunes Music Store, and making CDs difficult to copy. I'd like to address that last item here.

The music industry intends to create discs that cannot be copied easily. Although these discs look like CDs, technically, they're not; they don't adhere to the CD standard and, therefore, cannot be labeled as CDs. When you insert one of these things into your computer's media drive, the disc may not play—and even if it does, you might have a dickens of a time getting it out. Early versions of some of these discs have been known to lock up a computer's CD drive.

Fortunately, the music industry is now required to label these dangerous discs as a hazard to your computer. Should you encounter one of these things, take a good long look around the Web to see whether others have had success playing them. You don't want to be the one person who didn't get the word that your Mac or PC will lock up when such a disc is inserted into its media drive. Better yet, refrain from purchasing such tainted goods. If the music industry understands that customers will stay away from these loathsome discs, it may stop making them.

## Import Business: File Formats and Bit Rates

MP3, AAC, AIFF, WAV...is the computer industry incapable of speaking plain English!?

It may seem so, given the plethora of acronyms floating through modern-day Technotopia. But the lingo and the basics behind it aren't terribly difficult to understand.

MP3, AAC, AIFF, and WAV are audio file formats. The acronyms stand, respectively, for MPEG-1, audio layer 3 (if you must know, *MPEG* is an acronym for *Moving Picture Experts Group*); Advanced Audio Coding; Audio Interchange File Format; and Windows Audio Volume.

The compression methods used to create MP3 and AAC files are termed *lossy* because the encoder removes information from the original sound file to create these smaller files. Fortunately, these encoders are designed to remove the information you're least likely to miss—audio frequencies that you can't hear easily, for example.

AIFF and WAV files are uncompressed, containing all the data from the original. When a Macintosh pulls audio from an audio CD, it does so in AIFF format, which is the native uncompressed audio format used by Apple's QuickTime technology. WAV is a variant of AIFF and is used extensively with the Windows operating system.

Early versions of iTunes supported MP3, AIFF, and WAV encoding. iTunes 3 allowed you to play back AAC files but not encode them. The first two generations of iPods were incapable of playing AAC files, but with the introduction of iTunes 4 and the latest iPod software, all iPods can play them. iTunes 4 supports both the unencrypted .m4a AAC files created by iTunes and the encrypted .m4p AAC files sold at the iTunes Music Store.

As I mentioned earlier, iTunes 4.5 introduced the Apple Lossless Encoder. This is termed a "lossless" encoder because the encoder doesn't shrink the file by removing portions of the audio spectrum; rather, it removes redundant data. This scheme allows you to retain all the audio quality of the original file while producing a copy just over half the size of that original file.

Now that you're familiar with these file formats, let's touch on resolution.

You probably know that the more pixels per inch a digital photograph has, the crisper the image (and the larger the file). The number of pixels per inch helps describe the *resolution* of the image. The higher the resolution (the more pixels per inch), the better the quality.

Resolution applies to audio as well. But rather than using a standard of pixels per inch, audio defines resolution by the number of kilobytes per second (Kbps) contained in an audio file. *With files encoded similarly*, the higher the kilobyte count, the better-sounding the file (and the larger the file).

*continues on next page*

## Import Business: File Formats and Bit Rates *(continued)*

I emphasize "with files encoded similarly" because the quality of the file depends a great deal on the encoder used to compress it. Specifically, many people claim that if you encode a file at 128 Kbps in both the MP3 and AAC formats, the AAC file will sound better.

Before version 4, iTunes imported audio CDs as MP3 files encoded at 160 Kbps by default. This setting nicely balanced file size with sound quality and was a good choice for tunes downloaded to an iPod.

With iTunes 4, Apple changed the default import settings to AAC at 128 Kbps. The company claims that its AAC encoder produces better-sounding files at a lower resolution (and, thus, smaller files) than those created by its MP3 encoder.

The presence of this AAC encoder helps explain why Apple now claims that the current 20 GB iPod holds up to 5,000 four-minute songs, whereas, on release, the second-generation 20 GB models held 4,000 four-minute songs. Apple reduced the default resolution from 160 Kbps (for MP3 files) to 128 Kbps (for AAC files). When you understand that a four-minute song encoded with the MP3 encoder at 160 Kbps consumes 4.7 MB of hard drive space and that the same file encoded with the AAC encoder at 128 Kbps weighs in at only 3.8 MB, you see how Apple can make this claim. By default, iTunes 4 creates smaller sound files, allowing you to pack more tunes onto your iPod.

Although iTunes' default setting is perfectly swell, you have the option to change it. To do so, choose Preferences (located in the Apple menu in OS X and in the Edit menu in Windows and Mac OS 9.2 and earlier), and click the Importing tab (or the Importing button, in the case of iTunes 3 and 4) in the resulting iTunes Preferences dialog box.

The Import Using pop-up menu lets you choose to import files in MP3, AIFF, or WAV format in all versions of iTunes. iTunes 4 adds AAC encoding, and iTunes 4.5 adds the Apple Lossless Encoder. All iPods can play files encoded in the AAC, MP3, AIFF, and WAV formats. Only those iPods with the bottom Dock connector (third- and fourth-generation iPods and the iPod mini) can play songs formatted with the Apple Lossless Encoder.

The Configuration pop-up menu is where you choose the resolution of the AAC and MP3 files encoded by iTunes. In iTunes 4, the default setting is High Quality (128 Kbps). To change this setting, choose Custom from the Setting pop-up menu, and in the resulting AAC Encoder window, choose a different setting—in a range from 16 to 320 Kbps—from the Stereo Bit Rate pop-up menu (**Figure 2.5**). Files encoded at a high bit rate sound better than those encoded at a low bit rate (such as 96 Kbps). But files encoded at higher bit rates also take up more space on your hard drive and iPod.

## Import Business: File Formats and Bit Rates *(continued)*

**Figure 2.5**
AAC encoding options.

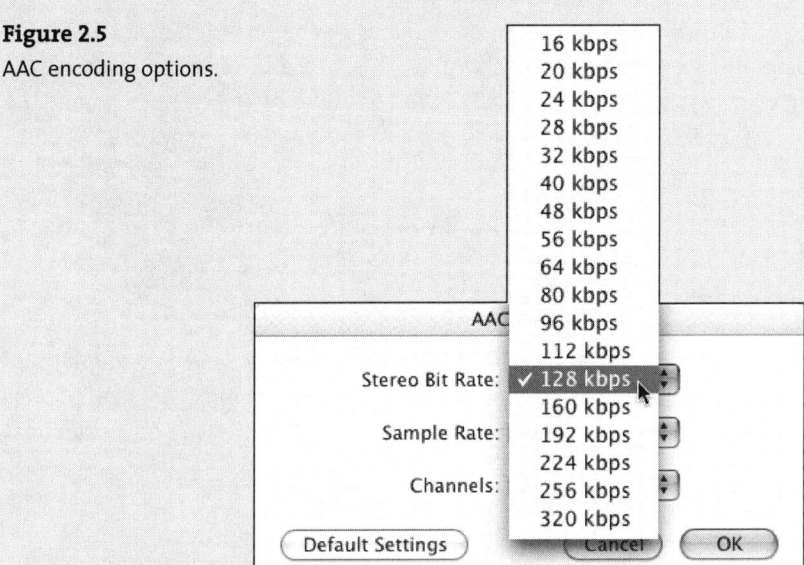

There are few good reasons to alter other settings in the AAC Encoder window. You have the option to change the sample rate to 48.000 kHz, for example, and the channel from stereo to mono. But a higher sample rate is useful only for professional audio gear (such as Digital Audio Tape decks and high-end audio editing applications), and converting stereo to mono is helpful only if you're Brian Wilson. (See, this former Beach Boy hears with only one ear and often mixed Beach Boys albums in mono because...oh, never mind.)

The default settings for MP3 importing (**Figure 2.6**) include Good Quality (128 Kbps), High Quality (160 Kbps), and Higher Quality (192 Kbps). If you don't care to use one of these settings, choose Custom from this same pop-up menu. In the MP3 Encoder dialog box that appears, you have the option to choose a bit rate ranging from 8 to 320 Kbps.

**Figure 2.6**
Three easy-to-choose MP3 encoding options.

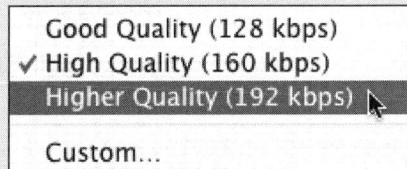

*continues on next page*

### Import Business: File Formats and Bit Rates *(continued)*

You can change other settings in the MP3 Encoder dialog box. By choosing the Use Variable Bit Rate Encoding (VBR) option, for example, you might produce better-sounding MP3 files (though they may be larger than if you hadn't chosen this option). You can also change the number of channels (mono or stereo) and stereo mode. For most people, the default settings work perfectly well.

It's up to you to balance quantity and quality. If you want to cram as many songs as possible onto your iPod and have what less-sensitive souls disparagingly term a "tin ear," feel free to use a low bit rate, such as 96 Kbps for AAC files and 128 Kbps for MP3 files. But unless you're listening to anything but narration (a "books on tape" kind of recording, for example), don't venture below these resolutions unless you *really* don't care about quality. And marching much above 192 Kbps—particularly if you're listening over headphones or computer speakers—is mostly a waste of time for all but those who have the most discerning ears.

## Songs from the Web

Apple has made getting music from the Web a far simpler (and far more defensible) enterprise with the opening of the iTunes Music Store. I discuss The Store in detail in the next chapter. But there are other avenues—legal and not-so—for finding music on the Web.

Finding free and *legal* music on the Web is getting easier by the day. Apple gives away a download each week from the iTunes Music Store (though you must have an account at The Store to download these files). And then there are the old standbys such as the Internet Underground Music Archives (www.iuma.com) and GarageBand.com (www.garageband.com). But recently, a number of Web sites devoted to pointing visitors to free music have begun to crop up. The Red Ferret Journal (www.enorgis.com/pmwiki/pmwiki.php), for example, boasts

## Legal Music-File Sources

Despite much of what you've heard about music file sharing on the Web, there are places to get perfectly legal free MP3 files. Some sites offer this music to expose unsigned bands; others give you a taste of an album in the hope that you'll purchase the CD. Such sources include:

- Internet Underground Music Archives (www.iuma.com)
- RollingStone.com (www.rollingstone.com)
- Billboard.com (www.billboard.com)
- Amazon.com (www.amazon.com)
- GarageBand.com (www.garageband.com)
- The iTunes Music Store (a free song download each week)
- Playlistmag.com (www.playlistmag.com)

Or, as I mentioned earlier, you can check out a Web site such as The Red Ferret Journal (www.enorgis.com/pmwiki/pmwiki.php) to find links to other Web sites that offer free music.

If you're looking for legal live recordings of such bands as the Grateful Dead, take a look at FurthurNET (http://furthurnet.com). This OS X-only Java application is a peer-to-peer file-sharing service that allows users to share live recordings. Note that many of the files shared on FurthurNET are complete shows that can take up hundreds of megabytes of storage. Use such a service only if you have a fast broadband connection and lots of room to store files.

links to more than 1 million free and legal music tracks. And of course, there are such far-from-legal sources as Internet newsgroups, HotLine servers, and peer-to-peer file-sharing clients. Let's put aside the legal and ethical arguments for now (I assure you that I'll address these important issues later in the book) and focus on getting music from the Web onto your iPod.

# Managing File Types

Remember, the iPod is capable of playing only AAC, MP3, Apple Lossless, AIFF, and WAV files (and remember, only those iPods with a Dock connector can play Apple Lossless files). Other audio formats exist on the Web, but these file formats are not supported by the iPod. Microsoft's Windows Media Player files (.wma), for example, will not play on the iPod. Neither will the music files offered by other online music stores, such as Napster and Musicmatch (in Chapter 5, I show you how to get around this limitation). Likewise, you can forget about Sony's Atrac format (which works only with Sony gear). Also, the iPod is incapable of playing files encoded with Ogg Vorbis—a popular music encoder in the Linux world.

If you'd like to use some other variety of audio file, you must convert it before you can bring it into iTunes. If you're running Mac OS 9, Norman Franke's free SoundApp application (**Figure 2.7**; www.spies.com/~franke/SoundApp) is a terrific utility for converting files to a form acceptable to the iPod. You may have to convert a file to AIFF format and then convert it to AAC within iTunes.

**Figure 2.7**
SoundApp can convert a multitude of audio file types in Mac OS 9.

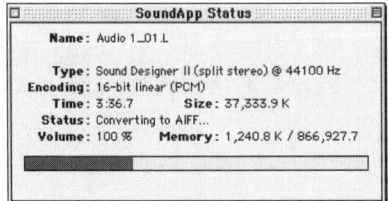

For those running Mac OS X 10.2 or later, Steve Dekorte's $10 SoundConverter (**Figure 2.8**; www.dekorte.com/Software/OSX/SoundConverter) is worth a look. SoundConverter supports just about every audio file type on earth.

Note, however, that you may never be able to convert certain types of files with an audio conversion utility. RealAudio files, for example, are generally streamed from the Web (meaning that the audio files are stored somewhere on the Web and played like a radio broadcast to your computer) and can't be stored in whole on your computer or converted to a form that your iPod understands.

**Figure 2.8**

SoundConverter converts sound files in Mac OS X.

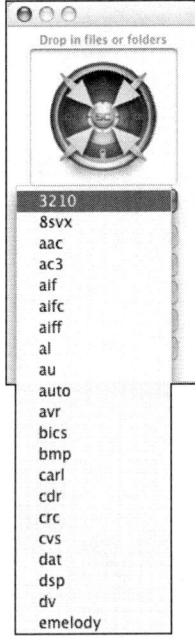

 Mac users can capture streaming audio (or any audio that plays through their computer's speakers, for that matter) and save it as an AIFF file with Ambrosia Software's (www.ambrosiasw.com) free WireTap application. Rogue Amoeba's (www.rogueamoeba.com) $16 Audio Hijack can also record the sound from just about any application running on your Mac; in addition it includes an equalizer and supports timed recording, allowing you to configure your Mac to record audio (such as a streamed radio broadcast) automatically. The $32 Audio Hijack Pro, in addition to having a wealth of features, can save hijacked files in MP3, AAC, and Apple Lossless formats.

If you're a Mac user interested solely in recording streaming MP3 radio broadcasts, take a look at Bit Cartel's $15 RadioLover (www.bitcartel.com/radiolover) or Fogware's $40 Internet Radio Recorder (http://www.fog-ware.com/irr.htm). As with Audio Hijack, these programs can be configured to record broadcasts on a user-defined schedule.

Windows users can record audio from running applications with 1st Benison Software's $30 All Recorder (www.allrecorder.com). All Recorder allows you to save files in the MP3, .wma, .ogg, .vqf, and .wav formats. Unless you'll want to convert these files later, save them in one of the two formats supported by the iPod: MP3 and .wav.

## Play Tunes over a Network

Once upon a time, streaming songs across a network from one computer to another was a cumbersome process. Now, thanks to built-in iTunes 4 support for OpenTalk (once called Rendezvous)—a networking technology that lets computers find one another effortlessly on a local network—streaming songs couldn't be easier. Here's how:

1. Launch iTunes 4.

2. Choose Preferences from the iTunes menu on a Macintosh and from the Edit menu in the Windows version of iTunes.

3. Click the Sharing button.

4. In the resulting window, enable the Share My Music check box.

   Below this check box, you'll see the option to share your entire library or just selected playlists. You'll also see options for naming your shared music and requiring a password to share your music (**Figure 2.9**).

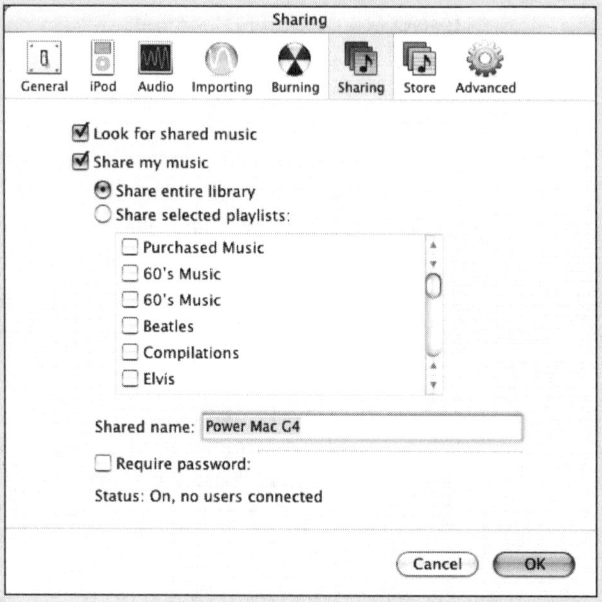

**Figure 2.9**
To share your music library—and view other shared libraries on a local network—visit iTunes 4's Sharing preference.

## Play Tunes over a Network (continued)

**5.** If you want other users' shared music libraries to be available to you, enable the Look for Shared Music check box.

**6.** Click OK to close the window.

Now when another computer is connected to your network—either wired or wirelessly—the music you've chosen to share will be available to that computer within iTunes 4. If you enabled the Look for Shared Music option in iTunes Preferences, and if that other computer is configured to share its music library, you'll be able to stream its songs to your computer (**Figure 2.10**).

**Figure 2.10**
The shared music library on another Mac.

To play those songs, simply click the shared-library entry in the Source list and wait for the shared songs to appear in iTunes' main window. If the password option is enabled on the other computer, you'll be asked for that password. (If you don't know the password, perhaps you're not welcome to share that music library.) When the songs appear, click the Play button to begin playing the playlist from the beginning, or select a song you want to hear and then click Play.

iTunes is set up in such a way that you can listen to the music from a shared library but not copy it to another computer.

Note that you may not be able to play all the songs in the shared library. For one thing, you can play songs purchased from the iTunes Music Store only if the computer you want to stream the songs to is authorized to play those songs. (For details on authorization and the iTunes Music Store, see Chapter 3.)

*continues on next page*

## Play Tunes over a Network *(continued)*

If you're a Mac user running an earlier version of iTunes, dread not. Here's a way for you to tune into another Mac's music:

1. Mount a network volume that contains music files that you want to stream to your Mac.

2. If you're using iTunes 3, launch iTunes, and choose Preferences from the iTunes menu. iTunes 2 users will find Preferences in the Edit menu.

3. In iTunes 3, click the Advanced button in the Preferences dialog box, and uncheck the Copy Files to iTunes Music Folder When Adding to Library check box.

   This option doesn't exist in iTunes 2; that version won't copy files to the music folder.

4. In either iTunes 2 or iTunes 3, choose the Add to Library command from the File menu.

5. In the resulting Add to Library dialog box (called Choose Object in iTunes 2), navigate to the mounted volume and then to a folder full of music files.

   This folder may be the iTunes Music folder on another Mac, for example. Note that if you're running Mac OS X, you must have sufficient privileges to access this folder. (You'll know you don't if you see a "Do Not Enter" icon slapped atop the networked computer's Music folder.)

6. With the folder highlighted, click Choose.

   Pointers to the music files within that folder are added to your iTunes Library. To play a song on the remote Mac, simply highlight its name and click iTunes' Play button.

Note: If you try to play a tune from a Mac that isn't mounted, iTunes prompts you to mount the volume.

You can play these files just as you'd play any other song in iTunes. The difference is that they're playing from a remote hard drive rather than from your Mac.

Better yet, because these files are in the Library, the iPod will add them the next time you update the iPod—one somewhat-sneaky way to add tunes that aren't located on the Mac that's sanctioned to work with the iPod.

# Moving Music into iTunes

After you've downloaded—and, if necessary, converted—the files you want, you have three ways to move them into iTunes:

- Choose an Add to Library command from iTunes' File menu.

  In the Macintosh version of iTunes, there's only the single Add to Library command. When you choose this command, the Add to Library dialog box appears (called Choose Object in iTunes 2). Navigate to the file, folder, or volume you want to add to iTunes, and click Open (**Figure 2.11**). iTunes decides which files it thinks it can play and adds them to the Library.

**Figure 2.11**
Those using earlier versions of iTunes can share music via the Add to Library command.

iTunes for Windows includes two commands: Add File to Library and Add Folder to Library. When you choose Add File to Library, up pops the Add to Library dialog box; you can navigate to individual music files and add them by clicking the Open button. When you choose Add Folder to Library, the Browse for Folder window opens, allowing you to browse the directories of My Documents, My Computer, and My Network Places. Select a directory and click OK; iTunes adds all compatible music files it finds in that directory.

- Drag files, folders, or entire volumes to the iTunes icon in Mac OS X's Dock, Mac OS 9's tear-off Applications menu, or the iTunes icon in either operating system (at which point iTunes launches and adds the dragged files to the Library).

   Windows users can drag files, folders, or volumes onto the iTunes shortcut on the Desktop or the iTunes icon in the Start menu (if you've pinned iTunes to this menu).

- Drag files, folders, or entire volumes into iTunes' main window. This method works for both the Mac and Windows versions of iTunes.

   By default, iTunes 2 keeps its songs in the iTunes Music folder within the iTunes folder inside the Documents folder. (In Mac OS 9, the Documents folder is at the root level of your startup drive; in Mac OS X, the Documents folder is inside your user folder.) When you add tunes to the Library via any of these methods, a dialog box will appear, warning you that should you move these files from their current location, iTunes won't be able to locate them later (**Figure 2.12**).

**Figure 2.12**
Early versions of iTunes issue a warning when you add songs to your Library.

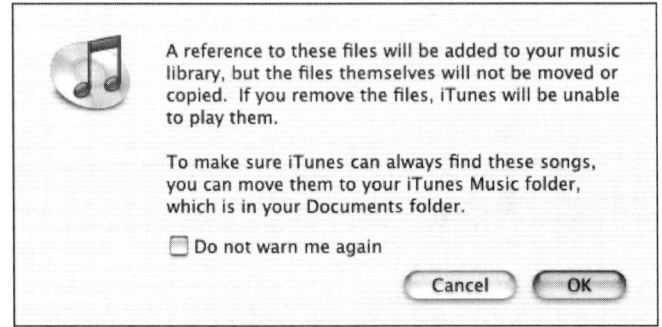

In the Mac versions of iTunes 3 and 4, you'll find songs in the iTunes Music folder within the iTunes folder inside the Music folder inside your OS X user folder. So, for example, the path to my iTunes music files would be chris/Music/iTunes/iTunes Music.

Windows users will find their iTunes Music folder by following this path: *yourusername*/My Music/iTunes/iTunes Music.

# Creating and Configuring a Playlist

If the iPod were like lesser music players, you'd have to select all the songs on the device from one enormously long list. Thank heaven Apple's engineers had more sense than to provide you such a limited interface. Among other options, you can navigate your iPod via the playlists you create in iTunes. Here's how to create a variety of playlists.

## Standard Playlists

You can create standard playlists in iTunes 2, 3, and 4. Follow these steps:

1. Click the large plus-sign (+) button in the bottom-left corner of the iTunes window (**Figure 2.13**), or choose the New Playlist command from the File menu (Command-N on the Mac, Ctrl-N in Windows).

**Figure 2.13**
Click the plus sign (+) to create a new playlist.

2. Enter a name for your new playlist in the highlighted field that appears next to the new playlist in the Source list (**Figure 2.14**).

**Figure 2.14**
Naming a new playlist.

3. Click the Library entry in the Source list, and select the titles you want to place in the playlist you created.

You can select multiple titles in a row by holding down the Shift key and clicking the first and last titles you want to include. All titles, including the ones you clicked, get selected via this technique. To select individual titles on the Macintosh, hold down the Command key and click the songs you want. In Windows, hold down the Ctrl key to select individual titles.

**4.** Drag the selected titles to the new playlist's icon.

**5.** Click the new playlist's icon.

The titles you selected are copied to the new playlist.

**6.** After you've dragged the titles you want into your playlist, arrange their order.

To do so, click the Number column in the main window, and drag titles up and down in the list. If you attempt to drag titles when any other column heading is selected (Song or Time, for example), the title plops right back where it came from when you let go of the mouse button. When the iPod is synchronized with iTunes, this is the order in which the songs will appear in the playlist on your iPod.

If the songs in your playlist come from the same album—you've ripped an audio CD, for example, or purchased an album from the iTunes Music Store—and you want the songs in the playlist to appear in the same order in which they do on the original album, click the Album heading.

 You may have noticed that I used the word titles in the preceding instructions, rather than songs. I did this to hint that you're not copying songs from one location on your hard drive to another. You're simply copying the song titles from the Library (the list of all the songs on your hard drive) to another list to make navigation easier. You can play the songs that appear in this playlist by selecting them in the Library as well.

## Playlist from Selection

iTunes 2, 3, and 4 also allow you to create a new playlist from selected items. Here's how to create such a playlist:

**1.** Select the songs you'd like to appear in the new playlist.

To select multiple items in a row, click the first item you want in the playlist and then Shift-click the last item. All the songs between (and including) the songs you clicked are selected.

2. Choose New Playlist from Selection from iTunes' File menu.

   A new untitled playlist containing all the selected songs appears in the iTunes Source list.

3. To name the playlist, type the name in the highlighted field.

## Smart Playlists

iTunes 3 introduced the *Smart Playlist*—a playlist based on user-generated criteria—and that feature remains in iTunes 4, albeit with some interface changes. When you invoke the New Smart Playlist command in iTunes 3, you get a window that contains two tabs: Simple and Advanced. iTunes 4 dispenses with this tab structure and instead presents the Advanced interface. Smart Playlists are not available in iTunes 2. Here's how they work:

1. Choose New Smart Playlist from iTunes' File menu.

   If you're using iTunes 3, you'll see two tabs—Simple and Advanced—in the resulting Smart Playlist dialog box. To create a simple Smart Playlist, make sure that you're in the Simple section of the Smart Playlist dialog box.

   If you're running iTunes 4, you'll see no tabs.

2. Choose your criteria.

   In iTunes 3, you'll spy a pop-up menu that allows you to select songs by artist, composer, or genre, followed by a Contains field. iTunes 4 offers more selection criteria. To choose all songs by Elvis Presley and Elvis Costello, for example, you'd choose Artist from the pop-up menu and then enter **Elvis** in the Contains field.

   You can limit the selections that appear in the playlist by minutes, hours, megabytes, gigabytes, or number of songs. You may want the playlist to contain no more than 1 GB worth of songs, for example.

   You'll also see a Live Updating option. When it's switched on, this option ensures that if you add any songs to iTunes that meet the criteria you've set, those songs will be added to the playlist. If you add a new Elvis Costello album to iTunes, for example, iTunes updates your Elvis Smart Playlist automatically.

**3.** Click OK.

A new playlist that contains your smart selections appears in iTunes' Source list.

To create an advanced Smart Playlist in iTunes 3, choose New Smart Playlist from iTunes' File menu, and click the Advanced tab in the resulting Smart Playlist dialog box.

iTunes 3's advanced Smart Playlist is the same as iTunes 4's regular playlist and allows you to choose songs in many ways (**Figure 2.15**). You can, for example, select songs by album, artist, bit rate, comment, date added, last played, genre, or play count. Clicking the plus-sign (+) button next to a criterion field allows you to add other conditions. You could create a playlist that contains only songs that you've never listened to by punk artists whose names contain the letter *J*.

**Figure 2.15**
iTunes 4's Smart Playlist dialog box.

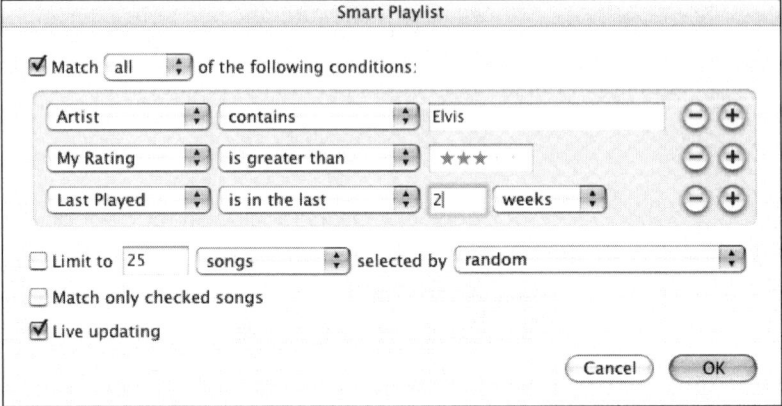

As you can with the simple Smart Playlist, you can limit what appears in the resulting playlist by minutes, hours, megabytes, gigabytes, or number of songs. Advanced Smart Playlists are also updated automatically if you choose the Live Updating option.

## Proposed Playlists

Stuck for ideas on how to create smarter Smart Playlists? Sample some of these recipes:

**The New Music All the Time playlist**

Select New Smart Playlist from iTunes' File menu, and configure the top row of pop-up menus to read *Play Count is 0*. If you like, enable the Limit To option, and limit the songs in your playlist by number of songs, duration of playlist, or cumulative size of the songs in the playlist (10 GB, for example). Enable the Live Updating option so that when a song has been played once, it's removed from the playlist.

**The iPod mini playlist**

When you plug an iPod (that's configured to update automatically) into your computer and your iTunes library contains more music than your iPod can hold, iTunes creates a playlist of music that will fit on your iPod. iTunes is the tiniest bit discerning about this playlist, in that it includes all songs on an album rather than giving you a taste of each album in your iTunes library. It's not terribly smart about using space effectively, however. It will, for example, copy AIFF, WAV, and Apple Lossless files to your iPod—files that take up a lot of space that could be better used for storing more music files in AAC and MP3 format.

For this reason, it's a good idea to create a Smart Playlist that excludes these massive songs and designate this list as the one to use when you update your iPod. To do so, create a series of conditions that read *Kind does not contain*. This list of conditions would include AIFF, WAV, Apple Lossless, and QuickTime. You might also want to exclude genres such as Holiday and Children's Music. If you have a lot of music on your computer, and you've rated that music, consider adding a rating condition that reads *My Rating is Greater than 3 Stars*.

Be sure to limit the size of this playlist with the Limit To option at the bottom of the Smart Playlist window. For an iPod mini, this option should read *Limit to 3500 MB selected by Album*. (You must use megabytes rather than gigabytes, because the GB field won't accept decimals, as in 3.5 GB.)

When you've created this playlist, select your mini in the Source menu, and click the iPod Preferences button. In the iPod Preferences window that appears, enable the Automatically Update Selected Playlists Only option, select the Smart Playlist you created for your mini, and click OK. The mini will be updated with your playlist—and will continue to be as long as you leave this option selected.

*continues on next page*

## Proposed Playlists *(continued)*

**The Monday Morning playlist**

On the first day of the work week, it can be difficult to get the juices flowing. What you need is a heart-pumping playlist. Creating such a playlist requires a bit of planning, however. When you next browse through your iTunes music library, keep an ear cocked for tunes that are likely to get your Monday-morning groove on. When you find one of these tunes, open its Get Info window and enter Monday in the Comments field. When you're ready to compile your playlist, configure the top row of pop-up menus to read *Comment is Monday*.

Using the Comments field is an excellent way to choose music by mood. Also consider Smart Playlists for raucous Saturday nights and hanging-around-in-bed-'til-noon Sunday mornings.

**The Subgenre playlist**

Some people find Apple's genres a little broad—Classical that encompasses the music of Bach, Schubert, and Glass; and Jazz that lumps together Chet Baker with Sun Ra. Here's a technique for using an album's Comment field to create subgenres:

1. Select all the cuts on an album, and choose Get Info from the File menu to produce the Multiple Song Information window.

2. In the Comments field, enter the appropriate subgenre for that music: Baroque, Bebop, Italian Opera, or Cool Jazz, for example.

3. Repeat for each album in your library.

To put your efforts to work, create a Smart Playlist that uses the Comments field to distinguish music—one that reads *Comment Contains Romantic*, for example. To create more-specific playlists, add other terms to an album or song's Comment field. You might enter such terms as *piano*, *concerto*, and *Classical* to place all the piano concertos by Haydn, Mozart, and Beethoven in a single playlist.

**The Back Up Your Purchased Music playlist**

If you lose the music you purchase from the iTunes Music Store, you lose it for good and all—Apple won't allow you to download purchased music a second time without paying for it. For this reason, you should routinely back up your purchased music. This Smart Playlist can help you do it.

## Proposed Playlists *(continued)*

1. Configure the top row of pop-up menus to read *Kind contains Protected AAC*, give it a name (such as Backup Library), and click OK.

   This places all the purchased music files in your iTunes music library in a single playlist. (Your Purchased Music playlist should contain these same songs, but if you've reorganized your iTunes Music folder, it's possible that some of the music you purchased won't appear in the Purchased Music folder.)

2. Select Preferences from the iTunes menu on the Mac or from the Edit menu on a Windows PC, and click the Burning tab in the Preferences window to open the Burning window.

3. In the Disc Format portion of the Burning window, select Data CD or DVD, and click OK.

   This option allows you to burn your iTunes files in their current format, rather than convert them to a format compatible with the audio CD standard (a format that creates much larger files).

4. Select your Backup Library playlist, and click iTunes' Burn button.

   If the number of files in the playlist exceeds the capacity of a CD-R disc, don't be concerned. iTunes will burn as many files as it can to the first disc and then ask for as many subsequent discs as necessary to back up everything in the playlist.

5. When you've burned that playlist, Control-click it (if you have a Mac) or right-click it (if you have a PC), and select Edit Smart Playlist from the contextual menu.

6. Click the + button next to the top row of pop-up menus, and configure the resulting row of menus to read *Date Added is in the Last 2 Weeks*.

7. Enable the Live Updating option, and click OK.

8. If you're using a Mac, launch iCal, and create an appointment two weeks hence called *Back up iTunes!* Configure the appointment so that it recurs every two weeks, and set an alarm that reminds you to back up your playlist.

   If you're using a PC, use the calendar within Outlook or an application such as Palm Desktop to create a similar alarm.

If you do lose your purchased music, open iTunes' Preferences window, click the Advanced tab, and be sure that the Copy Files to iTunes Music Folder When Adding to Library option

*continues on next page*

## Proposed Playlists *(continued)*

is enabled. Insert each backup disc, select the Add to Library command from iTunes' File menu, navigate to the disc, and click Open. The purchased music files will be copied from the disc to your computer and placed in your iTunes music library.

**The Audiobooks playlist**

The fourth-generation iPods place audiobooks in their own special playlist. If you have an earlier iPod, you can fake an audiobooks playlist. Just configure the top row of buttons to read *Genre contains audiobooks*.

**The Likely Hits playlist**

Pop albums invariably feature their strongest tracks in the number 1, 2, and 3 positions. To avoid those awful recitation-of-Elizabethan-poetry-over-soupy-strings tracks that often appear in the latter part of the album, configure the top row of pop-up menus to read *Track Number is less than 4*.

Note: If the album was recorded before 1980 (and, therefore, appeared originally on vinyl), consider creating a list that includes the first, seventh, eighth, and fourteenth tracks (thus grabbing the opening and closing tracks on each side of the record).

**The Prog-Rock Lover's playlist**

Configure the top row of pop-up menus to read *Time is greater than 15 minutes*. Click the + button, and configure the next row of pop-up menus to read *Genre is Rock* (or *Genre is AlternRock*). Click the + button once again, and configure this row of pop-up menus to read *Year is in the Range 1971 to 1979*.

Note: If you're not careful, this collection could turn into The Self-Indulgent Noodling Guitar/Bass/Drum Solo from Hell playlist. To guard against this fate, you might want to add one more line of pop-up menus that reads *Artist is not Grateful Dead*.

**The Down-and-Out Country playlist**

Country-music lovers know that the classics of their favorite genre have the words *whiskey*, *truck*, *pool hall*, and *dog* sprinkled throughout the libretto—and that the very cream of this crop feature at least one of these words in the song title. With that in mind, create four separate Smart Playlists, each featuring one of the aforementioned magic words. Take the contents of each Smart Playlist, dump them into a master playlist, pour that playlist into your iPod, strap on the headphones, heave the dog into the truck, and head on over to the pool hall for a couple of whiskies.

iTunes 4 includes four Smart Playlists: 60's Music, My Top Rated, Recently Played, and Top 25 Most Played. As their names imply, 60's Music (an homage to Steve Jobs' love for music of that decade) includes songs recorded in the 1960s, My Top Rated includes 25 songs selected at random that have a rating of four or five stars, Recently Played includes 25 songs selected at random that you've played in the past two weeks, and Top 25 Most Played includes the 25 songs you've played most often. These playlists have the Live Updating option enabled, which makes it possible for these playlists to be updated dynamically as conditions change (when you rate more songs, play different tunes, or play other tunes more often, for example).

To see exactly what makes these playlists tick, Mac users can Control-click a Smart Playlist and choose Edit Smart Playlist from the resulting contextual menu. Windows users simply right-click a playlist to see this command.

In iTunes 4.5, Apple enhanced the Smart Playlist in an important way. Previously, there was no easy way to keep sections of your library from appearing in a Smart Playlist. Let's say you'd digitized all your old phonograph albums, for the sake of posterity, but you didn't want any of the songs on them ever to appear in a Smart Playlist. Sure, you could have added a "phonograph" comment to each archived song and told the Smart Playlist not to include any song with the comment "phonograph," but wouldn't it be easier if you could simply tell the Smart Playlist to exclude all songs within certain playlists? That's exactly what iTunes 4.5 and later does for you by including the new Playlist criterion. Now you can tell Smart Playlists to harvest songs only within certain playlists.

## Playlist Helpers

iTunes 3 introduced such helpful features as *ratings*, the ability to pass judgment on a song by assigning it a rating of one to five stars; *play count*, a feature that keeps track of the number of times you've played a song in iTunes and on your iPod; and *recently played*, a feature that keeps track of when you last played a song. Here's a quick look at how these features enhance your iPoding experience:

**Ratings.** Although employing ratings is a fine way to vent your critical spleen ("I don't care how hefty a royalty it brought the composer, 'Brandy [You're a Fine Girl]' was a dreadful waste of vinyl!"), it's also quite useful. After you rate your songs, you can use those ratings as a playlist criterion.

You can, for example, create a Smart Playlist that contains nothing but songs with a rating of four stars or more, thus guaranteeing that you hear nothing but your personal favorites. Or if an ill-favored cousin has planted himself on the living-room sofa for one night too many, create a playlist made up of nothing but one-star wonders, and blast it from one end of the house to the other in a repeating loop.

You can assign ratings to the songs in your iTunes Library in two ways. The traditional way is to click the My Rating column in the main iTunes window and then drag the pointer to the right. This maneuver causes stars to appear in the column. Or, if you prefer doing things as inefficiently as possible, you can click a song title, press Command-I on the Mac or Ctrl-I on a Windows PC to produce the Song Information window, click the Advanced tab, and drag your pointer in the My Ratings field to produce the desired number of stars. (OK, one instance in which assigning ratings this way *isn't* inefficient is when you want to assign the same rating to a batch of songs. Just select all the songs to which you want to assign a rating; press Command-I on the Mac or Ctrl-I on the PC; and, in the resulting Multiple Song Information window, check the box next to the My Rating field. Now issue a rating in that field. The rating you create is assigned to all selected songs.)

The other way to go about it is to assign a rating directly on the iPod. To do so, start listening to a song, and press the Select button twice. You'll be whisked to a rating screen, where you use the scroll wheel to assign the one-to-five-star rating. When you next synchronize your iPod, the ratings you've entered on your iPod are transferred to iTunes. Note that you can rate songs only on third-generation and later iPods.

**Play count.** The ability to keep track of the number of times you've played a song is also helpful when you want to create a playlist. One might reasonably assume that if you've played some songs more than others, those tunes hold a special place in your heart. By using play count as a smart-playlist criterion, you could take all songs that you've played

> ### Playlist Helpers *(continued)*
>
> more than 10 times, shove them into a playlist, and—using the batch-rating technique I mention earlier in this sidebar—rate all the songs in that playlist with five stars.
>
> Or you could use play count as a way to limit the songs you've played to death. In this case, create a Smart Playlist of songs that you've never heard. Play this group of tunes when you'd like to listen to some fresh material.
>
> iTunes 3 and 4 keeps track of number of times you've played a song in the Play Count column of the main iTunes window. The iPod tracks the play count in the Top 25 Most Played playlist in the iPod Playlists screen.
>
> **Recently played.** The name says it all. iTunes 3, iTunes 4, and the iPod keep track of when you last played a song. This information is reflected in the Last Played column of iTunes' main window. On the iPod, songs most recently played appear in the Recently Played playlist in the iPod Playlists screen.
>
> You can also use the recently played criterion to create a Smart Playlist comprised of fresh material (or tunes you just can't get enough of).
>
> iTunes 3, iTunes 4, and the iPod keep track of play counts and recently played status. This status won't change on the iPod, however, until you connect the iPod to your computer and update it. You can play Nick Lowe's "Truth Drug" 17 times in a row on your iPod, for example, but it won't appear in the Recently Played or Top 25 Most Played playlist until you update your iPod in iTunes. (Note that the Live Updating option must be switched on in these playlists for this feature to work.) When you update the iPod, the play-count tally increases in iTunes to reflect the number of times you've played particular tunes on your iPod.

# Moving Music to the iPod

The conduit for moving music to the iPod is iTunes—which, fortunately, is fairly flexible in the way it goes about the process. The key to determining how you move your tunes is the iPod Preferences dialog box.

With the advent of iTunes 4.7, there are two ways to access iTunes' iPod Preferences window. To start, plug your iPod into your computer and launch iTunes. (By default, iTunes launches on its own when you connect the iPod.) The iPod will appear in iTunes Source list (**Figure 2.16**).

**Figure 2.16**
My iPod in the Source list.

In earlier versions of iTunes, you clicked on the iPod in the Source list to view a new icon that appeared next to the EQ icon in the bottom-right corner of the iTunes window (**Figure 2.17**). Clicking this iPod icon opened the iPod Preferences dialog box.

**Figure 2.17**
The iPod Preferences icon appears at the bottom of the iTunes window when you select the iPod in the Source list.

This option remains in iTunes 4.7. However, you can also reach this dialog box by opening iTunes' Preferences window and clicking the iPod tab. Doing so produces the dialog box you desire (**Figure 2.18**). Using this latter method offers the singular advantage of not requiring you to first select the iPod in the Source list.

**Figure 2.18**
The iPod Preferences dialog box.

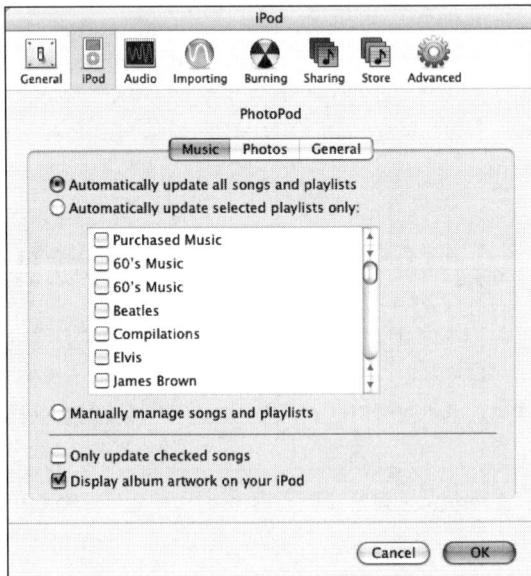

But what happens when you have two iPods plugged into your computer at the same time? Will the iPod preferences dialog box reflect it? Indeed it will. With two iPods attached to your Mac or Windows PC, a pop-up menu appears in the iPod preferences window. From this menu you simply choose the iPod you want to work with and you're ready to go. Alternatively, you can select the iPod you want to configure from the Source list and then click the iPod icon at the bottom of the iTunes window. The iPod preference dialog box will appear with that iPod chosen.

Aside from iPod preferences being incorporated into the iTunes Preferences window, there are some other differences. The major difference is the Photos tab that appears when you plug an iPod Photo into your computer. I discuss this tab and its effect on the iPod Photo in Chapter 3. The other differences are cosmetic. Where earlier iPod preferences dialog boxes placed all options in a single dialog box, the new preferences splits options into two or three tabs. If you've connected any iPod save the iPod Photo, the dialog box contains a Music and General tab. When an iPod Photo enters the picture, that third Photos tab appears.

## The Music Tab

Here are the settings you'll find within iTunes 4.7's Music tab (and within the single Preferences dialog box in earlier versions of iTunes).

### Automatically Update All Songs and Playlists

When you choose this option, iTunes updates the iPod to include all the music in the iTunes Library. Any songs currently on the iPod that aren't in the iTunes Library are erased from the iPod.

Although everyone will be pleased that iTunes automatically adds songs from the iTunes Library, not everyone may be tickled by the notion that it also erases songs. If you've removed songs from iTunes' Library and want them to remain on your iPod after the update, this option is not for you.

This option is on by default.

## Automatically Update Selected Playlists Only

This option updates only the playlists you've selected. Any songs stored on your iPod that don't belong to the selected playlists are erased when you select this option.

This option is a good one to use when several members of your family are sharing an iPod. Mom can pack a playlist with hits from the '60s, and when it's her day with the iPod, she can update only her playlist and—to make room for her tunes—erase Little Johnny's Speed Metal selections. When Dad can wrestle the iPod away from Mom, he can lose the '60s and update the iPod with his be-bop collection.

It's also a good option for those with large music collections who carry an iPod mini. Because the mini holds "only" 1,000 songs, it's possible that you'll fit just a portion of your music collection on it. This option could make it much easier to manage your music by allowing you to chunk up your collection into multiple playlists and then rotate those playlists in and out of your mini by selecting playlists 1, 2, and 3 one month, and 4, 5, and 6 the next.

Again, this option isn't a good idea when you don't want items to be removed from your iPod.

## Manually Manage Songs and Playlists

Ah, finally—the option to use when you want to add songs to your iPod without removing any tunes from the device. When you select this option, all the playlists on your iPod appear below the iPod's icon in iTunes' Source list. To add songs to the iPod, just select them in the Library or one of iTunes' playlists, and drag them to one of the iPod's playlists (**Figure 2.19**). Those songs appear at the top of the playlist. To move a song's position, click the top of the Number column, and drag the song to where you'd like it to appear in the list.

**Figure 2.19**

Moving music to the iPod manually.

If you don't care to add songs to an existing playlist on your iPod, feel free to create a new playlist. Just click the icon of your iPod in the Source list and then click the New Playlist button (the + button) at the bottom of the Source list to add an empty playlist to the iPod. Name the playlist by typing its name in the highlighted field.

Optionally, you can add songs by genre, artist, or album by using iTunes' browser. To do so, follow these steps:

**1.** Choose Show Browser from iTunes' Edit menu.

A pane divided into Genre, Artist, and Album columns appears at the top of iTunes' main window.

**2.** Click an entry in one of the columns.

If you want to copy all the Kate Bush songs in your Library to the iPod, for example, click Ms. Bush's name in the Artists column. To copy all the reggae tunes to the iPod, select Reggae in the Genre column.

**3.** Drag the selected item to the iPod's icon in the Source list or to a playlist you've created on the iPod (**Figure 2.20**).

**Figure 2.20**
Move a mass of music by dragging it from iTunes' browser.

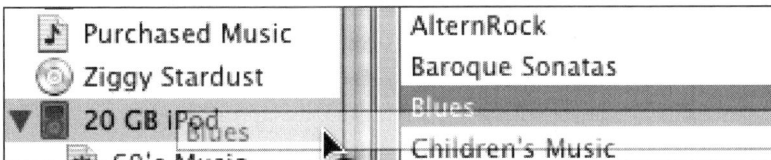

To remove songs from the iPod, select the songs you want to remove within the iPod entry in the Source list; then press your keyboard's Delete key (or Control-click on the Mac or right-click for Windows, and choose Clear from the contextual menu). Mac users can also drag the songs to the Trash on the Desktop (or, in the case of OS X, to the Trash in the Dock). You'll be asked to confirm that you really want to delete the songs. (You can disable this warning by clicking the Don't Ask Me Again check box in the warning dialog box.)

You can even copy entire playlists to other playlists by dragging one playlist icon on top of another. This method works for both iTunes and iPod playlists.

When you remove songs from your iPod, you don't remove them from your computer. Unless you select a song in iTunes' Library and delete it, the song is still on your hard drive.

When you choose to manage your songs and playlists manually, you'll be told that you have to disconnect the iPod manually—meaning that you have to take action to unmount the thing rather than simply unplug it from your computer. To do so, you can select the iPod in the Source list and then click the Eject button in the bottom-right corner of the iTunes window. Alternatively, Mac users can switch to the Finder and drag the iPod to the Trash. When its icon disappears from the Desktop, you can unplug your iPod. Windows users can invoke the Safely Remove Hardware command from the System Tray.

The iPod will also tell you when it's ready to be unmounted. When the iPod is mounted on your computer or busy accepting data from an application, the display flashes the international symbol for "Back off, Jack!" (the circle with a line through it), along with a "Do not disconnect" message. When you unmount it properly, the iPod displays a large checkmark and the message "OK to disconnect."

One more unexpected pleasure offered by the manual-update option is the ability to play songs on your iPod through the attached computer's speakers or via Apple's AirPort Express. (I discuss the AirPort Express at greater length in the Accessories chapter.) With manual update switched on, just select a song in your iPod, and press the computer keyboard's spacebar. The song streams off the iPod; through iTunes; and out your computer's speakers or headphones port, or to your AirPort Express and the stereo connected to it. To control the volume, you must use iTunes' volume control; the iPod's controls won't work in this mode.

## Only Update Checked Songs

As its name hints, this option tells iTunes to update those songs that are checked in iTunes' Library. This option can act as a safety measure, ensuring that any songs that are no longer available to iTunes (the songs you pulled from a networked volume by following the advice in the "Play Tunes over a Network" sidebar earlier in this chapter, for example) aren't erased from your iPod during an automatic update.

 Care to check or uncheck all the songs in a playlist at the same time? On the Mac, hold down the Command key and click any checkbox in the playlist. In Windows, hold down the Control key and do the same thing. By unchecking a box, all boxes will be unchecked. Check a box and all boxes will be checked.

# The General Tab

The General tab contains two non-musical options that effect how an iPod and iTunes interact when the iPod is plugged into your computer (**Figure 2.21**).

**Figure 2.21**
iPod Preferences' General tab.

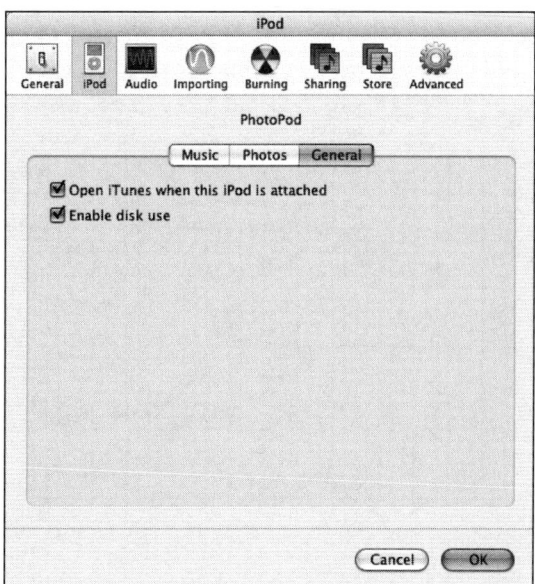

### Open iTunes When This iPod Is Attached

On by default, this option fires up iTunes when you plug your iPod into your computer's FireWire or USB 2.0 port. This option is reasonably convenient unless you're using your iPod strictly as an external hard drive. Because I do use my iPod for exactly this purpose, I keep this option switched off.

## Copy Restrictions

The iPod was designed to be a one-way copying device. You can move music from your computer to your iPod, but you can't move music from the iPod to the computer. Apple designed the iPod this way to discourage music piracy. The company might very well have run into some legal problems were the iPod shown to be a portable conduit for moving music from one computer to another.

For this same reason, the iPod is tied to one computer. When you plug your iPod into a computer other than the one it was originally plugged into, and that iPod is configured to be updated automatically, a warning dialog box appears, indicating that the iPod is linked to another iTunes Library (**Figure 2.22**). You'll be given the option to leave the iPod as is or have its contents replaced by the current computer's iTunes Library. If you choose to leave the iPod as is, you can't add songs to its Library until you open the iPod Preferences dialog box and choose the "manually manage" option. After you do, you can copy songs freely from that computer's iTunes Library to the iPod.

**Figure 2.22**

The iPod was designed to synchronize with one computer at a time.

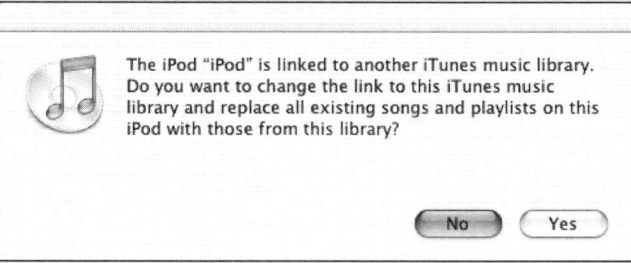

> ### Copy Restrictions *(continued)*
>
> But that leaves you in a bit of a quandary, for when you return your iPod to the original computer, if you turn on one of the automatic-update options, the songs you copied from the other computer are erased from the iPod, because they don't exist in the iTunes Library of the original computer. You could simply manage your iPod manually from that day forward, of course, but that pretty well ruptures the convenient relationship between iTunes and the iPod.
>
> Alternatives to this manual-mode scheme? You could copy the song you want from the original CD to both computers (provided that you own the CD, of course). Or you could burn a CD of music files stored on one computer and copy those files to the other computer (again, provided that you own the original material). If you *don't* own the original material—and no, downloading it from an illegal source on the Internet or borrowing your friend's copy of the CD doesn't count—do your conscience a favor and buy the CD or purchase the music from the iTunes Music Store.

## Enable Disk Use

This option allows your iPod to appear on the Mac's Desktop or within the PC's My Computer window, where you can use it just like any other hard drive. To copy files to the iPod, drag them to the iPod icon. Likewise, you can move files from the iPod by double-clicking the iPod to open it and then dragging the files from the iPod to your computer.

By default, you can't use this method to move your music files from the iPod to the computer. Music files that you drag to the iPod's icon won't appear in iTunes, either. I'll discuss this issue—and ways around it—at length in Chapter 5. Suffice it to say for now that the music files you play on your iPod are hidden away so that you won't be tempted to copy them to a multitude of computers.

When you choose the "manually manage" option, your iPod is configured as an external drive automatically, and this option is selected but grayed out. If you select one of the automatic options, you must enable this option for the iPod to appear on the Mac's Desktop or within Windows' My Computer directory.

Switching on this option is also necessary if you want to rummage around in an iPod Photo's Full Resolution folder after you've opted to copy full-resolution photos from your computer to the iPod. I'll discuss this option in greater detail in Chapter 3.

## Voice Recordings and iTunes

Apple added support for recording voice memos when it released the iPod Software 2.1 Updater. To record these memos, you need Belkin's Voice Recorder or Griffin Technology's iTalk. After you've recorded a few voice memos, here's how to interact with them in iTunes.

1. Connect the iPod to your Mac or PC.

   When iTunes launches, you'll see a message that reads "The iPod *YouriPod'sName* contains new voice memos. Would you like to copy these voice memos to your Music Library?"

2. Click Yes to copy the audio recording from the iPod to your computer.

3. Click the Library button at the top of the Source window.

   In the main window, your recordings are titled with their creation date and time—11/14/04 9:14 AM, for example.

4. Click iTunes' Play button to listen to the recordings.

5. To export the voice recordings, drag them out of iTunes and onto the computer's desktop.

   The .wav file is copied to the desktop.

   For more information on voice recordings, see Chapter 9.

## The Get Info Window

If you peek in iTunes' File menu, you'll find the Get Info command. Choosing this command produces the Song Information dialog box (**Figure 2.23**) for the selected song (or songs). You don't need to be concerned about a lot of what goes on in this dialog box; some settings apply only to iTunes. But it is worth your while to look at the portion of the dialog box that appears when you click the Info tab.

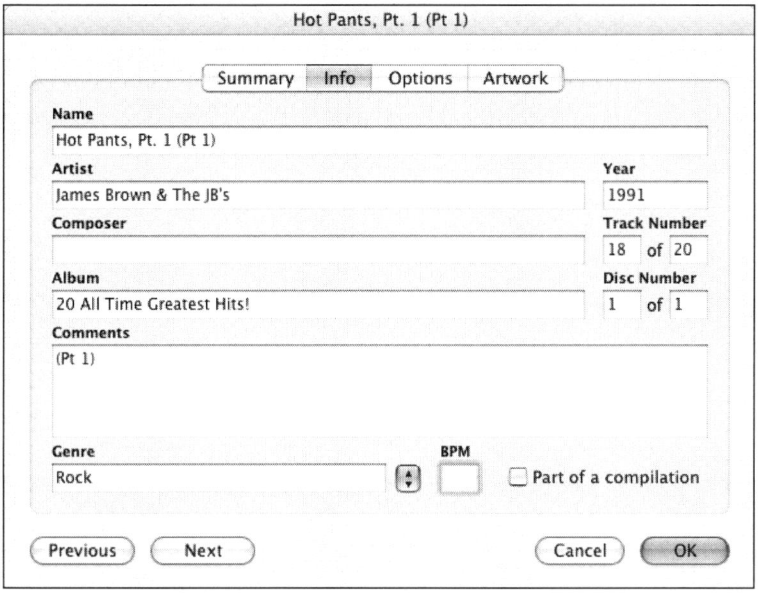

**Figure 2.23**
The Song Information dialog box.

In the Info tab, you'll find Artist and Album fields (along with the Name field, which appears at the top of every tab in this dialog box). The information in these fields—termed *ID3 tags*—is carried over to the iPod. You may find occasions when it's helpful to change the information in these fields. If you have two versions of the same song—perhaps one from the CD and another as a live recording—you could change the song title of the latter to include *(Live)*. Or if you discover that the iPod splits an artist into different groupings—Elvis Costello, and Elvis Costello and the Attractions, for example—and you'd like all the songs by that artist to appear below a single heading, you can edit the Artist field.

Although you could click the Next and Previous buttons to change the settings of adjacent songs in the Library, it's not always necessary to do that. To change these fields in a group of songs, select a bunch of tunes in the Library, Shift-click the first and last songs in the series of titles you want to edit, or Command-click (Mac) or Ctrl-click (Windows) to select individual songs and then choose Get Info. This action produces the Multiple Song Information dialog box (**Figure 2.24**), where you can change the Artist, Album, Genre, and Comments fields for every selected song in one fell swoop.

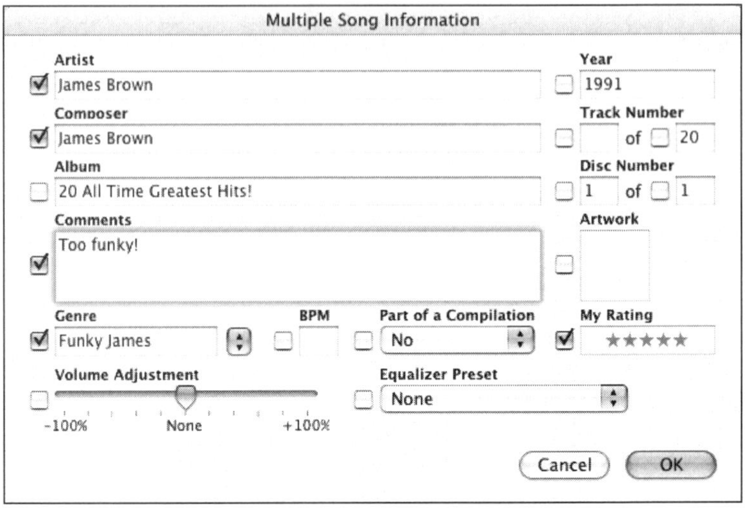

**Figure 2.24**
The Multiple Song Information dialog box.

## The Beats Go On

If you listened very carefully on the day iTunes 4 was announced, you heard a tiny whoop of joy from a small community of iTunes users who discovered that a beats-per-minute (bpm) tag has been added to the Info portion of iTunes' Get Info window. Why the hubbub? It seems that the iPod is very popular with DJs—for the obvious reason that it's a heck of a lot easier to carry a rave's worth of music on a device smaller than a pack of smokes than it is to lug around a crate full of records and CDs.

*Beat matching*—blending the beats of songs as you transition from one to the other—is an important part of the DJ trade. For this technique to work seamlessly, the number of beats per minute of the two songs must match; each must thump along at 121 beats per minute, for example.

Although iTunes 4 doesn't grant you the power to speed up or slow down a song to make it match another groove, it does allow you to sort songs and create playlists based on beats per minute. Have an early-evening gig where the crowd needs a bit of a push to get going? Cool—throw together a playlist with tempos of 130 bpm. When it's time to trance out in the wee hours, pull up the 96-bpm playlist.

You may recall from Chapter 1 that the equalizer settings you impose in iTunes carry over to the iPod. You can also change the equalizer preset for all the songs you've selected by choosing a preset from the Equalizer Preset pop-up menu. If you want to change the EQ settings for a single song, select that song, select Get Info, click the Options tab in the resulting Song Information dialog box, and choose a preset from the Equalizer Preset pop-up menu.

## Sound Check

Sound Check, added with the October 2002 iPods and iTunes 3, lives on in the current iPods and iTunes 4. (Sorry, it's not available in iTunes 2.) This feature attempts to address an all-too-common problem: The volume among songs (particularly songs from different albums) varies to the point that you must fiddle with the iPod's volume control constantly to maintain a consistent sound level.

When Sound Check is engaged, it analyzes the volume levels of all the songs in iTunes' Library and boosts the volume of quieter tunes so that their level more closely matches that of louder songs. This doesn't mean that Sound Check will alter individual volumes within a single tune—in other words, the *pianissimo* passages in the Rubinstein recording of Chopin's *Nocturnes* won't suddenly become *fortissimo*. Rather, the overall volume of those *Nocturnes* will be raised, so you won't feel compelled to crank the volume after listening to Mahler's *8th Symphony*.

In designing this feature, Apple had to make some trade-offs. For Sound Check to function flawlessly, it would have to spend hours analyzing your iTunes Library. Knowing that its customers were unlikely to put up with seemingly endless analysis, Apple designed Sound Check so that it brings volumes closer together than they were before—with the idea that although you may not be able to give up fiddling with the volume in iTunes and on the iPod, you'll fiddle less often.

To make Sound Check work on your iPod, you must first tell Sound Check to do its stuff with your iTunes Library. To do so, choose Preferences from the iTunes menu on the Mac or the Edit menu on the PC, click the Effects button to open the Effects dialog box, and check the Sound

Check checkbox (**Figure 2.25**). When you click OK in the Preferences dialog box, iTunes begins analyzing the songs in iTunes' library.

**Figure 2.25**
The Sound Check option.

When your iPod is next updated, its music files will be ready for the Sound Check feature. To switch it on, choose Settings in the iPod's main screen, select Sound Check, and press the Select button to choose On.

## Unsound Check?

Browse Apple's Discussions forums (http://discussions.info.apple.com), and you'll find more than one post that contests the effectiveness of Sound Check. If you're a Mac user who's disappointed with Sound Check, wander over to www.mani.de/en/software/macosx/ivolume/index.html and download iVolume. This $7 utility from Manfred Lippert sets all the songs in your iTunes Library to the same perceived loudness (**Figure 2.26**). Note that due to copy-protection issues, iVolume currently does not work with songs that were purchased from the iTunes Music Store since the release of iTunes 4.5, according to the plug-in's publisher.

**Figure 2.26**
iVolume in action.

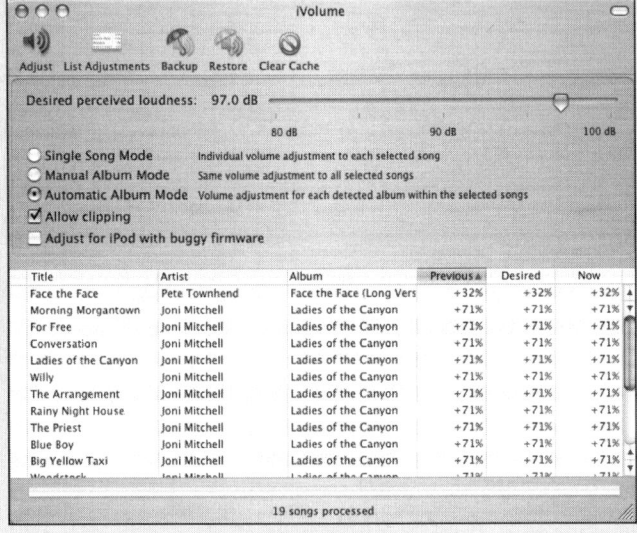

> **Unsound Check?** *(continued)*
>
> iVolume performs this feat by analyzing the tunes in your Library and adjusting the volume level (the one you see reflected in the Options area of a song's Get Info window) up or down to match a user-defined loudness level (90 dB, for example). When you move the songs that iVolume adjusted to your iPod, they retain their new individual volume settings.

## Other iTunes Tricks

What other changes can you make in iTunes that will make a difference to your iPod?

- **Show Duplicate Songs.** Prior to the release of iTunes 4.7, iTunes and iPod users were routinely vexed by an iTunes library that contained duplicate songs. Not only did these things clutter up the iTunes library, but they took up valuable space on the iPod. Apple decided to make tracking down duplicates a bit easier by adding a Show Duplicate Songs command to iTunes.

  The command works pretty much as advertised. Just select your iTunes library in iTunes' Source list and choose Show Duplicate Songs from the Edit menu. iTunes' main window will list all the duplicates it finds. Once these songs have been listed, you're welcome to delete any that you don't want.

  Before doing so, note that iTunes isn't terribly discerning about what is and isn't a duplicate. It filters tracks by only title and artist. This is fine if you've accidentally ripped the same CD twice, but you could run into trouble if you have both the live and studio versions of Led Zeppelin's "Black Dog." The Show Duplicate Songs command considers these to be duplicates even though you know better.

  And while I'm issuing notes, I might also mention that Show Duplicate Songs works only with songs in your iTunes library and its playlists. If you select your iPod—even if it's configured to be updated manually—the Show Duplicate Songs command is grayed out.

If you're a Mac user and would like a better filter—one that identifies duplicates by title, artist, album, and file size—take a look at Hyperbolic Software's free iTunes Dupes Barrier (http://www.hyperbolicsoftware.com/downloads.html).

- **Change the iPod's name.** When your iPod appears on the Mac's Desktop, within Windows' My Computer window, or in iTunes, it has a name—Mr. iPod, for example. If you've decided that your iPod is of the female, rather than male, persuasion, you might want to change its name to Ms. iPod. To do so, click the iPod's name on the Desktop or in the My Computer window, wait for the name to highlight, and enter its new name. Or click the iPod entry in the iTunes Source list to highlight the device, click the name to highlight it, and enter a new name.

  This new name will appear in the iPod's Info window the next time the iPod is updated.

- **Separately change the view settings for the iPod.** In iTunes' Edit menu, you'll find the View Options command. You use this command to determine the kind of information iTunes displays for items in the main window—the year songs were recorded and the date they were added to the Library, for example. Although you may want to sort tunes in the Library six ways to Sunday, you may be less inclined to do so when you view the information on your iPod (particularly because the iPod can't display a lot of these categories). Fortunately, you don't have to. You can create different view settings for every item in the Source List—including the iPod and each playlist on it.

- **Create a randomized playlist.** You're probably aware that you can randomize the playback of the songs in your iTunes library or in a selected playlist by pressing the Shuffle button, located next to the Create a Playlist button at the bottom of the iTunes window. With iTunes 4.6's Party Shuffle feature you can create a random playlist and then make adjustments to it—remove songs or shift their position in the playlist—as it plays. Just click the Party Shuffle entry in iTunes' Source list, and a selection of your music appears in random order in iTunes' main window. If you don't care for the order of the songs—or even for some of the songs that appear in the list—you can move songs by dragging them up or down the playlist or select a song you don't want to hear and press the Delete key on your computer keyboard to remove it from the playlist.

And this affects the iPod how? If you create a Party Shuffle playlist that you particularly like, select your iPod in the Source list, click the iPod Preferences icon, and flip the iPod into manual mode. Then drag the Party Shuffle entry in the Source list to your iPod's icon in the Source list. A new playlist is created on your iPod: Party Shuffle, which contains the same playlist as the one in the original Party Shuffle playlist on your computer.

If you prefer not to change your iPod from automatic syncing to manual mode, you can take the extra step to create a new playlist on your computer, call it Cool Party Shuffle, select all the songs in your Party Shuffle playlist, drag those songs into the Cool Party Shuffle playlist, and sync your iPod. The Cool Party Shuffle playlist is copied to the iPod.

- **Print the contents of your iPod**. Another recent addition to iTunes is the ability to print CD jewel-case inserts and lists of songs for the selected playlist. As far as iTunes' Print command is concerned, your iPod is just another playlist. To print the contents of your iPod, just select it in iTunes' Source list, choose Print from the File menu, enable the Song Listing option in the resulting Print dialog box, and choose Songs from the Theme pop-up menu. Then click the Print button, and before you know it, you'll have page after page of songs, artists, and albums you can flap in front of the faces of your iPod-less friends.

- **View iTunes Visuals**. Yes, when you play songs from the iPod through your computer (see the "Manually Manage Songs and Playlists" section), you can switch on iTunes Visuals—the program's groovy light-show feature. Visuals respond to the iPod's music just as they would to a song played directly on your computer, though you may find that they react a bit more slowly when you play from the iPod.

- **Use iTunes AppleScripts (Macintosh only).** Apple offers a host of helpful AppleScripts for iTunes that allow you to do such things as look up the entire output of an artist on the Web. Included in these AppleScripts is the iPod Library Summary script, which you'll find in the AppleScript menu when you add these scripts (**Figure 2.27**). When you highlight your iPod's name in the Source list and sort your iPod's tunes by Artist, this script generates a text file that includes the artist, album, song title, and play time of every song on your iPod. This file is tab-delimited and can be imported easily into a spreadsheet application such as AppleWorks or Microsoft Excel. You can find these scripts at www.apple.com/applescript/itunes/index.html.

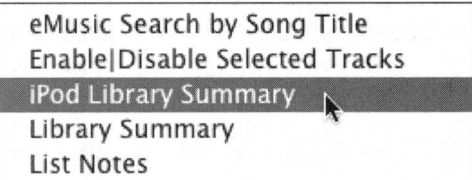

**Figure 2.27**
A helpful AppleScript can be yours for the downloading.

- **Get iPod help.** If you have an iPod, you know that the manual provides the basics, but not much more. When you want to get help with your iPod (I mean, other than in the pages of this quite-helpful book), choose iPod Help from iTunes' Help menu (**Figure 2.28**).

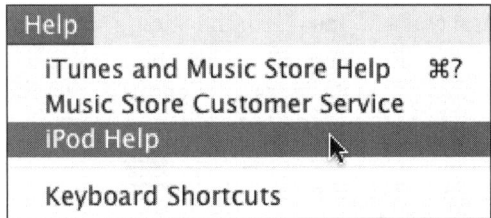

**Figure 2.28**
Need help? You'll find it here.

# 3
# Picture Perfect: iPod Photo

Don't look now, but within nearly all of us resides the selfish soul of a 3-year-old. Do you doubt me? Riddle me this, then. Apple releases a faultless music player in the form of the iPod, and what do you hear? "But I want my iPod to do *more! Now! Gimme, gimme, gimme....*"

And thank goodness, say I, that this is the case. Without consumers' constant desire for bright shiny objects, the world's economy would crumble, and Apple's engineers would spend their days cracking open older iPods to replace their exhausted batteries.

This ceaseless carping not only keeps dollars, drachmas, and deutschemarks circulating, but also drives companies such as Apple to produce the Next Big Thing. In the case of the iPod, that NBT is a device that not only holds and plays thousands of tunes, but displays scads of pictures as well. This is the iPod Photo.

# A New iPod or No?

Following the October 26, 2004, announcement of the iPod Photo, many people were confused about what wonders the iPod Photo held. Before I dip into the small details of the device, let me make a few points clear.

## Some of the Same

In regard to its form and its music- and data-handling capabilities, the iPod Photo is virtually indistinguishable from a fourth-generation iPod. It bears the same controls as this iPod; it transfers data the same way over the same FireWire and USB 2.0 connections; its menu structure is very similar; it handles contacts, calendars, and notes just like its fourth-generation sibling; and until you switch the thing on, it looks exactly like a fourth-generation iPod. Unlike earlier iPods, however, it does require iTunes 4.7 or later.

## Expectations vs. Reality

When Steve Jobs unveiled the iPod Photo, he quickly dispelled the notion that Apple had any interest in developing a video iPod (at least in developing one at that time). Though he felt that few people would be interested in viewing video on his beloved player, he had no doubt that it would be a wonderful platform for displaying pictures. What he didn't spell out is how necessary a personal computer is to making the transaction between iPod and digital camera work.

Many had hoped that an iPod with photo capabilities would be able to download pictures directly from a digital camera and then display those pictures on the iPod—thus making the device a useful tool for photographers who want to preview scads of pictures in the field without having to swap media cards or drag along a laptop. This is not that iPod.

The iPod Photo requires that its pictures be converted and stored in special files. Currently, the iPod Photo is incapable of performing either of these jobs. Rather, iTunes 4.7 or later converts the files, stores them in the proper format, and then downloads the photos to the iPod. As I explain later in the chapter, although you can copy full-resolution images to the iPod, as well as transfer images via a device such as Belkin's Media Reader for iPod, these images won't display on your iPod until they're copied to your computer, converted, and then transferred back to the iPod via iTunes.

## It Comes in Colors

Though you'd have some difficulty differentiating a 40 GB fourth-generation iPod and a 40 GB iPod Photo when the two are switched off and placed side by side, once you turn them on, the difference becomes startlingly clear. The iPod's 2-inch, 65,536-color liquid crystal display is glorious (**Figure 3.1**). Despite the iPod's name, it uses colors in ways other than flashing photographs across its screen. Its interface sports a look similar to the blue "Aqua" theme used by Apple's Mac OS X operating system. The battery indicator has been colorized, so a full battery appears green, and a nearly drained battery shows red. The device's calendars and games have been colored to make them easier to read and play. The iPod's Volume and Timeline thermometers are a soothing blue, as are the stars on the Rating screen. Songs that have embedded album art can display album covers when played. And, of course, this iPod can play your pictures singly or in a slideshow

**Figure 3.1**

With grayscale pictures, it's hard to see just how colorful and crisp the iPod Photo's screen is. Take my word for it—it is. Photo courtesy of Apple Computer.

But not all of this iPod's graphic enhancements come from color. Apple also employed a thinner font—similar to what's used on the iPod mini—that gives the menus a cleaner look. And to make it easier to discern your music, entries that don't fit on one of the iPod Photo's screens (an entry in the Artists or Songs screen, for example) scroll across the screen in ticker-tape fashion when selected. On other iPods, names that don't fit are cut short and end with an ellipsis—Mary Chapin Carp..., for example.

### iPod Photo and Album Art

The iPod Photo can display album art, but it doesn't *have* to. The trick to switching album art on and off is iTunes 4.7's Display Album Artwork on Your iPod option (located in the Music tab of the iPod Preferences window). With this option on, the iPod will do what the option suggests: display album art for those files that have art embedded in them. When the option is off, no album art is displayed, though the art won't be removed from the file.

So given that files won't be any smaller when you disable album art, why do it? Displayed album art adds an extra click to navigating the iPod. On older iPods, when you click the Select button while a song is playing, you're taken to the Scrub screen. On an iPod Photo, clicking a Now Playing screen that displays artwork takes you to a window that shows you a full screen of artwork. Some people find clicking through this intermediate screen inconvenient. Turning off album art eliminates this step.

## Television Network

Although the iPod Photo's ability to display pictures on its 2-inch display earns it a certain "gee-whiz" respect, showing pictures and slideshows on a pocket-packed device is hardly news to those who carry late-model cellular phones and PDAs. These devices are just as useful for boring the pants off your former friends with your summer-vacation slides.

Ah, but suppose that the iPod could also project those pictures on a television set. Let's see your Nokia do that, buddy. (No, really, let's not.) Yes, broadcasting slideshows to a TV is another of this iPod's charms. Apple helps this process along by including an AV cable that features two audio jacks and a composite video plug. String this cable between a TV and the iPod's specially engineered headphone port (engineered to output video, that is), and it's showtime! For higher-quality video, take advantage of the S-Video port on the back of the iPod Photo's bundled Dock (no S-Video cable is included, however).

Yes, the iPod does all this and a tiny bit more. Now that you're hip to its trip, let's examine how it performs these wondrous feats.

# Porting Pictures

In one hand, you've got a passel of pictures; in the other, your iPod Photo. How do you marry the two? No shotgun necessary; just follow along.

## iTunes Delivers

Just as iTunes delivers music to your iPod, so does it handle the transaction between the pictures stored on your Mac or Windows PC and the iPod Photo. Those without an iPod Photo attached to their computer won't see this added functionality as it makes itself known only when you've made that connection between computer and iPod.

With that in mind, make such a connection and whistle in admiration when you choose Preferences from the iTunes menu, click the iPod tab, and notice that a Photos tab has magically appeared within the resulting window. This tab is the key to moving pictures from your computer to the iPod. It works this way:

1. Enable the Synchronize Photos From option.

    When you do, you'll see an alert that asks if you're really sure you want to enable photo support. If this is your first time adding photos to your iPod, you may wonder why Apple would question your desire to have the iPod perform the job for which you paid so dearly. iTunes does this to warn you that any photos currently on the iPod will be replaced. Although you have the option to synchronize music manually, you don't have the option to manage photos manually on the iPod; thus, you have to be more careful about accidentally erasing pictures when you plug your iPod Photo into another computer and that other computer replaces your photos with photos of its own.

iTunes is smart enough to keep its music- and pictures-synchronization options separate. If you attach an iPod whose music and photo libraries are associated with a different computer, you're given the option to synchronize each library separately. You can, for example, tell iTunes not to update its music with the music library of the currently connected computer, but to update the iPod with the pictures on this new computer.

**2.** Choose a source of photos.

On a Macintosh, you'll see iPhoto listed in the Synchronize Photos From pop-up menu (**Figure 3.2**). On your Mac, you also have the option to choose images from the Pictures folder in your user folder or select any other folder you'd like. This works pretty much as you'd expect.

**Figure 3.2**
iPhoto as a photo source in the Mac version of iTunes 4.7.

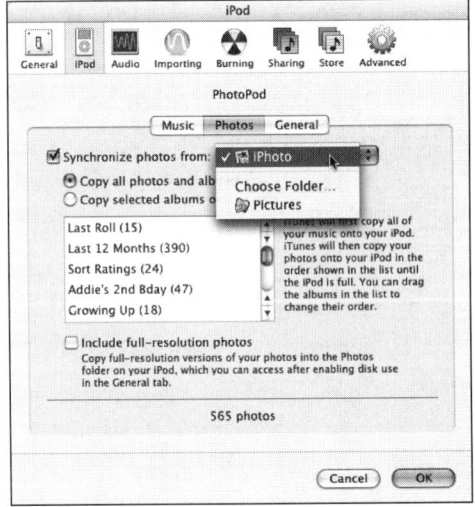

When you choose iPhoto, the entry below reads Copy All Photos and Albums. When you enable this option, all the pictures in your iPhoto library will be converted and copied to the iPod. You also have the choice to Copy Selected Albums Only. This works much like the Automatically Update Selected Playlists Only option in the General tab of iPod Preferences. Here, you can choose to add photos from a select group of iPhoto albums. Regardless of which option you choose, whenever you add new images to a selected album, the iPod automatically updates its photo library when it next synchronizes.

If you choose Pictures from this pop-up menu, the options below change to Copy All Photos and Copy Selected Folders Only. The principles of iPhoto import apply here as well. If you choose Copy All Photos, iTunes rummages around in this folder and looks for compatible graphics files. (iTunes 4.7 for Mac can recognize JPG, TIFF, PICT, GIF, PNG, JPG2000 or JP2, PSD, SGI, and BMP files; on a Windows PC, iTunes 4.7 recognizes JPG , JPEG, BMP, GIF, TIF, TIFF, and PNG.) If you choose Copy Selected Folders Only (**Figure 3.3**), you can direct iTunes to look in only those folders that you select.

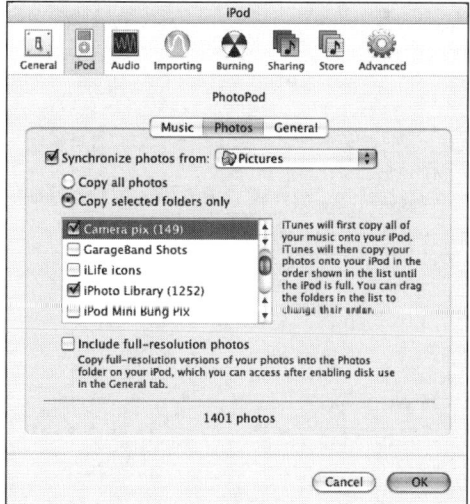

**Figure 3.3**
Copying photos from select folders within a host folder.

Finally, you can select Choose Folder. When you do, up pops a Change Photos Folder Location navigation window. Just traipse to the folder you want to pull pictures from, and click Choose. When you do this, the folder you've chosen replaces Pictures in the pop-up menu.

 This is a good way to copy every picture from your hard drive to your iPod. As far as iTunes is concerned, your hard drive is just another folder. Select it as the source folder with the Copy All Photos option selected, and iTunes grabs all the compatible graphics files it can find, converts them, and plunks them onto your iPod.

This process is no more complicated for Windows users. The main difference is that the Windows version of iTunes offers no iPhoto option (and because there is no version of iPhoto for Windows, that's probably a good thing). Instead, you'll see the option to Copy All or Selected photos from your My Pictures folder or a folder of your choosing.

If you've installed Adobe Photoshop Elements 3.0 or later or Adobe Photoshop Album on your PC, the Synchronize Photos From pop-up menu will also contain entries for these programs, allowing you to import pictures from the albums these programs create (**Figure 3.4**).

**Figure 3.4**
Adobe Photoshop Album as picture source.

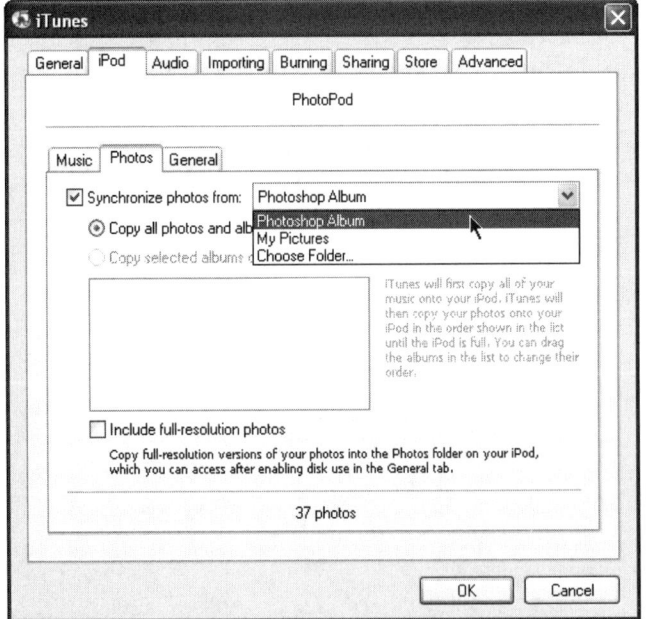

 The tip I proposed for copying all the pictures from your Mac to your iPod works with Windows as well. In this case, choose your C drive as the source. When you do, every compatible graphics file will be converted and copied.

**3.** Include full-resolution photos (or don't).

Near the bottom of the Photos tab of the iPod Preferences window, you'll see the Include Full-Resolution Photos option, followed by this text:

*Copy full-resolution versions of your photos into the Photos folder on your iPod, which you can access after enabling disk use in the General tab.*

This is a useful hunk of text, in that it hints at where your full-resolution images are stored, but were room to allow, it might be even more useful if it continued with these words:

*Oh, and don't get your hopes up thinking that just because you've copied these full-resolution images to your iPod, you'll be able to view these exact images on your iPod or project them to a television. No, sir (or madam, as the case may be), this option is provided only as a convenient way to transfer your images to the iPod so that you can later attach it to a different computer and copy your pictures from here to there. I mean, heavens, the iPod Photo is a little miracle worker, but for the love of Steve, do you really expect it to decipher images of heaven-knows-how-many-resolutions and convert them to a form compatible with your el-cheapo boob tube? Cut us some slack. We here at Apple are pretty smart, but we can't walk on water.*

Unlike the iPod's invisible iPod_Control folder, the iPod Photo's Full Resolution folder, which appears within the iPod's Photos folder, is organized in a logical way. When you open the Full Resolution folder, you'll see a folder that bears the year the pictures were created. Within this folder are folders marked with the month of creation. Within one of these folders is a folder denoting the day of conception. So the folder hierarchy might look like this: Photos/Full Resolution/2005/2/28/yourphotos.

**4.** Click OK.

If the iPod's photo library is linked to the computer it's currently attached to, clicking OK tells iTunes to convert your photos and load them onto the iPod. If the iPod has a photo library loaded from a different computer, you'll once again see the "Are you sure?" dialog box, warning you that the pictures currently stored on the iPod will be vaporized and replaced with the photos on the attached computer. Click Yes, and the iPod will be updated.

## Image Storage and the iPod Photo

If you're the curious sort, you're probably wondering where and how the iPod Photo stores its images. Here's the dope:

Unlike music files—which, as I reveal later in the book, are made invisible so you won't monkey around with them in an unsavory way—the iPod's photos are in plain view.

Well, sort of.

I waffle because, although the Photos folder is plain to see (it's at the root level of the iPod), when you open that folder, you'll find no other folder that contains your pictures in accessible-by-your-computer form. Instead, you'll find a Photo Database file and a folder called Thumbs. It's this Thumbs folder that your pictures call home (**Figure 3.5**).

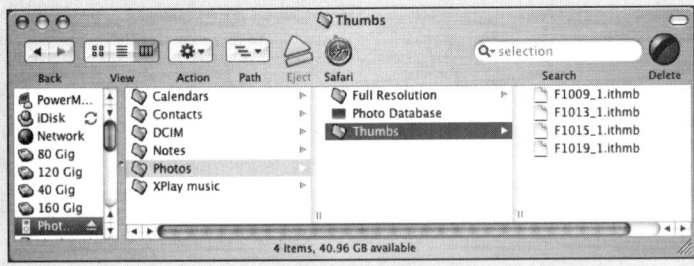

**Figure 3.5**
The iPod Photo's pictures are embedded in a proprietary .ithmb file.

Wait—before you dash off to peer into this folder, I should warn you that it contains a series of files with the .ithmb extension. These files contain your pictures. Regrettably, these files can't be opened by any program I've come across (though it's still early days as this book goes to press—some enterprising shareware author may come up with a utility that can read these things).

If you've asked iTunes to save full-resolution images of your photos to the iPod, you'll find these images in the aptly named Full Resolution folder. This is the folder you'll copy to another computer when you want to transfer your pictures.

You might also find another folder full of images on your iPod—a DCIM folder, for example. Such a folder appears if you've transferred images to your iPod via a media reader or USB camera connection. In Chapter 9, I go into detail about how these devices interact with your iPod and computer. For the purposes of this chapter, suffice it to say that you can't load these pictures onto your iPod without first transferring them to your computer and running them through iTunes, using the technique I outlined earlier in this chapter.

# Viewing Pictures

Having more colorful menus and a Solitaire game that's finally worth playing are all well and good, but you probably dropped five or six C-notes so you could view pictures on your iPod. Doing so couldn't be much easier:

1. Select Photos in the iPod's main screen, and press Select.

2. Choose an album from the list that appears in the Photos screen.

    If you don't see any albums listed, you need to use iTunes to export some pictures to the iPod.

3. Press Select to move to a thumbnail view of your pictures.

    The thumbnail view presents you with a five-by-five grid of pictures representing the contents of your photo album. A scroll bar to the right of the window appears if you have more pictures than will fit on a single screen.

4. Use the click wheel to select a picture.

    Running your thumb up or down the click wheel moves you forward or back through the thumbnails. You can move through the thumbnails pretty quickly with very little movement of your digit.

5. With the proper picture selected, press the Select button.

    And there's your picture.

6. Use the Forward and Back buttons or click wheel to advance and retreat.

    Pressing Forward presents you with a full-screen view of the next image. Back moves you back one screen to the previous image. You can also rotate your thumb around the click wheel to move from picture to picture.

## The iPod Photo Flip Book

A couple of turns through a photo album using the click wheel will remind people of a certain age of an old-fashioned "flip book." For those who are unfamiliar with the term, a flip book is a do-it-yourself animation technique in which you draw a figure on the first page of a book, slightly change the figure on the next page, and on and on until you have multiple varied copies of the figure. Then, if you flip rapidly from one page to the next (using a motion like shuffling a deck of playing cards), the figure will appear to move.

After wheeling his way through a couple of photo albums on an iPod Photo, Dan Frakes, my partner in crime at Playlistmag.com and *Macworld* magazine, had a flash of inspiration: What if you segmented a movie into still frames, loaded those frames onto an iPod Photo as a photo album, and then scrolled through them at the proper speed?

Who says the iPod Photo can't do video (albeit really cheesy video)? Here's Dan's technique:

1. Open a QuickTime movie file—preferably, a movie without sound—in Quick Time Player.

   (Note that this trick requires QuickTime Pro.)

2. Choose File > Export.

3. In the Export dialog box, choose Movie to Image Sequence from the Export pop-up menu.

4. Click the Options button, and choose a frame rate (15 fps works well) and an image format (I use JPEG).

5. Save the movie to a new folder.

6. Open the new folder containing the exported movie.

   The folder will be full of images.

7. Drag the images into a new iPhoto Album, and make sure that the images are in the right order within the album.

8. Copy the new album to your iPod Photo (via iTunes' Preferences).

So now you have the individual frames from your video on your iPod Photo. Unfortunately, the fastest "playback speed" provided by the iPod's standard slideshow options is 2 seconds per image, which is far too slow to get smooth video. Instead, select your album and then select the first image in the album (the first frame of your video) to display it in full-screen mode. Now use the iPod's click wheel to "play" the movie (by scrolling clockwise) at whatever speed you like. You've just created the first electronic photo flipbook!

Smart guy, that Dan Frakes.

# Slipping into a Slideshow

Showing individual pictures is great for that "pass the picture of your dog around the restaurant table" experience, but when you're ready to tell the complete story, a slideshow's the only way to go. Follow along and I'll show you how to present one of your own.

## Slideshow Settings

The key to the perfect iPod slideshow is the iPod Photo's Slideshow Settings screen. To access the screen, choose Photos from the iPod's main screen, and press the Select button. In the resulting Photos screen, you'll find the Slideshow Settings entry, along with a list of all the photo albums on your iPod. For now, select Slideshow Settings, and press Select again (**Figure 3.6**).

**Figure 3.6**
The iPod Photo's Slideshow Settings screen.

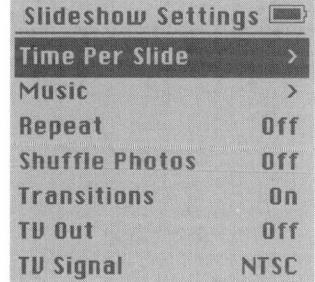

You've arrived at the Slideshow Settings screen, where you can configure such important settings as how long each slide will play, the music that will accompany your slideshow, and the type of TV signal the iPod will output. Let's run through all this screen's commands.

### Time Per Slide

Simple enough. You have six choices: Manual, 2 Seconds, 3 Seconds, 5 Seconds, 10 Seconds, and 20 Seconds. It's none of *my* business how you go about *your* business, but I might offer a couple of hints here.

The first is that if you plan to narrate your pictures, choose Manual. This option allows you to decide when to advance to the next slide.

If you won't be narrating your slides, and you want to give your audience a reasonable amount of time to *ooh* and *ahh*, choose 3 Seconds or 5 Seconds. The 2 Seconds setting gives the crowd barely enough time to know what they're looking at before the next slide rolls in.

Ten seconds is a long time to look at a picture unless you're really interested in the subject. And 20 seconds is darned near an eternity unless that picture is of your latest newborn or that hottie from Chemistry class. Before choosing one of these longer settings, be sure that your audience will be engaged for the length of each slide. And if you're showing a lot of slides, be very, very careful unless your intention is to move your guests out of your home as quickly as possible.

## Music

Another simple one. From this screen, you choose the playlist you'd like to accompany your slideshow. What's that? You say you just want to play one song, not an entire playlist? No problem; just use the iPod's On-The-Go feature to create a one-song playlist. On-The-Go is the last choice in the Slideshow Music screen. And if you'd like a silent slideshow, just choose Off.

## Repeat

This is a simple binary command: On or Off.

## Shuffle Photos

Here's another either/or command. If you'd like the pictures from the selected album to be displayed randomly, switch Shuffle Photos to On.

## Transitions

Making this command plural is slightly deceiving to the extent that it may lead you to believe that the iPod Photo offers more than one transition. Currently, it doesn't. When this command is set to On, a left-to-right wipe transition is placed between each slide.

## TV Out

You have three options here: Off, Ask, and On.

Off means that no slideshow will display on a TV attached via the iPod's A/V cable or the Dock's S-Video port. When you play a slideshow, that show displays normally on the iPod.

Choosing Ask causes the iPod to display the Start Slideshow screen, where you'll see one of two messages:

*Slideshows can also be started by pressing the center button on any full screen photo.*

or

*Slideshows can also be started by pressing the play button on any highlighted photo or album.*

Useful as all get-out, I agree, but the most helpful things about these screens, from my perspective, are the TV Off and TV On commands at the bottom of the display. If you have a TV attached to the iPod, choose TV On. If there's no TV present, choose TV Off.

 Ask is a nice option if you routinely show slideshows on both the iPod and on your TV. Sure, it's one more click, but it saves you from continually jumping back to the Slideshow Settings screen.

Finally, On lets the iPod know that you'd like it to project its slideshow on an attached TV. If you haven't connected a television and leave this option on, you'll see a different sort of display on your iPod when you play a slideshow. A slideshow with TV Out off does what you'd expect—shows a series of full-screen pictures. With TV Out on and no connected TV, you'll see a preview screen—one that shows the current slide in the center of the screen, the previous slide in a smaller view to the left, and the next slide in a smaller view to the right. Yes, this is a way to preview your slides, but it's almost completely useless when you're watching the show on the iPod alone.

 Having TV Out on while watching a slideshow also drains your iPod's battery charge much more rapidly than if you have TV Out off. Apple tells us that the iPod Photo can play a slideshow continuously for up to five hours (my tests indicate that it does a bit better than that). But this figure holds only if TV Out is switched to Off. With TV Out set to On, you'll get no more than two hours of continuous play time from a slideshow.

### TV Signal

This is the command you'll likely have to set exactly once in the iPod's life unless you're a jet-setter. You can choose between NTSC and PAL output. NTSC is the television standard used in North America and Japan. PAL is the standard just about everywhere else. Choose the setting that makes sense for your television.

> **TV Only?**
>
> With the Slideshow Settings screen populated with two TV settings, one couldn't be blamed for thinking that the iPod *must* be connected to a television to project its pictures. But let's take a moment to think outside the box.
>
> The iPod can output to any device that's willing to accept an S-Video or composite video connection. Take a look at your camcorder, and you'll likely find inputs for one or both of these video standards. Likewise, many Windows PC users will find a video card planted inside the PC that accepts one or both varieties of video. Why not put these inputs to good use by recording the video output of your iPod Photo?
>
> Doing so works along the lines I've outlined for connecting the iPod to a television. Simply find that appropriate input on your computer, camcorder, or projector, and string the cable from here to there. After you've done this, you'll need to configure the input device to accept the iPod's signal. On a camcorder, this may mean digging down through a few menus to a Record Control function. On a PC, it might require delving into a program's preferences to select the correct input on your video card. And you will likely have to configure a projector to align with the iPod's chosen output refresh rate and resolution (60Hz, 640 × 480 is always a good place to start).

## Projecting Pictures

You've packed your iPod with the photos of your latest tour of Okeechobee, you've primed your audience with caffeine, and you're ready to rock. Rather than pass the iPod from hand to hand (and risk never seeing it again), why not put your pictures up on the big screen? Here's how:

1. Plug 'er in.

The iPod can project to a TV either through the included A/V cable or via the S-Video port on the iPod's Dock. The A/V cable's yellow connector is for composite video; the red connector is for the right audio channel; and the white connector is for the left audio channel. (Note that this cable bears a special three-ring miniplug sleeve—the end that goes into the iPod's headphone port—that's designed to work specifically with the iPod. Other A/V cables are unlikely to work with the iPod Photo.)

If you have the option to use S-Video, do so. It will produce a better-looking picture, plus it gives you the option to use a *really* long cable. The iPod's A/V cable is just under 5 feet long, and if you plan to narrate over a manually controlled slideshow, you're going to be tethered fairly closely to your TV. Fifteen feet of S-Video cable will allow you to sit comfortably on the couch and control the show from the iPod planted in its Dock.

If you've configured your slideshow to be accompanied by music on your iPod, be sure to make an audio connection—either from the two audio RCA plugs on the A/V cable or via the Audio Out port on the Dock, if you're using the Dock's S-Video connection.

**2.** Switch on TV Out.

Your iPod won't play on the television unless you tell it to.

**3.** Know what to expect.

If you have a picture on the iPod's screen, don't be surprised when it doesn't flash up on the TV screen the moment you plug in the iPod. Video from the iPod won't appear on the TV until you start a slideshow.

**4.** Start the show.

Choose an album from the iPod's Photos screen, and press Select. On the subsequent screen, you'll see thumbnail images of the pictures in the album on a five-by-five grid. Use the scroll wheel to move to the first picture you want to display, and press Play.

Pressing Play again will pause the slideshow.

**5.** Stop the show.

After everyone's fallen asleep, there's no need to tax your iPod's battery further. Press Menu to stop the slideshow and return to the thumbnail screen.

## Pocketful of Presentation

I understand that there's a powerful lot of pleasure in housing the pictures of your second child's birth on a device as sleek as the iPod, but its picture-projecting powers can also be turned to more serious purposes. And if you're like me, when you hear the phrase "serious purposes" dropped into a casual conversation, you think one thing: PowerPoint.

That's right—your iPod Photo can also be used as a portable PowerPoint presenter. Although the businesslike nature of the task may make it sound like a daunting undertaking, it's a cinch. Here's how:

**1.** Create or open a PowerPoint presentation.

**2.** Choose Save As from PowerPoint's File menu.

**3.** From the Format pop-up menu in the resulting Save As dialog box, choose TIFF (Tagged Image File Format); then click Save.

PowerPoint will save each slide as a separate TIFF image in a folder of your choosing.

I suggest TIFF rather than JPEG because TIFF is a lossless graphics format, whereas JPEG strips out information to create smaller files. When iTunes converts the slide for the iPod, it will do its own stripping. I see no reason to strip the file twice.

**4.** Connect your iPod Photo to your computer.

**5.** Launch iTunes 4.7 or later, choose Preferences from the iTunes menu, click the iPod tab, and then click the Photos tab in the iPod Preferences window.

**6.** Select Choose Folder from the Synchronize Photos From pop-up menu, and navigate to the folder full of images you exported from PowerPoint.

**7.** Click OK to load the images to your iPod.

**8.** Connect your iPod to a projector or television, configure its Slideshow Settings for a manual slideshow, and run your presentation from the iPod.

# 4

# The iTunes Music Store

In the latter days of the 20th century, you would have been hard-pressed to find a more contented group of executives than those who ruled the recording industry. Prices of new audio CDs remained high; the threat of digital copying via such devices as digital audio tape (DAT) recorders had largely been eliminated, thanks to efforts of the industry's legislative lobbyists; and young consumers couldn't seem to get their fill of boy bands and the overexposed navels of blonde chanteuses.

Enter the Internet and an online enterprise named Napster—a service that allowed people to "share" music files among themselves. Suddenly, if you had a broadband connection and the will to do so, you were able to help yourself to free music by the bucketful. And, by the hundreds of thousands, people did.

The recording industry eventually put an end to the "pirate" version of Napster through litigation (the Napster name has since been applied to a commercial music service), but the genie had fled the bottle. Napster was replaced by decentralized peer-to-peer file-sharing services that could not be shut down easily. Music piracy was rampant, and the music industry saw its profits erode quickly.

One might argue that the industry shared a portion of the blame for fostering an environment in which piracy could grow by charging a premium for CDs and promoting artists that many consumers found blandly homogeneous. Although the recording industry may not have understood the part that it played in its own difficulties, it certainly recognized that consumers found online distribution to be a workable—and desirable—means of bringing new music into their lives. The times they were a-changin', and if the recording industry intended to remain viable, it had to find a way to adapt to these changes.

The trick to doing this properly was to create a service that both protected the industry's assets—the music it produced at substantial cost—as well as allowed consumers a fair measure of freedom in how they put those assets to use. (You were unlikely to woo file-sharing enthusiasts from such unlimited—though illegal—sharing schemes as Limewire, KaZaA, and select Internet newsgroups by limiting consumers' listening options.) Consumers were accustomed to listening to music on multiple devices—computers, home stereos, portable music players, and automobile CD decks—and any service that limited their freedom to do so was unlikely to gain popular acceptance.

Not that some third parties haven't tried. Such services as the now-defunct press*play* charged you a monthly subscription fee to listen to music streamed over the Internet and download some of that music to your computer. One reason press*play* failed is because the music remained yours only as long as you continued to pay press*play*'s subscription fee; as soon as you left the service, the music files were disabled. Also, if you wanted to download that music and retain a permanent copy, you had to pay an additional fee per song.

Apple looked at the available legal music services and examined the desires of both the recording industry and consumers—and it saw an opportunity to create a service that would blow the subscription companies out of the water. After months of hush-hush negotiations with the major recording companies, Apple unveiled what it considered to be the best alternative to file-sharing and music-subscription services—a service that gave consumers the freedom to download individual songs and albums permanently for a reasonable price, yet protected the interests of the music industry by encoding those songs in such a way that they couldn't be pirated rampantly.

So successful was this service that subscription outfits such as press-*play* folded quickly; they couldn't justify such limited methods of distribution after Apple demonstrated that you could sell downloadable music without treating customers like criminals. Because success breeds imitation, it wasn't long before wannabes such as Napster, Musicmatch Downloads, and Microsoft's MSN Music Service appeared. Although these services offer some of the same features as Apple's online music service, they sport cumbersome interfaces; they don't offer audio books; they're incompatible with the Mac OS; and they offer files that, by default, can't be played on the world's most popular portable music player, the iPod.

In this chapter, I look at the original (and best) online music outlet: the iTunes Music Store.

# The One-stop Shop

Realizing that the iTunes Music Store (hereafter known simply as *The Store*) would be most successful if it were easy to use, Apple eschewed the typical Internet-commerce model of creating a Web site that users accessed through a Web browser. Although this model worked reasonably well for countless merchants, it invariably required customers to slog through Web page after Web page to find and pay for the items they desired. Apple wanted a service as immediate as the experience of going to a record store, gathering the music you want, and taking it to the counter.

To replicate this experience, Apple placed The Store inside an application that was already built for music browsing and that many of its customers were likely to be familiar with: iTunes 4.

Incorporating The Store into iTunes offered several benefits:

- It's easy to access. Just open iTunes (version 4 or later), and click the Music Store icon in the Source List. If your computer is connected to the Internet, the iTunes Music Store interface appears in the main iTunes window.

Starting with iTunes 4.6, Apple made visiting The Store even easier (or, some may say, more annoying). The first time you connect your iPod to your computer (or restore your iPod), iTunes launches and displays the iTunes Music Store page. To stop it from doing so, simply click the small X in the information window at the top of the iTunes window, and select a different item in iTunes' Source list.

- It's a cinch to find music. First, enter a search term in the Search Music Store field, located in the top-right corner of the iTunes window. (This term can be an artist, album or song title, or even a single word.) Then press the Mac's Return key or the PC's Enter key. In very little time, a list of matches (including songs, album titles, and artists), sorted by relevance, appears in iTunes' main window. If you type **Louie** in the Search field, for example, you'll find links to multiple versions of the perennial frat-house favorite "Louie, Louie," as well as songs performed by Louis Armstrong, Little Louie Vega, and 88 Fingers Louie.

- It's tough to purchase music you don't want. The Store allows you to hear a 30-second preview of every song it sells. Just highlight the song you want to listen to, and click iTunes' Play button. Depending on the speed of your Internet connection, the preview quickly or slowly streams to your Mac or PC and into your ears. If you don't care for the song, cool; you've just saved yourself the trouble of purchasing the entire album, as you would have had to do in the bad old days. Continue to preview songs, and purchase just the ones you like.

If you do purchase something you don't like, you're not out as much money as you would be if you shopped at a real record store. Individual songs at The Store cost $.99, and on average, single albums cost $10.

- It couldn't be much easier to purchase music. Simply create an Apple account, locate the music you want to buy, and click the Buy Song or Buy Album button next to the pertinent song or album. After iTunes confirms your decision to purchase, it downloads the music to your computer.

- Finally, when the music is on your computer, you can copy it to your iPod, play it on up to five computers, and burn it to an audio CD that you can play anywhere you like—all without leaving the iTunes application.

In short, the entire process is about as complicated as ordering and eating a Big Mac and fries (and a whole lot healthier!). Easy to use as it may be, however, The Store has hidden depths. In the following pages, I'll explain all that there is to know about The Store and tell you how you and your iPod can put it to the best use.

## What's in Store?

When Steve Jobs flung open the doors of the iTunes Music Store on April 28, 2003, he boasted that The Store offered more than 200,000 songs from the Big Five recording companies: BMG, EMI, Sony, Universal Music, and Warner. This is quite a passel of music by anyone's standards. In the following months, Apple bulked up its catalog to the tune of one million songs (and counting), adding more music from the Big Five as well as incorporating the catalogs of several independent labels.

Although The Store carries a wide variety of audio recordings—everything from comedy to country to rock to classical to world music—the bulk of the material is of the variety that my college music-theory professor termed "pop tunes." As we go to press, the pop catalog has some fairly glaring gaps—you won't find recordings by the Beatles or Led Zeppelin, for example—and offerings by such popular artists as The Beach Boys, Elvis Costello, and King Crimson are limited (okay, so I'm showing my age).

Such gaps can't be attributed to anyone's lack of forethought, because Apple would love to have these artists in its catalog. The difficulty is that the works are so popular that the artists and their representatives can afford to hold out for better terms, requiring Apple to cut a special deal with them. (Such a deal was made for the Eagles' catalog, for example.) As these deals continue to be cut, you'll see a better-rounded catalog.

*continues on next page*

### What's in Store? *(continued)*

You may never see the Beatles at The Store, however. Apple Records (the Beatles' label) and Apple Computer don't see eye to eye on this whole music-merchant business. Apple Records maintains that it's the only Apple entity entitled to sell music. The two Apples have been to court a couple of times over this issue (Apple Records has prevailed each time), and they're at it again. Perhaps when the Apples work this one out, the Beatles' catalog and the solo works of its members will find their way to The Store.

If you're interested in music that's not played on VH1 and MTV, you'll find The Store's inventory to be a little spotty. Soundtracks for musicals, for example, are virtually nonexistent; you'll find no soundtrack recordings for *West Side Story*, *The Wizard of Oz* (though the audio book is available), *South Pacific*, or *Camelot*. And if you're a classical-music buff, you'll find recordings of many of the compositions you enjoy, but not necessarily recordings by a particular conductor, orchestra, artist, or opera company.

## Prepare to Shop

Ready to shop? Great. Let's make sure that you have the tools you need to get started. After you have those tools, we'll get you signed up with an account and then take an extensive tour of The Store.

## What You Need

As these pages go to print, The Store is available in Austria, Belgium, Canada, Finland, France, Germany, Greece, Italy, Luxembourg, Netherlands, Portugal, Spain, the United Kingdom, and the United States.

 Which store you're allowed to purchase music from depends on the issuing country of your credit card. If you have a credit card issued in Germany, for example, you can purchase music only from the German iTunes Music Store (though you don't physically have to be in Germany to do this—again, the credit card determines where you can shop).

To get started with The Store, your computer must meet these specifications:

Macintosh users must be running Mac OS X 10.1.5 on a 400 MHz G3 processor or better. To share music and burn DVDs, you need Mac OS X 10.2.4 or later. Your Mac must have at least 128 MB of RAM (Apple recommends 256 MB). Your Mac must also have copies of iTunes 4.5 or later and QuickTime 6.2 or later. If you want to use Apple's AirPort Express to stream music, you must be running Mac OS X 10.3 or later. To use purchased music in Apple's iLife applications (iMovie, iPhoto, iDVD, and GarageBand), you must have QuickTime 6.5.1 or later installed. You can download iTunes 4 from www.apple.com/itunes/download and the latest version of QuickTime from www.apple.com/quicktime/download.

An easier way for Mac users to download these files is to fire up the Software Update application built into Mac OS X. This application (which you access through Mac OS X's System Preferences) can download both iTunes 4 and the latest version of QuickTime automatically. Just choose System Preferences from the Apple menu, click Software Update in the resulting System Preferences window, and then click the Check Now button. Software Update ventures out onto the Web to determine which of your OS X components (including iTunes and QuickTime) require updating. If updates are available, another Software Update window appears, listing those updates. Check the updates you'd like to acquire, and click the Install button. Software Update downloads the updates, installs them, and (if necessary) instructs you to restart your Mac.

Windows users must be running Windows XP or 2000 on a 500 MHz Pentium-class processor or better, and 128 MB of RAM or more is recommended. To purchase music you must also have iTunes 4.5 or later and QuickTime 6.4 or later installed. (The current version of QuickTime—6.5.2 as we go to press—is included with iTunes for Windows.)

Although you can access The Store via any Internet connection, you'll find it far more fun to shop with a broadband connection. A four-minute song weighs in at around 4 MB. Such a download over a DSL or cable connection takes next to no time at all but can be terribly slow over a poky modem connection.

Because you've bothered to read a book titled *Secrets of the iPod and iTunes*, I assume that you have more than a passing interest in Apple's portable music device. Although it's not necessary to have an iPod to take advantage of The Store—music purchased at the store can be played on your computer and burned to CD—the iPod technically is the only portable music player capable of playing music purchased at The Store. (I'll show you how to skirt this limitation later in the chapter.) Okay, yes, Apple *has* cut a deal with Motorola to allow some of that company's phones to play tunes purchased from The Store, but in my book, a phone that stores a limited number of tunes hardly counts as a portable music player (though as phones begin to offer gigabytes of storage, the phones and I will both change our tunes).

## Limited for Your Protection

Earlier in the chapter, I suggested that for commercial online music distribution to be successful, the interests of both consumers and the music industry must be addressed. If an overzealous copy-protection scheme keeps consumers from playing their purchases on different devices, those consumers will look for less limited (and, perhaps, less savory) ways to obtain music online. And if consumers can share purchased music easily across the Internet, music companies will lose money and quickly withdraw support for the service.

With every intention of creating a successful distribution system, Apple has tried to address the desires of both consumers and the music industry. Consumers should be pleased that they're allowed to play music purchased at The Store on a variety of devices: computer; portable music player (the iPod); and any commercial CD player, including the ones in your home stereo, boom box, and car. And the music industry's fears of rampant piracy should be calmed because consumers can play that music on a limited number of computers; purchased music files are linked to the person who purchased them; only so many copies of a particular playlist can be burned to CD; and by default, the only music player that can play that music is the iPod.

Following are the specific restrictions Apple imposes on purchased music:

- Purchased music is encoded in a protected version of Dolby Laboratories' Advanced Audio Coding (AAC) format, which bears the .m4p extension (versus the .m4a extension of the standard AAC files that iTunes 4 can create). These files are encoded in a way that makes pirating difficult.

- You may play purchased music on up to five computers, which can be a mix of Macs and Windows PCs. All these computers must be authorized by Apple. If you attempt to play purchased music on an unauthorized computer, you'll be instructed to register the computer online before you can play the music. I describe the ins and outs of authorization later in this chapter.

### Limited for Your Protection *(continued)*

- You may burn up to seven CD copies of a particular playlist that contains purchased music. When you change that playlist—add or subtract a song, for example—you may burn another seven copies. Change the playlist again for another seven burns.
- You cannot burn purchased music on CDs formatted as MP3 discs.
- The name and Apple ID of the person who purchased the music are embedded in each purchased song. Apple does this to discourage buyers from making those songs widely available on the Web (and to trace songs to the rightful owner, should they find their way to the Web).
- You can download purchased music one time. If you need to download it again—because your hard drive crashed, for example, and you lost your music library—you must purchase it again. This is reason enough to back up your music library (preferably by burning it to CD).
- All purchases are final. If you download Highway 9's "Heroine," thinking that it's the Velvet Underground's "Heroin," you're stuck with it.
- You can play purchased music on as many iPods as you like, as long as those iPods are running iPod Software 1.3 Updater or later. Earlier versions of the iPod software won't recognize AAC-encoded music (either standard AAC encoding or the protected AAC format used for purchased music).

## Signing On

Creating an account at The Store isn't difficult. Just follow these steps:

**1.** Make sure that your computer can get onto the Internet.

Configuring your computer to access the Internet is beyond the scope of this book. I suggest, however, that if you don't have an always-on Internet connection (a DSL, cable, or satellite broadband connection), you should configure your modem so that it automatically dials into your ISP when an application such as iTunes needs to get onto the Web.

**2.** Launch iTunes 4.

3. Click the Music Store entry in iTunes' Source list (**Figure 4.1**).

**Figure 4.1**
The iTunes Music Store in the Source list.

Your computer will venture out onto the Web and connect to The Store. When The Store is ready for action, its interface will appear in iTunes' main window.

4. Click the Sign In button in the top-right corner of the iTunes window (**Figure 4.2**).

**Figure 4.2**
Click the Sign In button to create an Apple ID.

In the resulting window, you'll have the opportunity to create an account or enter your Apple ID and password or your AOL screen name and password.

This AOL business is relatively new. Apple and AOL recently formed a strategic alliance whereby AOL members can log onto The Store with nothing more than their screen name and password. Any purchases these folks make are charged to the credit cards they use to pay their monthly AOL fees.

This same alliance placed links to The Store within AOL and made Sessions@AOL recordings—live performances by a few of today's popular artists—available to customers of The Store.

It's possible that you already have an Apple ID. If you've made a purchase at the online Apple Store, for example, or bought pictures through iPhoto, you've signed up for Apple's 1-Click shopping system. Not long ago, Apple converted 1-Click accounts to Apple ID accounts. Your user name and password for your 1-Click account is now your Apple ID.

5. If you have either an Apple ID and password or an AOL screen name and password, enter them and click the Sign In button; otherwise, click the Create Account button.

   If you click Create Account, you'll be given a brief rundown on what you can do at The Store and asked to agree to The Store's terms and conditions.

6. Agree to the terms and conditions to move to the next page, where you'll create an Apple ID. Far be it for me to suggest that you forgo reading a document by which you'll be legally bound, but the fact is that unless you agree to the terms spelled out on this screen, you'll be barred from shopping at The Store.

7. In the next window (**Figure 4.3**), you'll do the following:

**Figure 4.3**
Enter your email address and a hard-to-guess password on this screen.

- Enter a valid email address in the Email Address field.

- Concoct a hard-to-guess password, and place it in both the Password and Verify fields.

- Enter a question and answer that can help Apple identify you, if need be. You might enter "How many telephone poles does it take to reach the moon?" in the Question field, for example, and answer it with "One, if it's long enough."

- Use the Month and Day pop-up menus to enter your month and date of birth, which also help Apple identify you.

- If you don't want to receive emailed marketing material from Apple, uncheck both the options in the I Would Like to Receive the Following Via Email section.

- If you want to view Apple's privacy policy, click the Privacy Policy button.

**8.** Click the Continue button to move to the Credit Card and Address screen, where you enter your Visa, MasterCard, American Express, or Discover number and contact information, including name, address, and phone number.

**9.** Click Done.

You're a member in good standing at The Store. From now on, your account name should appear in the Account field in the top-right corner of the iTunes window when you click the Music Store entry in the Source list.

## Tooling Around

As I tap out these words, The Store carries more than a million songs. Fortunately, you needn't trudge through an alphabetical list of all these titles. Instead, Apple offers you multiple ways to browse its catalog of compositions. Let's look at The Store's floor plan and the best ways to navigate it.

# Navigating The Store's Floors

The Store's main page offers a host of links for finding the music you need (**Figure 4.4**). Much like a "real" record shop, The Store places the day's most popular picks up front.

**Figure 4.4**
The Store's main page.

Here's what you'll find on the home page.

## Primary links

Across the top of the main page, you'll see a banner that changes from time to time. This banner may promote hot new singles or albums, exclusive tracks, or music videos available only at The Store.

Below the banner are side-scrolling windows that contain picture links to New Releases, Exclusive Tracks, Pre-Releases (a cut from an upcoming album, for example), Just Added, and Staff Favorites (yup, *Dark Side of the Moon* is bound to grace this list on a regular basis—and honestly, is there anyone over the age of 30 who *doesn't* own this album already?). Click the arrows to the side of each list to scroll forward or backward through the list of selections. These lists generally contain 16 selections each.

On a slowish connection, it takes a while for these lists to scroll. You can scan these categories far more quickly if you click the See All link in the top-right corner of each category. When you do, you'll be taken to a page that contains all the entries for that category (as well as album cover art) on one page—with the exception of the New Releases and Just Added links, for which you'll see all the new releases from the past few weeks displayed as text links.

Arrayed along the top-left side of the main page are text links that direct you to many of The Store's most interesting features. They include:

## Search links

The two links at the top of the list—Browse Music and Power Search—hint that there are more efficient ways to find music than clicking the song and album titles you see on The Store's home page.

### Browse Music

The Store offers a Browser view much like the view you see when you select your library or a playlist and choose Show Browser from iTunes' Edit menu. (In point of fact, selecting this command produces the same result as clicking the Browse Music link.) Click Browse Music, and iTunes' Browser columns appear, listing Charts, Radio Charts (we'll get to those in a minute), and The Store's various Genres in the leftmost column. Click a Genre entry, and a list of artists appears in the middle column.

Click an artist's name, and available albums by that artist appear in the last column. Click an album title, and the music contained on that album appears in the Results area below.

The Results area is divided into columns titled Song Name, Time, Artist, Album, Genre, and Price (**Figure 4.5**). You can sort the list by any of these criteria by clicking the appropriate column head. Click Artist, for example, and the list is sorted alphabetically by artist. Click Time, and the list is sorted by shortest to longest playing time.

**Figure 4.5**

The Store's no-nonsense Browser view.

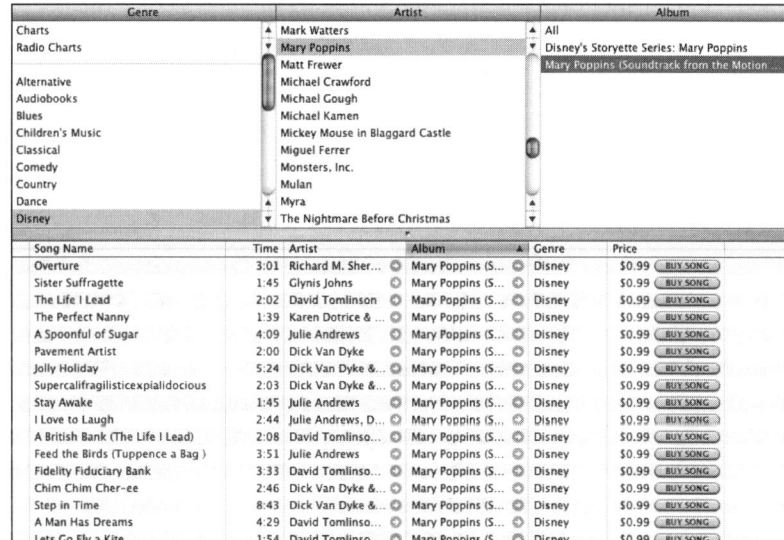

You'll notice that a right-pointing arrow appears on the right side of entries in both Artist and Album views. Clicking this arrow allows you to travel to the page devoted to that album or artist—a great way to explore an album or an artist's catalog after searching for a single song.

## Biography and Influences & Contemporaries

The first iteration of The Store provided a lot of great ways to explore new music—Staff Favorites, top songs and albums, and listener links—but Apple wanted to do a bit more to help you locate and buy music that might be to your liking. Thus, the Biography and Influences & Contemporaries links were born.

Situated on the pages of popular artists, the Biography link does exactly what you'd expect: transports you to a detailed biography of the artist, along with a discography (which includes all the artist's albums, not simply those available at The Store), a list of compilation albums, a videography, a bibliography, and (where appropriate) a filmography (**Figure 4.6**). If songs and albums mentioned on these pages are available from The Store, you'll see live links.

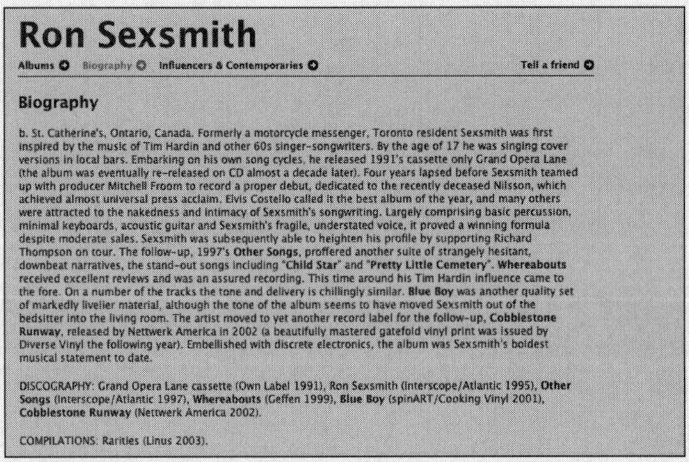

**Figure 4.6**
Learn about the lives of your favorite artists.

### Ron Sexsmith

Albums  Biography  Influencers & Contemporaries                                          Tell a friend

**Biography**

b. St. Catherine's, Ontario, Canada. Formerly a motorcycle messenger, Toronto resident Sexsmith was first inspired by the music of Tim Hardin and other 60s singer-songwriters. By the age of 17 he was singing cover versions in local bars. Embarking on his own song cycles, he released 1991's cassette only Grand Opera Lane (the album was eventually re-released on CD almost a decade later). Four years lapsed before Sexsmith teamed up with producer Mitchell Froom to record a proper debut, dedicated to the recently deceased Nilsson, which achieved almost universal press acclaim. Elvis Costello called it the best album of the year, and many others were attracted to the nakedness and intimacy of Sexsmith's songwriting. Largely comprising basic percussion, minimal keyboards, acoustic guitar and Sexsmith's fragile, understated voice, it proved a winning formula despite moderate sales. Sexsmith was subsequently able to heighten his profile by supporting Richard Thompson on tour. The follow-up, 1997's Other Songs, proffered another suite of strangely hesitant, downbeat narratives, the stand-out songs including "Child Star" and "Pretty Little Cemetery". **Whereabouts** received excellent reviews and was an assured recording. This time around his Tim Hardin influence came to the fore. On a number of the tracks the tone and delivery is chillingly similar. **Blue Boy** was another quality set of markedly livelier material, although the tone of the album seems to have moved Sexsmith out of the bedsitter into the living room. The artist moved to yet another record label for the follow-up, **Cobblestone Runway**, released by Nettwerk America in 2002 (a beautifully mastered gatefold vinyl print was issued by Diverse Vinyl the following year). Embellished with discrete electronics, the album was Sexsmith's boldest musical statement to date.

DISCOGRAPHY: Grand Opera Lane cassette (Own Label 1991), Ron Sexsmith (Interscope/Atlantic 1995), **Other Songs** (Interscope/Atlantic 1997), **Whereabouts** (Geffen 1999), **Blue Boy** (spinART/Cooking Vinyl 2001), **Cobblestone Runway** (Nettwerk America 2002).

COMPILATIONS: Rarities (Linus 2003).

The Influences & Contemporaries link is both helpful and occasionally amusing. And what makes it so?

It's helpful because every so often, you'll learn about artists you might normally miss. The Followers portion of Elvis Costello's Influences & Contemporaries page, for example, directed me to a charming Canadian singer/songwriter, Ron Sexsmith. I'm now a fan.

## Biography and Influences & Contemporaries
### (continued)

I find some of these links amusing because it turns out that—according to The Store, at least—nearly every popular musician who's had a hit in the past 40 years was influenced by the same seven Bob Dylan albums (**Figure 4.7**). And why do so many R&B artists on the site prefer James Brown's 20 All Time Greatest Hits rather than the album Brown aficionados cite as most influential—*Can Your Heart Stand It!!*?

**Figure 4.7**
Gee, this Zimmerman fella is one influential cat.

Larger forces are at work, of course. *Can Your Heart Stand It!!* isn't available from The Store and, thus, is not cited as an influence. Likewise, because the Beatles' repertoire is currently unavailable at The Store, you'll find that the Fab Four were far less influential than you might have imagined.

The list of Contemporaries is helpful to the extent that you gain a very general idea of the kind of music you might like if you care for the work of a particular artist. But the entries in this list are often off by a wide margin. The Stevie Nicks/Lindsay Buckingham-era Fleetwood Mac, for example, is cited as a contemporary of the Yardbirds—a British R&B band (featuring, at one time or another, guitarists Eric Clapton, Jeff Beck, and Jimmy Page) that broke up when Nicks and Buckingham were still eyeing each other during second-period geometry class at Menlo Atherton High School.

Obviously, work in this area remains to be done. But because there are hours of entertainment value in trying to discover just how many artists owe their livelihoods to the work of Misters Dylan and Brown, I sincerely hope that the work isn't done until after you've read this book.

### Power Search

If you want to be a power shopper, you must learn to take advantage of The Store's Power Search function.

When you click the Power Search link on the main page or choose Power Search from the pop-up menu below the magnifying-glass icon in the Search field, you're taken to a page where you can search for music based on such factors as song title, artist, album, genre, and composer. This feature comes in handy when you want to really narrow your search (**Figure 4.8**).

**Figure 4.8**
Power Search.

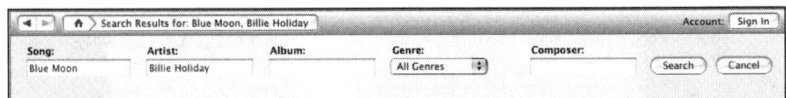

If you performed a simple search for the song "Blue Moon" by entering its title in the Search field, you'd be presented with 532 matches. Even if you search by song title, you'll get just over 200 results. Invoke Power Search, however, and you can narrow things down quite nicely.

If you're interested in vocal renditions of "Blue Moon," for example, enter **Blue Moon** in the Song field and then choose Vocal from the Genre pop-up menu. Aha—now you get just 19 matches. Had you entered **Billie Holiday** in the Artist field, you'd see only five matches.

Power Search is also useful when you aren't quite sure what you're looking for. You may recall hearing a David Bowie song that set your toes a-tapping, but all you can remember of the lyrics is the word *Detroit*. Just launch Power Search, and enter **Bowie** in the Artist field and **Detroit** in the Song field. *Woo-hoo!* Up pops a link to "Panic in Detroit" from Bowie's *Aladdin Sane* album.

## Feature links

The next group of links directs you to specific features offered by The Store. Some are music-related, whereas others are present to highlight a new or particularly attractive Store add-on. They include:

## Audiobooks

When The Store first opened its doors, it included a Books & Spoken genre. Despite the implications of this name, material within this genre did not include "books on tape" material; rather, it meant comedy records (Bill Cosby, Firesign Theatre, and Richard Pryor, for example) and excerpts from radio broadcasts and literary readings, such as William S. Burroughs reading a portion of *Naked Lunch*.

When The Store was updated to accommodate Windows users, Apple dropped the Books & Spoken genre and introduced Audiobooks, a collection of more than 5,000 "books on tape" items provided by Audible.com.

And what has Apple done with all the material that used to be in the now-absent Books & Spoken genre? That material is still available in the new Comedy genre—a genre listed in the Power Search window but not in the Genre pop-up menu on the main page. Not everything listed in this genre is comedy—the aforementioned William S. Burroughs reading, for example—but enough of the material is humorous that the classification generally makes sense. Perhaps Apple will have constructed a Comedy page by the time you read this book. If not, use the Search or Power Search function to find the laughs you like.

The easiest way to access The Store's literary section is to choose Audiobooks from the Genre pop-up menu on the main page. When you do, you'll be taken to the Audiobooks page, which looks remarkably like any other Store genre page (**Figure 4.9**).

**Figure 4.9**
The Audiobooks page.

When you click the Audiobooks link, you'll be taken to a page that looks very much like one of the music pages. As this book goes to press, the Audiobooks page is divided into easy-to-understand categories: New & Noteworthy, Behind the Music (music-oriented books), Fiction, Nonfiction, and Classics. The New & Noteworthy, Fiction, and Nonfiction categories include the kind of material you'd find in a well-stocked airport bookstore—fairly current titles that are likely to appeal to a broad audience. The Classics selections include titles that many people are required to read by the time they've finished their freshman year of college: *Atlas Shrugged*, *Crime and Punishment*, *1984*, and *Moby Dick*, for example. Regrettably, this page doesn't include a Staff Favorites category (and given the generic nature of the books in the categories that do appear on the page, it could use one).

The left side of the Audiobooks page offers links to more-specific categories of books, including Business, Comedy (books, not recordings), History, Mystery, Religion & Spirituality, Sci Fi & Fantasy, and Technology. Click one of these links, and you'll go to a browser view, where you can search by author.

On the right side of the Audiobooks page, you'll find a list of the day's 20 top-selling books, along with a link to the top 100 books The Store has sold that day. Much like the music top 100 lists, the page of 100 top-selling books includes a picture of the cover of the book, the price of the book, and a Buy Book link. To get more information about a particular title, click its picture. You'll go to a page where you can read a description of the book and listen to a 90-second preview.

Inexplicably, the list of authors is sorted by first name. This isn't a terrible burden with modern authors whose first and last names are well known—Stephen King, Amy Tan, and Chris Breen, to name a few of today's most prominent writers—but I pity the high-school student who wasn't paying attention when a teacher casually mentioned that Mr. Balzac was christened Honoré. If you get flummoxed in such situations, feel free to use iTunes' Search field.

# Fresher Air

The Store carries several radio shows originally broadcast by National Public Radio, including the hysterically funny "Car Talk" and Ira Glass' thought-provoking "This American Life." The Store also carries a selection of Terry Gross' wonderful interview program, "Fresh Air." Anyone who's anyone in the performing and literary arts has been a guest on this show (as have many prominent journalists, business leaders, and politicians).

If you enter **Fresh Air** or **Terry Gross** in the Search field, however, you'll find that it's difficult to find the program you want, because the resulting page contains hundreds of entries. As this book goes to press, 1,027 "Fresh Air" broadcasts are available for purchase (at $2.95 each), so trying to locate that Tony Bennett interview may be difficult unless you know this secret:

Use Power Search.

To find the "Fresh Air" program you want, choose Power Search from the pop-up menu in the Search field. In the Artist field, enter **Terry Gross**; and in the Album field, enter the name you're looking for, such as **Eddie Izzard** (**Figure 4.10**). In a short while, "Fresh Air" broadcasts that match your search appear.

**Figure 4.10**

Use Power Search to track down your favorite "Fresh Air" interviews.

At the risk of taking money out of Apple's pockets, I should mention that you can get recordings of "Fresh Air" programs recorded after the year 2000 by visiting http://freshair.npr.org. Unlike the shows sold at The Store, these files are formatted for Real Networks' RealPlayer—meaning that you can't save them unless you use such programs as Rogue Amoeba's Audio Hijack (Mac), Ambrosia Software's WireTap (Mac), or 1st Benison Software's All Recorder (PC) to record them as they stream to your computer (see Chapter 2 to be reminded how to do this). What might take the sting out of this inconvenience is that the NPR site offers more "Fresh Air" programs than The Store does—and they're free from NPR.

You needn't worry that you'll have to jump through extra hoops to purchase audio books from The Store. Unlike Audible.com, The Store doesn't make you decide which format you want the book delivered in: a lower-quality file that takes up less space (and downloads faster) or a higher-quality file that takes longer to download because of its larger file size. That's because The Store delivers audio books in only one format. When you purchase an audio book, you can expect to receive a mono file, encoded in The Store's protected AAC format at a bit rate of 32 Kbps and a sample rate of 24 kHz.

The audio-savvy among my readers may issue a rude *"Phhhhhttttppp..."* after reading these specifications. But let me assure you that although I wouldn't care to live on a diet of music encoded at these settings, spoken-word content is perfectly listenable.

## Book Burning

Unless the narrator of your purchased audio novel or work of nonfiction reads *very* quickly, the play time for your purchase is likely to be measured in hours. Yet a recordable CD can store only about 80 minutes of audio. How do you cram all that narration onto a single CD?

You can't. When iTunes burns a book to disc, it converts the file to the AIFF format required by audio CDs—a format that consumes 10 MB of hard disk space per minute of stereo audio.

Fortunately, iTunes provides an easy way to record your audio books to disc. When you select a file that will exceed the recording capacity of an audio CD and ask iTunes to burn a disc, the program offers to split the file into lengths that can fit on a CD. (If you must know, each segment is 1 hour, 19 minutes, and 56 seconds.) When iTunes fills one CD, it spits it out and asks for another blank disc. It continues to spit and ask until it finishes burning the entire file to disc.

The resulting discs won't be named in an intuitive way—"War and Peace" I, II, and III, for example. Rather, each will simply read "Audio CD" when you insert it into your Mac or PC. For this reason, you should keep a Sharpie at the ready to label each disc as it emerges from your CD burner.

You may notice that the audio books you purchase begin with a short advertisement from Audible.com. Although I understand that advertising helps turn the wheels of capitalism, I slightly resent paying for a product and then being subjected to ads. For this reason, when I purchase an audio book, I click it in iTunes, choose Get Info from the File menu, click the Options tab, enter **0:09** in the Start Time field, and click the OK button. This procedure truncates the first nine seconds of the file—which, coincidentally, is exactly as long as the Audible.com advertisement. Then I can listen to the file advertisement-free.

### Disney

If you follow the tittle-tattle of Hollywood, you're aware that the relationship between Disney and Apple CEO Steve Jobs' movie company, Pixar, is a little strained (and if you don't follow the aforementioned TT, I'll just say that currently, Pixar and Disney mix about as well as oil and water). The two companies' music relationship seems fairly chummy, however, as evidenced by this featured link to soundtracks from Disney movies. Whether you crave music from such Disney classics as *Mary Poppins* and *101 Dalmatians* or recordings of Disney/Pixar's recent offerings, you can find it here.

### iMix

A recent addition, iMix is your chance to inflict your musical values on the rest of the world by publishing a playlist of your favorite (or, heck, your least-favorite) songs (**Figure 4.11**). When you click the iMix link, you're taken to a page that contains three columns marked Top Rated, Most Recent, and Featured. Click an album cover to view (and purchase, if you like) the songs in it.

**Figure 4.11**
Share your musical tastes with the world.

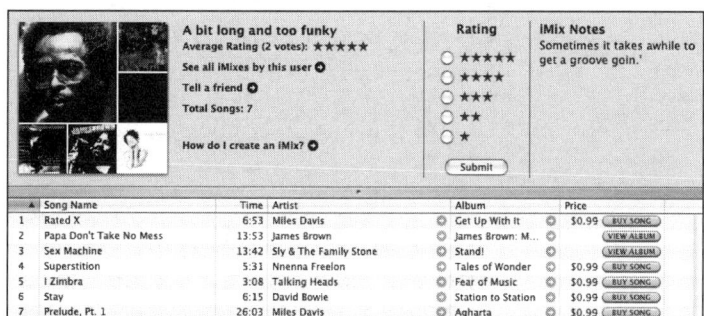

As enjoyable as it may be to view others' iMixes, it's more fun to create your own. You can do so by following these steps:

1. Create a new playlist in iTunes, and give it a really cool name.

   I hate to rain on your parade, but your iMix is going to get very little attention if you call it "My Favorite Songs." Part of the joy of creating these things is grouping songs in unexpected or humorous ways. A recent meander through The Store's Top Rated iMixes revealed Big Hair Songs (tunes by such hair-apparents as Bon Jovi, Warrant, Poison, and Cinderella) and The Periodic Table (song titles such as "Helium," "Carbon," "Chlorine," and "Iodine").

2. Cruise through your iTunes library, and drag into it songs you'd like to publish as an iMix.

   Note that your iMix can contain only songs available for purchase from The Store. If the iMix contains songs not available at The Store, those songs won't appear in the published playlist.

3. Round out your list with songs at The Store that you don't own.

   An iMix doesn't require that you actually own the music you're recommending. You can now drag previews of any of The Store's songs or audio books into a playlist in iTunes' Source list. Feel free to add these previews to your iMix playlist.

4. Click the arrow to the right of your playlist's name.

   Clicking this arrow produces a dialog box that warns you that you're about to create and upload an iMix.

5. Click Create.

   You'll be taken to The Store, and iTunes' main window will show you a picture of the cover of your album (a collage of album covers from songs you've included).

6. Edit the title and description to suit your iMix.

7. Click Publish.

   Your iMix will be published to The Store and will remain there for one year. You'll receive an email confirmation of the iMix's publication.

**8.** Tell a friend.

The window that tells you that your iMix has been published also offers the Tell a Friend button. Click this button to view the Tell a Friend screen, where you can send an email announcement to whoever you like. When your announcement has been sent, you have the option to send another.

**9.** Click Done when you're finished.

Your iMix won't appear in the Most Recent column right away. Apple vets these things, and if it doesn't approve of your iMix's title, it won't appear.

Suppose that you created your iMix under less-than-optimal conditions—you were in a bad mood, you'd just seen Avril Lavigne pouting her way across the late-night airwaves and decided to exact your revenge by creating an "Oh, do grow up!" iMix, or you mistook a bottle of gin for Gatorade and then created an ill-advised iMix. What can you do to erase your work? Simple. Click the Account button at the top of the iTunes window, enter your Apple ID and password when prompted, and click the Manage iMixes button on the resulting Apple Account Information page. In the resulting page, you'll find controls for removing any of your iMixes.

When Apple first offered iMixes, it left out an important component—the ability to search other customers' iMixes. You could spend days creating the perfect playlist, but unless it rose to the top of the ratings or you spammed the entire world with announcements for it, very few people saw it. With the release of iTunes 4.7, that's all changed. Click the magnifying glass icon in the search field, and you'll spy the iMixes entry. Select this entry, enter any search term you like, and you'll be transported to a page that includes any iMixes that match your search.

## Billboard Charts

Clicking the Billboard Charts link takes you to The Store's browser view. Apple, in league with *Billboard* magazine, has collected the Billboard Hot 100, Billboard Top Country, and Billboard Top R&B lists for the past umpteen years (*umpteen* in this case meaning as far back as 1946).

These charts list only those songs that are available at The Store, so you'll find gaps in them. During the mid- and late '60s, for example, the Beatles owned many of the top spots on the Billboard charts, yet the lads from Liverpool appear nowhere in these charts. When a song isn't available, numbers are simply skipped. The top three spots in 1968's Hot 100 are missing, for example.

### Radio Charts

If you've been following along at The Store while reading this chapter, you know that the same browser view that displays Billboard Charts is also the home of Radio Charts. This is a relatively new feature and an incredibly helpful one. It works this way:

When you click Radio Charts, you'll see a list of cities in the browser's second column. Click a city, and a list of FM radio stations in that city appears in the browser's third column. Click a radio station, and a list of 60 or fewer songs available at The Store that are routinely played on that station appear below. These lists not only help you learn what music is topping the charts from coast to coast, but they're also a nice way to find music you've heard on the radio and failed to get the name of. Chances are that if a song's in constant rotation, it will appear in iTunes' Radio Charts.

## Video links

The next logical step for The Store is to move into the movie market—sell videos as well as music. That day has yet to dawn, but Apple's toe is definitely in the water, as indicated by The Store's Music Videos and Movie Trailers links.

### Music Videos

The Music Videos link takes you to a page of...well, music videos. Click a video, and you're offered the option to watch the small or large version of a QuickTime video that's streamed to your computer (if you have a small monitor, you may have to scroll the window to see the size buttons). Viewing a video requires that you have Apple's QuickTime installed (as of course you do, because iTunes requires it). Choose the version you want, and a black movie window appears, after which the movie begins to stream across your Internet connection. When enough of the movie has been downloaded to ensure smooth playback of the entire thing, the movie begins playing.

You'll find two links on these video pages: one in the video window that will take you to the artist's page and the traditional purchase/preview link to the song played in the video.

### Movie Trailers

Apple has offered QuickTime movie trailers on its Web site for quite some time (www.apple.com/trailers). Now it's brought trailers to The Store as well. Rather than simply showing off the wonders of QuickTime (as is the case on its original trailers site), Apple offers trailers at The Store in part to sell soundtrack albums. When you click the Movie Trailers link, you'll be taken to a page that displays links to current movie trailers; trailers for recently released DVDs; and, of course, links to popular soundtrack albums available for purchase at The Store.

By default, you're not allowed to keep copies of any of the music videos and few of the movie trailers, but there are ways around it. If you're a Mac user, you can download iGetMovies from http://homepage.mac.com/djodjodesign and save a copy of the video to your Mac. If you're working on a Windows PC, you can use a screen-capture utility to record these videos. Note that the audio in these videos is recorded at a resolution of 32kHz—quality noticeably inferior to that of songs sold at The Store. Rather than steal the music that accompanies these videos by capturing it, pay the $.99 Apple asks for. Your conscience and ears will feel better for it.

## Gift and support links

The final group of links in the first pane of The Store's home page direct you to an area for bestowing the gift of music on your nearest and dearest, an area for redeeming those gifts, and a Support link that directs you to The Store's Web page.

### Allowance

An iTunes Allowance can best be described as a gift certificate (which I'll describe in a moment) that keeps on giving. After you create an allowance, the recipient of your largesse will have his or her Store credit bumped up by the amount that you've designated (values include $10–$100 in ten dollar increments and $150 and $200) on the first day of each month. Just as when you purchase a gift certificate, your credit card will be charged, not the recipient's.

Why set up an iTunes Allowance when you can simply give a gift certificate? Convenience, mostly. Sure, if your 17-year-old faithfully does her chores each month (and also refrains from damaging the family car too badly), you could send her a gift certificate each month. But in many households, it's easier to give her a monthly music allowance and then, should her bed remain unmade for three weeks or the minivan return a little mini-er than when it left, pull the plug until she's made amends.

Creating an iTunes Allowance is very similar to giving a gift certificate. Just follow along:

1. Click the Allowance link.

   Alternatively, you can click the Account button in the top-right corner of the iTunes window; enter your Apple ID when requested to do so; and in the resulting Apple Account Information page, click the Setup Allowance button.

2. In the Set up an iTunes Allowance window before you, you'll be asked to provide your name, the recipient's name, and a value for the monthly allowance. You'll also be given the option to send the allowance now or wait until the first of the next month. If your recipient doesn't have an Apple ID, you must create one for him or her. Otherwise, enter the ID in the Apple ID field. You can also append a personal message (**Figure 4.12**).

**Figure 4.12**
Making allowances.

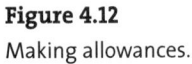

**3.** Click Continue.

You'll be asked to enter your Apple ID and password. Then you're presented with the Confirm Your Purchase screen.

**4.** After you've checked everything twice, click Buy.

The next screen tells you that the allowance has been created.

**5.** Click Done to return to the Apple Account Information page.

 Unfortunately, you can't create an allowance for your own account—and that's too bad, because this is a great way to put yourself on a budget. Those who can't resist the many temptations of The Store may want to create an additional Apple ID to issue an allowance from one ID to another. When you get close to exceeding your monthly allowance, you know it's time to pull in the reins. To create another Apple ID, you'll need to use a different email address from the one connected to your original Apple ID. I have one Apple ID set up for my .Mac address and another for an AOL address. I used the same credit card for both IDs, and The Store raised no objections.

After you've created an allowance, a new Manage Allowances button appears on your Apple Account Information page. When you click this button, you go to the Edit Allowances page, where you can add allowances or suspend or revoke any that you've created. When you revoke an allowance, any balance placed in the account remains; it won't be credited back to you.

If you think you're going to reinstate that allowance—for when your daughter has started making her bed again, for example—use the Suspend button. If you click Remove, you won't be able to put that allowance back into service; you must create a new one. To reactive a suspended account, return to this screen, and click the Activate button next to the account name. When you do, a dialog box will appear, asking whether you'd like to send the allowance immediately or wait until the first of the next month.

## Gift Certificates

Just in time for the 2003 holidays, Apple updated The Store so that you could easily give someone the gift of music and audio books. It created iTunes Gift Certificates—electronic certificates in denominations ranging from $10 to $200 (specifically $10, $20, $30, $40, $50, $75, $100, $150, and $200) that you email to the objects of your affection.

To let your loved ones know how much you care (or how little you care to jump in the car and go to a bricks-and-mortar music store), follow these steps:

1. Click the Gift Certificates link.

   Alternatively, you can click the Account button in the top-right corner of the iTunes window; enter your Apple ID and password when requested to do so; and in the resulting Apple Account Information page, click the Gift Certificates button.

2. In the iTunes Gift Certificates window before you, click the Buy Now button.

3. In the next window, provide your name, the recipient's name, and the recipient's email address; choose a value for the certificate; and, if you want to, enter a personal message (**Figure 4.13**).

**Figure 4.13**
Preparing an iTunes Gift Certificate.

Optionally, you can choose to send the gift certificate by snail mail (at least, you can with the U.S. iTunes Music Store). Clicking the Send via U.S. Mail button launches your Web browser and takes you to an Apple Store page, where you can create a gift certificate that Apple will mail to your recipient.

4. Click Continue.

You'll be asked to confirm that the information you entered was correct.

5. After you've checked everything twice, click Buy.

The next screen tells you that the certificate has been sent.

6. Click Buy Another, if you're feeling particularly generous, or click Done to return to the Apple Account Information page.

Because I know my audience is comprised of quality people—people who are likely to receive countless gift certificates—you might want to know what to expect should someone send a gift your way.

You'll receive an email message alerting you to the fact that some generous soul sent you a gift from The Store in an amount from $10 to $200 (**Figure 4.14**). If your email client is configured to load images, the message will display a green gift certificate, along with a button that reads Redeem Now and another labeled Download iTunes (just in case you don't have a copy of iTunes 4.1 or later already). If your email client displays text only, you'll still see the message from the sender, along with a link that you click to redeem your certificate.

**Figure 4.14**
It couldn't be much easier to redeem a gift certificate.

Clicking this link or the Redeem Now button launches iTunes and then opens The Store. Shortly after The Store loads, a dialog box asks whether you'd like to redeem your certificate. Click Redeem Gift Certificate, and another screen appears to tell you that you've successfully redeemed your certificate. You can confirm the truth of this statement by the appearance of a Credit field next to the Account button in iTunes. This field contains the amount of credit you have left on your certificate (or certificates, if you've received more than one). Click Done to return to The Store's main page.

 There's another way to redeem gift certificates. Just click the Account button in the top-right corner of the iTunes window; enter your Apple ID when requested to do so; click the View Account button; and in the Apple Account Information page, click the Gift Certificates button. Click the Redeem button in the resulting iTunes Gift Certificate page. In the next page, enter the Gift Certificate confirmation number exactly as it appears in the email you received. Then click Redeem. If you entered the number correctly, you should see the confirmation page.

Now whenever you purchase items from The Store, the prices of those items will be deducted from the amount shown in the Credit field. Should the price of the items you're purchasing exceed the amount in the Credit field, your credit will be used up, and the balance will be charged to your Store account.

 Gift certificates can be redeemed only from The Store from which they were issued. A gift certificate purchased at the German iTunes Music Store cannot be redeemed at the U.S. iTunes Music Store, for example.

## Prepaid Cards

Apple and Target have joined forces to sell prepaid iTunes Music Store cards in $15 denominations. If you can't obtain a Store account because you lack a credit card or are looking for an easy-to-give gift, one of these cards is a nice way to go. If you've received such a prepaid card and want to redeem it, just click the Prepaid Cards link, enter the 16-digit code that appears on the back of the card, and click Redeem. In next to no time, your account will be credited.

## Redeem

To redeem your gift certificates easily, click this link. When you do, iTunes main window will be taken up with the Enter Code screen, where you enter a 12-digit gift certificate code to redeem your store credit.

## Support

With this book at your side (or, better yet, open in front of your face), you shouldn't need to click The Store's Support link, but should you come across a problem that's arisen since the publication of this edition, click this link to be taken to Apple's iTunes Support Web page. Here, you'll find answers to frequently asked questions about both iTunes and The Store.

## iTunes Essentials

Although you can purchase entire albums from The Store (and are occasionally required to purchase an entire album to get all the songs on it), it's mostly a song-based enterprise. By this, I mean that The Store encourages you to pick and choose just the pieces of music you like.

Given this idea, it makes sense that Apple would offer compilations of songs, organized by some catchy sort of theme—Women in Bluegrass, Animation Classics, and It Came From TV!, for example. Apple calls these compilations iTunes Essentials, and you'll find a listing of recent iTunes Essentials smack-dab on The Store's home page.

Yes, these are essentially Apple's own iMixes—collections of songs the folks who work at The Store think you'll like (**Figure 4.15**). Unlike most of The Store's other albums, you get no discount for buying these compilations. If an iTunes Essential contains 17 songs, you pay $16.83, or $.99 per song.

**Figure 4.15**

The iTunes Essentials page.

Given that you realize no price break, what's the attraction? These compilations are likely to expose you to unfamiliar music that you might like. Many people appreciate Apple's expertise in this regard and are willing to pay extra for that guidance.

## Celebrity Playlists

If you'd like to know what rocks the worlds of Moby, Fred Durst, Patti Smith, and The Presidents of the United States (no, I'm not exactly sure whether it was Millard Fillmore or Gerald Ford who picked the tunes for this particular list), click these links. The resulting page offers a list of tunes an artist thinks worthy. Of course, you can preview and purchase songs—either individually or the entire list—directly from this page. Some artists, such as Herbie Hancock and Sting, offer generous descriptions of why they chose a particular song. These recommendations can be enlightening—who wouldn't be interested in the music that Wynton Marsalis admires, for example—as well as amusing (R.E.M.'s Michael Stipe loves Neil Diamond's "I Am...I Said"!?).

## Top of the pops

The right side of the main page offers its share of navigation links as well. Here, you'll find links to Today's Top Songs and Today's Top Albums. These lists include the top 10 recently downloaded songs and albums. Should you care to view the top 100 downloaded songs or top 100 downloaded albums, click the Top 100 Songs and Top 100 Albums links, respectively.

These Top lists don't point to the best music around. Remember, the technical requirements of The Store necessarily determine who shops there. The Store's clientele is confined to Macintosh owners running Mac OS X and Windows users running Windows XP or 2000, most of whom have a reasonably fast connection to the Internet. This demographic doesn't favor fans of Perry Como or Bix Beiderbecke, so don't be disappointed if your favorite artists never rise to the top of the charts.

### Expedient iTunes Music Store Browsing

If you're weary of first visiting the home page of the iTunes Music Store and then traveling to the areas of The Store that really interest you, this tip will help.

Launch iTunes, and drag your favorite links from The Store onto your Desktop. If you want to view the page that displays The Store's Top 100 Songs, for example, drag the Today's Top Songs entry to the Desktop. When you do this, the entry turns into a Web Internet Location file.

To put this file to good use, launch iTunes; then double-click the file. Your default browser will launch. Then iTunes will come to the fore and load the page associated with the link.

## A practical pop-up

Given the links to New Releases, Exclusive Tracks, Pre-Releases, Staff Favorites, videos, iTunes Essentials, Billboard and radio charts, Celebrity Playlists, and Today's Top Songs and Albums, as well as access to the Search and Browse functions, you should be well on your way, right?

Perhaps. But don't leave the main page without checking out the Choose Genre pop-up menu (**Figure 4.16**).

**Figure 4.16**

The Choose Genre pop-up menu.

You'll find this menu in the top-left corner of the main page. It's a great tool to use when you're in the mood for a particular style of music. Just click the menu and pick the genre that appeals to you, such as Folk or Dance.

Choosing an item from the Genre menu takes you to a page devoted to that genre (**Figure 4.17**). This page is laid out similarly to the main page, containing at least New Releases, Staff Favorites, and Just Added sections, plus an Up & Coming section, where appropriate. (You won't find an Up & Coming section for Soundtracks or Classical, for example.) Some genre pages include subcategory listings. On the Folk page, for example, you'll find links to '60s folk music. The Electronic page includes Chill Groove and Trip-Hop subcategories. And the last time I looked, the Jazz genre page included a Verve Vault subcategory featuring recordings from the classic jazz label.

**Figure 4.17**
A genre page.

The Today's Top Songs and Today's Top Albums lists change to reflect the most popular songs and albums within that genre. On these pages, you'll also find links to the top 100 songs and top 100 albums for that genre.

## The Search field

Looking for a song, artist, or album in a hurry? Click in the Search field in the top-right corner of the iTunes window, enter your query, and press Return (**Figure 4.18**). After a few moments, you'll see a list of matches in the iTunes window.

**Figure 4.18**
The Search field.

You can narrow your search by clicking and holding the magnifying-glass icon in the Search menu and then choosing Artists, Albums, Composers, or Songs from the pop-up menu. (You can also access the iMixes and Power Search features from this pop-up menu.)

## Fast Lane to The Store

With version 4.6 of iTunes, Apple incorporated one more quick way to get to The Store—the arrow links that, by default, appear next to song names, artists, and albums in your iTunes library and playlists. These arrows appear regardless of whether you ripped the songs from CD, purchased them from The Store, or obtained them by more nefarious means. As long as a song includes title, artist, or album information in its ID3 tags (a portion of a music file that holds this kind of information), it will sport an arrow link (**Figure 4.19**).

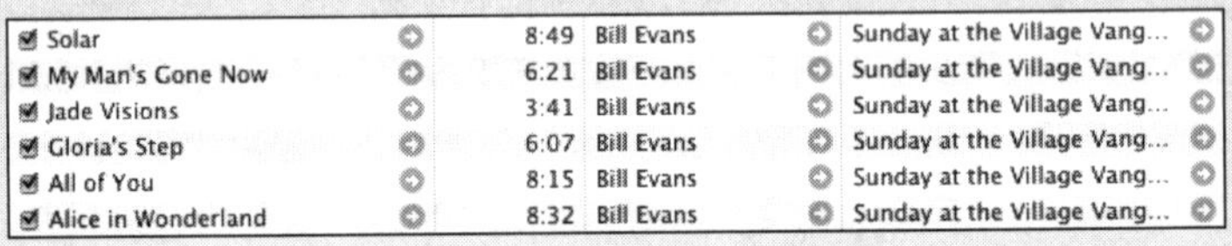

**Figure 4.19**

Click these arrows in your iTunes library to be taken to identical or similar items in The Store.

| | | | |
|---|---|---|---|
| ☑ Solar ⊙ | 8:49 Bill Evans ⊙ | Sunday at the Village Vang... ⊙ |
| ☑ My Man's Gone Now ⊙ | 6:21 Bill Evans ⊙ | Sunday at the Village Vang... ⊙ |
| ☑ Jade Visions ⊙ | 3:41 Bill Evans ⊙ | Sunday at the Village Vang... ⊙ |
| ☑ Gloria's Step ⊙ | 6:07 Bill Evans ⊙ | Sunday at the Village Vang... ⊙ |
| ☑ All of You ⊙ | 8:15 Bill Evans ⊙ | Sunday at the Village Vang... ⊙ |
| ☑ Alice in Wonderland ⊙ | 8:32 Bill Evans ⊙ | Sunday at the Village Vang... ⊙ |

These links work this way:

Suppose you've ripped Crowded House's "Don't Dream It's Over" from an audio CD. Click the arrow next to its name, and The Store opens, revealing the album page for the group's album *Recurring Dream: The Very Best of Crowded House*. Click the arrow next to Crowded House in your library's Artists column, and The Store takes you to the Crowded House artist page. As you might guess, clicking the arrow link in the Album column takes you to that album's page at The Store—if it exists. If the album isn't available, you're either directed to an artist page (click a link next to the Beatles' *Abbey Road* album, for example, and you're sent to The Store's Beatles page) or to the Power Search page, where you can use its powers to find the music you seek.

If you're a Mac user and would like to use these links to navigate to other songs in your library, hold down the Option key and click a link. When you do, songs connected to the link you clicked—all songs by an artist or the songs on an album—will appear in the iTunes window.

Not everyone is thrilled by these links. If you'd rather not see them, open iTunes' Preferences window, click the General tab, and disable the Show Links to Music Store option.

## The Browse button

Have a slow connection to the Internet and find searching The Store painful because of the time it takes to download The Store's graphics? You can skip the eye candy by clicking the Browse button.

Doing so brings up a Browser view similar to the one I described earlier. Here's how to use it:

1. Click the Browse button.

   The top portion of the iTunes window divides into three sections: Genre, Artist, and Album.

2. Click a genre you want to search (Electronic, for example).

   iTunes accesses The Store, and after a while, a list of all artists linked to that genre appears in the second section.

3. Click an artist whose albums you'd like to view.

   iTunes once again goes to The Store and downloads a list of available albums (or partial albums) by that artist.

4. Click the album you want to explore.

   A list of songs available for purchase from that album appears in the Results Area.

NOTE: When you double-click entries in the browser, you go to one of The Store's graphics-heavy pages. Double-click Pop in the Genre section, for example, and the page devoted to The Store's Pop selections appears, complete with colorful background and album covers. Likewise, double-clicking an artist or album entry transports you to the page devoted to that artist or album.

## The way home

Should you ever wander into one of the scarier sections of The Store (say, the polka aisle), it's easy to find your way back to the main page. Simply click the Home icon at the top of the iTunes window (**Figure 4.20**), and you're transported to the main page.

**Figure 4.20**
The Home icon and the Back and Forward buttons.

Next to the Home icon, you'll see a path from your present location to the main page—Home/Rock/Peter Gabriel/Secret World Live, for example. To move up a level or two, simply click one of the entries in this hierarchy.

Another way to retrace your steps is to use the Back and Forward buttons just to the left of the Home icon. These buttons are similar to the Back and Forward buttons in your Web browser. Click the Back button to move to the page you viewed previously. If you've backtracked and want to go forward again, click the Forward button.

# Audio Appetizers: Previewing Songs

How many times have you purchased a CD because you liked one track and discovered that the rest of the disc was utter dreck? Thanks to The Store's Preview feature, those days are over.

You can listen to 30 seconds of every song available from The Store. I can't stress strongly enough how cool this is. It's like waltzing into the kitchen of any restaurant on earth, whipping out a spoon, and taking a nibble of every dish on the menu.

"Mmm, I *love* this."

"Whoa, too spicy!"

"I'm sorry—did I accidentally sample something intended for your *dog?*"

## Say What!?

If you haven't listened to urban music in the past couple of decades, you may not realize that some of this material is peppered (quite liberally, in some cases) with what can be politely termed "colorful" language (words such as &*(@#, $^%**&!, and the ever-popular %&^%#$%!!!). Rather than risk offending those who find such language offensive, The Store appends an EXPLICIT label to such material. If there's a version of the song edited to remove objectionable language, that song bears a CLEAN label.

That's right—no need to buy the entire five-course meal. At The Store, you can preview music and shop à la carte, buying just the songs that you like.

Previewing music is easy. Just select a song title and initiate the preview by clicking iTunes' Play button, double-clicking the song title, or pressing the spacebar on your keyboard. Your computer will access the Web, download the preview, and play 30 seconds of the song you selected (**Figure 4.21**).

**Figure 4.21**
The Playing Speaker icon next to a playing preview.

| 3 | Across the River | 5:56 | Peter Gabriel |
| 4 | Slow Marimbas | 1:45 | Peter Gabriel |
| 5 | Shaking the Tree | 9:18 | Peter Gabriel |
| 6 | Red Rain | 6:14 | Peter Gabriel |

To preview the previous or next song in a list while a preview is playing, press the left-arrow key to play the previous song or the right-arrow key to play the next song.

If you have a slow connection to the Internet, you may notice that playback of previews stutters or stops in the middle and then, after an interruption, begins again. iTunes does its best to begin playback of previews only when it thinks it can complete the download and play the preview without interruption. Sometimes, though, iTunes guesses incorrectly, or an interruption of your connection forces the preview to stop playing while the remainder of the preview is downloaded.

If you suffer from *previewus interruptus*, choose Preferences from the iTunes menu on the Mac or the Edit menu on a Windows PC; click the Store button in the resulting window; and enable the Load Complete Preview Before Playing option, which tells iTunes to download the entire preview before playing it back.

> ### Firewalls, Proxies, and Previews
>
> If your computer sits behind a firewall or gains its access to the Internet via a shared proxy, you may not be able to listen to The Store's previews or even download music from The Store. The vagaries of firewalls and proxies are not within the scope of this book. (For readers who are somewhat savvy about such things, however, I will mention that The Store, like many of Apple's services, uses HTTP Port 80 to do its work.) Suffice it to say that if you double-click a song expecting to hear a preview, a small window that reads *Opening URL* pops up and disappears—and then you hear nothing, cock a curious eye at your Internet connection. If you're using a proxy, try to get away from it by establishing a direct connection to the Internet. If you can configure your firewall to be less vigorous, do so.

## Learning About New Music

Suppose you're slavishly devoted to a particular artist. Wouldn't it be great if someone from The Store called you up to tell you that Your Very Favorite Artist had a brand new track ready for download? iTunes 4.7 offers the next best thing.

Just click on an artist's name to be taken to that artist's page. Glance over at the upper right corner of the page and you'll see the Artist Alert link. Click this link and up pops The Store's sign in dialog box. Enter your Apple ID and password, click Add, click OK in the confirmation dialog box, and the artist is added to your list of faves. When a new song from this artist becomes available, you'll receive an email alerting you to that fact.

## Getting the Goods

Now that you have an account and can find your way around The Store, it's time to stop manhandling the merchandise and actually buy something. You'll be amazed by how easy (and addictive) this can be.

## The Pick-and-pay Method

The pick-and-pay method is akin to going to a record store, picking up a CD, taking it to the counter, purchasing the disc, returning to the store to pick another CD, purchasing it, going back to the store once again, and...well, you get the idea. You pay as you go. This is how The Store operates by default. Pick-and-pay works this way:

1. **Pick your Poison (or Prince, P-Funk, or Procol Harum).**

   Using any of the methods I suggested earlier, locate a song or album that you desperately need to own.

2. **Click the Buy Song or Buy Album button.**

   To purchase a song, click the Buy Song entry in the Price column that appears in iTunes' main window. To purchase an album, look in the first pane of the browser and then click the Buy Album button. The price of your purchase is listed next to each of these buttons. As I wrote earlier, songs are priced at around $1, and single albums go for around $10 on average.

 At times, you can't download an entire album. Instead, The Store may list a partial album—one from which you can purchase only individual songs.

3. **Enter your Apple ID or AOL screen name and password in the resulting window.**

   Should you not want to see this window in the future, check the Remember Password for Purchasing check box.

   If you've forgotten your password, click the Forgot Password? button. When you do, you'll be taken to a secure page on Apple's Web site that offers you two options: have Apple email your password to you, or ask Apple to display the hint that you entered when you signed up for your account. This procedure works the same whether you're seeking the password for your Apple ID or AOL account.

4. **Click the Buy button (Figure 4.22).**

**Figure 4.22**
The Store allows you to cancel a purchase before you download a song, unless you disable this warning.

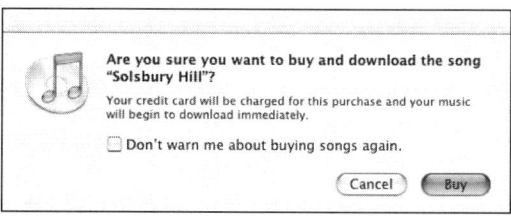

Just to make sure you weren't kidding around when you clicked the Buy button, a new window asks you to confirm your intention to make your purchase. Should you care to banish this window forevermore, check the Don't Warn Me About Buying (Songs/Albums) Again check box.

If you've decided not to purchase the song or album, click Cancel and go on with your life.

5. Click the Buy button again.

The song or album you purchased begins downloading, and your credit card is charged for your purchase. As each song downloads, it appears in the Purchased Music playlist, accessible from iTunes' Source window. The progress of the download is displayed at the top of the iTunes window.

## Altering Your Account

If you have an Apple ID and care to change your account or credit-card information, view an accounting of your online music purchases, or reset the warnings iTunes issues when you're about to purchase music, follow these steps:

1. Launch iTunes 4, and choose Music Store from the Source list.

2. Sign into The Store.

3. Click the Account button in the top-right corner of the iTunes window (the clear button that contains your Apple ID or AOL screen name).

4. Enter your password in the resulting window.

5. Click the View Account button.

In the Apple Account Information window that appears, you'll see a series of buttons: Edit Account Info (this button does not appear if you're using an AOL account), Edit Credit Card, Purchase History, Manage iMixes (this button doesn't appear if you haven't created an iMix), Gift Certificates, Setup Allowance, and Reset Warnings (**Figure 4.23**). For the most part, these buttons are self-explanatory. (I detail iMixes, gift certificates, and allowances earlier in this chapter.)

## Altering Your Account *(continued)*

**Figure 4.23**
You can edit your account information and view your purchase history in this window, as well as access Gift Certificate and Allowances options.

If you find that you're a little too enamored of shopping at The Store, it's not a bad idea to click the Purchase History button every so often. In the Purchase History window, you'll see the details of your last purchase, along with an overview of earlier purchases—though no total for all your purchases (which, given the condition of your heart and/or your pocketbook, may be a good thing).

# The Shopping-cart Method

If you intend to bulk up your music library significantly in a single shopping session, you might find the pick-and-pay method tedious. The Store offers an alternative—piling all your music into a single shopping cart and checking out in one fell swoop. To do so, follow these steps:

1. Choose Preferences from the iTunes menu on your Mac or the Edit menu on your PC.

2. Click the Store icon in the resulting window.

**3.** Select the Buy Using a Shopping Cart option.

**4.** Click OK to dismiss the window.

A Shopping Cart entry appears in iTunes' Source list.

**5.** Whirl around The Store until you find a song or album you want to purchase.

The buttons in the Price column and below the album entry read Add Song and Add Album, respectively.

**6.** Click the Add Song or Add Album button to add a song or album to your shopping cart.

**7.** Repeat steps 5 and 6 until you can shop no more.

**8.** Click the Shopping Cart entry in the Source list (**Figure 4.24**).

**Figure 4.24**
The Store's Shopping Cart in the Source list.

The main iTunes window displays all the songs and albums you've piled into your cart. (Album titles appear with a triangle next to them. Click the triangle to reveal the contents of the album.)

At the bottom of the window, you'll see the total you'll owe if you proceed. This total does not include sales tax (which—yes—you will be charged).

**9.** Remove any songs and albums you don't want.

If, after viewing the potential cost of your mad dash through The Store, you decide that you really can live without *The Definitive Collection: Tony Orlando & Dawn*, click the Remove button next to its entry in the Price column.

**10.** Take a gander at the recommendations in the browser portion of the iTunes window.

Get this: When you pick songs for the shopping cart, The Store generates a selection of albums that it thinks you'll enjoy, based on the songs and albums you intend to buy. When you have items in the shopping cart and click the Shopping Cart entry in the Source list, those recommendations appear in the browser portion of the iTunes window.

I fear that these recommendations may disconcert some people. On one hand, you may be exposed to music you hadn't considered before. On the other hand, you may feel that these recommendations malign your musical tastes, implying that said tastes are, shall we say, unrefined ("What on *earth* leads you to believe I'd be interested in Doris Day's *Greatest Hits*?").

As a Just-for-Fun game, see if you can force The Store to offer up a particular recommendation. Without adding a Billy Joel album to your shopping cart, for example, try to select the kind of songs and albums that are likely to generate such a recommendation.

**11.** Buy your music.

Within the shopping cart, you can buy songs or albums individually by clicking Buy Song or Buy Album, or buy everything in the cart by clicking the Buy Now button at the bottom of the iTunes window.

Unless you've instructed iTunes not to warn you about shopping-cart purchases, a window asks you to reconfirm your intention of buying the items in your cart. If you're sure you want to proceed, click Buy. The items in the cart will be downloaded and placed in the Purchased Music playlist, and your credit card will be charged for the purchase. Click Cancel to nullify the transaction.

The items in your shopping cart remain there even when you log out of The Store or quit iTunes. To remove them permanently, either buy them or click the Remove button next to each item.

## Portable Previews

When discussing iMixes, I hinted that you can drag previews out of The Store and into playlists you've created in iTunes. This is handy not only for recommending music you don't own, but also for creating a wish list of music you may one day buy.

If you're a little short on cash this month, for example, but want to remember to eventually purchase a few songs from *Tom Jones: Reloaded—Greatest Hits* and *16 Most Requested Songs: Engelbert Humperdinck*, just drag the tunes you want to own to a playlist you've created. When your ship finally comes in, you can buy these tunes in a couple of different ways.

The more tedious way is to select the playlist and click Buy Song for each tune in the list. The zippier way is to delve into the Store tab of iTunes' Preferences window, enable the Buy Using a Shopping Cart option, and drag your playlist atop the Shopping Cart entry in iTunes' Source list. In a matter of moments, the songs in your playlist will be added to your shopping cart, ready to purchase with a single click of the Buy Now button.

# Playing with Your Purchases

After the purchased music has found a home on your hard drive, you have several ways to put it to work.

## Play It

If you're like 99 percent of the people who shop at The Store, the first thing you'll want to do is play the music you've purchased. When you first play a purchased song, iTunes checks to see that your computer is authorized to play purchased music.

As you may recall, you are allowed to play purchased music on up to three computers. When you play a purchased song for the first time, iTunes checks to see whether the computer is authorized to play purchased music. If so, the music plays back with no problem. If the computer hasn't been authorized, you'll be prompted for your Apple ID or AOL screen name and password. That name and password, along with some information that identifies your computer, are sent to Apple, where that Mac or PC is counted against your limit of five authorizations.

If you've used up your authorizations on five other computers, you'll be notified that you must deauthorize one of your computers before you're allowed to play the purchased music. Fortunately, deauthorizing a computer is as simple as choosing Deauthorize Computer from iTunes' Advanced menu (**Figure 4.25**). When you select this command, your computer connects to the Internet, and Apple's database is updated to reflect the deauthorization of that particular computer.

**Figure 4.25**
The Deauthorize Computer command.

After you deauthorize a computer, of course, you can't use it to play back purchased music until you authorize it again. (Yes, this means that if you own more than five computers and intend to play purchased music on all of them, you're going to spend some time playing the deauthorization shuffle.)

 Reformatting the computer's hard drive (or replacing that hard drive) does not deauthorize the machine. Before passing your computer along to someone else, be sure to deauthorize it.

 One way to gain additional authorizations is to maintain both an Apple ID and an AOL account at The Store. Each account allows you to authorize five computers, for a total of ten authorizations—and yes, they can be the same computers. Of course, songs purchased with a particular account—your AOL account, for example—will play only on a computer authorized for that account. But this scheme does allow you a neat way to purchase music from the office PC, if you've already used up your five authorizations among the family's computers at home.

## Lost Authorizations

When working on an earlier edition of this book, my PC crashed badly, making it impossible for me to log on to my usual user account in Windows XP. After I created a new user account, I attempted to play some of the music I'd purchased from The Store on that PC.

No go. According to iTunes, I'd exhausted the three authorizations allowed at the time. (Apple now allows you to authorize as many as five computers.)

Counting on my fingers, I checked the tally of my authorizations against Apple's:

My Power Mac G4. That would be authorization one (index finger).

My PowerBook G4. Authorization two (ring finger).

My PC. Uh-oh, *my PC!* The third authorization had died along with the corrupted user account (middle finger).

*Dagnabbit!*

Dashing to iTunes, I quickly selected Music Store Customer Service from iTunes' Help menu in the hope that somehow, Apple would take pity on me and heft me out of the soup.

This command launched my Web browser and whisked me to a page where (after the site identified my computer as a PC) I entered my Apple ID and password. Toward the bottom of the page, I found the Get Help With Computer Authorization link. On the resulting Computer Authorization page, I looked under the Still Having Trouble? heading (because the trouble I was having was not addressed elsewhere on the page); chose Computer Authorization from the Specific Request pop-up menu; and, in the politest terms possible, described my situation in the provided field. Then I clicked the Submit button and crossed my fingers.

A few hours later, I received this reply:

*Dear Mr. Breen,*

*Thank you for contacting iTunes Music Store Customer Service.*

*We have manually deauthorized your registered systems from the Music Store. You can now reauthorize the computers that you intend to use. To protect our customers' privacy, this is not a service that is generally performed. However, given the nature of your situation, we have made an exception. If you're selling a computer or plan to no longer use it, make sure you've deauthorized it before you no longer have access to it.*

*Sincerely,*

*The iTunes Music Store Team*

> ## Lost Authorizations *(continued)*
>
> Had I the opportunity to respond to that Team, I might have written:
>
> *Dear iTMST,*
>
> *Thank you for your prompt attention. Having a provision in place for a regrettable (though inevitable) situation such as this saved my bacon (and will undoubtedly do the same for others). Your efforts shall not go unnoticed (except by those readers who stubbornly refuse to read helpful sidebars). Keep up the good work!*
>
> *Your pal,*
>
> *Chris*

## Burn It

People play music on all kinds of devices and in all kinds of environments—on computers, boom boxes, home stereos, and portable music players, and in cars, boats, and planes. (I've even seen a system that allows you to play music in your hot tub.) Forcing you to listen to music only on your computer is silly. And because Apple Computer is anything but silly, it made sure that you'd be able to take your purchased music with you on something other than an iPod, iBook, or Windows PC. It does so by allowing you to burn purchased music to CD.

When you do so, the .m4p files are converted to red-book audio files—the file format used by commercial audio CDs. These CDs are not copy-protected in any way and behave just like regular ol' audio CDs. Pop 'em into a standard CD player, press Play, and out comes the music.

As I indicated earlier in this chapter, burning your music to CD involves a few limitations. You can burn up to seven copies of a particular playlist. If you attempt to burn an eighth copy, you'll be told that you can't. If you alter that playlist after the seventh burn—by adding or removing a song—you can burn another seven copies. Alter that playlist, and you get seven more copies. Also, you cannot burn purchased music to MP3-formatted CDs. (MP3 CD is one of the options in the Burning section of iTunes Preferences.)

### From .m4p to AIFF to MP3

Technically adept readers are undoubtedly thinking, "Wait a sec. If the protected .m4p files are converted to unprotected AIFF files when they're burned to CD, what's to keep me from turning around and using iTunes to re-rip the files on that CD as unprotected AAC or MP3 files?"

Not a darned thing.

Yes, you'll lose some quality by going from a compressed format (.m4p) to an uncompressed format (AIFF) back to another compressed format (AAC or MP3), but the files will still sound remarkably good.

Why would you want to do such a thing?

Devices other than the iPod use MP3 files. My TiVo video recorder offers an option that allows me to stream music wirelessly from my computer to my TiVo (which is connected to my home stereo). The catch is that it will stream only MP3 files—not the encrypted AAC files that I've purchased from The Store. If I want to listen to those files on TiVo, I must convert them to MP3.

And if I dare suggest such a thing in a book devoted to the iPod, there are other (lesser-quality, of course) MP3 players in the world. If I want to play my purchased music on an old Rio device that I picked up at a garage sale for a couple of bucks, I must convert that music to MP3.

By the way, you needn't go to the trouble of burning a CD and then re-ripping it if you have a Macintosh and have installed Apple's $49 iLife '04 suite. iTunes and QuickTime Pro are configured in such a way that they refuse to convert an .m4p file to MP3. But you can use Apple's own applications, iMovie 4 and GarageBand, to import .m4p files as audio tracks and export just those audio tracks as AIFF files.

## Beyond The Store: Audible.com

The availability of audio books at The Store is a marvelous feature, but the iTunes Music Store currently doesn't have as wide a selection of material as Audible.com does, and in some cases, you'll find that the same material is less expensive on Audible.com. Luckily, you can still play Audible.com material on your iPod. In the following pages, I'll show you how.

# Downloading and Playing Audible.com Files (Macintosh)

iTunes 3 and the iPod Software 1.2 Updater brought Audible.com compatibility to iTunes and the iPod for Macintosh. The feature works this way:

1. Launch iTunes 3 or 4, choose Preferences from the iTunes menu, click the General button in the resulting window, and click the Set button next to Use iTunes for Internet Music Playback.

2. Log onto the Web, and point your browser to www.audible.com.

3. When you're on the site, find something that you'd like to download (a novel, for example), and click the Add to Basket button.

4. Click the Checkout button on the page that appears.

5. If you don't have an Audible.com account, you'll be asked to set one up.

   Doing so requires that you submit your name and email address and that you create a user name and password. When you make a purchase, you'll be asked for a credit-card number and more-extensive contact information (street address and phone number).

6. Review the charges on the next page, and click the Proceed with Purchase button.

   The purchase will be processed. After the file is processed, you'll be taken to a page that lists the order number of your purchase and provides links to My Library, a storage area for any Audible.com files you've purchased.

7. Click the My Library link.

   You should see your file (or files, if you've purchased more than one).

8. Click the Get It Now button next to the file you want to download.

9. In the window that appears, select a format for the file you want to download.

   The Mac and iPod support formats 2, 3, and 4. Format 2 files are the smallest and the lowest-resolution (meaning that they don't sound very good). Format 3 files are larger (and sound better) than Format 2 files. Format 4 files are the largest of all and, as you might expect, are of the highest quality.

10. After you select a format, click the Download button.

    Don't worry—you haven't committed to downloading the file in this one format alone. You're welcome to return to My Library and download the file again in another format (or this same format, if you like).

11. Double-click the downloaded file.

    The file should open in iTunes. (If it doesn't, launch iTunes 3 or 4, and drag the file into iTunes' main window.)

12. If this is the first time you've used an Audible.com file, enter your Audible.com user name and password when iTunes asks you to do so.

    After you enter that information, iTunes will log onto the Web and register your Mac with Audible.com.

When you next update your iPod, any Audible.com files that you've downloaded will be moved to your iPod.

# Downloading and Playing Audible.com Files (Windows)

Version 4 of Audible's AudibleManager application supports the iPod on a PC running Windows Me, 2000, or XP. Here are the steps for using AudibleManager:

1. Create an Audible.com account as I outline in the previous section.

2. Launch AudibleManager.

3. Download an Audible file in format 2, 3, or 4 (the iPod doesn't support format 1 files).

**4.** Locate the .aa file that corresponds to the audible file you've downloaded (usually on this path: program files\Audible\programs\downloads\).

**5.** Drag the file into the main iTunes window. When you next update your iPod, the Audible.com file will be copied to your iPod.

Note that iTunes may ask you to authorize your computer to play Audible.com files. If so, enter your Audible.com user name and password.

# Audiobooks and Audible.com Tips

Apple and Audible.com have done their best to make downloading and playing these files as easy as possible, but you should know a few tricks:

- You needn't worry about losing your place when you're playing an audio book file. When you stop playing the file in iTunes 3 or 4 or on your iPod, the file will be bookmarked, so when you play the file next, it begins playing from the spot where you left off.

  Better yet, if you listen to the file in both iTunes and on your iPod—a chapter of a novel on your iPod while you're driving to work and a chapter on your office computer when you're supposed to be preparing the company's quarterly earnings statement, for example—the bookmark will be synchronized between the iPod and the Mac or PC the next time you update your iPod. If you most recently played the file on your computer, iTunes will update the bookmark on your iPod so that it matches the bookmark in iTunes.

- Some Audible.com files are chunked up into sections—by chapters, for example. On a third- or fourth-generation iPod, iPod Photo, and iPod mini, you can navigate through these sections easily by playing an audio book file and pressing the Select button. In the resulting screen, you'll see a timeline with a number of lines that mark each section. Press the iPod's Forward button to move to the next section. Pressing the Back button sends you to the previous section.

- If your computer relies on a proxy server to access the Internet, iTunes won't be able to register your computer with Audible.com; therefore, you won't be able to play Audible.com files. If you're in such a situation, find another way to get to the Web—via a dial-up connection, for example. You need to make this alternative connection just once, long enough for the computer to be registered with Audible.com.

## Put It on Your iPod

You may recall that this book is also about the iPod. Given the subject matter of this volume, maybe it's appropriate to discuss the partnership between The Store and the iPod.

## Requirements

As I said in the early part of this chapter, there's no limit to the number of iPods on which you can play purchased music. If, for example, you've pungled up for every iPod made by Apple—the original 5 GB iPod; the second-generation 5, 10, and 20 GB models; the updated second-generation 10, 15, and 30 GB iPods; the 15, 20, and 40 GB third-generation iPods; and today's iPod mini, the 40 and the 60 GB iPod Photos, the iPod Special Edition: U2, or the 20 and 40 GB fourth-generation iPods—you can play a single purchased song on all 16 iPods (19, if you count the three iPod models made exclusively for Windows). You must update these iPods with a computer that has been authorized, of course. If you attempt to copy purchased music to an iPod from an unauthorized Mac or PC, you'll be told that the operation cannot proceed.

The only other requirement for using your iPod with purchased music is that your iPod must be running version 1.3 or later of the iPod software. If you have a third- or fourth-generation iPod, an iPod Photo, or an iPod mini, you're set. These iPods ship with version 2.0 or later of the iPod software. If you have a first- or second-generation iPod, you must download the iPod Updater 2004-07-15 (or later, if a newer version has been released) and update your iPod. This updater includes installers for all iPod models and updates first- and second-generation iPods to version 1.4. You can find links to the latest iPod software at www.apple.com/ipod.

# Moving Music to Your iPod

Considering the number of pages I've devoted to The Store, I wish I could finish the chapter by revealing a series of convoluted steps for adding purchased music to your iPod, but the truth is, augmenting your iPod with these tunes is no more complicated than transferring any other kind of music file. If your iPod is configured to auto-update when it's plugged into your computer (and that computer is authorized to play purchased music), any music you've purchased will be moved to your iPod automatically. That music will appear in a Purchased Music playlist (**Figure 4.26**), as well as in any playlists you've created that contain purchased music.

**Figure 4.26**
The Purchased Music playlist.

If you've purchased Kate Bush's "Wuthering Heights" and added it to a playlist on your computer for songs inspired by the works of the Brontë sisters, it will appear on your iPod in both the Purchased Music and Brontë playlists. And just like other music files you've transferred, it appears in the Song, Album, and Artists sections of the iPod.

If you've chosen to update your iPod manually, you can copy purchased music from your iTunes library in the same way that you copy other kinds of music. Just select the songs or albums you want to copy and then drag them to the iPod icon in the Source list, or click the triangle next to the iPod's icon to reveal the playlists on the iPod and then drag the songs or albums into one of the playlists. (Remember, as I mentioned in Chapter 2, you can't drag music into a Smart Playlist—only into a playlist you've created.)

 If you use one of the methods outlined in Chapter 6 of this book to transfer music from your iPod to your computer, you still won't be able to play purchased music files that were on your iPod unless your computer is authorized to play this variety of file.

## About Album Art

One nice feature of The Store is that when you purchase a song or album, you also get a picture of the album cover. To view that cover in iTunes, select a song you've purchased and click the Artwork button in the bottom-left corner of the iTunes window.

If you listen to music primarily on your iPod, this album art does you no good unless you have an iPod Photo—you can't view the covers on iPods other than the iPod Photo—and it may actually be doing some harm. You see, the album art is included within each song you purchase from The Store, and that art makes those song files bigger. How much bigger depends on the complexity of the art. I've found that some songs are just 15 KB heavier with included album art, whereas others balloon by nearly 135 KB. On average, let's say that album art adds 80 KB to each purchased song. If you have 1,000 songs on your iPod that include album art, you've wasted 80 MB of space—enough for 20 four-minute songs.

The slow, painful way to remove album artwork is to select a song, press Command-I to bring up the song's info window, click the Artwork tab, click the album cover, and then click the Delete button (**Figure 4.27**).

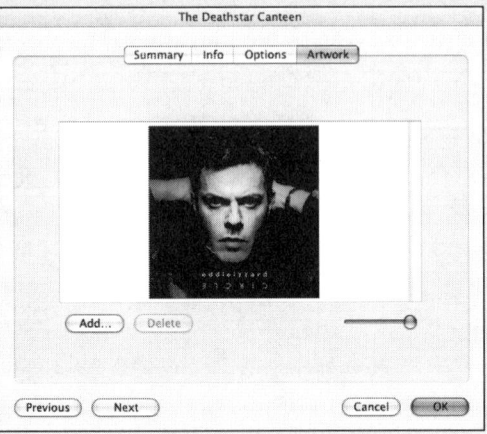

**Figure 4.27**
Click the Delete button to remove album artwork.

If you're a Mac user, you have a more efficient way. Travel to http://www.malcolmadams.com/itunes/scripts/scripts09.php?page=3#removeartwork, and download Peter Vendlegård's free Remove Artwork 2.0 AppleScript.

My hope is that an enterprising software developer will create a utility that makes it easy to remove artwork from iTunes for Windows.

# Troubleshooting The Store

The Store is a nicely conceived enterprise and works remarkably well, but like all things made by the human hand, it has its little quirks. Here are some minor difficulties you might run into.

## "I can't purchase music from The Store with my old copy of iTunes!"

That's correct, you can't. When Apple brought iTunes 4.7 online, it drew a line in the sand so you could purchase music only with versions of iTunes later than iTunes 4.5. If you have a version of iTunes previous to iTunes 4.5, you must upgrade in order to purchase music from The Store.

## "How do I get rid of The Store?"

Being the kind of person who balances his checkbook once every decade whether it needs it or not, I'm the last person to pass judgment on those who have difficulties managing their personal finances. If you're spending more money in The Store than has proved to be wise, you can remove a measure of temptation by following these steps:

1. Choose Preferences from the iTunes menu on your Mac or from the Edit menu on your Windows PC.
2. Click the Store button.
3. Uncheck the Show iTunes Music Store check box.
4. Click OK.

This method won't disable your ability to use The Store; it simply removes the Music Store item from the Source list. If you want to bar your access to The Store permanently, you might try defaulting on your credit-card payments for a couple of years.

## "How do I keep others from using The Store?"

If you're tasked with keeping the company computers in line and find that employees are spending far too much time listening to 30-second previews of Massive Attack's latest electronic musings, configure the company firewall to block the phobos.apple.com Internet host.

### "I purchased a song, but it didn't download! Do I have to buy the song again?"

No. If access to downloading has been blocked (either by a firewall or proxy that needs to be fixed or by a glitch on Apple's end), you should be able to download your purchased music after the trouble has cleared up. To do so, choose Check for Purchased Music from iTunes' Advanced menu. If there are songs that you've purchased but not downloaded, they should download when you invoke this command.

### "My hard drive crashed and took all my purchased music with it! How do I replace it?"

If the purchased music resides only on your computer's hard drive, you buy it again. Regrettably, although Apple keeps track of the music you've purchased (as indicated by the fact that you can view your purchase history), the company has made no provisions for allowing you to download music again.

For this reason, I recommend that you back up your purchased music (to an audio or data CD, for example). Fortunately, because you're likely to be an iPod owner, you have a backup of your songs on your iPod. Just use the techniques I outline in Chapter 6 to recover purchased music from your iPod.

### "I have a bone to pick with Apple over a purchase I made."

For such bone-picking, you'll need to contact Music Store Customer Service. You can do this easily from within iTunes by choosing Music Store Customer Service from iTunes' Help menu. This command opens your default Web browser and takes you to the Music Store Customer Service page, where you can learn about different avenues for dealing with problems related to The Store.

Alternatively, you can visit www.apple.com/support/itunes/musicstore.html.

## "When I try to play purchased music on my Mac, I get some weird error message!"

This can happen on a Mac when your computer's clock is set incorrectly. Usually, you'll see an alert that indicates a -9800, -9815, or -9814 error. To correct the problem, go into the Date & Time system preference, and set your Mac to the correct date and time.

## "How can I politely suggest to Apple that The Store would benefit from offering the complete works of Frank Zappa?"

My ardent hope is that Mr. Zappa's *oeuvre* will be in The Store by the time you read this book, but if it isn't, launch iTunes, and select the Provide iTunes Feedback command located in the iTunes menu on a Mac and the Help menu on a Windows PC. Your browser will open and take you to the iTunes & Music Store Feedback page. On this page, choose Music Requests from the Feedback Type pop-up menu, and make your musical wishes known in the Comment field.

This page is useful for offering other kinds of feedback to Apple—sending a correction, making a suggestion, or submitting a bug report, for example.

# 5

# Of iPods and PCs

By now, you're probably aware that although the iPod is an Apple product from cover to core, Microsoft Windows users are just as welcome to slide into the iPod groove as their Mac-using companions.

This hasn't always been the case. When the iPod was first released, it was intended to be compatible with Macs only (though a couple of third-party utilities allowed you to use a Mac iPod with Windows—I'll show you how later in this chapter). But it didn't take Apple long to realize that a fair number of Windows users were also enthusiastic about owning an iPod.

Apple hoped that these Windows folk would be so enthralled with this diminutive device that they'd purchase a Mac simply so they could use it with an iPod. And some did.

Once Apple determined that it had sold about as many iPod/Macintosh combo platters as it was likely to, it set about creating an iPod for Windows. This model would vary little from the Mac iPod. It would require a hard drive formatted to be compatible with the Windows operating system, Windows-compatible software for downloading music to the device, and a FireWire adapter for use with FireWire cards that bore the smaller 4-pin FireWire connector used on some PCs.

This is the Windows iPod that Apple announced in July 2002 and shipped the following September.

When Apple introduced the third-generation iPod in April 2003, it dispensed with the "this one's for Macintosh and this one's for Windows" scheme, instead issuing a single iPod model that works with either Macintosh or Windows. In the hope of making the iPod even easier for Windows users to enjoy, Apple dropped the requirement that data be transferred via FireWire (a connection type not used on a lot of PCs) and designed the latest iPods to support both FireWire and USB 2.0.

Apple completed its plan for iPod parity in October 2003 when it unveiled iTunes for Windows, thus allowing Windows and Mac users to share a similar iPod experience from beginning to end. I say *similar* rather than *exact* because differences remain in how you treat the device on each platform. Most PCs don't bear a FireWire port, for example, so docking a Windows iPod is a slightly different experience on a PC than it is on a Mac. And unlike their Macintosh counterparts, Windows users have a choice of software: iTunes for Windows; Musicmatch Jukebox (the software that originally shipped with the Windows iPod); and a couple of third-party applications that offer capabilities iTunes and Musicmatch don't, as well as support for earlier versions of Windows that aren't compatible with iTunes or Musicmatch. Finally, Windows users have access to online music services other than the iTunes Music Store (and may want to play some of that music on their iPods).

In this chapter, I'll discuss all these topics and offer tips for making your Windows-formatted iPod comfortable with either computing platform.

# Configuring Your PC

If you have a fourth-generation iPod, iPod Photo, or iPod mini and a fairly new PC, you're in clover. These iPods can be charged by a high-power USB 2.0 port (you can use this port to swap data between the iPod and PC as well), and Apple includes a cable in the iPod box that sports a USB 2.0 connector on one end and the iPod's proprietary data/power connector on the other. With the iPod software installed on your PC, just string this cable between the iPod and computer, and you're well on your way.

If you have an earlier iPod or an older PC, things get trickier. For example, although third-generation iPods can transfer data via a USB 2.0 port, you can't power these iPods by such a port. If you have one of these iPods, you must use Apple's $19 iPod Dock Connector to FireWire and USB 2.0 Cable. On one end of this cable sits the proprietary data/power connector that plugs into the bottom of the iPod or the iPod's Dock. From this connector extend two cables—one that sports a USB 2.0 plug (for transferring data to and from the iPod) and another that bears a FireWire connector (for plugging into a FireWire port or the iPod's power adapter).

But what happens if your PC lacks a USB 2.0 port, or you have a first- or second-generation iPod that doesn't support USB 2.0?

You have a couple of options:

- If you have a third-generation iPod, you can add USB 2.0 to your PC with an inexpensive PCI card, or you can skip USB 2.0 altogether and add a FireWire PCI adapter. Such an adapter provides power to your iPod, works with many digital camcorders, and obviates the need for Apple's special USB 2.0 cable.

- If you have a first- or second-generation iPod (these models don't support USB 2.0), you must add a FireWire PCI adapter. When doing so, be sure that you add an adapter that bears a 6-pin FireWire port. Some FireWire adapters include a 4-pin port (the kind of port you usually find on digital camcorders). Although such ports can be used to transfer data, they won't power an iPod.

# Making the Connection: Hardware

The means to get FireWire on your PC is a FireWire host adapter card. If you have a desktop PC, this card will be designed for your PC's PCI slots (**Figure 5.1**). If you have a laptop with a PC Card slot, look for a FireWire PC Card. These FireWire cards are made by such companies as Adaptec (www.adaptec.com), Belkin (www.belkin.com), Keyspan (www.keyspan.com), and Orange Micro (www.orangemicro.com). PCI FireWire cards cost $35 to $75, and FireWire PC cards hover around $100.

**Figure 5.1**
A PCI FireWire card.

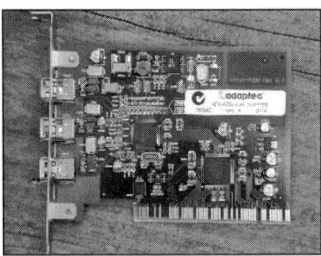

You might also consider purchasing a PCI card that carries both FireWire and USB 2.0 connectors. The vendors I listed earlier offer such cards priced at just over $60.

To add a FireWire, USB 2.0, or FireWire/USB 2.0 combination card to your PC, that PC must have an available PCI or PC Card slot (FireWire/USB 2.0 combination cards aren't available in PC card configurations) and should be equipped with a 266 MHz or faster processor. (A 350 MHz processor really is the base limit if you also plan to use this card for digital video.) You must be running Microsoft Windows 98 Second Edition (SE), Me, 2000, or XP (both the Home and Professional editions support FireWire and USB 2.0).

 If you're running Windows 98 SE, consider upgrading. FireWire made its first appearance in Windows 98 SE, and quite frankly, Microsoft didn't do a terribly good job of implementing it. Transfer rates can be slower than in later revisions of Windows, and these early FireWire drivers don't always see eye to eye with the iPod.

## Installing a PCI card

Now that you're sure that your PC is up to snuff, here's how to install the card in a desktop PC:

1. Turn off the PC, and disconnect the cables running into it: video, mouse, keyboard, USB, modem, Ethernet, sound, and power.

2. Open the PC.

   See your PC's manual if you're unsure how to do this.

3. Touch the PC's power supply (that big silver box on the inside) to discharge any static electricity you may be carrying around with you.

   Static electricity can destroy delicate computer components.

4. Remove the PCI card from its static proof bag.

5. Locate a free PCI slot (**Figure 5.2**)—it's probably white with a single notch—and remove the metal cover that blocks access to the slot from the back of the PC.

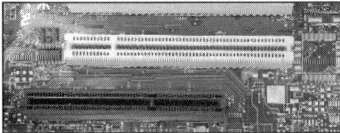

**Figure 5.2**
PCI slots are usually white.

6. Insert the card, and screw it into place (**Figure 5.3**).

**Figure 5.3**
The FireWire PCI card in place.

7. Close the PC.

8. Reconnect any cables you disconnected.

9. Restart your PC.

### Installing a PC Card

The PC Card slot was designed so that adding devices such as Ethernet, modem, USB, media reader, and FireWire cards to your laptop would be a dead cinch. It is. To install a FireWire or USB 2.0 PC Card, simply shove the card into the PC Card slot. You should be able to do this with the laptop running, but check the instructions that came with the card, in case the manufacturer wants things done differently.

A FireWire PC Card may not provide power to your iPod (and a USB 2.0 PC Card certainly won't). (Check the documentation that comes with the card to learn whether power is part of the package.) This means that you can't charge your original iPod from your laptop PC. If your card doesn't provide power, you must charge the iPod before plugging it into your laptop or use a device, such as SiK's FireJuice adapter or Apple's USB 2.0 + FireWire cable. (For more information on the SiK adapter, see Chapter 9.)

You can power a fourth-generation iPod, iPod Photo, or iPod mini from a PC laptop if that laptop bears a high-power USB 2.0 port. Note, however, that Apple suggests that you'll get better results if your laptop is plugged into a power outlet before connecting your iPod to your laptop.

## Completing the Connection: Software

You may have to do a little or a lot to configure your new card, depending on the card you get and how Windows likes it. Windows can be the tiniest bit unpredictable, and you may have to install some kind of driver software to make your PC work with the card. Or Windows may be more than happy to do the job for you by installing its own drivers. Please let the manual be your guide.

After you install your card and reboot Windows (or, in the case of a laptop and PC Card, insert the card), Windows may see the card and install the appropriate drivers automatically when the PC boots up. If Windows does install the drivers, it may ask you to reboot your PC. Do so.

Thereafter, these are the steps you're likely to take in Windows XP:

1. After Windows has rebooted, right-click My Computer, and choose Properties from the resulting contextual menu (**Figure 5.4**).

**Figure 5.4**
Choose Properties from My Computer's contextual menu.

The System Properties dialog box opens.

2. Click the Hardware tab and then the Device Manager button, and look for the appropriate entry for your card.

   On my PC, my FireWire card is listed below SBP2 IEEE 1394 Devices.

3. Click the plus sign next to the 1394 entry to reveal the name of the FireWire card you've inserted (**Figure 5.5**)

**Figure 5.5**
The FireWire card recognized by Windows.

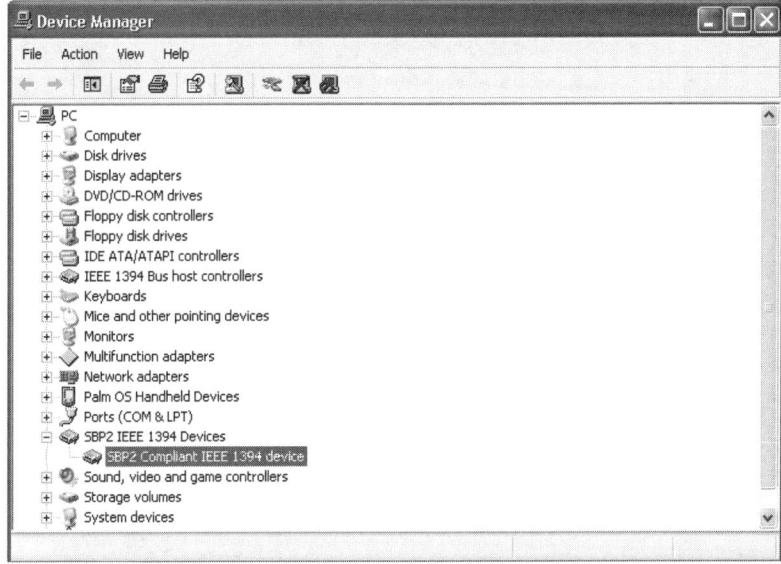

If you've installed a USB 2.0 or FireWire/USB 2.0 combo card, you'll find the USB portion of the card listed under the Universal Serial Bus Controller entry.

4. Right-click this name to reveal the contextual menu, and choose Properties from this menu.

In the Device Status section of the resulting window, you should see the message "This device is working properly" (**Figure 5.6**).

**Figure 5.6**
Windows' reassurance that the FireWire card actually works.

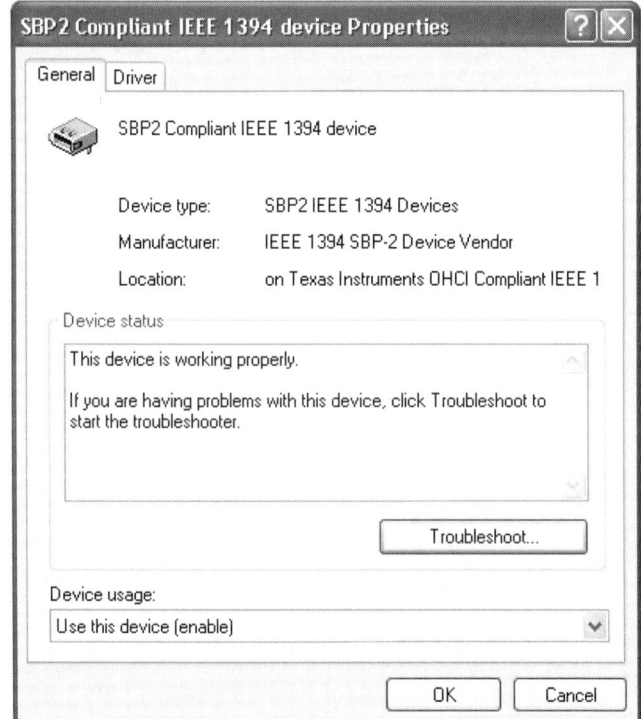

If you see anything other than this message, check the manual that came with the card, and pray that it features a troubleshooting section. If no help is offered there, check the card manufacturer's Web site for help. You may have to get an updated driver or reconfigure Windows.

# iPod for Windows Software

Included with the latest iPods is a CD-ROM that contains the drivers necessary for the iPod to be recognized by Windows, a Windows version of the iPod Software Updater (a utility necessary for updating or restoring the iPod's software), and a copy of iTunes for Windows. If you have an iPod shipped before the release of iTunes for Windows, your CD-ROM includes a copy of Musicmatch's (www.Musicmatch.com) Musicmatch Jukebox Pro. The latter application, like iTunes, lets you play the music files on your PC and iPod, burn music files to CD-R and CD-RW discs, and download music to your iPod.

## Installing the iPod Software

If you've installed just about any other Windows application, there are no surprises here. When you insert the iPod disc, an installer application opens and walks you through the installation process. Although installing the software is anything but challenging, a few points are worth mentioning.

Out of the box, all iPods are formatted for the Macintosh. To convert them to an iPod formatted for Windows, you must restore (reformat) them with the Windows iPod Software. The easiest way to do this is to install the iPod software and, during the installation process, wait for a window to appear that reads: "Your new iPod needs to be configured. Do it now?" Click OK and another window prompts you to plug in your iPod.

The installation will proceed apace—installing first the iPod system software and then iTunes and QuickTime. When these components are installed, the appropriate version of the iPod Updater Software will launch and offer you a single choice: Restore. *Restore* in this case is little more than a euphemism for *reformat*. When you restore an iPod, you erase all the data on it. When you restore an iPod on a Windows PC, its hard drive is formatted as a FAT-32 volume. When you restore an iPod on a Mac, it's formatted as a Mac OS Extended volume (also known as HFS+).

If your iPod is connected to your PC via a powered FireWire connection, pressing Restore sends the firmware update to the iPod, restarts the iPod, and updates the firmware (thus erasing the data from it). All this happens with the iPod plugged into the FireWire port.

If your iPod is connected to your PC via USB 2.0, this process works a bit differently. When you click Restore, the firmware update is sent to the iPod; then you're asked to plug the iPod into a power source before the update can proceed. (Apparently, the USB 2.0 connection can't guarantee the kind of uninterrupted power the iPod wants to complete the update.) A cute little icon of the iPod's power adapter and a wall plug appears on the iPod's screen. When you provide that power—which can be either the adapter-in-power-socket setup outlined on the iPod's screen or a powered FireWire connection—the update proceeds, with the firmware installed and the data removed.

Because an update or restore via USB 2.0 won't proceed unless you connect your iPod to a power source, be sure you have the iPod's power adapter nearby before performing such an operation.

When you quit the installer, iTunes will launch and display a screen where you can name your little musical buddy, as well as register the iPod. It's up to you to decide whether to register the iPod or not. Registering the device may help, should you need repair or replacement service at some point, but your sales receipt works just as well.

## The Small Print

If you decide to register your iPod, you'll be asked for your iPod's serial number. If you have extraordinarily good vision (or a decent magnifying glass), you may be able to make out the miniscule number printed on the shiny back of the iPod. I can't.

Fortunately, you can find the serial number in two other locations. The first is the iPod's display screen. Just fire up the iPod, choose the About command in the main iPod screen, and press Select. You'll find the serial number at the bottom of the resulting About screen. You can also find the iPod's serial number on the outside of the box that the iPod came in (not the outer sleeve, but the black or white inner box).

You'll also see that the Automatically Update My iPod option is checked. If you don't want iTunes to dump all its music into your iPod when you get through this naming process, uncheck this option. When this option is unchecked, you must update the iPod manually. (See Chapter 2 for details on how to switch from manual to automatic updating.) Click Finish to exit this window.

If you've configured your iPod to be updated automatically, iTunes will proceed to copy all the compatible music on your PC to the iPod. During this process, it will also take you to the iTunes Music Store if you have an active Internet connection. If you'd rather not visit The Store right away, click the small X in the display that reads "Accessing Music Store" to stop the connection.

## Converting Windows Music Files

One feature of the Windows version of iTunes that's not present in iTunes for the Mac is the ability to convert files saved in the unprotected .wma format (the default audio file format used by Microsoft's Windows Media Player) to Apple's AAC format. Before you dash to iTunes in search of a Convert From .wma command, you should know that Apple has made this as transparent as possible by performing this operation semi-automatically when you drag files into iTunes or invoke the Add File to Library or Add Folder to Library command.

To convert a file, be sure that you're running iTunes 4.5 or later and have installed Windows Media Player 9 or later (available from www.microsoft.com/windows/windowsmedia/default.aspx). With these applications on board, drag unprotected .wma files into iTunes' main window (or use one of the Add To commands). iTunes will alert you that it would like to convert the file to AAC format. Click Convert, and it will happen; iTunes creates a new AAC file and places it in the iTunes Music folder, leaving the original .wma file intact.

And what, exactly, is an unprotected .wma file? Just like Apple, Microsoft offers unprotected and protected versions of its audio files. Unprotected audio files are generated by Windows Media Player when, for example, you rip a CD. These files are also commonly found on the Internet. Protected .wma files are generally sold on the Internet through online commercial music services such as Napster and Musicmatch. These files are protected so that they're more difficult to trade (steal). iTunes can't convert protected .wma files.

# Musicmatch Jukebox

When I sat down to update this book for the latest edition, I had to think long and hard about whether to excise any mention of Musicmatch Jukebox—the Windows software Apple bundled with the iPod before it released iTunes for Windows. After all, iPods now ship with versions of iTunes for both Mac and Windows; Musicmatch Jukebox doesn't provide that all-important connection to the iTunes Music Store; it doesn't support AAC file encoding or playback; it doesn't support the fourth-generation iPod, iPod Photo, or iPod mini; and quite honestly, I find that Musicmatch Jukebox is more difficult to work with than iTunes.

On the other hand, Musicmatch Jukebox still works with the first three generations of iPods; it provides a couple of useful features that iTunes doesn't have; and it works with more flavors of Windows than iTunes does. (Musicmatch Jukebox is compatible with Windows Me, XP, and 2000, whereas iTunes requires you to run Windows XP or 2000.) So why deny those who prefer the Musicmatch Way some helpful advice on how to put it to best use?

Note that if you've installed iTunes for Windows, Musicmatch Jukebox will no longer function with your iPod (see the sidebar "Musicmatch Jukebox Reinstallation"). Before attempting to use Musicmatch, make sure that your iPod will work with it.

Current versions of Musicmatch Jukebox aren't compatible with any iPods. The last version that worked with the iPod (the first three generations only) is version 7.5, which you can find at http://partners.musicmatch.com/archives. The file you're specifically looking for is called mmsetup_7.50.5005_ENU_Apple.exe.

# Musicmatch Jukebox Installation

If your iPod didn't come bundled with iTunes for Windows, and you'd like to use Musicmatch Jukebox, these instructions are for you.

When the installer finishes updating your PC's hard drive with the components necessary for Windows to work with the iPod, the Musicmatch Jukebox installer launches. This installer would like a little personal information.

As you can in the iPod registration screen, you can refrain from providing your name and email address. You must, however, indicate the year you were born. Apparently, there are laws on the books that lend a greater degree of privacy to those under the age of 13. If you enter a year of birth that places you among this group, the registration screen won't allow you to enter personal information.

The Personal Music Recommendations window follows. In this window, you can choose to allow Musicmatch to collect data on the kind of music you listen to so that it can send you links to downloadable music it thinks you'll like. Just between us, I consider my musical habits to be my own business, so I selected the No option in this window. But if you find such a service desirable, click Yes with my blessing.

After you've made your choice and clicked Next, the installer proceeds, installing the application and plug-in driver necessary for Musicmatch Jukebox to recognize the iPod as a portable music device.

Next, you'll be asked to enter a user upgrade key. This key, which is the number on the outside of the iPod Software CD sleeve, enables Musicmatch Jukebox Pro's features—the ability to rip music files and burn CDs faster, for example. Enter this number, and you're good to go. The installation process completes, and Musicmatch Jukebox opens by default.

When the installer finishes, you'll be asked to restart your PC. Do so.

## Musicmatch Jukebox Reinstallation

When you install iTunes for Windows on a PC that includes a copy of Musicmatch Jukebox, some of the files necessary for Musicmatch Jukebox to work with the iPod are deleted. Some people contend that Apple did this intentionally to grab a greater share of the music-player market. Others who have broad experience with PCs understand that it's the Windows way for a new program to muscle aside an older program that offers similar capabilities (Windows Media Player being the outstanding example). Regardless of why iTunes disables Musicmatch, the fact remains that it does.

If you've installed iTunes for Windows and long for the days of Musicmatch Jukebox, Musicmatch offers the following steps for bringing Musicmatch Jukebox back to life (and, ironically enough, removing iTunes for Windows):

1. Disconnect the iPod from your computer, if it's still connected.
2. Double-click My Computer.
3. Double-click Control Panel.
4. Open the Add or Remove Programs control panel.
5. Select and uninstall the iTunes item.
6. Select and uninstall the iPod for Windows item.
7. Select and uninstall the Musicmatch iPod Plugin item.
8. Select and uninstall iPod System Software Update and any other iPod-related items that might be listed.
9. Select and uninstall the Musicmatch Jukebox item.
10. Close the Add or Remove Programs control panel.
11. Restart your computer.
12. Delete the contents of the iPod directory by dragging the files to the Recycle Bin and then emptying the Recycle Bin.
13. Navigate to the \program files\Musicmatch\Musicmatch Jukebox\ folder.
14. Delete the files in the Musicmatch Jukebox folder—but not the folder itself.
15. Reinstall Musicmatch Jukebox from the installation CD that came with your iPod, or download the iPod software from Musicmatch.com.
16. When the installation finishes, reboot your computer.
17. When the computer finishes rebooting, connect the iPod to your system.
18. Open Musicmatch Jukebox.

# The iPod Manager

As I mentioned earlier, when you connect an iPod and format it for Windows, and iTunes launches, iTunes takes care of the iPod's initial configuration (its name and whether you want it to be updated automatically when you plug it in) in the first screen. Musicmatch Jukebox does the same sort of things with the help of the iPod Manager application, which is installed with the iPod 2.0 Software Updater. (Version 2.1 of this software doesn't include it.)

When you install this earlier version of the Windows software with a third-generation iPod, you'll find the iPod Manager in the Windows System Tray.

The iPod Manager window gives you access to the following options:

- **Enable Disk Mode**. Enabling this option allows you to use the iPod as a removable hard drive.

- **Change Home Application**. Ostensibly, clicking this button allows you to choose which application you'd like to use to manage music on your iPod. Regrettably, this feature doesn't include a Browse button, so there's no way to direct iPod Manager to use an application other than Musicmatch Jukebox. All you get is a pop-up menu that doesn't list alternatives to Musicmatch Jukebox.

- **Launch 2.0 Updater**. Click this button to launch the iPod Software 2.0 Updater, which lets you update the iPod's software or restore (reformat) the iPod.

- **Check Apple Website for Latest**. Clicking this button launches your Web browser and takes you to Apple's home page. Unfortunately, it doesn't take you directly to Apple's iPod page, where you're more likely to find the update you desire. A more direct approach would be to point your browser to www.apple.com/ipod.

- **Show in System Tray**. If you disable this option, the iPod Manager icon disappears from the System Tray.

- **Automatically Launch Home Application on iPod Plug In**. Enabling this option causes Musicmatch Jukebox to launch when you plug in your iPod.

One option that's not apparent in the iPod Manager window is the ability to rename your iPod. Just click the name that's displayed below the icon of your iPod in the top portion of the window, and type a new name.

 Newer versions of Musicmatch Jukebox are not compatible with your iPod. For this reason, you should steer clear of the Update Software command in the Options menu.

## Musicmatch Jukebox Overview

Musicmatch Jukebox is comprised of a few windows. The main window contains the play controls to the left and the Playlists area to the right (**Figure 5.7**). You can hide the Playlists area by clicking the left-pointing triangle on the right side of the window.

**Figure 5.7**
Musicmatch Jukebox's Main window, with play controls and Playlists area.

The My Library window contains a column view of all the songs in your music library (**Figure 5.8**). You can change the view in which your library is displayed—by artist, album, or genre, for example. Songs are clumped together in folders, depending on the view you've selected. If you've chosen to view by artist, for example, all John Cale songs are placed in a single folder. View this same library by album, and you'll see John Cale's *Paris 1919*, *Helen of Troy*, and *Slow Dazzle* albums broken into separate folders.

**Figure 5.8**

The Musicmatch Jukebox Library window.

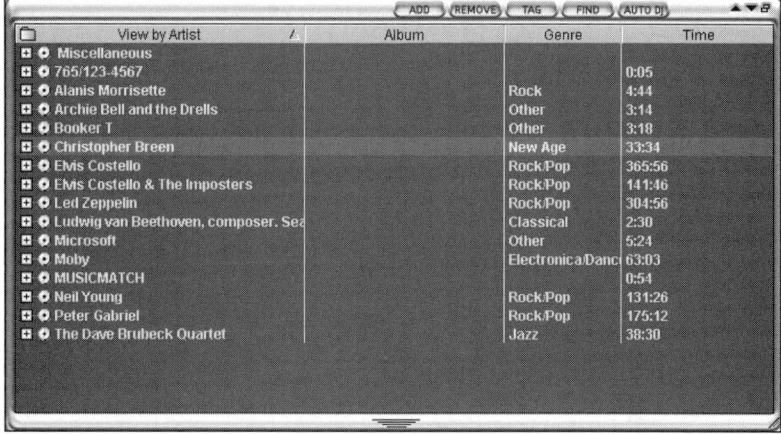

When you plug in your iPod and launch Musicmatch Jukebox, the Portable Devices window appears (**Figure 5.9**). In this window, you view the songs on your iPod, manually synchronize your music library and iPod, and gain access to the iPod's options via the Option button (including the ability to edit the iPod's name and determine whether it's updated automatically when you plug it into your PC). I'll discuss each of these windows and functions at greater length later in this chapter.

**Figure 5.9**

Musicmatch Jukebox's Portable Devices window.

# Ripping a CD

Your iPod wouldn't be much of a music player if it had no music on it. The first thing you'll want to do is move some music from the most likely source—an audio CD—into Musicmatch Jukebox. Here's how to go about it:

**1.** Launch Musicmatch Jukebox.

**2.** Insert an audio CD into an available CD drive.

Older versions of Windows may open and play the CD with Musicmatch Jukebox. If you're running Windows XP (Home or Professional), a window will appear, asking what you'd like to do with the CD: play it with Windows Media Player, play it with Musicmatch Jukebox, view the files it contains with Windows Explorer, or take no action. For now, choose the option to play the audio CD in Musicmatch Jukebox.

If your PC has an always-on connection to the Internet (such as a cable modem or DSL connection), Musicmatch Jukebox will venture out onto the Web and download such track information as title, artist, and length of each song on the CD. If you have a penchant for tedious tasks (or no information is available online for the CD you've inserted), you're welcome to enter song information manually.

**3.** To convert (or *rip*) the audio files on the CD to your hard drive, click the red Record button in Musicmatch Jukebox's main window (**Figure 5.10**).

**Figure 5.10**
Click the Record button to rip an audio CD.

— Record button

When you do, the Recorder window appears.

**4.** Specify which tracks on the disc you'd like to rip.

By default, all tracks are selected.

**5.** Click Record in the Recorder window.

Musicmatch Jukebox begins ripping the CD, showing the progress it's making as a percentage of each song ripped.

When Musicmatch Jukebox finishes ripping the CD, a fanfare erupts from your PC's speakers, and the disc is ejected.

 By default, Musicmatch Jukebox rips CDs as MP3 files encoded at 128 Kbps. (As you recall, it doesn't support ripping or playing AAC files.) When Apple's iTunes rips in the MP3 format, it does so at 160 Kbps, which produces larger—and better-sounding—files than those ripped at 128 Kbps. If you want your files to sound as good as the other guy's or gal's, choose Settings from Musicmatch Jukebox's Options menu, click the Recorder tab in the resulting Settings window, enable the Custom Quality option, and move the slider so that the quality reads 160 Kbps.

# Moving Music into Musicmatch Jukebox

Ripping a CD isn't the only way to get music into Musicmatch Jukebox. You can download music from the Web, for example, or you may have moved some music that you own from another computer to your PC via a network connection. You can add this music to Musicmatch Jukebox as well, and there are a few ways to do it.

- Choose Add New Music Track(s) to Music Library from Musicmatch Jukebox's File menu.

  When you issue this command, the Add Tracks to Music Library dialog box appears. From this dialog box, you can navigate to specific folders that contain music. Or you can take the shotgun approach: Select a volume (your C drive, for example), and click the

Add button (**Figure 5.11**). Musicmatch Jukebox scans that volume for compatible music files and adds any that it finds to the library.

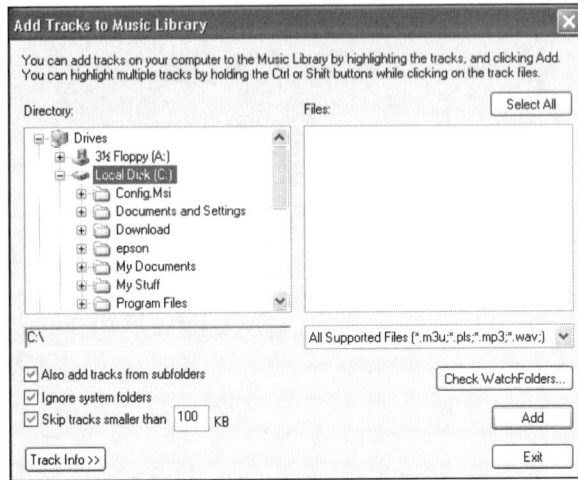

**Figure 5.11**

Adding tracks to your music library.

The shotgun method is likely to turn up such interesting musical tidbits as the Microsoft toe-tapper "Windows Welcome Music" (all 5 minutes and 24 seconds of it!).

Fortunately, the latest version of Musicmatch Jukebox (version 7.5) that shipped with the iPod includes an option for skipping tracks smaller than a certain size (100 KB, by default). This option helps ensure that such extraneous audio files as system alert sounds aren't added to your music library.

- Drag a compatible music file into Musicmatch Jukebox's Playlist or Library window.

  Dragging the file into the Playlist window causes the song to begin playing immediately but doesn't add it to Musicmatch Jukebox's library. To add the file to a playlist, click the Save button just below the Playlist window. To add the file to your library, drag the file into the Library window.

- Use Musicmatch Jukebox's WatchFolders feature.

  By default, Musicmatch Jukebox stores its songs in the My Music folder within the My Documents folder (which is inside your user folder, if you're running Windows XP). You can instruct Musicmatch Jukebox to use additional folders for music storage by choosing WatchFolders from the File menu.

In the resulting WatchFolders window (**Figure 5.12**), click the Add button to create a watch folder. When you want to add music to your library, drop the music files into a watch folder. Musicmatch Jukebox will add to its library any files that it finds in watch folders.

**Figure 5.12**
The WatchFolders window.

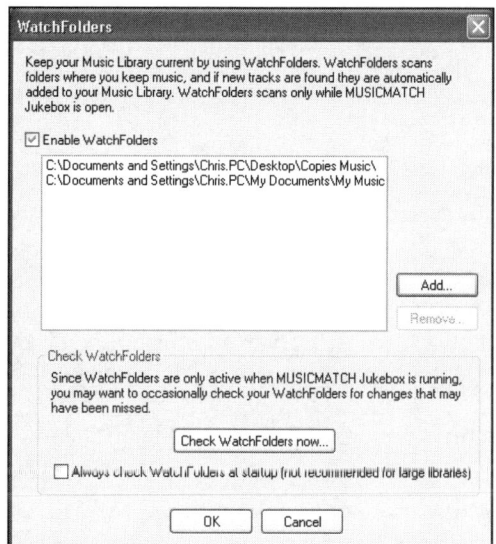

## Creating and Configuring a Playlist

Like iTunes and the Macintosh iPod, Musicmatch Jukebox allows you to organize your library of songs in playlists. To create such a playlist, follow these steps:

**1.** Launch Musicmatch Jukebox.

If the Library window doesn't appear, click the My Library button in the bottom-left corner of the Musicmatch Jukebox window.

**2.** Select the songs you'd like to add to your playlist.

3. Right-click one of the selected songs, and choose Add Track(s) to Playlist Window from the contextual menu (**Figure 5.13**).

**Figure 5.13**
Select some tunes, and invoke this command to add tracks to a playlist.

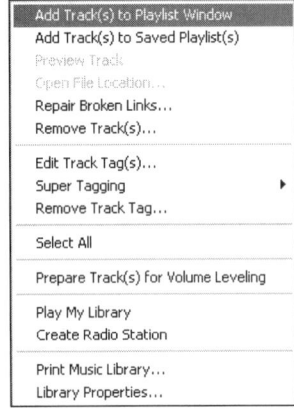

*or*

Choose Music Library from Musicmatch Jukebox's Options menu and then choose Add Track(s) to Playlist Window from the submenu.

4. After the songs appear in the Playlists window (**Figure 5.14**), arrange the order in which you'd like the songs to play simply by dragging songs up or down in the list.

**Figure 5.14**
Your songs appear in the Playlists area.

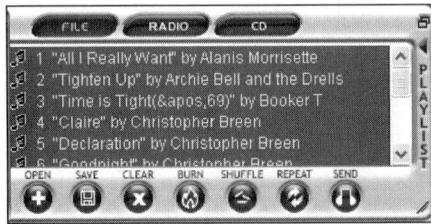

5. When you have the playlist configured to your satisfaction, click the Save button that appears just below the Playlist window.

The Save Playlist dialog box appears.

6. Enter a name for your new playlist, and click Save.

**7.** To clear the songs from the playlist, click the Clear button below the Playlists window.

This action doesn't remove the songs from your library; it simply clears the playlist so that you can create or call up other playlists.

**8.** To call up a playlist, click the Open button below the Playlists window, click the Playlists button in the resulting Open Music dialog box, and then click the Play button.

The playlist will load in the Playlists window, and the first song in the playlist will begin playing.

If you'd like to add music to an existing playlist, you can skip steps 3 through 6. Just select the songs you'd like to add to the playlist, right-click one of the selected songs, and choose Add Track(s) to Saved Playlist(s) from the contextual menu. When you do, the Select Playlist window appears. Click the playlist to which you want to add the tracks; then click OK. The selected tracks are added to the playlist.

# Moving Music to the iPod

Musicmatch Jukebox offers you a couple of ways to transfer music from your PC to the iPod. As with iTunes and the iPod, you can cause the iPod to update each time you plug it into your PC, or you can update it manually. The key to managing music on your iPod is the Options dialog box, available from Musicmatch Jukebox's Portable Devices window. Let's take a look.

## The Portable Devices window

By default, when you plug your iPod into your PC, Musicmatch Jukebox opens, along with the Portable Devices window. The iPod appears below the Attached Portable Devices entry in the left pane of this window.

If you click the iPod in this window and then click the Options button that rests in the bottom-right corner of the Portable Devices window, you'll get the aptly named Options dialog box. Within this dialog box, you'll find options for adding music to your iPod.

## The Options dialog box

The Options dialog box is broken into four tabs.

- **General tab**. What a waste of a perfectly good tab. Other than providing a place to post Musicmatch Jukebox's product information, this area allows you to reset those "Don't ask me again" messages so that, indeed, Musicmatch Jukebox *will* ask you again.

- **Audio tab**. This tab is slightly more useful to iPod users. This area allows you to apply current digital sound enhancements to your files; apply volume leveling, a process that attempts to maintain a consistent volume among the songs on your iPod; and resample audio files encoded at more than a certain resolution at a different rate. (Files encoded at 160 Kbps can be resampled at 128 Kbps, for example.)

  Regrettably, only one of these options works on the Windows iPod. Sound enhancements within Musicmatch Jukebox such as EQ aren't copied to the iPod from a PC (though they are if you use iTunes for Windows), and you can't apply volume leveling to songs on the iPod (though you can apply volume leveling to files on the PC and then transfer them to the iPod).

  If you choose the resampling option, however, when you download songs to your iPod, they will be resampled at the settings you requested. This resampling takes some time—about 45 seconds on a not-terribly-fast PC—so unless you're really pressed for space, don't bother using this option.

- **Synchronization tab**. Ah, now we're cookin'. The settings in the Synchronization tab let you decide whether to synchronize your entire music library when you sync your iPod or synchronize only selected playlists (**Figure 5.15**). This area also includes the Automatically Synchronize on Device Connection option. When this check box is unchecked, you can manage the contents of your iPod manually and mount your iPod on your PC without fear that its contents will be wiped out because the library on the PC doesn't match the songs on the iPod.

**Figure 5.15**
Musicmatch Jukebox's synchronization options.

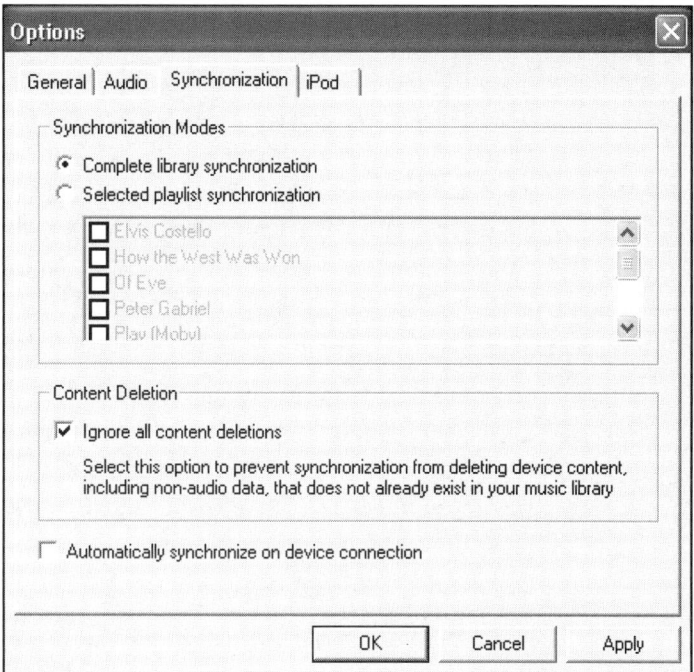

 Included with Musicmatch Jukebox 7.5 is the new Ignore All Content Deletions option. If you disable this option, Musicmatch Jukebox will delete not only audio files on the iPod that aren't in your computer's music library, but also nonaudio files. That's right—if you disable this option, Musicmatch Jukebox may delete the PowerPoint presentation and email database that you copied to your iPod for "safekeeping." Why Musicmatch included an option that puts your data at risk is beyond me. Suffice it to say that you do not want to disable this option.

- **iPod tab**. Finally, the iPod tab includes options for automatically launching Musicmatch Jukebox when you plug the iPod into the PC, enabling disk use (in which your iPod appears as a removable hard drive), and naming your iPod. You'll also find the iPod's version number in this tab.

## Moving music

If you've chosen to have your iPod updated whenever Musicmatch Jukebox launches, all you need to do to move new songs to your iPod is plug it into your PC. Musicmatch Jukebox will launch, and the songs in your library will be synchronized with the songs on your iPod. Even if you haven't chosen to update the iPod automatically, it's easy to synchronize Musicmatch Jukebox's music library with your iPod. Just open the Portable Devices window, select the iPod in the left pane, and click the Sync button.

To add songs to your iPod when you've configured it to be updated manually, select your iPod in the Portable Devices window, open the My Library window, and drag the songs you want into the main Portable Devices window. You can also drag and drop files from outside the program (from the desktop or a window, for example) into the Portable Devices main window.

Finally, you can create playlists in the Playlists area of Musicmatch Jukebox's main window and click the Send button to move that playlist (and the music it includes) directly to your iPod.

Musicmatch Jukebox will not let you move anything but MP3 and WAV files to your iPod. Although you can play unprotected AAC files on an iPod formatted for Windows, Musicmatch Jukebox doesn't support that file type; therefore, you can't use Musicmatch Jukebox as a conduit for moving those files from your PC to the iPod.

# Editing Track Tags

Editing track information in Musicmatch Jukebox is just as easy as carrying out a similar operation in iTunes. To produce the Edit Track Tag(s) window (**Figure 5.16**), just click the Tag button in the My Library window, right-click a track in your music library, and choose Edit Track Tag(s) from the contextual menu. Or select a track, choose Music Library from the Options menu, and then choose the Edit Track Tag(s) command from the resulting submenu.

**Figure 5.16**

The Edit Track Tag(s) window.

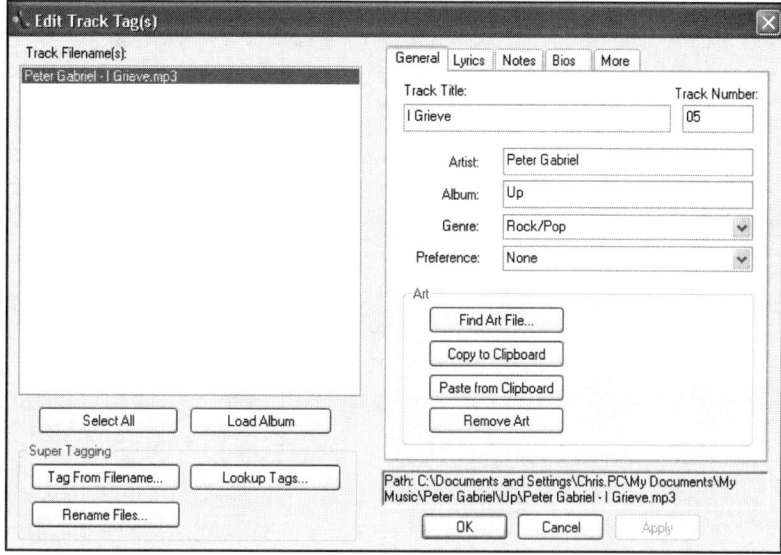

In this window, you can enter such information as track title, track number, artist, album, genre, preference (akin to iTunes' ratings), lyrics, notes, bios, tempo, and mood. You're welcome to knock yourself out filling in each field for every song in your library, but before you do, you should understand that the iPod will use only the information in the Title, Artist, Album, and Genre fields.

This window offers some features you won't find in iTunes. Take the Load Album button, for example. I can best explain how this button works by providing this for-instance: You've chosen to edit the track information for the Beatles song "If I Fell." When you click the Load Album button, all the songs from the album *A Hard Day's Night* appear in the Track Filename(s) list. If you then click the Select All button, you can edit tag information for all the songs on that album at the same time.

You'll also find options for looking up tags on the Internet (helpful if you've obtained music that hasn't already been tagged) and for batch-renaming selected files. And unlike iTunes, Musicmatch's tagging feature can download album artwork for the songs in your library. Currently, iTunes provides album artwork only for music purchased from the iTunes Music Store.

# Other Musicmatch Jukebox Tricks

What other changes can you make in Musicmatch Jukebox that will affect your iPod?

- **Make volumes consistent.** If you scroll through your iPod's Settings screen, you'll see the Sound Check option. This feature is peculiar to the iPod and iTunes. When you switch Sound Check on in iTunes, the songs in the iTunes library are processed so that songs play at a consistent volume (some songs aren't wildly louder or softer than others). You can toggle this effect on the iPod.

  Although Sound Check appears in the Windows iPod's Settings screen, the feature isn't supported if you're using Musicmatch Jukebox (it is if you use iTunes for Windows). This doesn't mean, however, that you can't produce a similar effect in Musicmatch Jukebox.

  Musicmatch Jukebox uses the Volume Leveling feature to generate this effect. Much like Sound Check, Volume Leveling processes songs in your music library so that they play at a volume similar to other Volume Leveling-processed songs. The difference between Sound Check and Volume Leveling is that you can't turn Volume Leveling off on the iPod. (Also, unlike Sound Check, Volume Leveling doesn't have to be applied to every song in your library; you can process only a selected group of songs.) After the songs have been processed on the PC, that volume setting is maintained on the iPod, regardless of whether the Sound Check feature is turned on or off in the Settings screen.

  To employ Volume Leveling, open the My Library window, select the songs to which you'd like to apply the effect, and right-click a selected file. From the resulting contextual menu, choose Prepare Track(s) for Volume Leveling. You can also invoke the Volume Leveling command in the Playlists window. Just select the songs you want to process in the playlists, right-click a selected file, and choose Prepare Track(s) for Volume Leveling from the contextual menu that appears.

Alternatively, you can ask Musicmatch Jukebox to apply Volume Leveling to songs when they're imported from a CD. To do so, choose Settings from the Options menu, click the Recorder tab in the resulting Settings window, enable the Prepare Tracks for Volume Leveling option, and click OK to close the Settings window.

**NOTE** Those who are using Musicmatch instead of iTunes may be ready to throw up their hands and finally shift to iTunes because this process is more complicated than it is in iTunes. Bear in mind, however, that the results of Musicmatch's method may be more to your liking. As I explain in Chapter 2, Sound Check isn't all it's cracked up to be, and other schemes that crank up the volume on each individual track can be more effective. Such is the case here.

- **Generate random playlists**. Musicmatch Jukebox includes a feature similar to iTunes' Smart Playlists, called AutoDJ, which generates playlists for you based on three criteria. It works this way:

  Click the AutoDJ button in the My Library window. The AutoDJ window appears (**Figure 5.17**). In this window are three scrolling lists, each accompanied by a list of search criteria (Album, Artist, and Genre, for example). To generate a random playlist, select different criteria in each list, and enter the play time for the resulting playlist.

**Figure 5.17**

AutoDJ's not-as-smart-as-iTunes playlist.

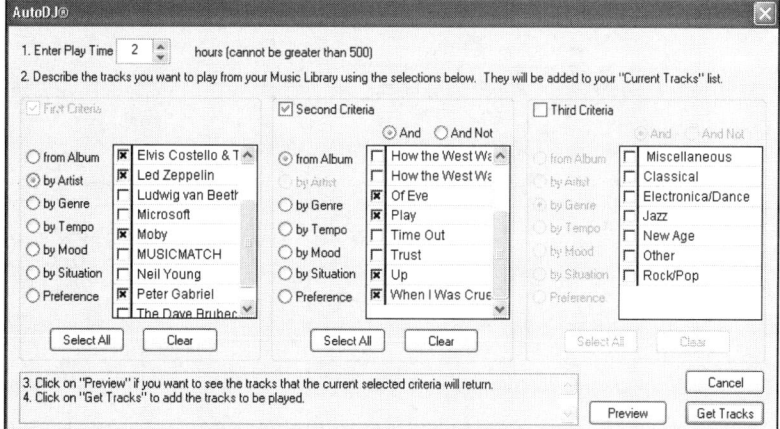

If I chose By Album for the first list, for example, AutoDJ would display all the albums in my library. Then I'd check the albums from which I was willing to accept songs. In the second list, I might choose By Artist. All the artists in my library would appear in the list, and I'd select those that I was willing to have appear in my playlist. And in the third list, I might choose By Genre and select Jazz and Rock/Pop, thus ensuring that only jazz and rock/pop tunes would appear in my playlist.

Next, I'd enter a play time of three hours and click the Get Tracks button to generate the playlist. AutoDJ would grab three hours' worth of songs from my library that met my criteria and randomly place their titles in Musicmatch Jukebox's Playlists window. Then I could save that playlist and later transfer it to my iPod.

## Software Alternatives

Although the Windows iPod ships with iTunes and used to ship with Musicmatch Jukebox, those two programs aren't your only options for moving songs to your iPod. Three other fine applications originally designed to let Macintosh iPods function with Windows PCs now also work with the Windows iPod. Those utilities are Mediafour's (www.mediafour.com) $30 XPlay 2, Red Chair Software's $25 Anapod Explorer (www.redchairsoftware.com), and Joe Masters' free EphPod (www.ephpod.com).

## XPlay 2

Mediafour is known among Mac users primarily for its MacDrive product, which allows Mac volumes to be viewed and manipulated on a PC running Microsoft Windows. In January 2002, the company held a press briefing for a product called XPod, claiming that the product would give Windows users the same kind of access to the iPod that Mac users have.

Somewhere along the way, Apple suggested that the name *XPod* was a little too close to *iPod*, and Mediafour obligingly changed the name to XPlay. Though the name changed, the product's capabilities did not.

The betas of XPlay released in the spring of 2002 showed a program with a lot of promise: the capability to mount and manipulate an iPod formatted for the Macintosh as an external drive on the desktop or through Windows Explorer, the option to have Windows Media Player 7.x and later recognize the iPod as a portable music player (letting you see and play the music on the iPod, as well as copy compatible music files from Windows Media Player to the iPod), and the capability to update your iPod's music files automatically when the iPod is attached to the PC.

Now in final form, XPlay lives up to its promise, providing users of Mac and Windows iPods, iPod Photos, and iPod minis a way, other than through iTunes or Musicmatch, to organize the music on their portable players.

 Note that you must be running XPlay 2 1.0.11 or later to use the program with an iPod Photo. Earlier versions of XPlay don't recognize this colorful iPod.

## Installing and configuring XPlay

Follow these steps to set up XPlay on your PC:

1. On a PC running Windows 98SE, Me, 2000, or XP, install XPlay.

2. Restart your PC.

3. When the PC is fully booted, plug your iPod into the PC with a FireWire cable (or USB 2.0 cable, if you have a fourth-generation iPod, iPod Photo, or iPod mini).

   Your iPod will mount as a removable drive (**Figures 5.18**, this page and **5.19**, next page), and a small icon will appear in the System Tray. (When you click this icon, you can unmount the iPod.) In short order, the XPlay iPod Setup Wizard appears.

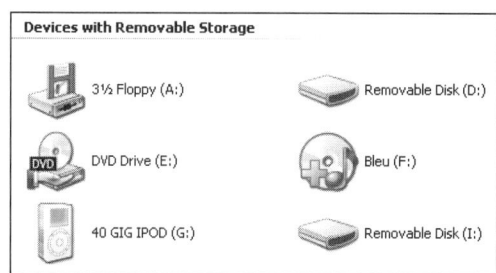

**Figure 5.18**
The iPod as a removable drive.

**Figure 5.19**
The contents of the drive are as accessible to your PC as any other removable drive.

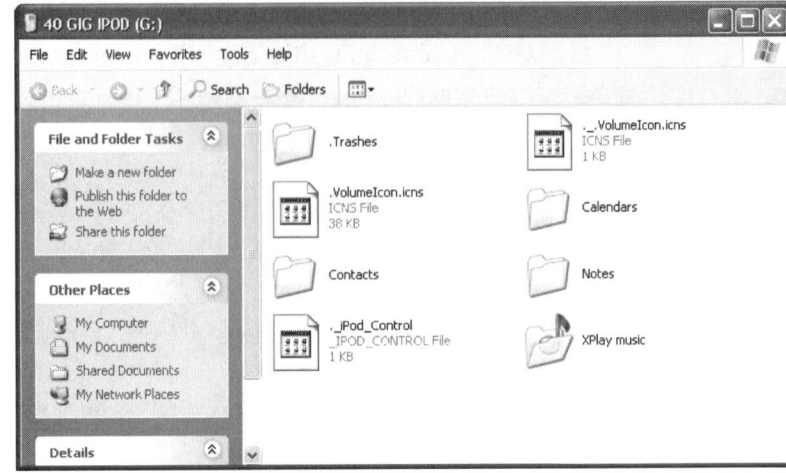

4. Click Next to begin the setup process.

5. In the first screen, change your iPod's name, if you want (**Figure 5.20**), and click Next.

**Figure 5.20**
XPlay offers you the option to rename your iPod.

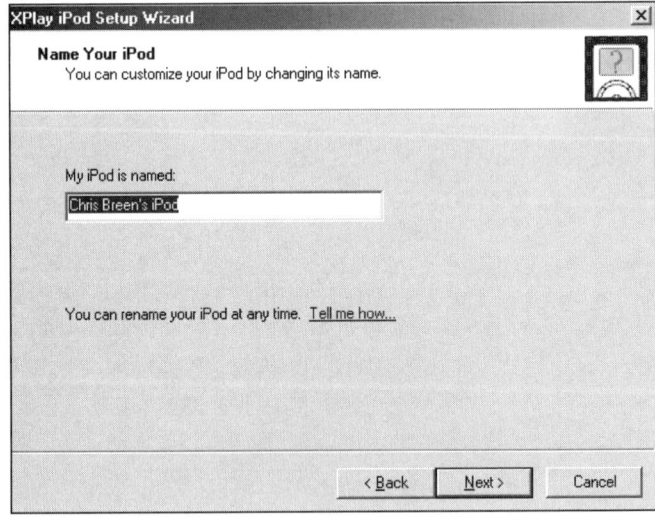

In the resulting synchronization option screen, you can specify whether you'd like the iPod to be updated automatically when you plug it in or whether you want to update the iPod yourself (**Figure 5.21**).

**Figure 5.21**

Choose your synchronization options in the XPlay iPod Setup Wizard.

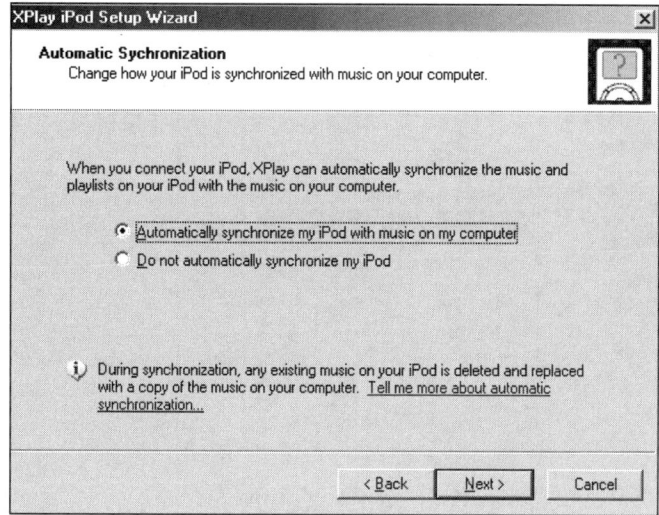

6. Make your choice, and click Next.

   Next, you are asked to select a music collection to synchronize with: Windows Media Player or a folder of your choosing. Which you choose depends largely on where you have your music stored on your PC. If it's already in Windows Media Player, choose this option. If you're using iTunes or have dropped your music into a folder somewhere else on your PC, you may prefer to synchronize to the iTunes library or to another folder on your PC.

7. Make your choice, and click Next.

   In the next screen, you're offered the option to register your iPod with Apple. If you choose it, XPlay will launch your Web browser and take you to Apple's registration site. If you haven't already registered your iPod, feel free to register it this way. You don't have to register for XPlay to work, however.

8. Again, make your choice, and click Next to complete the setup process.

   XPlay and your iPod are ready to use.

If you'd like to change the way that XPlay is set up later—to update your iPod manually rather than have it updated automatically, for example—right-click the XPlay icon in Windows' Notification area, and choose Change Synchronization Options from the contextual menu (**Figure 5.22**). Choosing this command walks you through the latter part of the XPlay setup process.

**Figure 5.22**
Accessing XPlay's options from the System Tray.

## Playing with XPlay

XPlay offers you two ways to get to the music on your iPod: browsing the items inside the XPlay folder that XPlay places on your iPod, or going through the default media player. In this section, I'll look at both methods.

When you finish the XPlay setup, the installer places an XPlay music folder at the root level of your iPod. The contents of this folder (**Figure 5.23**) are arranged similarly to the iPod interface. Inside the XPlay music folder, you'll find:

**Figure 5.23**
The XPlay folder.

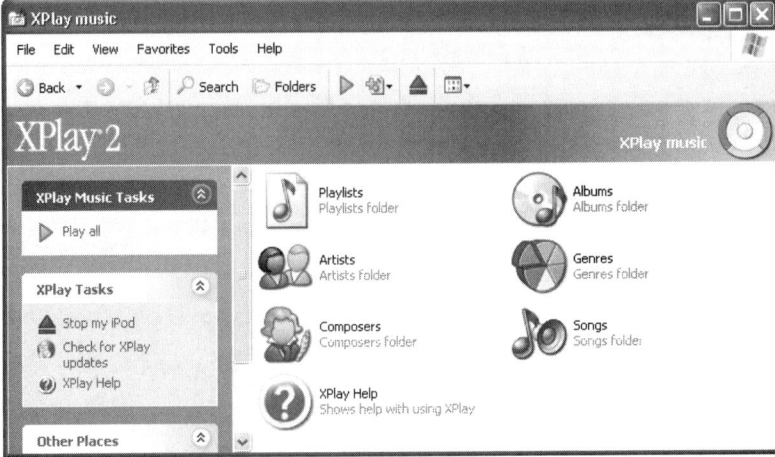

- **Albums**. Inside the Albums folder, you'll find a list of all the albums on your iPod, as well as another folder called (all songs on all albums). Opening this folder reveals—as you might expect—all the songs on all the albums on your iPod.

- **Artists**. Here, you'll see file icons that represent all the artists on your iPod. Double-click an artist folder, and you'll spy another folder called All Songs by "artist", in which "artist" is the name of the artist. If you click the James Brown folder, for example, you'll see another folder called (all songs by James Brown). Double-click this folder, and you'll see a list of all the songs on your iPod by that artist: "Prisoner of Love," "Papa's Got a Brand New Bag," and "I Got the Feelin,'" for example. Inside an individual artist's folder, you'll also see the artist's songs broken down by albums—*Can Your Heart Stand It!!* and *Ain't That a Groove*, for example. Finally, the Artists folder contains the (all songs by all artists) folder that...well, you can probably guess.

- **Composers.** XPlay 2, released in the spring of 2004, includes two new folders. The first is Composers, a folder that organizes songs by their composers. How does XPlay know who wrote the tunes in your music library? It finds this information within a song's ID3 tags (part of a music file that stores such info). If someone has entered information in a song's Composer field, XPlay will use that information to sort the song. Double-clicking the Composers entry might show Lennon/McCartney if you have any Beatles songs on your iPod, for example.

In addition to seeing individual songwriters when you double-click the Composers icon, you'll spy All Albums by All Composers and Unknown Composer. Double-clicking the first reveals album entries for every song on your iPod that has information in the Album ID3 tag. Even if you have just one song from an album, if that one song has something written in the Album field, it will appear here as an album. Double-click these albums to reveal any songs you have from that album. Double-clicking Unknown Composer presents a list of albums that don't have any information entered in their Composer ID3 tag.

- **Genres.** This folder works much like the Composers folder. If a song has Genre ID3 tag information—Acoustic or Jazz, for example—it will be sorted into the appropriate genre folder within this folder. Double-click a genre folder to reveal all the songs that fit that genre.
- **Playlists.** This folder contains all the playlists on your iPod. Double-clicking a playlist reveals all the files within that playlist.
- **Songs.** Double-click this folder to display all the songs on your iPod.
- **XPlay Help.** Double-click this file to view XPlay's help file.

## Copying via drag and drop

Using this hierarchy, you can add audio files to your iPod simply by dragging them from a drive on your PC to a folder on the iPod that contains songs. Note that XPlay doesn't allow you to copy protected AAC files (the kind you purchase at the iTunes Music Store) to your iPod.

## Copying music back to your PC

The iPod was designed to be a one-way device—allowing you to copy music from your computer to it but not copy music from it to your computer. But obviously, it's something a lot of people want to do (for reasons both pure and not-so). XPlay allows this second kind of copying via its Copy To contextual-menu command. To invoke it, simply right-click any of XPlay's items save playlists—Artists, Albums, Genres, Composers, or Songs—and choose Copy To from the resulting contextual menu. Pick the destination for the copied files in the Browse for Folder window that appears, and click OK. The files you've selected will be copied to your PC's hard drive.

## Copying via Windows Media Player

If you've chosen to use Windows Media Player in conjunction with XPlay, follow these steps to copy songs from your PC to the iPod.

1. Launch a copy of Windows Media Player.

**2.** Click the Copy to CD or Device button.

The main Windows Media Player window splits in two, with the left side devoted to files on your PC and the right side devoted to files on your iPod (**Figure 5.24**). If your iPod doesn't appear in the list to the right, choose it from the Device List pop-up menu above the right pane of the Windows Media Player window.

**Figure 5.24**

The iPod as a portable player in Windows Media Player.

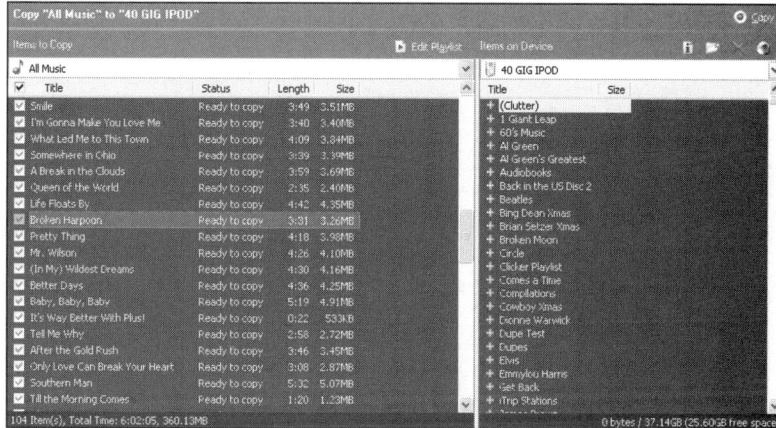

After churning away for a while, Windows Media Player displays all the songs on your iPod.

**3.** If you want to play files on your iPod from Windows Media Player, return to the XPlay music folder on your iPod, navigate to a song or playlist you want to play, right-click that item, and choose Play from the contextual menu.

Unfortunately, you can't play the songs in the list by double-clicking the song title. Neither can you copy the songs back to your PC with Windows Media Player (but you already know how to do that with XPlay).

Note that the files on your iPod must be configured to play with Windows Media Player. Invariably, when you install a new Windows multimedia application, it wants control of your PC's media files.

iTunes and Musicmatch Jukebox are no exceptions. During installation, these applications will ask if you'd like them to be the default media player for supported file types—MP3, AIFF, and WAV among them. If you allow this to happen, choosing Play from XPlay's contextual menu will cause the selected file(s) to play in the default music player.

If you'd like XPlay's files to play in Windows Media Player, but they insist on opening in another application, open Windows Media Player, and choose Options from the Tools menu. Click the File Types tab, and in the File Types list, check the MP3 Audio file (mp3) check box (**Figure 5.25**). Then click Apply to direct MP3 files to play in Windows Media Player.

**Figure 5.25**
Configuring Windows Media Player to play media files.

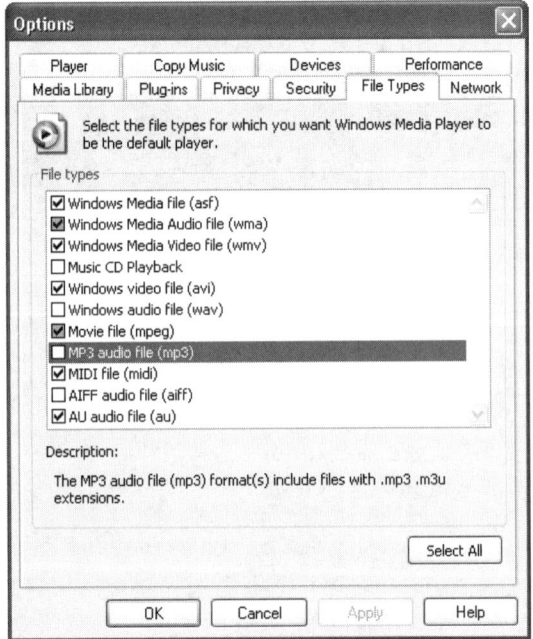

4. To copy songs from your PC to the iPod, select a compatible music file (MP3, AIFF, or WAV) in the left pane of the Windows Media Player window, and click the Copy Music button (above the right pane).

The song is copied to your iPod. If you try to copy a song in any other format (Windows Media format or protected AAC, for example), the song title will turn red, and in the status column, you'll see an entry that reads "An error occurred." (At this point, you're welcome to thank Microsoft for developing proprietary standards that fail to work with non-Microsoft products.)

### Converting .wma files

When you drag a .wma-formatted file to one of the XPlay folders, XPlay will attempt to convert it to an MP3 file. But this works only if you've installed a third-party MP3 encoder such as Intervideo's $10 XPack for Windows XP (www.intervideo.com/products/custom/ms/windowsxp/media_pack.jsp). Without such an encoder, you'll receive an error message when you drag a .wma file into an XPlay folder. This error message directs you to Mediafour's support site, which in turn directs you to Microsoft's site, which in turn directs you to a few encoders. My fervent wish is that future versions of XPlay will include such an encoder, thus saving users the trouble of seeking one out.

## Anapod Explorer

I'm a bit chagrined that it took five editions of this book to get around to discussing one of the finest Windows tools for managing music on an iPod: Red Chair Software's Anapod Explorer. Granted, unlike iTunes, it won't rip CDs; neither does it provide access to the iTunes Music Store. But when it comes to file conversion, two-way file transfers, and remote access to your iPod, Anapod Explorer trumps iTunes at every turn.

### Exploring Anapod Explorer

Anapod Explorer requires Windows 98SE, Me, 2000, or XP. As with all these applications, if you're running Windows 98SE (and really, isn't it about time you upgraded?), you should look for updated FireWire drivers, as the drivers that shipped with this version of Windows aren't terribly robust. The program is offered in four editions: the free Trial Edition, the $25 iPod Edition (for white iPods), the $25 iPod mini Edition, and the $30 Universal Edition (which works with all iPod models). The Trial Edition offers enough features to give you a feel for the program but doesn't offer the program's best features, such as streaming music from your iPod across a network or batch transfer of music from the iPod to your PC. The iPod and iPod mini Editions have the same features; they're simply built for different iPod models. The Universal Edition allows you to use more than one iPod with the program.

It's easy to get going with Anapod Explorer. Just follow these steps:

1. Install and launch the application.

   If you've purchased one of the pay-for editions, you'll see a request in the Anapod browser that you double-click an entry to begin the activation process. Double-click the requested entry, and an activation window appears.

2. Click the Go to Online Activation Form button.

   Clicking this button opens your browser and takes you to a page on Red Chair's Web site where you register your software. Red Chair suggests that an activation code will be emailed to you in less than an hour.

3. When you've received your activation code, attach your iPod to your PC via a FireWire or USB 2.0 connection (if your iPod supports USB 2.0).

4. Right-click the Anapod Explorer item in the System Tray, and choose Connect iPod from the contextual menu.

5. Click the Anapod Explorer icon in the System Tray, and choose Open Anapod Explorer from the resulting contextual menu.

## A familiar interface

Whereas XPlay was designed with the Mac user in mind—as evidenced by the fact that Mac folk are accustomed to browsing their files by opening folders—Anapod Explorer has a distinctive Windows feel. What lends it this feel is its striking similarity to Windows Explorer (thus, the name). Just like Windows Explorer, Anapod Explorer presents files in a two-column window—with the left column containing volumes and directories that can be expanded to reveal enclosed items, and the right column displaying the contents of whatever is selected in the left column.

Specifically, when you click the Anapod Explorer item, the column to the right displays a list that represents your iPod (**Figure 5.26**). This list doesn't mirror what's actually stored at the root level of your iPod's drive; rather, it represents the music and data stored on your iPod and the special features offered by Anapod Explorer. Among the entries you'll see are Audio Tracks (all the songs on your iPod), Playlists, Artists, Albums, and Genres, as well as Contacts and Notes for storing exactly these kinds of files.

**Figure 5.26**

The contents of your iPod as Anapod Explorer sees them.

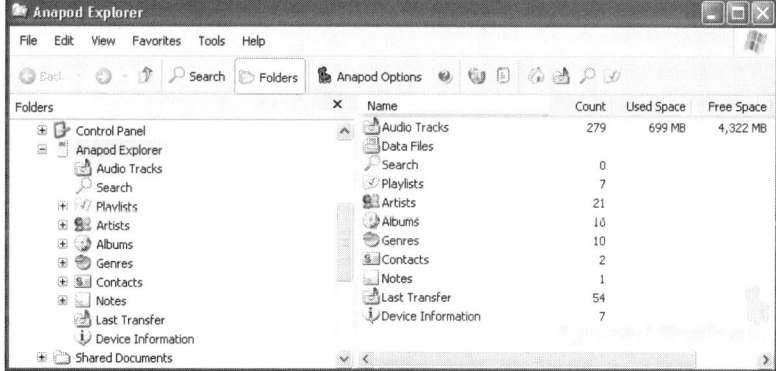

 Anapod Explorer also includes a Data Files folder, which it places at the root level of your iPod. If you care to store other kinds of files on your iPod—word processing or movie files, for example—and you want those files to be visible within Anapod Explorer, copy them to this folder. Although you're welcome to copy data files or folders to the root level of the iPod, they won't appear in Anapod Explorer unless you copy them to this specific folder.

The program tosses a few additional helpful entries into this list. You'll find a Search entry that allows you to conduct simple and advanced searches (the difference being that Simple Search allows you to search by one criterion, and Advanced Search lets you gang together multiple criteria—album, artist, and genre, for example—to find the music you seek.

You'll also find a Last Transfer entry, which provides details on the music files you last transferred to your iPod, as well as a Device Information entry, which reveals such arcane details as your iPod's hardware, firmware, and driver version.

If you click the small plus sign (+) that appears next to the Anapod Explorer entry in the left column, you can easily browse the contents of any of the entries within it by clicking that entry. The contents of that entry—the albums on your iPod when you click the Album entry, for example—are revealed in the right column. Use the + buttons in the left column or double-click an item in the right column to reveal that item's contents—the songs on an album, for example (**Figure 5.27**).

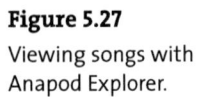

**Figure 5.27**

Viewing songs with Anapod Explorer.

Arrayed across the top-right side of the Anapod Explorer window are buttons that take you to some of these destinations more quickly. Here, you'll find a Top Level button that displays Anapod Explorer's default view, an Audio Tracks button that displays all the songs on your iPod in a long list, a Search button that reveals the program's Search view, and a Playlists button that shows you all the playlists on your iPod.

## Transferring music with Anapod Explorer

Moving music into Anapod Explorer is easy. If you're the drag-and-drop type, simply drag a music file or folder full of music to the Anapod Explorer entry in the left column. The program will copy the music to your iPod. If you've copied a folder full of music to the iPod, Anapod Explorer will offer to create a playlist from that folder, giving the playlist the name of the host folder.

If you prefer to move a mass of music at once—and have Anapod Explorer scour your computer for all the music on it at the same time—follow these steps:

1. Click the Anapod Options button at the top of the window.

2. In the resulting Anapod Explorer Options window, click the Speed Sync entry below the iPod entry.

3. Click the Add Folder button, and navigate to the directory where you'd like Anapod Explorer to look for music (your My Music folder, for example, or, if you want to find all the music on your PC, your C drive).

4. Click OK to dismiss this window, and click the Sync button at the top of the Anapod Explorer window.

5. In the resulting SpeedSync window, click the Begin Comparison button.

    Anapod Explorer will root around in the directory you designated, looking for music that isn't currently stored on your iPod. When it finishes, the "PC Files Not on iPod" tab lists all the music it finds that isn't on your iPod.

**6.** Enable the Transfer These Files to Your Player option, and click the Synchronize button (**Figure 5.28**).

The music from the PC will be copied to the iPod.

**Figure 5.28**
Transferring masses of music to your iPod with Anapod Explorer.

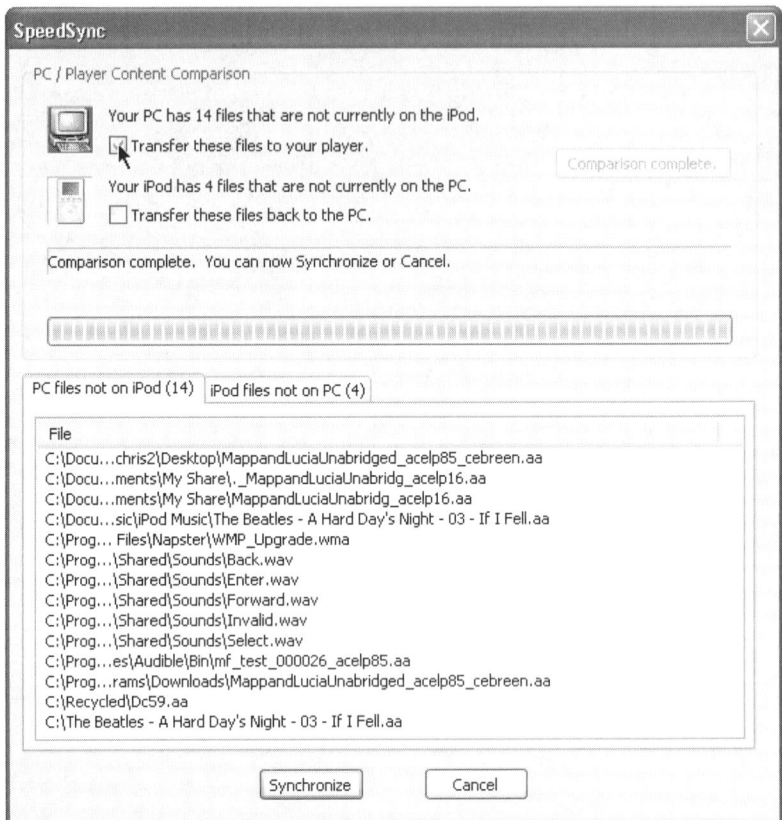

If you've been following along in Anapod Explorer while you read these pages, you've undoubtedly noticed that some entries within the Anapod Explorer Options and SpeedSync windows hint at greater things—specifically, that the program is more than willing to copy files on the iPod to the PC. It works this way:

**1.** Repeat steps 1 and 2 above.

2. In the PC Target Folder area of the SpeedSync area of the Anapod Explorer Options window, enter a path to a folder where you'd like to store music copied from the iPod (such as C:\Documents and Settings\chris\My Documents\My Music\iPod Music).

3. Click OK to dismiss this window, and click the Sync button at the top of the Anapod Explorer window.

4. In the resulting SpeedSync window, click the Begin Comparison button.

5. Enable the Transfer These Files Back to the PC option, and click Synchronize.

Those files on your iPod that aren't stored on your PC's hard drive will be copied to the folder that you designated in Step 2.

 Alternatively, you can right-click items on the iPod from within Anapod Explorer—a playlist or album, for example—and choose Copy to Computer to copy the selected item to your PC.

## Complete Conversion

Anapod Explorer includes an AudioMorph feature that, with near transparency, converts files that are incompatible with the iPod—.wma, FLAC, and Ogg Vorbis, for example—to something the iPod can digest without altering the original file on your PC. AudioMorph can also convert the bit rate of a file during transfer—changing MP3 files encoded at 256 Kbps to 160 Kbps, thereby allowing you to put more files on your iPod.

I say "near" transparency because this works only with files for which you have a suitable plug-in. You can find compatible plug-ins by clicking Anapod Options, clicking the AudioMorph entry in the resulting window, and clicking the Help and More Plugins button. Doing so takes you to Red Chair's Web site, which contains links to suitable plug-ins. As with XPlay, I'm disappointed that Red Chair didn't include plug-ins for converting common file types (.wma to MP3, for example).

## Playing music with Anapod Explorer

As with Windows Explorer, much of the power of Anapod Explorer is hidden in its contextual menus, such as a method of playing the tunes on your iPod when it's connected to your PC. To do so, right-click an appropriate entry—a song, album, artist, genre, or playlist, for example—and choose Play Track (or Play These Tracks, if the item contains multiple tracks) from the contextual menu. Music will play through the PC's default music player.

To force the files to play in a different player—Windows Media Player if you want to play MP3 files, for example—simply right-click an item, choose Play Track (or Play These Tracks) from the contextual menu, and select Choose Playback Software from the submenu. In the Anapod Explorer Options window that appears, choose an application from the window's Playback Software pop-up menu. If the application you want to use doesn't appear in this pop-up menu, click the Register Application button, navigate to the application you desire, and click Open.

## Other Anapod Explorer tricks

Despite its understated interface, Anapod Explorer has a lot going on under the surface. Here are a few of the highlights:

### *Anapod Xtreamer*

If you've dutifully read this book from page 1, you understand that iTunes allows you to listen to music stored on computers running on the same local network. Anapod Explorer offers a similar capability—with a twist. With a feature called Anapod Xtreamer, you can listen to the music stored on an iPod that's connected to a computer on a network.

When you choose Browse Anapod Xtreamer from the Anapod Explorer icon in the System Tray, your PC's default browser launches to reveal a Web page representing the musical contents of the iPod connected to your PC—including entries for All Tracks, Search, Playlists, Artist, Albums, and Genres. Click the link associated with one of these entries, and the contents of that entry are displayed on a subsequent page. From there, you can click the Stream All Tracks in This Folder link to play all the tracks in that folder, or click the STR entry next to an individual track for that track to stream to your default music player and play (**Figure 5.29**).

**Figure 5.29**
Anapod Xtreamer's browser view.

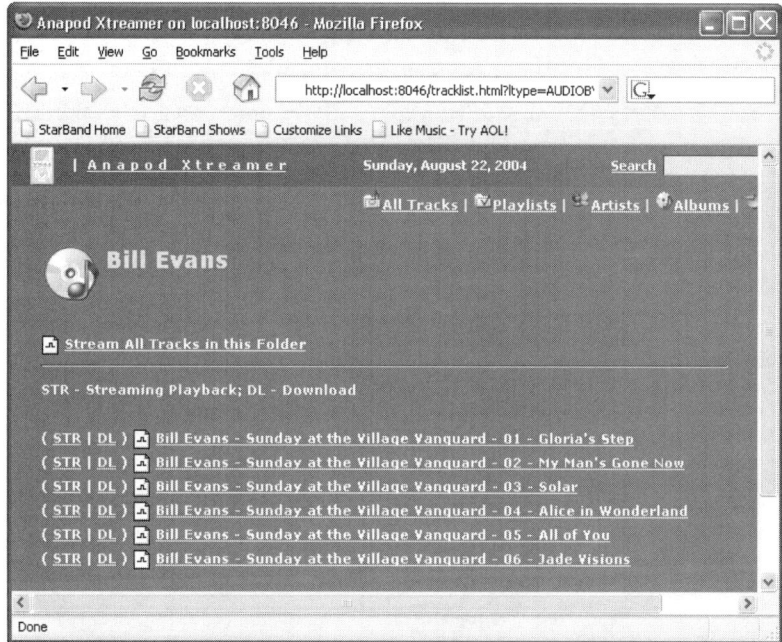

Should you want to download a track from the iPod to your PC in this view, just click the DL link next to a track. The track will download from the iPod to your PC just as though it were a Web-based file.

"But wait a minute," your interior voice interrupts, "if I can access my iPod via a browser, what's to keep someone who knows my IP address from also accessing—and possibly downloading—the music on my iPod?"

Nothing, except your skill at setting up a firewall.

Although Anapod Xtreamer was created so you can stream music from an iPod across a local network, let's not kid ourselves. If you have a static IP address, an always-on broadband connection to the Internet, and the will to do so, you can allow the rest of the world to listen to the music on your iPod (and grab the tunes on it).

It doesn't take a great legal mind to know that using Anapod Xtreamer in this way is anything but kosher. So don't.

### File recovery

You may know that when you toss a file into the Recycle Bin and empty the bin, the file isn't really wiped from your computer's hard drive. Rather, the database that keeps track of these kinds of things makes a note that the hard drive sectors occupied by that file may now be written to. Similarly, when an application such as iTunes or Anapod Explorer replaces one music library with another—as is the case when an iPod is associated with one computer and then automatically synchronized with another—the music files supposedly vaporized from your iPod may still be on it.

Anapod Explorer includes a feature that may allow you to recover such files. To access it, right-click the Anapod Explorer System Tray icon, and select Anapod Manager Options. Click the iPod Devices link; then click the Recover Missing Tracks button. Anapod Explorer scours the hidden folder on the iPod that holds the device's music and attempts to recover any that aren't currently recognized as part of the iPod's current roster of tunes. You'll find a list of these recovered tunes when you click the Last Transfer entry.

### And more...

Anapod Explorer lets you do a load more stuff: adjust track volume, transfer items quickly from one playlist to another, create playlists similar to iTunes Smart Playlists (though not as smart as Apple's offering), and create contacts within the application. If it's not abundantly clear by now, I'm pretty fond of this program. If you're a Windows user who's interested in an alternative to iTunes, Anapod Explorer is worth a long look.

## EphPod 2

Joe Masters' EphPod 2 is a free application that allows you to manage the music on your iPod. Like Musicmatch Jukebox, it lets you move files to the iPod from Windows, launch songs in the designated media player (iTunes, Windows Media Player, or Musicmatch Jukebox, for example), and create contacts and calendar events. EphPod uses a spreadsheet-style columned interface to represent the layers of the iPod, rather than XPlay's folders. Unlike XPlay, EphPod does most of the work internally, rather than through Windows Explorer or Windows Media Player. Also, unlike Musicmatch Jukebox, EphPod lets you copy unencrypted AAC files from your PC's hard drive to the iPod. (EphPod, like XPlay, doesn't support copying the encrypted AAC files available from the iTunes Music Store to your iPod. Anapod Explorer will allow you to play these files if your computer has been authorized by iTunes.)

## Setting up EphPod

EphPod requires that your PC be running Windows 98SE, Me, NT, 2000, or XP. If you're running Windows 98SE, you may want to search for upgraded FireWire drivers or upgrade your version of Windows before you start.

Also, EphPod works perfectly well with an iPod formatted for Windows. But if you'd like it to work with a Macintosh iPod (the purpose for which it was designed), you need to install an application that allows the PC to "see" the Mac iPod.

XPlay uses Mediafour's own MacDrive for this purpose—and EphPod can, too—but EphPod's creator has had better success with DataViz's $40 MacOpener. Mr. Masters offers a version of EphPod that contains a 15-day trial version of MacOpener so that you can try it for yourself. You can find this version at www.ephpod.com/download.html.

Then follow these steps to make EphPod work for you:

**1.** Install EphPod.

**2.** Connect your iPod to the PC with a FireWire or USB 2.0 cable.

**3.** Launch EphPod.

The EphPod Installation Wizard starts. You don't have much to do other than click a Next button if your iPod is attached and recognized by the PC. (You can tell that the iPod is recognized if it appears as a removable drive.) During the setup process, EphPod creates a database of all the songs, playlists, artists, and albums on your iPod's hard drive.

## Why Use a Third-Party Application?

Given that iTunes (or Musicmatch Jukebox, with older iPods) is included with the iPod, and considering that Macintosh iPod owners can easily use the Windows software on the iPod CD to convert their iPods to Windows-compatible devices, why bother with XPlay, Anapod Explorer, or EphPod?

If you're a Mac iPod user looking for a way to use your iPod on a PC without reformatting the iPod's hard drive, XPlay is an attractive option. Unlike EphPod, XPlay includes the software necessary for a Windows PC to mount and use a Mac iPod. Mac iPod owners must purchase a separate utility (at $10 more than the price of XPlay) to use their iPods with EphPod. And XPlay now supports the iPod's EQ features and lets you copy music files from the iPod to your PC easily.

Longtime Windows users are likely to be attracted by Anapod Explorer's interface; nothing else out there resembles Windows Explorer so closely. Those who are looking for powerful ways to move music from PC to iPod (and back again) will be pleased by what Anapod Explorer has to offer. And if you'd like to serve up the contents of your iPod to those on your network (or across the world), Anapod Xtreamer makes it darned easy to do so.

EphPod is an enticing alternative for those whose iPods are already formatted for Windows, not only because it's free, but also because of all the things it can do that iTunes and Musicmatch Jukebox can't: create contacts, edit calendars, download news stories, and copy songs from the iPod to your PC's hard drive.

### Using EphPod

EphPod's interface is similar to Windows Explorer (**Figure 5.30**). The top half of the EphPod window—called iPod View—is divided into panes that represent navigation layers on the iPod. The bottom half of the window—called Songs—lists songs. Navigating EphPod is a simple matter of choosing entries in the iPod View section, selecting subentries in the second and third panes, and then selecting songs in the song list in the bottom half of the window.

**Figure 5.30**
EphPod's interface.

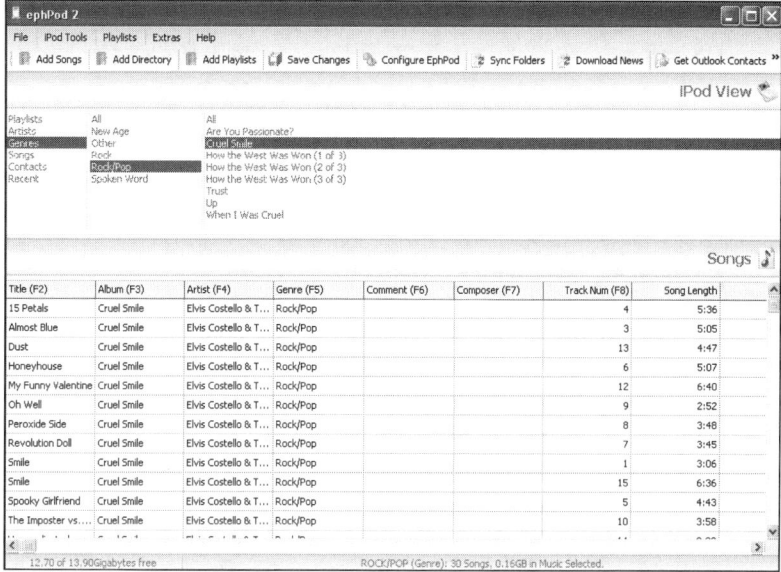

In the first pane at the top of the window, you'll find Playlists, Artists, Genres, Songs, Contacts, and Recent. These entries work this way:

- Click the Playlists entry, and the playlists on your iPod appear in the second column. Click a playlist, and the songs in the playlist appear in the third column. Double-click a title in the third column, and the song list scrolls to the point where that song appears at the top of the song list.

- Click the Artists entry in the first column, and the second column reveals all the artists on your iPod in the second column. Click an artist, and that artist's albums appear in the third column. Click the All entry in the second column, and all the albums on your iPod appear in the third column. Click an album in the third column, and all the songs on that album appear in the song list.

- Click the Genres entry in the first column, and the second column displays a list of the styles of music—rock, jazz, and classical, for example—on your iPod. EphPod gets this information from each song's ID3 tag information.

## File Ripping and Windows

One feature that XPlay, Anapod Explorer, and EphPod don't have is the capability to rip music files from audio discs. Fortunately, this feature isn't necessary, because you have a copy of iTunes or Musicmatch Jukebox. But you Mac users who are reading this chapter in the hope of using your Mac iPods with Windows are in for a slight shock when you attempt to rip an audio CD with Windows Media Player.

Yes, you can shove an audio CD into your PC and ask Windows Media Player to extract the audio files from that CD; the application will oblige. Regrettably for you as an iPod owner, however, the form that those extracted files take is not compatible with your iPod. Windows Media Player encodes files in a format that's friendly only to Windows Media Player. If you try to copy such files to your iPod, you'll receive an error message indicating that the iPod can accept only MP3, AIFF, and WAV files.

If you want to extract audio files from a CD in a format that the iPod *can* understand, you'll have to use iTunes, Musicmatch Jukebox, or a utility such as the free Audiograbber (www.audiograbber.com-us.net).

- Click the Songs entry in the first column, and all the songs on the iPod appear in the song list. You can sort songs by several criteria, including Title, Artist, Album, Genre, Comment, Track Number, Song Length, Encoding (the song's bit rate), File Type (MPEG, AIFF, or WAV), File Date, File Size, File Name (the path to the file), and Song ID (the number assigned to the song in EphPod's database).

- Click the Contacts entry, and the subject headings for all your contacts appear in the second column. If you double-click a contact, the Contact Information window appears. You can edit that information in this window.

To play a song in EphPod, double-click its title in the song list to launch the default media player and play the song. To load all the songs in a playlist into the default media player (**Figure 5.31**), right-click a playlist, and choose Play Playlist from the resulting contextual menu (**Figure 5.32**).

**Figure 5.31**
A playlist in Windows Media Player.

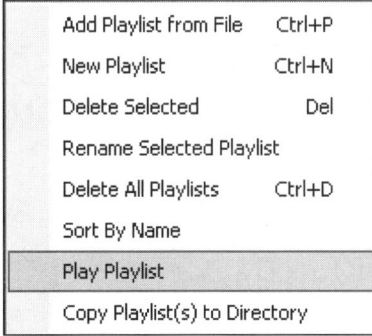

**Figure 5.32**
Right-click a playlist to play all the songs in the default media player.

## Transferring music with EphPod

EphPod helps you move audio files on and off the iPod. Here's how to do so:

**1.** Click the Add Songs button in EphPod's toolbar, or choose Add Songs from EphPod's File menu (**Figure 5.33**).

**Figure 5.33**
EphPod's Add Songs command.

The Select Songs dialog box opens.

**2.** Navigate to a folder that contains MP3 or AAC files you'd like to add to your iPod.

Note that EphPod doesn't allow you to add AIFF files to the iPod, but it does support WAV files. Also unlike Musicmatch Jukebox, it supports Audible.com files.

**3.** Control-click to select more than one file, and click Open.

The Writing Songs window appears, displaying the progress of the copy (**Figure 5.34**). This window disappears when the copy is complete.

**Figure 5.34**
Making progress.

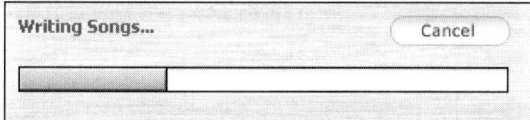

Alternatively, you can choose the Add Songs From Directory command from the File menu and add songs through a Windows Explorer interface.

## Using EphPod's other options

EphPod has its own unique features, including these:

- **Contact creation**. As this book goes to press, not even iTunes can do this. For more information on how to create contacts in EphPod, see Chapter 7.

- **Calendar Editor**. EphPod includes a feature for editing vCalendar files on your iPod. For more information on this feature and other calendar-related iPod functions, see Chapter 8.

- **Memo creation**. This is another not-yet-done-in-iTunes feature. Choose New Memo (As Contact) from the File menu, and a window appears where you can put down your most personal thoughts (or, perhaps, your grocery list). For those who are interested in such things, EphPod places your memo in the vCard's Title field.

- **The option to create playlists from a variety of sources**. From the Playlists menu, you can create playlists based on album title, genre, all songs, or orphan songs (songs that aren't associated with a particular album).

- **Copy Songs to Directory**. Then there's a feature guaranteed to pique the interest of those on both sides of the music-piracy fence. When you right-click a song or group of selected songs in the song list, you'll see the Copy Songs to Directory command in the resulting contextual menu (**Figure 5.35**). When you invoke this command, you can copy files from the iPod to the PC. If you chose to, you could take your iPod to a PC-packing friend's house and copy songs from your iPod to your friend's PC. This practice would go against Apple's "Don't steal music" admonition, however.

**Figure 5.35**
EphPod allows you to copy songs from your iPod to your PC.

| Edit Tag | Ctrl+I |
|---|---|
| Set Start Time | Ctrl+Alt+S |
| Play Song | |
| Adjust MP3 Volume | |
| Select All Songs | Ctrl+A |
| Deselect | Ctrl+D |
| Add Song | |
| Delete Selected | Del |
| Add Selected Songs to Playlist | Ins |
| Make Playlist from Selected | |
| Copy Songs to Directory | |
| Make Playlist from Album | |
| Make Playlist from Genre | |

- **News service**. New to EphPod is the capability to download news stories from such sources as BBC World News, CNET News.com, and SlashDot (**Figure 5.36**). You can also download local weather forecasts. To configure such downloads, choose Configuration from the Extras menu, and click the Download Options tab in the resulting dialog box.

**Figure 5.36**

EphPod's news-service option.

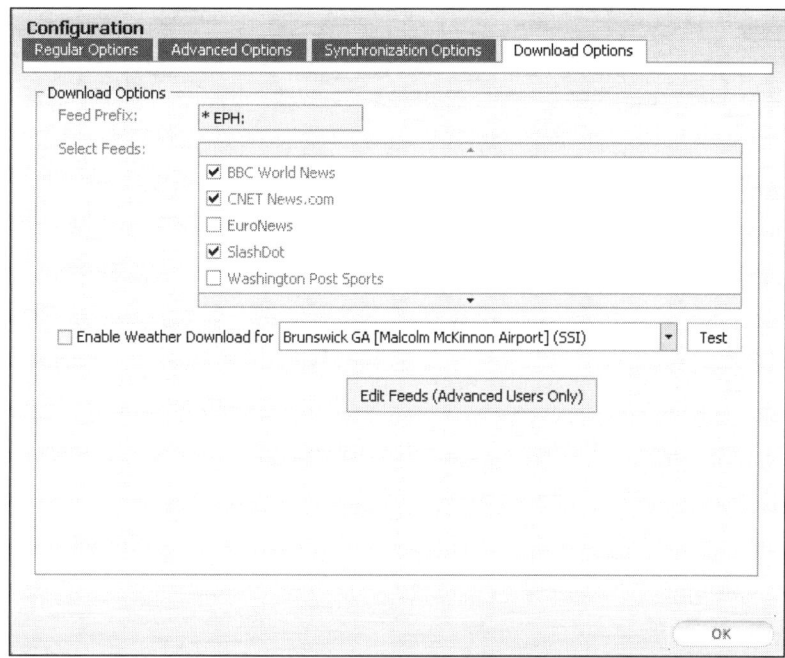

## Purchased Music Alternatives

Speaking of alternatives, it's no secret that there are commercial online music outlets other than the iTunes Music Store. Napster, Real Networks, and Musicmatch are following Apple's lead by selling songs for 99 cents and most albums for just under $10. As we go to press, Microsoft has launched a beta version of its MSN Music Service as well. Mac users are barred from these services (Napster won't even allow a Mac browser to access its site) because their computers can't play files encoded in the protected .wma format that these services employ.

I presume that because you're reading this chapter, you're a Windows user. And because you are, you can frequent these sites and purchase the music they offer. Yet because the files sold by these sites are in a format that's incompatible with the iPod, are they worth your while?

Perhaps. Some offer selections that aren't available at the iTunes Music Store, and all of them—after you've slogged through their impotent interfaces—will make you appreciate the iTunes Music Store that much more on your next visit.

*continues on next page*

## Purchased Music Alternatives *(continued)*

To play the music you purchase from these sites on your iPod, you must convert it. This is easier said than done, because .wma files are protected (as are the AAC files sold by the iTunes Music Store), so direct conversion with a player such as Windows Media Player is out.

The trick is to purchase the music, burn it to CD (where the files are converted to a format that's friendly to iTunes and the iPod), and then rip that CD in iTunes in either AAC or MP3 format. Sure, you'll lose a bit of the quality of the original file, because you've converted it from a compressed file to an uncompressed file and then smushed it again with a different compressor (.wma to AIFF to AAC), but currently, that's the only way to go about it.

# The Removable Drive

6

Given the praise heaped upon the iPod for its musical capabilities, it's easy to overlook the fact that it's more than a music player equipped with a hard drive. The iPod is also a capable FireWire/USB 2.0 drive that happens to play music. This distinction may not seem terribly important until the day you're sitting in front of an Apple PowerBook whose hard drive has suddenly gone south while your co-workers—many of whom have flown in from overseas—anxiously await the now-vanished PowerPoint presentation you slaved over for the past six weeks.

If you'd set aside a portion of your white iPod for a system capable of booting your Mac and a teensy bit more room for a copy of PowerPoint and that presentation, what could have been a disaster would turn into an opportunity to demonstrate why you're more deserving of an executive parking space than that schlep Henderson, who smells of garlic and routinely pinches your yogurt from the office mini-fridge.

And although Windows users can't boot their PCs from an iPod, the iPod can still serve as a useful backup and storage solution for those who are not running the Mac OS.

In this chapter, I'll show you how the iPod operates as an external storage device, how you can exploit it in this regard, and—yes—how to move music off your iPod and onto all the computers you own (as well as discuss the moral ramifications of doing so).

## FireWire to Go

When Apple introduced its fast serial input/output technology, FireWire, it didn't do so by hailing the benefits of this technology as they might relate to video and audio applications. Rather, Steve Jobs demonstrated FireWire by plugging a small hard drive into a Mac. What's the big deal?

To begin with, the hard drive wasn't powered. Second, the Mac was.

Again, *what's the big deal?*

Before this, external hard drives—most of which used the Small Computer System Interface (SCSI) technology—had to be plugged into an electrical source. And the computer intended for use with this SCSI drive had to be powered off when you plugged the SCSI device into it. Otherwise, you possibly were in for a heap of trouble—trouble that might include a corrupted hard drive or a fried motherboard on your computer.

This FireWire stuff was remarkable because it could pull power from the device it was plugged into via the FireWire cable, and you could plug and unplug devices with the drive and computer switched on—a process known as *hot swapping*.

This trip down memory lane serves to explain that because the iPod is, in essence, a FireWire drive with a few components thrown in (OK, *elegantly* thrown in) to make it play music, it operates in a similar fashion to any other FireWire drive. Just like some other FireWire drives, the iPod doesn't require external power when it's plugged into a computer. Just like other FireWire drives, an iPod can be plugged into a running computer, and (if you've configured the iPod to mount as a FireWire drive, as I suggested in Chapters 2 and 5) you have a reasonable expectation that its icon will appear shortly on your Mac's Desktop or within Windows' My Computer window.

With the release of the third generation of iPods, the iPod became both a FireWire *and* a USB 2.0 drive. This USB 2.0 functionality is a boon to both Mac and Windows PC users. Mac users with late-model Macs (that sport a USB 2.0 port) can mount and charge a fourth-generation iPod, iPod Photo, and iPod mini via a USB 2.0 connection just as they can with FireWire—thus freeing the Mac's FireWire ports for other devices. (A third-generation iPod can be mounted via USB 2.0 but not charged.) Windows PC users will appreciate support for USB 2.0 because they're more likely to find a USB 2.0 connector on their computers than a FireWire port.

Regrettably, USB 2.0 can't work miracles. As I mentioned earlier, the iPod can't be used to boot a PC. This is a limitation of the Windows operating system, not of the iPod, so if you feel shortchanged as a Windows user, please direct any testy letters to Redmond rather than to Cupertino. Because the iPod can't boot a PC, my Windows readers may feel a little left out in the early part of the chapter. For this, I apologize, but I promise to deliver a few Windows-centric tips later in the proceedings.

Some iPods can, however, boot a Mac—meaning that the hard drive inside the iPod can start up your Mac if your Mac supports being booted from a FireWire drive. (The Blue & White Power Mac G3 and Power Mac G4 [PCI Graphics] don't support FireWire booting.) This feat may not seem so remarkable until you try the same trick with another FireWire drive that doesn't support booting.

You'll notice my careful use of the word "some" in the previous paragraph. By that I mean that all four generations of the white iPod, the iPod Special Edition: U2, and the iPod Photo will boot a Mac, but an iPod mini won't. Although installation of Mac OS X 10.3 seems to go successfully, the iPod mini refuses to boot. For this reason, any reference in the following pages to installing a bootable operating system on an iPod refers only to standard-issue iPods, not the iPod mini.

There's no trick to getting a white iPod to boot your Mac, however. Plug it in, designate the iPod as the startup device, and restart your computer. The trick is installing a bootable operating system on the iPod. With

Mac OS 9, this is no big deal unless you have a Mac made in the past couple of years; no Macs sold today can boot into Mac OS 9. If you want to boot your newish Mac from an iPod, you must install Mac OS X on that iPod. On earlier Macs, Mac OS 9 installs as you'd expect.

In early versions of Mac OS X, this process was also nearly painless (as it is with Mac OS X 10.3, Panther). But installing Mac OS X 10.2 (Jaguar) on an iPod is a bit more challenging (though not impossible). In the next few pages, I'll show you how to place each of these operating systems on your iPod and, when they're in place, how to boot into them.

## The Low-Capacity iPod

Those Mac users who own an early iPod—a 5 GB model, for example—are undoubtedly jotting numbers in the margins as they read this chapter.

"Let's see, a full installation of Mac OS X 10.3 requires about 3 GB of hard drive space. My iPod holds approximately 4.6 GB of data. If I subtract 3 from 4.6, just how crazy would I have to be to install the Mac OS on an iPod with this kind of limited storage capacity?"

The answer: a little bit.

There are things you can do during the installation of Mac OS X to slim down the system. For example, you can click the Installer's Customize button when it makes itself known, and choose to not install such applications as Internet Explorer and the various components of the iLife suite (iMovie, iPhoto, iTunes, iDVD, and GarageBand). You can also uncheck the options to install additional printer drivers, fonts, text-to-speech voices, and language files. Doing all this creates an installation that consumes about 1.1 GB of space.

But honestly, if you wanted a music player that stored only a couple of gigabytes of songs, you could have saved yourself a lot of money and purchased a less-expensive player (or replaced your old iPod with an iPod mini). Because Mac OS X does take up so much room, it doesn't make a lot of sense to create a bootable 5 GB iPod with the intent of keeping it in this state forevermore.

In a pinch, however, it could make a lot of sense. When I speak at computer conferences, I often create a bootable iPod that duplicates the essential elements of the startup drive on my Mac at home. Or if I need to troubleshoot a client's Mac, it's often easier to create a bootable iPod that also contains my troubleshooting tools than to try to perform the operation with a PowerBook and a load of disc-based troubleshooting utilities.

# Installing the Mac OS on Your iPod

Placing Mac OS 9 and versions of Mac OS X before Mac OS X 10.2 on your iPod is remarkably similar to configuring any Mac's hard drive as a startup disk. To start, just plug your iPod into a Mac running either Mac OS 9 or Mac OS X.

If the iPod's icon doesn't appear on the Desktop, launch iTunes 2, 3, or 4; click the iPod in the Source list; click the iPod Preferences button at the bottom of the iTunes window; and select Enable Disk Use (called Enable FireWire Disk Use in older versions of iTunes) in the resulting iPod Preferences window. Then quit iTunes.

Insert a Mac OS installation disc into your Mac's CD/DVD drive. Note that a Software Restore CD won't allow you to install a copy of the Mac OS on your iPod. You must have a separate installer disc, such as the Mac OS 9 or Mac OS X 10.1.x installation disc.

Now I'll show you the steps for installing Mac OS 9 and Mac OS X 10.1.x.

Throughout this section, I refer to Mac OS X 10.1.x. I do this to distinguish this earlier version of Mac OS X from the later 10.2.x (Jaguar release) and Mac OS X 10.3 (Panther release). Any time I refer to Mac OS X 10.1.x, you can assume that I'm also referring to earlier versions of Mac OS X. I specifically mention 10.1.x because, quite frankly, any earlier versions of Mac OS X were pretty marginal. If you haven't upgraded Mac OS X to at least 10.1, you should, and quite honestly, you'll find your Mac is far more functional with even more recent versions of the Mac OS.

## Installing Mac OS 9

Just follow these steps to install Mac OS 9 on your iPod:

1. Insert the Mac OS 9 CD, and choose Restart from the Special menu.

2. As soon as you hear the Mac's startup sound, press and hold down the keyboard's C key.

3. When you see the happy Mac face, let go of the C key.

   Now the Mac is booting from the CD-ROM you inserted. The CD window should open, revealing the Mac OS Install application.

4. Double-click this application to launch the installer.

5. Click the Continue button in the resulting Welcome screen.

6. In the Destination screen that appears next, choose your iPod from the Destination Disk pop-up menu (**Figure 6.1**); then click Select.

**Figure 6.1**
Select your iPod in the Mac OS 9 Installer's Destination screen.

7. Click through the Important Information and License Agreement screens after reading every word in them carefully.

   I'm kidding. No one reads these things. But agree to the license agreement, because if you don't, the installer quits, and then where are you?

8. Click Start in the Install Macintosh Software screen to begin the installation (**Figure 6.2**).

**Figure 6.2**
Click Start to begin the installation.

9. Go have a cup of coffee; the installation takes a while (**Figure 6.3**).

**Figure 6.3**
Sixteen minutes is plenty of time to get a cup of coffee while your Mac creates an iPod you can boot from.

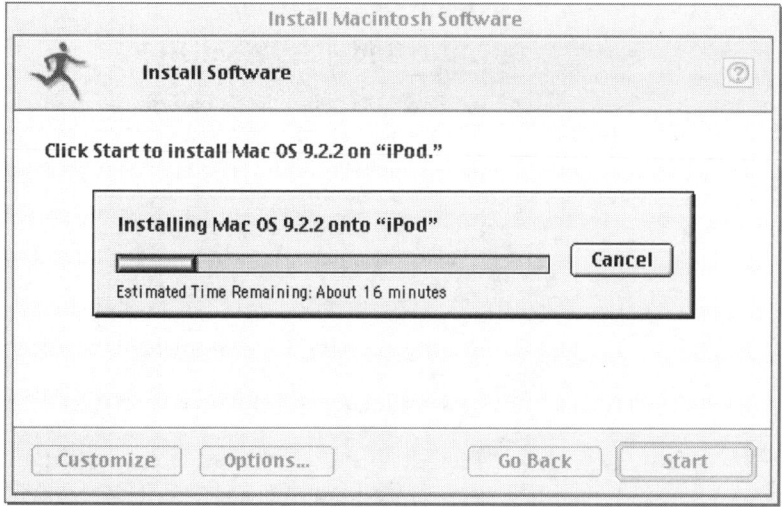

10. When the installer is finished, click Quit.

11. Choose Control Panels and then Startup Disk from the Apple menu.

    Your iPod appears as one of the startup-disk choices (**Figure 6.4**).

**Figure 6.4**
The Mac OS, cozily tucked away on your iPod.

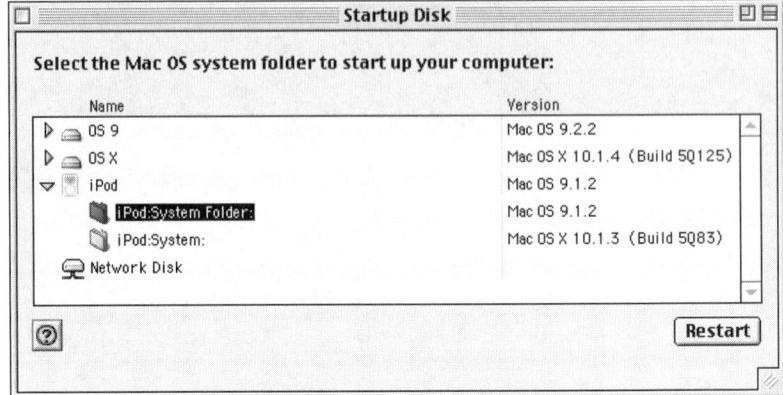

12. Click the iPod; then click the Restart button to boot from your iPod.

## Installing Mac OS X 10.1.x

And to install Mac OS X 10.1.x on your iPod, follow these instructions:

1. Insert the Mac OS X Installer disc.

2. Either restart your Mac and hold down the C key to boot from the Installer disc or double-click the Install Mac OS X application on the CD.

3. Click the Restart button in the resulting Install Mac OS X window.

    The Mac will restart and boot from the OS X Installer disc.

4. When the installer appears, select the language you'd like your Mac to use, and click Continue.

5. In the Welcome screen, click Continue again.

6. Click through the Important Information and License Agreement screens after memorizing every word in them (yeah, right...).

Agree to the license agreement because if you don't...well, you know.

7. In the Select a Destination screen, select your iPod, and click Continue.

In this screen, you'll see the option to erase your hard drive and format it as either a Mac OS Extended or a Unix File System volume. Do not select this option. It will not only erase every bit of information on your drive (including all the songs on your iPod), but also may cause your iPod to stop working until you reset it with the iMac Software Updater. (See Chapter 10 for information on troubleshooting your iPod.)

8. In the next Easy Install screen, specify whether you want to proceed with the installation as is or perform a customized installation.

Because you want both a bootable iPod and one on which you can store as much music as possible, click the Customize button.

9. In the Custom Install screen that results, select only the language options that you're likely to use.

These languages take up space on your iPod's hard drive that could be devoted to storing tunes.

10. Click Install, and go have two cups of coffee; this installation takes longer than the Mac OS 9 installation.

11. When the installation is complete, click Restart.

Don't worry if you're not around to click Restart; the Mac will restart on its own 30 seconds after the installation is complete. Your Mac will boot into Mac OS X 10.1.x from your iPod.

12. When the Mac reboots, go through the Mac OS X setup procedure.

When you finally get to the Desktop, Software Update will launch automatically. Mac OS X gets better with each update, and it's likely that a few updates are waiting for you.

13. If Software Update discovers updates, install them (**Figure 6.5**).

**Figure 6.5**
Software updates undoubtedly await you.

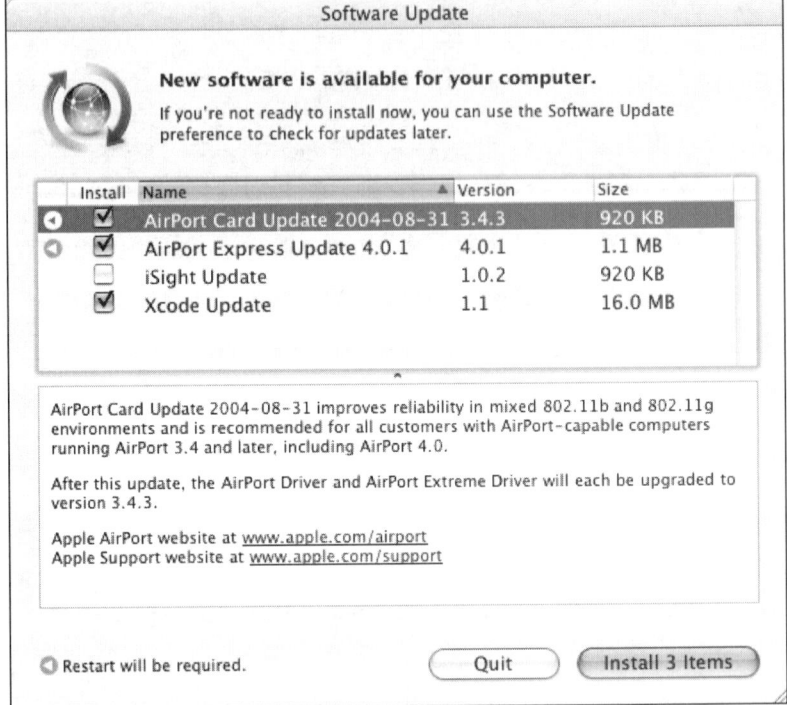

14. After the updates are installed, restart (if necessary), and run Software Update again.

Certain updates become available to System Update only when other updates are installed. This situation used to be a real inconvenience that required you to install—separately—one update after another. Apple has ganged groups of these updates into a single installation package, such as the Mac OS X Update Combo 10.1.5. But such dependent installations haven't disappeared completely—and who knows what the future might hold—so it's a good idea to run System Update a couple of times in a row to be sure that you've got all the latest updates.

Your iPod is ready to boot your Mac into Mac OS X 10.1.x.

# Installing Mac OS X 10.2.x (Jaguar)

A reader of the first edition of this book wrote in to say that even though he followed the instructions in the book, he was unable to install Mac OS X 10.2 on his iPod. What did I—"Mr. *Secrets of the iPod*," as he put it—have to say on the subject? Just this:

As you've observed, you cannot place a bootable copy of Mac OS X on your iPod by using the Mac OS X 10.2 installer. When I attempted to do so, the OS X installer got as far as installing the contents of the first installation disc (there are two installation discs in the commercial release of the OS), but the iPod refused to boot to allow the installation of the second disc.

Sometime later, I attempted to install Jaguar on an iPod from the installation DVD that accompanies a Dual 1.42 GHz Power Mac G4. Although the installation process completed, the iPod refused to boot beyond Jaguar's initial gray startup screen.

But because I am "Mr. *Secrets of the iPod*," allow me to let you in on this little secret: You can install a copy of Mac OS X 10.2.x on your iPod, and your iPod will boot from it. The trick is that you must move an existing copy of Mac OS X 10.2.x from your Mac's hard drive to the iPod. To do this, I use Mike Bombich's $5 Carbon Copy Cloner (www.bombich.com/software/ccc.html)—a utility that "clones" a Mac OS X installation from one volume to another and allows you to make that cloned volume bootable. Here's how to go about it:

1. With your iPod configured to mount on your Mac's Desktop, plug it into your Mac.

    The iPod's icon will appear on the Desktop (or, if Finder Preferences isn't configured to display hard drives on the Desktop, in the Computer window).

2. Download, install, and launch a copy of Carbon Copy Cloner.

    Version 1.4 and later versions are compatible with Mac OS X 10.2.x.

3. From the Source Disk pop-up menu in the Cloning Console window, choose a volume on your Mac that contains Mac OS X 10.1.2.x or higher. (As we go to press, the latest Jaguar-compatible version of Carbon Copy Cloner is 2.3.)

Although Carbon Copy Cloner allows you to select which items at the root level of your OS X volume to clone, it doesn't allow you to choose files and folders within those root-level items. In other words, you can't tell Carbon Copy Cloner to clone only one or two applications within the Applications folder. You either clone the entire Applications folder (and all its contents) or none of the Applications folder.

For this reason, it's a good idea to clone an OS X 10.2 volume that isn't packed with extra files and applications. Cloning a 12.4 GB OS X 10.2 volume to your 15 GB iPod will leave you precious little space for songs, contacts, and calendars.

4. Choose your iPod from the Target Disk pop-up menu.

5. In the Items to Be Copied list, Command-click the items that you don't want to clone to your iPod (**Figure 6.6**).

**Figure 6.6**

Use Carbon Copy Cloner to create a bootable iPod running Mac OS X 10.2.

Items that you should copy to create a bootable (and useful) startup disk include:

- .hidden
- Applications
- Library
- System
- Users
- bin
- mach_kernel
- private
- sbin
- usr

6. Click the Remove button (just above the Items to Be Copied list) to exclude the selected files from the cloning process.

7. Click the Preferences button, and in the resulting sheet, make sure that the Make Bootable option is selected, and click Save or Cancel to dismiss the sheet (**Figure 6.7**).

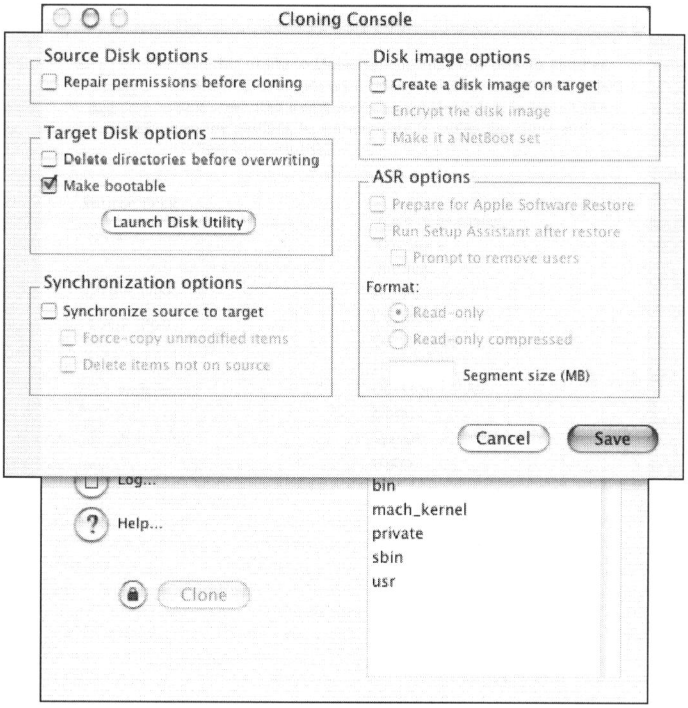

**Figure 6.7**

Make sure that Carbon Copy Cloner's Make Bootable option is enabled.

8. Click the Lock icon, and enter your administrator's password when you're requested to do so.

9. Click the Clone button to begin cloning the source volume to your iPod.

10. When the process is complete, quit Carbon Copy Cloner, choose System Preferences from the Apple menu, and click the Startup Disk system preference.

    Your iPod will appear in the list of bootable volumes.

11. Click the iPod's System folder; then click Restart to boot from your iPod.

## Installing Mac OS X 10.3.x (Panther)

I'm pleased to report that Apple did something to its Mac OS X 10.3 installer that lets you install Panther on an iPod without jumping through these hoops. With the Panther installer, the iPod behaves exactly like any other removable drive, and the installer does its job without a hitch.

To install Panther on your iPod, insert the first Panther disc; double-click the Install Mac OS X icon; wait for your Mac to boot; designate the iPod as the target for the installation; and click the Customize button to keep from installing unnecessary language, printer, and application files (and save yourself up to a gigabyte of space on the iPod).

### Why Create a Bootable iPod?

After reading the last few pages, you may wonder why you'd bother to install Mac OS 9 or Mac OS X (or both) on your iPod. The truth is, you may not need to. You may own the one Macintosh in the world that will never, ever suffer from hard-disk corruption, extension conflicts, and buggy software. For you, having a reliable bootup disk that contains all your troubleshooting utilities isn't necessary.

Or, your musical cravings may be so intense that if you can't cram in every minute of the 666.66 hours of music that the 40 GB iPod is capable of storing, you'll wind up with a bad case of the heebie-jeebies (or, worse yet, the jim-jams).

> ### Why Create a Bootable iPod? *(continued)*
>
> I'm not one of these people. Because I troubleshoot Macs for a living, I find the ability to store all the tools I need on such a portable, bootable hard drive to be a real benefit. And although I love music, I hardly find it limiting to store only 100 hours of music on my iPod. It's so easy to replace songs on the device with new material that when I get bored with my current selections, I spend a couple of hours transferring a different 100 CDs to my iPod, and my listening needs are met for the next couple of months.

## Additional Data Storage

Being able to boot your Macintosh from an iPod is a good first step, but it's only a first step. To make your iPod both bootable and useful, consider using its data-storage capabilities for the following purposes:

- **Macintosh: Installing your troubleshooting utilities.** The most important reason for making a bootable iPod is that it allows you to repair the hard drive that should be booting your Mac. If your Mac's hard drive is on the fritz and won't boot your Mac, it's a godsend to have another hard drive that can boot your Mac *and* that contains all your troubleshooting utilities. Currently, those utilities might include Disk Warrior from Alsoft (www.alsoft.com), a splendid tool for repairing low-level corruption; TechTool Pro from Micromat (www.micromat.com); Data Rescue from ProSoft Engineering (www.prosofteng.com); and Norton Utilities from Symantec (www.symantec.com).

- **Macintosh: Keeping the applications you need close at hand.** If it's your job to chair the next meeting, and you absolutely need a PowerPoint presentation to make that meeting a success, install both a copy of your presentation and a working copy of PowerPoint on your iPod.

- **Macintosh: Keeping the drivers and accessories you need close at hand.** Fat lot of good it does you to boot from your iPod, fire up your graphing application, and then not be able to print that all-important flow chart because your iPod doesn't have a copy of the driver that allows it to use the company printer.

- **Macintosh and PC: Keeping network settings, serial numbers, and passwords close at hand.** When you configure your iPod as an external drive, configure it fully. Nothing is more frustrating than being unable to get on the Internet because you neglected to configure your network settings. Likewise, it's all well and good that you've installed Applications X, Y, and Z on your iPod, but if you haven't run them and entered the serial numbers that allow them to function, you could be up a creek when you're on the road and don't have those serial numbers at hand.

- **Macintosh and PC: Taking your user folder with you.** Under Mac OS X and Windows XP, your user folder holds most of your computing life: your Documents folder, music files, pictures, movies, network settings, the works. If you keep a copy of your user folder on your iPod, copy that folder to a Mac running Mac OS X or a PC running Windows XP, create a new user on that computer, and copy the information from your user folder to that new user, you've got a configuration darned close to the computer at home or work.

- **Macintosh and PC: Keeping a backup of important documents.** If you're working on something that you absolutely can't afford to lose—the company's yearly financial statement, your term paper, or the digital movie of your daughter's second birthday—keep a backup copy on your iPod. It's also worthwhile to keep a backup of your Address Book data, emails you might need to refer to, and your Web-browser bookmarks.

It's not necessary to keep a copy of absolutely everything on your computer—just those few items that will make you tear your hair out if they're missing.

- **PC: Transferring your files and settings.** You can select the iPod as a destination for files and settings transferred with Windows XP's Files and Settings Transfer Wizard. (To access this wizard, open the Start menu and follow this path: All Programs > Accessories > System Tools > Files and Settings Transfer Wizard.)

  Just run the wizard, select the iPod as the destination disk, and let Windows copy your files and settings to the iPod. If you need to restore those files to your PC or transfer them to another PC, run the Files and Settings Transfer Wizard once again, select your iPod as the source disk, and copy the files to the PC.

### All iPod, All the Time?

Although you can boot your Mac from your iPod, does that mean that you always should?

No.

The iPod was designed as a music player—one whose diminutive hard drive wouldn't be asked to spin for days on end. When that drive rotates for long stretches of time—as it will when you boot from it—the iPod heats up. If you take a gander at your music player, you'll see that there's no way to vent that heat out of the iPod. Excessive heat plus hardware is usually a formula for disaster.

For this reason, I suggest that when you boot from your iPod, you do so for short periods of time—long enough to troubleshoot your Mac or get through a lecture or demonstration. When you've accomplished your task, boot from your Mac, and let the iPod carry on with its main job: rocking your world.

 Fun Fact. So if you boot from your iPod, does it behave both as a startup drive and as an iPod? In other words, can the iPod sync its calendars, contacts, and songs to itself?

Why, yes, it can. When you launch iTunes, the iPod transfers the songs in the iTunes Music folder to the area on your iPod where songs are stored. And just where, exactly, is that storage area? Read on.

# The Hidden Revealed: Song Storage on the iPod

If you mount your iPod as an external storage device and double-click its icon, you'll be surprised to find that it contains just a few folders: Contacts, Calendars, and (if you have a third- or fourth-generation iPod, iPod Photo, or iPod mini) Notes. You know that the iPod contains your entire library of Bill Frisell CDs, yet they're nowhere in sight. Has Apple created a stealth partition that stores only song data? Do the songs sit in some kind of temporary storage buffer and disappear when the battery drains? Is the iPod really some remarkable wireless receiving device that plays songs beamed from Apple's super-secret orbiting satellite?

No, no, and no.

Apple has done no more than create a scheme whereby the iPod's music files are placed in an invisible folder. Those music files sit right alongside the Contacts, Calendars, and Notes folders; you just can't see them.

Why would Apple do such a thing? Simple: to make it harder to copy files from your iPod to a Macintosh or PC.

And why would Apple want to discourage such a procedure? Because Apple doesn't want the iPod to facilitate the practice of sharing music illegally. Leaving these files out in the open could tempt people who would not otherwise pirate music, and it might leave Apple open to criticism (and lawsuits) from the stodgier elements of the entertainment industry.

If this is the case, why didn't Apple come up with some impossible-to-crack encryption system, rather than this invisibility scheme? I'll let Apple's CEO, Steve Jobs, answer that one:

"Piracy is not a technological issue. It's a behavior issue."

If I may be so bold as to interpret Mr. Jobs' words, I believe he's saying that no matter how secure the knot you tie is, someone will come along and untie it. And he's correct. Countless bright individuals take it as a personal challenge to outwit any copy-protection scheme that comes along. Those who are bent on piracy will always find a way to defeat any copy-protection scheme they encounter. And because copy-protection schemes *will* be defeated, companies that embrace copy protection risk creating an expensive and time-consuming cycle of devising protection schemes, waiting for them to be broken, devising new protection schemes, waiting for *them* to be broken, and on, and on, and on.

Apple decided that it didn't care to jump aboard this merry-go-round. Parties that have a greater stake in the game (the recording industry, for example) can spend their time and money on copy-protection schemes and Washington lobbyists. Apple was content to make sharing files difficult enough to discourage casual pirates and to include the words "Don't steal music" in iPod packaging and advertisements. Beyond that, it's up to the individual user to decide whether it's morally responsible to enjoy the work of others without paying for it.

Which brings us, of course, to this question:

# Music Sharing: Right or Wrong?

Excuse the rampant editorializing, but here are the issues surrounding music sharing as I see them. Feel free to agree or disagree, as the mood strikes you.

- Taking music that the owner would like you to pay for—whether by copying it from an iPod, duplicating someone's audio CD, or downloading the music from an illegal source on the Internet—is wrong. If you intend to keep the music, you should pay for it. Someone (or a group of someones) created that music with the intention of being rewarded for that toil in ways other than your undying admiration. If you respect an artist's work, you should also respect the artist's desire to be paid for that work.

Music that's intended to be shared—such as live concert performances, when the artists care not a whit whether you swap recordings with your friends—is a different matter.

- As a professional musician, I'm well aware that musicians have been sorely abused by the recording industry. Your mother was correct, however, when she suggested that two wrongs don't make a right. Striking back at the recording industry by denying artists their paltry royalties is no way to punish record executives. If you're concerned about the rights of recording artists, visit the Recording Artists Coalition Web site (www.recordingartistscoalition.com), and lobby your elected officials to enact legislation that protects artists' rights.

- As a consumer, I believe that it's my right to play music I own on any compatible device I own, as long as it's for my personal enjoyment. Currently, the law agrees. That means that if I have one iPod, four Macs, two PCs, one car stereo, two home stereos, a boom box, and a portable CD player, I may make copies of that music for each and every device I own and, if I feel so inclined, play that same recording on every one of these devices at the same time.

  By creating the iTunes Music Store, Apple agrees that I'm also allowed to play purchased music—in its raw form—on up to five computers. Given that I can easily burn purchased music to CD-R and play it on any CD player I like (including the CD drive in any of my computers), I can live with this very minor limitation.

Because I believe in the rights of both musicians and consumers, I will now reveal how to move the music you legally own from your iPod to any computer you also own. Music that you don't own shouldn't be on your iPod in the first place; neither should you take the music you own and dump it on your best friend's computer. Piracy is, indeed, a behavior issue. So please watch your behavior.

# Moving Music

The iPod stores music in an invisible folder called iPod_Control. This folder is located at the root level of your iPod's hard drive. If you're a do-it-yourselfer, you can make this folder and its contents visible and then drag the files from the iPod to your computer's hard drive. Alternatively, a variety of utilities for the Mac and PC give you access to this invisible folder and its contents. I'll show you both the manual and assisted methods in the following sections.

If you use one of these methods to transfer music from your iPod to your computer, you still won't be able to play music files you purchased from the iTunes Music Store that were on your iPod unless your computer is authorized to play those files. For more information on authorizing your computer, see Chapter 4.

## The manual method (Mac OS 9)

Download a utility that's capable of turning invisible files visible. For this example, I'll use Daniel Azuma's $10 FileTyper (http://dazuma.freeshell.org/filetyper), though a host of other utilities, including Apple's ResEdit, can do the job (**Figure 6.8**).

**Figure 6.8**
FileTyper reveals the hidden iPod_Control folder.

Then follow these steps:

1. While you're running Mac OS 9, launch FileTyper.

2. Choose Open from the File menu.

3. In the Open dialog box, navigate to the mounted iPod, and click Open.

4. Locate the iPod_Control folder, and click Select.

   Two windows will appear: one marked Folder Attribute Editor, and one marked File Attribute Editor.

5. If the Folder Attribute Editor is not active, click it.

   The entry in the first field in this window should read Device.

6. Click the Cancel button.

   Now the first field should read iPod_Control (**Figure 6.9**).

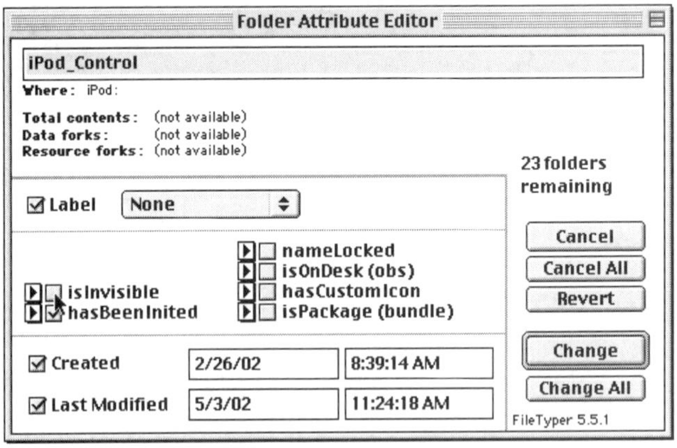

**Figure 6.9**
Uncheck the isInvisible check box and then click Change All to make the iPod_Control folder (and all folders within it) visible.

7. In this window, uncheck the check box titled isInvisible.

8. Click the Change All button.

9. When you're asked to confirm that you really want to do this, click OK.

   The Folder Attributes Editor window disappears, leaving the File Attributes Editor window open. This window has the word *Preferences* in the first field.

10. Click the Cancel All button.

11. Quit FileTyper.

12. Double-click the iPod's icon on the Desktop to open the iPod's hard drive.

   Inside, you'll see that the iPod_Control folder is visible (**Figure 6.10**). Inside this folder are two folders: iTunes and Music. The Music folder contains all your music files inside folders that begin with the letter *F*—F00, F01, F02, and F03, for example.

**Figure 6.10**
The hidden revealed.

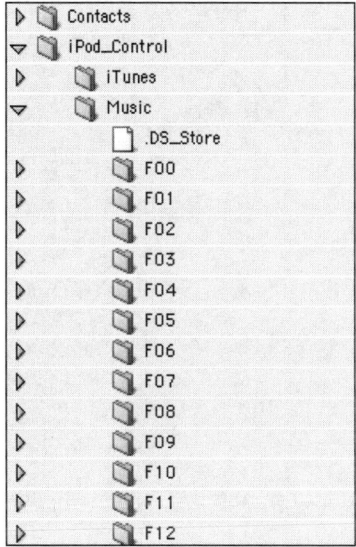

13. Use Sherlock to seek the songs you want to copy to your Mac.
14. To copy the songs, just open the appropriate folder and drag the files to your Mac's hard drive.

## The manual method (Mac OS X)

The process is even simpler in Mac OS X. Here's how:

1. Mount your iPod on the Desktop.
2. Download and install a copy of Marcel Bresink's free TinkerTool (www.bresink.com/osx/TinkerTool.html).
3. Launch TinkerTool.

4. In the Finder Options section of the Finder tab, check the Show Hidden and System Files check box (**Figure 6.11**).

**Figure 6.11**
In TinkerTool, select Show Hidden and System Files and then click the Relaunch Finder button to reveal the invisible files and folders on your iPod.

5. Click the Relaunch Finder button at the bottom of the dialog.

6. Move back to the Desktop, and double-click your iPod to open its hard drive.

   Inside, you'll see that the iPod_Control folder is visible.

7. Open this folder and then the Music folder within it.

   Inside this folder, you'll find your music files inside folders that begin with the letter *F*—F00, F01, F02, and F03, for example (**Figure 6.12**).

**Figure 6.12**
The hidden revealed (redux).

8. Use Mac OS X's Find feature to seek the songs you want to copy to your Mac.

9. To copy the songs, just open the appropriate folder and drag the files to your Mac's hard drive.

## The manual method (Windows XP)

Revealing the iPod's hidden song files is child's play under Windows XP. Here's how:

1. Mount your iPod on your PC.

2. Open the My Computer window, and double-click the iPod.

3. Choose Folder Options from the Tools menu to open the Folder Options dialog.

4. Click the View tab.

5. Below the Hidden Files and Folders entry, click Show Hidden Files and Folders (**Figure 6.13**).

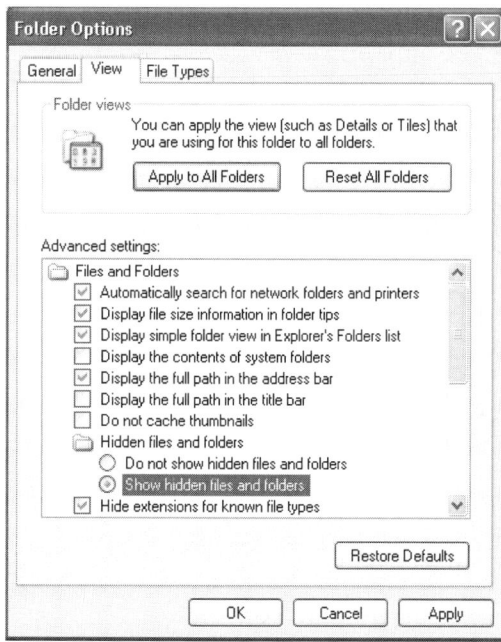

**Figure 6.13**
Select the Show Hidden Files and Folders option to reveal invisible items in Windows.

6. Click Apply.

   The iPod_Control folder is visible.

7. Open this folder and then the Music folder within it.

   Inside this folder, you'll find your music files inside folders that begin with the letter *F*—F00, F01, F02, and F03, for example (**Figure 6.14**).

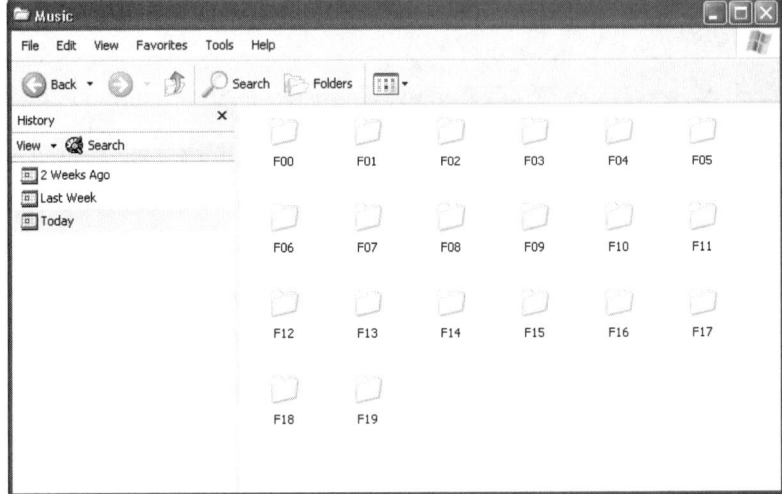

**Figure 6.14**
The return of the son of the hidden revealed (redux).

8. Click the Search button in the window's toolbar, and search your iPod for specific songs to copy to your PC's hard drive.

9. To copy the songs, just open the appropriate folder and drag the files to your PC's hard drive.

## The assisted methods

Go to VersionTracker (www.versiontracker.com), and enter iPod in the Search field. You'll turn up a fair number of utilities that can assist you with moving music files from your iPod onto your computer's hard drive. Here are some of my favorites.

- **Senuti** (Mac OS X)

  http://wbyoung.ambitiouslemon.com/senuti

Whitney Young's free Senuti offers a straightforward interface for moving music off your iPod. Like similar utilities, it allows you to select songs on the iPod and then copy them to a location of your choosing. Unlike with other utilities, you can copy not only single songs and songs grouped by artist and album, but also complete playlists from the iPod (**Figure 6.15**).

**Figure 6.15**
Senuti lets you copy songs within your iPod's playlists.

This solves a tricky problem that has plagued some iTunes users. Suppose that you lost your computer's entire iTunes library. You could recover your songs from the iPod, but how would you recreate your carefully wrought playlists? Now, as long as those playlists were copied to the iPod, you can recreate them by copying a playlist at a time from the iPod, creating a new playlist in iTunes, and adding the songs copied from the iPod's playlist to the playlist you created in iTunes.

- **PodManager** (Mac OS X)

    http://podmanager.brunoblondeau.com

    Bruno Blondeau's $8 PodManager couldn't be simpler. Plug in your iPod, launch PodManager, select the songs you want to copy from your iPod to your Mac, and click the Copy Selected Songs on Disk button (**Figure 6.16**). PodManager does as you request, copying music from the iPod to a folder you designate.

**Figure 6.16**
PodManager lets you sort your iPod's music files by song, artist, or album.

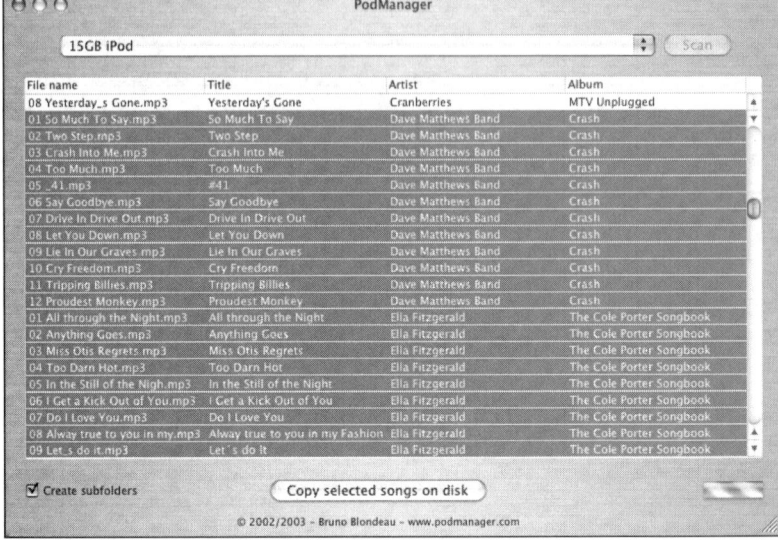

PodManager offers a couple of attractive features. The first is that you can sort songs by Title, Artist, or Album. The other is that you can sort copied files into subdirectories. You can create a folder called Beatles, for example, and place tunes from *A Hard Day's Night* and *Abbey Road* in separate folders.

 Unlike some iPod utilities, Senuti and PodManager identify AAC files as well as MP3 files. (Some other utilities recognize only MP3 files.)

- **iPod Tracks -> Desktop** (Mac OS X 10.1.3 or later)

    www.faqintosh.com/risorse/as/AS_ipodtracks2desktop.html

    Marco Balestra's clever (and free) AppleScript makes it easy to move files you've selected in iTunes to your Mac's Desktop. Just run the installer script included with iPod Tracks -> Desktop, and launch iTunes 3 or 4. In the AppleScript menu, you'll find two new additions: iPod Tracks -> Choose and iPod Tracks -> Desktop. Invoking the first command throws up a dialog that asks you to choose a destination for the selected songs on your iPod. Choose the iPod Tracks -> Desktop command to copy the songs that you've selected on the iPod to the Desktop.

iPod Tracks -> Desktop can copy both MP3 and AAC files (even the encrypted AAC files sold by the iTunes Music Store).

- **PodMaster 1000** (Mac OS 9 and Mac OS X)

  http://homepage.mac.com/podmaster/FileSharing1.html

  The $8 PodMaster 1000 from Flying Mouse Software is a nice little tool that sports an iPod-like interface (**Figure 6.17**). PodMaster 1000 not only allows you to copy any number of MP3 files (sorry, AAC files are not supported) from your iPod to your Mac, but also lets you play songs from the iPod through your Mac (and its speakers). Additionally, you can view a file's ID3 tag information. Heck, it even includes a cute little Mac OS X clock that appears when you click the Apple logo in the top-left corner of the PodMaster window.

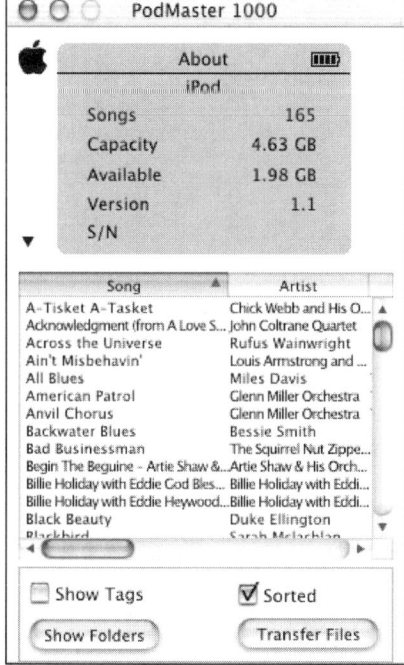

**Figure 6.17**
PodMaster 1000 is among the most flexible of the iPod assistance utilities (and one of the few that's compatible with Mac OS 9).

- **Pod 2 iPod** (Mac OS X)

  www.ifthensoft.com

  This program from If Then Software takes a different tack from other iPod utilities. Although it can copy an entire music library from an iPod to your Mac, its main purpose is to copy the music library from one iPod to another—making it a handy tool for those who own two iPods and would like the music libraries on each to be coordinated (**Figure 6.18**). Pod 2 iPod is donationware.

**Figure 6.18**
Clone one iPod to another with Pod 2 iPod.

- **OmniWeb** (Mac OS X)

  www.omnigroup.com/applications/omniweb

  Wait a minute—isn't OmniWeb a Web browser? Why, yes it is. But OmniWeb has a special feature that's not available in any other Mac Web browser: the capability to display the iPod's iPod_Control folder and its contents. To invoke this feature in this free-unless-you-feel-guilty-about-using-it-for-free-in-which-case-you-can-pay-$30-for-it browser, just launch OmniWeb, and drag the iPod's icon to OmniWeb's main window. In a flash, all the files on your iPod are revealed in the browser (**Figure 6.19**). Double-click the iPod_Control folder to reveal the Music folder and the *F* folders within it. To copy a song to your Mac, just double-click the song or drag it to your Desktop. You can copy entire folders of songs—the *F* folders I mentioned earlier—by dragging their links to the Mac's Desktop. The folders will be "downloaded" to your hard drive.

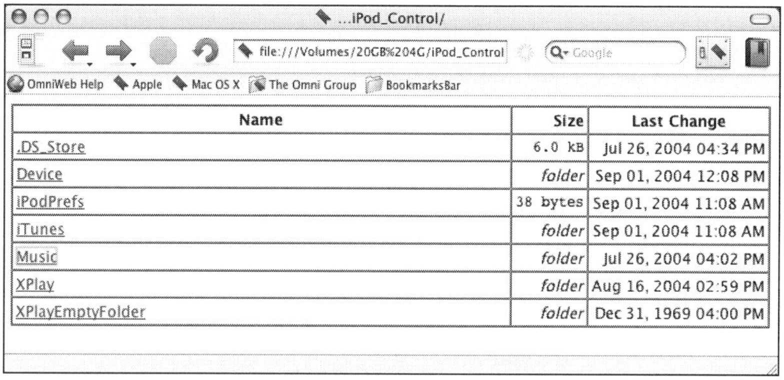

**Figure 6.19**
Drag and drop your iPod into OmniWeb to reveal hidden folders and files.

- **Open Pod** (Mac OS X)

    http://homepage.mac.com/beweis/b_ipod.html

    Open Pod, a free script, creates a new playlist within iTunes that displays all the songs on your iPod (**Figure 6.20**). You can copy songs from your iPod by dragging them from this playlist to your Mac's Desktop. Don't let the fact that you have to download Open Pod from a Webpage written entirely in German deter you. It's worth the effort.

**Figure 6.20**
Select the OPEN iPod playlist to drag songs from your iPod to your Mac.

- **Anapod Explorer** (Windows)

  www.redchairsoftware.com

  I write at length about Red Chair Software's Anapod Explorer in Chapter 5. As I mentioned there, you can copy songs from your iPod to your PC by right-clicking items on the iPod from within Anapod Explorer—a playlist or album, for example—and choosing Copy to Computer from the contextual menu (**Figure 6.21**).

**Figure 6.21**
Copying files with Anapod Explorer.

- **XPlay 2** (Windows)

  www.mediafour.com

  I also write at length about Mediafour's $30 XPlay in that same Chapter 5. I'll just remind you that the latest version of XPlay includes a Copy To contextual-menu item (**Figure 6.22**). Just select the items you want to copy, right-click, choose Copy To, and choose a destination for the copied tunes.

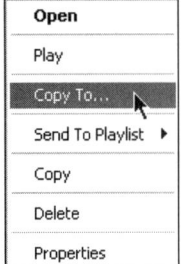

**Figure 6.22**
XPlay allows you to copy files from your iPod to your PC's hard drive.

- **EphPod** (Windows)

    www.ephpod.com

    You also read plenty about Joe Masters' free EphPod in Chapter 5. As I stated earlier, among its many talents is its capability to copy songs from the iPod to the Windows directory of your choosing. Just select the songs you want to copy in the Songs portion of the EphPod window, right-click one of the selected songs, and choose Copy Songs to Directory from the contextual menu (**Figure 6.23**). Navigate to the directory where you'd like to copy the songs, and click OK. The songs are copied.

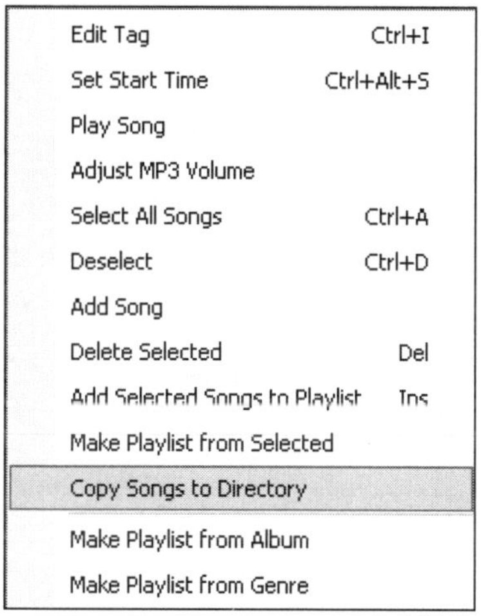

**Figure 6.23**
EphPod also lets Windows users move music from the iPod to a PC.

# 7

# Making iContact

In many ways, Apple is a victim of its own success and history. How else can you explain the flood of "Is that all?!?" comments that followed the initial release of the world's finest portable music player? People expect great things from Apple, and even when Apple delivers those great things—such as the first iteration of the iPod—the many-headed aren't satisfied.

Apple's first major upgrade to the iPod software—iPod Software 1.1 Updater—clearly demonstrated that Apple had further plans for the iPod. If iPod users desired more from their music players, Apple was willing to provide it in the form of a simple contact manager. If those users wanted to free space in their bandolier of gadgets by leaving the Palm device at home, fine. From this day forward, the iPod will display your contacts (and more, as you'll learn in this chapter).

# Getting Addressed

The iPod wasn't always a contact manager...or was it? Let's look at the history and state of the art in configuring iPod contacts.

## First on the Block: iPod Organizer

It would be incorrect to credit Apple with being the first to think of using the original Macintosh-compatible iPod as a personal information manager (PIM). It didn't take savvy users more than a couple of days after the iPod's general release to figure out that by creating very short, empty MP3 files and editing the Artist, Album, and Song information to include names and phone numbers, you could construct a crude contact database of your own (see the sidebar "Crude Contacts" in this section).

Only someone with few contacts or the patience of a saint would be willing to go through this kind of rigmarole. Fortunately, not long after the release of the iPod, ProVue Development (www.provue.com) released iPod Organizer, a $20 Macintosh application created with the company's Panorama database package.

iPod Organizer basically is a run-time version of Panorama that allows you to add information to the iPod's Song, Artist, and Album fields. It works this way:

An iPod Organizer *record* (entry) contains seven fields: Category, First Name, Last Name, Organization, Data, Source, and Notes (**Figure 7.1**). The first five fields are transferred to the iPod; the program uses the last two for internal housekeeping and for notes you want to keep on the Mac. Data entered in the Category field—something like My Friends or Burger Joints, for example—appears in the iPod's Artist screen. First Name, Last Name, and Organization appear in the Album screen. And data—phone numbers and addresses, for example—appears in the Songs screen (the information that scrolls in the iPod's display).

**Figure 7.1**

ProVue Development's iPod Organizer.

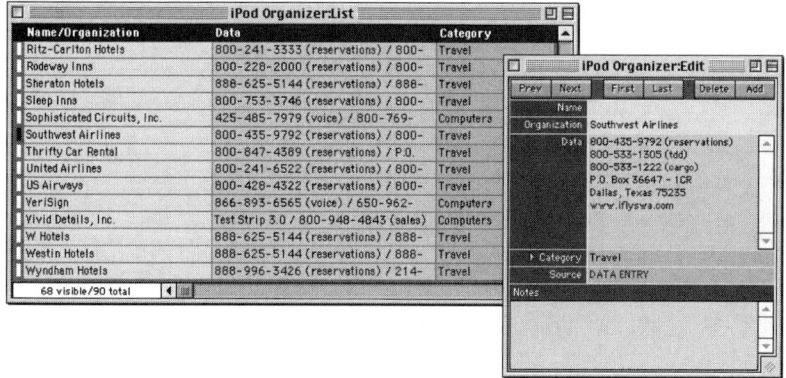

 If you care to enter information other than phone numbers and addresses in iPod Organizer, you're welcome to do so. Create a to-do list. Jot down the few items you need to pick up at the store. Or squirrel away the computer passwords you routinely forget. Knock yourself out.

After you've entered the information you want to use in your records, iPod Organizer moves the data to iTunes. When you next update your iPod, the information you entered in iPod Organizer transfers to the iPod.

There's a lot of power and convenience on iPod Organizer's front end, thanks to the driving force of the run-time version of Panorama. But the process that takes place within iTunes and on the iPod is no different from the one I outline in the sidebar "Crude Contacts." iPod Organizer simply creates the number of empty MP3 files it needs and copies the data into the Song, Artist, and Album fields in iTunes; then iTunes transfers those MP3 files to the iPod. Very clever.

## Crude Contacts

With today's iPod software, you can easily create and add contacts to your Mac or Windows iPod. But if you'd care to re-create a bit of recent history and cobble together your own crude contacts, here's how:

**Mac OS 9: Creating Short Audio Files with SimpleSound**

**1.** Create and save an audio file about 5 seconds long.

If you're running Mac OS 9.2 or earlier, you can do this by launching SimpleSound (usually located in the Apple Extras folder inside the Mac OS 9 Applications folder) and clicking the Add button in the resulting Alert Sounds window.

**2.** When the recording window appears, click the Record button, allow SimpleSound to record 5 seconds of silence, click Stop (if necessary), and then click the Save button (**Figure 7.2**).

**Figure 7.2**
Mac OS 9's SimpleSound application.

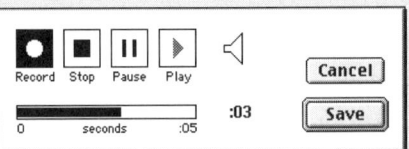

**3.** Give the file a descriptive name, such as Blank MP3, when you're prompted.

**4.** Quit SimpleSound and any other running applications.

**5.** Open the System Folder; then double-click the System file.

**6.** Drag your Blank MP3 file out of the System file and onto your Desktop.

**Mac OS X: Creating Short Audio Files with AudioX**

**1.** Create and save an audio file about 5 seconds long.

OS X doesn't include a utility for recording sound, so you'll have to grab one from the Web. The $20 AudioX (www.realmacsoftware.com/audiox.php) is an easy-to-use recording application.

**2.** Using AudioX or a similar tool, record 5 seconds of silent audio, and save your file (**Figure 7.3**).

## Crude Contacts *(continued)*

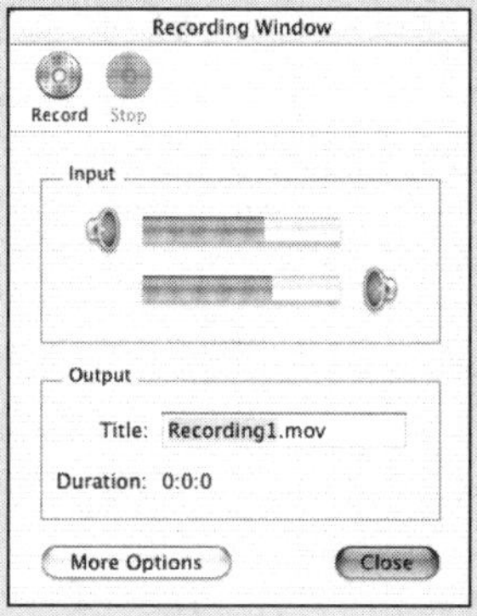

**Figure 7.3**
AudioX, an easy-to-use audio recorder for Mac OS X.

3. Launch iTunes, and choose the Preferences command (in the Edit menu in Mac OS 9.2 and earlier and in the iTunes menu in Mac OS X).

4. In the iTunes Preferences dialog box, click the Importing tab, choose MP3 Encoder from the Import Using pop-up menu, and click OK (**Figure 7.4**).

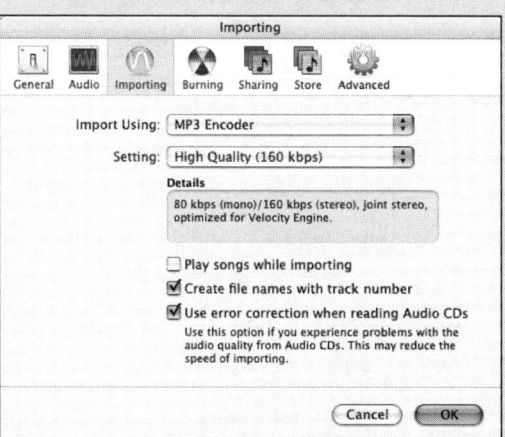

**Figure 7.4**
Select the MP3 Encoder in iTunes to convert AIFF audio files to MP3 files.

5. Choose Convert Selection to MP3 from iTunes' Advanced menu, and navigate to the Blank MP3 file you created.

   iTunes converts that file to MP3 format.

*continues on next page*

> ## Crude Contacts *(continued)*
>
> **Windows XP: Creating Short Audio Files with Sound Recorder**
>
> 1. Launch Sound Recorder (located in the Entertainment folder within Windows' Accessories folder).
>
> 2. Record 5 seconds of silent audio.
>
> 3. Choose Properties from the File menu.
>
> 4. Choose Playback Formats from the pop-up menu, and click Convert Now.
>
> 5. In the resulting Sound Selection window, choose PCM from the Format pop-up menu and 44.100 kHz, 16-bit Stereo from the Attributes pop-up menu; then click OK.
>
> 6. Name and save your file.
>
> 7. Launch iTunes, and choose Preferences from the Edit menu.
>
> 8. In the resulting window click the Importing tab and choose MP3 Encoder from the Import Using pop-up menu. Click OK to dismiss the window.
>
> 9. Drag your silent sound into the iTunes window, and select it.
>
> 10. Choose Convert Selection to MP3 from the Advanced menu.
>
> **Adding Your Contact Information**
>
> To edit the tag information necessary for creating your contact, follow these steps in iTunes for Macintosh or Windows:
>
> 1. After you've recorded a short audio file, click the Blank MP3 "song" that's now in iTunes' main window, and press Command-I to produce the Song Information window.
>
> 2. Where the song title appears, enter your contact's name and any bit of information you'd like to scroll across the screen of your iPod—an address, for example.
>
> 3. In the Artist field, enter a bit of information that will fit on the iPod's screen—a phone number, perhaps.
>
> 4. Use the Album field for some similarly small bit of information (**Figure 7.5**).

## Crude Contacts *(continued)*

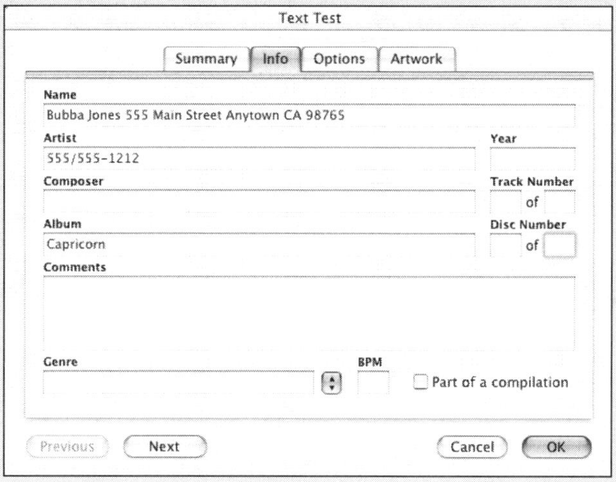

**Figure 7.5**
Rolling your own contact with iTunes.

*[Screenshot of iTunes "Text Test" Info tab showing fields: Name: Bubba Jones 555 Main Street Anytown CA 98765; Artist: 555/555-1212; Album: Capricorn; with Summary, Info, Options, Artwork tabs and Previous, Next, Cancel, OK buttons]*

5. Click OK.

6. Update your iPod.

7. Select your iPod in the Source list, and choose Update Songs on *the name of your iPod*.

8. Detach your iPod from your computer, navigate to the Songs screen, scroll down until you find the contact you just created, and click the Select button.

   The information you entered in the Song Title field scrolls across the screen from right to left, and the Artist and Album information appears below. If the information advances too quickly to the next song (after all, the iPod thinks that it's a 5-second song and will go on to the next tune after it's finished playing your short ditty), click the Play/Pause button to pause playback.

   To refine this technique but lose one of your fields, create several of these files, and enter the same information in the Album or Artist field—My Family, for example. This method allows you to group contacts.

   You can also group contacts by creating *group playlists*—playlists that contain nothing but the names of members of your family or the members of your company softball team.

9. Breathe a sigh of relief that you no longer have to do this kind of thing to get contacts into your iPod.

# Viva vCard

Whether iPod Organizer motivated Apple to add its own contact management to the iPod is something that only Apple knows. All that really matters is that Apple was motivated thusly, and contacts became part of the iPod experience with the release of iPod Software 1.1 Updater (and remained part of that experience in subsequent software updates).

The magic behind contact management on the iPod is the vCard standard.

## The vCard standard

In the mid-1990s, Apple, AT&T, IBM, and Siemens founded an initiative called Versit that created the *vCard* standard. This standard allows you to store electronically such information as names, addresses (business, home, mailing, and parcel), telephone numbers (home, business, fax, pager, mobile, ISDN, voice, data, and video), email addresses, and Internet addresses on computers, personal information managers, and cellular telephones. The standard also offers graphics support for photographs and logos. Audio and time-zone information is supported as well.

The standard is platform-agnostic, so you can share vCards among computers running a variety of operating systems—Mac OS, Windows, and Linux, for example—as well as with cellular phones and personal digital assistants, such as devices running the Palm operating system. vCard support is built into products from such vendors as Apple, IBM, Lotus, Lucent Technologies, Netscape, Now Software, and Microsoft.

## vCard and you

Fascinating as the history of the vCard format may be, its story becomes a lot more gripping when you understand that with very little muss or fuss, you can move information from products that support versions 2.1 and 3.0 of the vCard standard to your iPod. Before you break out the champagne, however, you should know that the iPod supports only a portion of the vCard standard. You can't view a graphic, for example, or listen to a sound contained in a vCard file stored on your iPod.

Here's the information that your iPod *can* display:

- **Contact's formatted name.** Bubba Jones, for example.

- **Contact's name.** The name as it appears in the contact (Jones, Bubba, Dr., for example).

- **Contact's address(es).** The address types supported by vCard (business, home, mailing, and parcel).

- **Contact's telephone number(s).** The phone numbers supported by vCard.

- **Contact's email.** The email addresses in the contact.

- **Contact's title.** Dr., Ms., Mr., and so on.

- **Contact's organization.** The company name displayed in the contact.

- **Contact's URL.** The Internet address contained in the contact.

- **Contact's note.** The note field in the contact.

vCard support wouldn't mean much if common applications didn't support it. Fortunately, the universal nature of the standard means that most information-management and email applications you're likely to run across support vCard. As this book goes to press, vCard support is present on the Mac in OS X's Address Book, Qualcomm's Eudora, Bare Bones Software's Mailsmith, Microsoft's Entourage email clients, and Palm's Palm Desktop 4.x and Now Software's Now Contact information managers. For Windows, you'll find vCard supported in such mainstays as Windows' Address Book, Microsoft Outlook, and Palm Desktop. (The Windows version of Qualcomm's Eudora doesn't support vCards.)

### iPod Sorting

Before the release of the iPod Software 1.2 Updater, you had limited ways to sort contacts on the iPod. If a contact's name within the vCard began with his or her first name, by gum, that's how it would be displayed on the iPod. Sure, you could edit the vCard file to swap the position of each contact's first and last name, but what an unholy bother.

Fortunately, Apple has made contact sorting much easier. Just highlight the Settings entry in the iPod's main screen, press Select, and scroll down to Contacts. Press Select again, and you'll find the Sort and Display options. Each option allows you to select First and Last or Last and First, thus allowing you to sort by last name but display your contacts' first name first and last name...well, last.

## Working with Contacts

Now that you understand the underlying structure of the iPod's contacts, you're ready to put them to practical use. In the following pages, you'll create contacts in various applications and export them to the iPod. Along the way, I'll show you ways to move unexpected information to your iPod.

## The Manual Method: Macintosh

Much like their paper counterparts, vCards are amenable to being dropped where they can be most helpful. In the case of vCards, this means that you can drag them from their host application (Mac OS X's Address Book application or Microsoft Entourage 2001 running under Mac OS 9, for example) onto your Mac's Desktop or into another vCard-friendly application.

Wouldn't it be swell if you could drop them into your iPod just as easily?

You can. Here's how.

### Step 1: Locating contacts in host applications

To find vCard-compatible contact information in the following programs, follow these instructions.

### Address Book (Mac OS X)

**1.** Open Address Book.

You'll find it in Mac OS X's Application's folder at the root level of your startup drive. All the contacts appear in the main window.

**2.** To select all the contacts, press Command-A; to select individual contacts, Command-click each contact you want to select.

Alternatively, you can select your contacts and select Export vCards from the File menu. The selected contacts will be placed into a single vCard, which you can drag into the iPod's Contacts folder in Step 2 ("Moving contacts into the iPod manually") on the next page.

### Microsoft Entourage 2001
### (for Mac OS 9.2 and earlier and OS X's Classic environment)

**1.** Open Entourage 2001 (inside the Microsoft Office folder).

**2.** In the Folder List field, click the Address Book entry, choose Address Book from the Window menu, or press Command-2 to display your contacts in the main Entourage window.

**3.** Click a contact; then press Command-A to select all the contacts, or Command-click to select numerous individual contacts.

### Microsoft Entourage v.X and Entourage 2004 (Mac OS X)

**1.** Launch Entourage (inside the Microsoft Office folder).

**2.** Click the Address Book button in the top-left portion of the main window, choose Address Book from the View menu's Go To submenu, or press Command-2 to produce the Address Book.

**3.** Click a contact; then press Command-A to select all the contacts, or Command-click to select numerous individual contacts.

### Palm Desktop 4.x for Macintosh

**1.** Open Palm Desktop.

**2.** If the Address List window isn't visible, choose Address List from the Window menu.

**3.** Click a contact; then press Command-A to select all the contacts, or Command-click to select numerous individual contacts.

**NOTE** Versions of Palm Desktop before version 4.x do not support the vCard standard.

**Eudora 6.1 and Now Contact 4.x for Macintosh**

Although the current versions of Eudora and Now Contact support the vCard standard, dragging contacts from these applications' address books onto the Desktop does not create vCard files. Later in this chapter, I'll show you some utilities you can use to extract vCard contacts from Eudora and Now Contact.

## Step 2: Moving contacts into the iPod manually

Now that you've located the contacts you want to move, you can move them. Follow these steps:

1. If your iPod's not connected to your Mac, make the connection, and wait for its icon to appear on the Desktop.

2. Configure your iPod so that it mounts on the Mac's Desktop as an external hard drive.

    To do this in iTunes, open the iPod Preferences dialog box, and check the EnableDisk Use check box (**Figure 7.6**).

**Figure 7.6**
Choose Enable Disk Use to mount your iPod on the Desktop.

3. Double-click the iPod icon on the Desktop to open the iPod's hard drive.

4. Locate and open the Contacts folder on this hard drive (**Figure 7.7**).

**Figure 7.7**
The iPod's Calendars and Contacts folders.

5. Open the application that holds the vCards you want to add to your iPod.

6. Select the vCards in that application, and drag them into the Contacts folder.

7. Disconnect your iPod by dragging its icon to the Trash.

8. Wait for the iPod to reboot, and navigate to the Contacts screen.

The contacts you copied are displayed in the Contacts list.

# The Manual Method: Windows

Moving contacts manually from Windows applications to the iPod isn't terribly different from performing the operation on the Mac. Here's how to go about it.

## Step 1: Locating contacts in host applications

To find vCard-compatible contact information in the following programs, follow these instructions.

**Address Book (Windows)**

1. Launch Address Book.

2. If it's not already selected, choose Main Identity's Contacts in the Address Book window's left pane.

3. Press Ctrl-A to select all the contacts, hold down the Ctrl key while clicking noncontiguous contacts to select multiple contacts individually, or hold down the Shift key while clicking two contacts (those two contacts and all contacts between them will be selected).

**Microsoft Outlook (Windows)**

1. Open Microsoft Outlook.

2. Click the Contacts button in the Outlook Shortcuts portion of the Microsoft Outlook window.

3. Press Ctrl-A to select all the contacts, hold down the Ctrl key while clicking noncontiguous contacts to select multiple contacts individually, or hold down the Shift key while clicking two contacts (those two contacts and all contacts between them will be selected).

**Palm Desktop 4.x for Windows**

1. Open Palm Desktop.

2. If the Address List window isn't visible, click the Address button in the left portion of the Palm Desktop window.

3. Press Ctrl-A to select all the contacts, hold down the Ctrl key while clicking noncontiguous contacts to select multiple contacts individually, or hold down the Shift key while clicking two contacts (those two contacts and all contacts between them will be selected).

## Step 2: Moving contacts into the iPod manually

Regrettably, not all the Windows applications I mention support drag and drop. But there's more than one way to skin a contact. To move contacts from each of these applications, follow these steps.

**Address Book and Microsoft Outlook (Windows)**

1. Open the Contacts folder inside your iPod.

    You'll find your iPod by double-clicking My Computer.

2. Switch to Address Book or Outlook, and drag and drop your contacts into the iPod's Contacts folder.

    Your contacts have been moved to the iPod as individual vCard files.

3. Unmount your iPod by clicking the iPod icon in the System Tray and choosing Unmount from the resulting contextual menu.

4. When the iPod displays the message "OK to disconnect," detach the data cable.

5. Wait for the iPod to reboot; then navigate to the Contacts screen.

    The contacts you copied are displayed in the Contacts list.

**Palm Desktop 4.x for Windows**

1. With your contacts selected in Palm Desktop, choose Export vCard from Palm Desktop's File menu.

2. In the resulting Export As window, navigate to your iPod's Contacts folder.

3. Making sure that vCard File (*.vcf) is displayed in the Export Type field, enter a name for your contact file in the File Name field, and click the Export button.

   Your contacts are moved to the iPod as a single vCard file.

4. Unmount your iPod by clicking the iPod icon in the System Tray and choosing Unmount from the resulting contextual menu.

5. When the iPod displays the message "OK to disconnect," detach the data cable.

6. Wait for the iPod to reboot; then navigate to the Contacts screen.

   The contacts you copied are displayed in the Contacts list.

You've probably heard (and if not, you'll soon learn) that many utilities for automating this process are available. If so, why use the manual method? To begin with, as this book goes to press, on a Windows PC, such utilities work only with Microsoft's Outlook. And many of the Mac utilities work only with Mac OS X. If you run Mac OS 9.2 or earlier, or don't use Outlook but want to move your contacts from a particular application, moving vCards manually may be your only choice. Also, I can't anticipate which future applications will offer vCard support or whether those applications will provide an expedient way to move contact information between your computer and the iPod. As long as the host application supports exporting contacts as vCards, the manual method should see you through until something more convenient comes along.

## Multiple Contacts in a Single File

If you drag multiple vCards into the iPod's Contacts folder, that folder will be jammed with files. If you're keen on both tidiness and repetitive tasks, you can place your contacts in a single .vcf file. To do so, just select a .vcf file as a master file, and open it in a text editor. Then open each .vcf file in the Contacts folder in that same text editor, and cut and paste the information in the file into the master file.

Your master file will look something like this:

```
begin:vcard
fn:Costello\, Elvis
n:Costello;Elvis;;;
email;type=internet:thebestelvis@mcmanus.com
end:vcard
begin:vcard
fn:Blow\, Joe
n:Blow;Joe;;;
tel;type=work:555/555-1212
email;type=internet:joe@blow.com
org:Joe Blow Inc
end:vcard
begin:vcard
fn:Jones\, Bubba
n:Jones;Bubba;;Dr.;
adr;type=work:111 Main Street;Anytown;AK;99988;USA
adr;type=home:543 Home Street;Anytown;AK;99988;
tel;type=home:555/555-1213
tel;type=work:555/555-1212
tel;type=cell:555/555-1234
email;type=internet:bubba@bubba.com
org:Bub Industries
url;type=home:www.bubba.com
note:Bubba loves chocolate cake!
end:vcard
```

# The Automated Method: Macintosh

Now that you've learned to crawl through iPod contact management when you need to, it's time to spread your wings and fly. The following automation methods will make working with contacts on your Mac much easier.

## iSync

Before the release of the iPod Software 1.2 Updater, Apple provided AppleScripts for automating the transfer of contacts between Mac OS X's Address Book, Microsoft's Entourage, and Palm's Palm Desktop and the iPod. Apple has since removed those AppleScripts from its site.

Why? Because Apple believes that it has a better solution: a utility called iSync.

iSync, as the name implies, synchronizes contact and calendar data between the Mac and such devices as the iPod, Palm computing devices, compatible cell phones, and—if you have a .Mac account (Apple's online service)—other Macs. Regrettably, iSync works only with the data stored in Mac OS X's Address Book and Apple's calendar application, iCal. (Dry those tears, Entourage and Palm Desktop users; see the sidebar "I Need Contact!" in this section to learn how to move your contacts into Address Book.)

iSync requires that you be running Mac OS X 10.2 (Jaguar) or later. As this book goes to press, 1.5 is the latest version of iSync. To sync your iPod with Address Book, follow these steps.

1. If iSync isn't on your Mac, download it from www.apple.com/isync.
2. Launch iSync, and choose Add Device from the Devices menu.

    Your iPod should appear in the resulting Add Devices window.

3. Double-click the iPod's icon.

The icon is added to iSync's window, which expands to reveal the synchronization options (**Figure 7.8**).

**Figure 7.8**
Synchronization options within Apple's iSync.

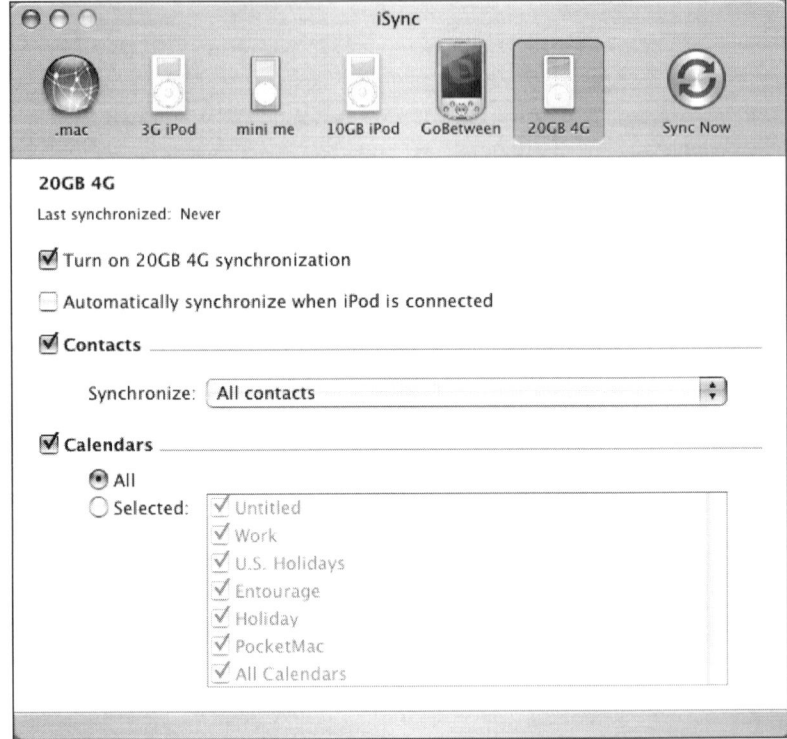

In the iSync window, you can switch on synchronization with the iPod, as well as choose whether you want to synchronize your iPod automatically when it's connected. You can also enable contact and calendar synchronization by checking the Contacts and Calendars check boxes (which are checked by default). Within the Contacts portion of the window, you can choose to synchronize all your contacts or choose a group you created in Address Book. (These groups appear in Address Book's aptly named Group column.) The Calendars portion of the window provides similar options, allowing you to synchronize your iPod with all your calendars or a selection of calendars (your work and home calendars, but not your child's soccer-schedule calendar, for example).

4. To synchronize your contact and calendar data between the iPod and Address Book and iCal, click the Sync Now button in the iSync window.

   The synchronization process begins. Before iSync moves a significant amount of data from the iPod to your computer, it issues a warning via the Safeguard window (**Figure 7.9**). If you've enabled synchronization between both Address Book and iCal, the first Safeguard window indicates how many contacts will be added to your iPod, how many will be removed, and how many will be modified.

**Figure 7.9**

iSync's not-so-subtle Safeguard window.

5. To finish synchronizing your contacts, click the Proceed button in the Safeguard window; to cancel the operation, click Cancel.

   A different Safeguard window appears if you've also enabled calendar synchronization. Here, iSync tells you how many calendar and To Do items will be added, removed, and modified. Again, click Proceed to synchronize your data.

 Don't be alarmed if you see a message indicating that the synchronization failed. If more than one device appears in the iSync window—such as your iPod and Palm Computing device—and not all devices are present and accounted for (you haven't plugged in your Palm cradle, for example), iSync will synchronize the devices it can find and then report a failure for those devices it can't find.

## I Need Contact!

If, like many Mac users, you've carefully squirreled away your contacts in Microsoft's Entourage or Palm's Palm Desktop, you may be disappointed that iSync works only with Address Book. But as Aristotle was so fond of saying, "It's no use crying over spilled goat's milk."

If you want to use iSync and you don't care to pay for a third-party utility, you must use Address Book. Fortunately, it's not difficult to move contacts from either program into Address Book. Here's how.

**Entourage**

1. In Mac OS X 10.2 or earlier, open the AppleScript folder inside Mac OS X's Applications folder and double-click the Script Menu.menu item (in Mac OS X 10.3, double-click the Install Script Menu application in this same location).

   This places an AppleScript menu in the Mac's menu bar.

2. From this menu select Mail Scripts and then choose the Import Addresses script in the submenu.

   When you run this script a window appears that gives you the option to import addresses from Entourage, Outlook Express, Palm Desktop, Eudora, Claris Emailer, or Netscape into Mac OS X's Address Book.

3. Choose Entourage and click OK.

   The script will run and copy your Entourage addresses to Mac OS X's Address Book.

Alternatively, Michael Zapp's iPod It (described later in this chapter) can extract addresses from Entourage into a single vCard that you can then drag into Address Book. Likewise, PocketMac's PocketMac iPod Edition (also described later in this chapter) can sync Entourage contacts, calendars, tasks, notes, and email to your iPod.

**Palm Desktop (version 4.0 and later)**

You can also move Palm Desktop contacts to Address Book with the script I just described, but if you'd like to try a different method, follow these steps:

1. Launch Palm Desktop, and choose Address List from the Window menu.

2. Select the contacts you'd like to move to OS X's Address Book in Palm Desktop's Address List window.

3. Choose Export from the File menu.

## I Need Contact! *(continued)*

4. In the resulting Export: Palm Desktop window, name your file, select the Desktop as the destination for your saved file, and choose vCard from the Format pop-up menu.

5. Click the Export button.

   A vCard containing all the selected contacts is saved to the Desktop.

6. Open Address Book, and drag the vCard into either the Group or Name portion of the window.

   In a flash, your contacts appear in Address Book, ready for exporting to your iPod via iSync.

**Older Contact Managers**

Those who use older contact managers, such as TouchBase and DynoDex, may believe that they've been left out of the party. Not so. Although these contact managers won't run in Mac OS X (or, likely, in Mac OS 9), you can still pull their data into Address Book. The means for doing so is Palm Desktop.

Palm Desktop began life as Claris Organizer, and it retains the file compatibility that it had in its Claris incarnation. Just use Palm Desktop's Import command to open your old contact-manager file (you may need to move a few fields around during the import process to make the data line up correctly) and then export it as a vCard file.

## Eudora 6.1 (Mac OS 9 and OS X)

Although the Macintosh version of Qualcomm's Eudora 6.1 supports the vCard standard (as does Eudora 5.1), contacts in the program's Address Book are not saved in vCard format. To move your Eudora addresses to the iPod, therefore, you must convert them.

To do so, download Andreas Amann's free Eudora vCard Export utility from http://homepage.mac.com/aamann/Eudora_vCard_Export.html. Then, to use the program, follow these steps:

1. Launch Eudora vCard Export, and choose the sort order you prefer from the Sort Order pop-up menu: first name, last name; or last name, first name (**Figure 7.10**).

**Figure 7.10**
Eudora's vCard Export preferences.

2. Locate your Eudora folder (inside the Documents folder, which is inside your Mac OS X Users folder), and drag it on top of the Eudora vCard Export icon.

   When the program finishes converting Eudora's contacts, it creates a Contacts folder on the Mac's Desktop and places the converted .vcf files in that folder.

3. Drag the .vcf files into the Contacts folder inside the iPod.

   Your iPod must be mounted on the Desktop for you to do this.

 The Eudora vCard Export utility can't pull contact information from mailing-list entries that contain groups of contacts. The program can handle only individual contacts.

## Now Contact (Mac OS X and OS 9)

Two tools are available for moving contacts out of version 4.x of Now Software's Now Contact personal information manager application. The first is NowPak for iPod (ftp://ftp.poweronsoftware.com/pub/software/nowsoft/NowUpToDate/nowpakforipod.sit), a free, OS X–only AppleScript produced by Now Software that transfers both contact and calendar information from Now's Now Contact and Now Up-to-Date. The other is NETsettings NowPod (www.netsettings.com/nowpod.html), a free utility that works with both Mac OS 9 and Mac OS X. The two utilities work in slightly different ways. Here's how to export your contacts with each utility.

**NowPak for iPod (Mac OS X 10.2 and earlier only)**

1. Make sure that the iPod is mounted on the Desktop.

2. Launch Now Contact.

3. Launch Now Contact to iPod.

4. When you're prompted, pick an iPod to update (and if you have more than one on your Desktop, aren't you the lucky duck); then click Select.

5. If you've already run this script once, you'll see a warning that an entry already exists for this address book.

    You can cancel the process, append contacts that you've added since you last ran the script, or overwrite the preceding entry.

6. When you're given the option to display names by last name first or first name first, make your selection and then click Select.

    The script does its work and informs you of its success when the job is done.

7. Click Done to complete the process and quit the script.

8. Drag the iPod to the Trash to unmount it.

    When the iPod reboots, you'll find your contacts listed in the iPod's Contacts screen.

    Note: As we go to press, the current version of NowPak (v 1.0) doesn't work under Mac OS X 10.3 (Panther).

**NETsettings NowPod (Mac OS 9 and OS X)**

1. Make sure that the iPod is mounted on the Desktop.

2. Launch Now Contact.

3. Launch NETsettings NowPod.

4. Choose Preferences from the Edit menu to open the Preferences dialog box.

5. Click the General Preferences tab (**Figure 7.11**), and choose the Reverse Names option to have the iPod display names in reverse order from the way that they're displayed in Now Contact (last name first, for example).

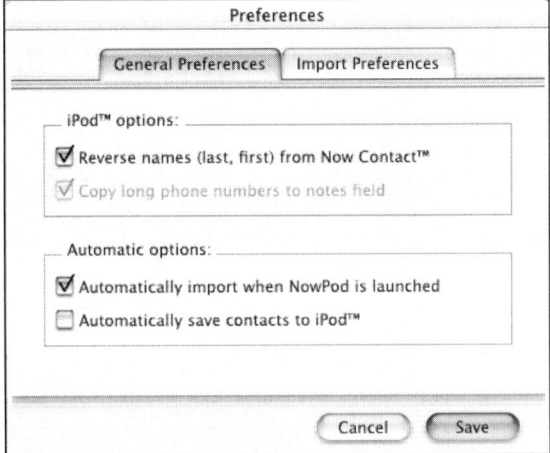

**Figure 7.11**
NowPod's General preferences.

6. Choose the Automatically Import When NowPod Is Launched option (if that sounds like a good idea) or the Automatically Save Contacts to iPod option (if you prefer not to copy contacts to the iPod manually).

7. Click the Import Preferences tab (**Figure 7.12**), and select the information you'd like to import to your iPod.

**Figure 7.12**
NowPod's Import preferences.

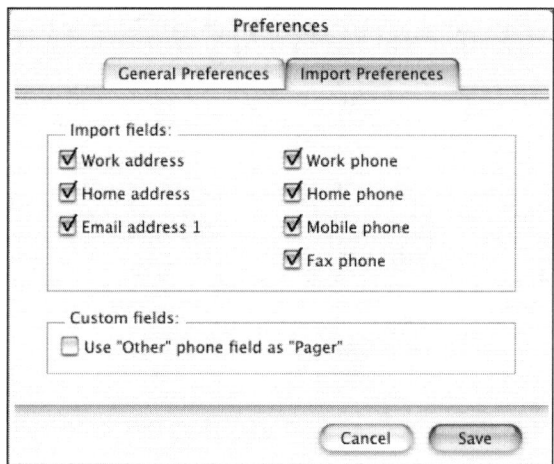

Options include work address, home address, email address, work phone, home phone, mobile phone, and fax phone.

**8.** Check the Use "Other" Phone Field as "Pager" check box if this option appeals to you.

**9.** Click Save to save your choices.

**10.** Switch to Now Contact, and display only those contacts that you want to import to the iPod.

Select all the contacts that begin with the letter *B*, for example, and choose Find Selected from the Find menu to display just those contacts. NowPod will import only the contacts that are displayed.

**11.** Switch back to NowPod, and click Import.

Unless you've configured NowPod to place your contacts on the iPod automatically, you'll be prompted for a location in which to save the exported .vcf file.

**12.** If you've chosen to move your contacts to the iPod manually, drag the .vcf file you just created to the iPod's Contacts folder.

# The Automated Method: Windows

Increasingly, more utilities are available for moving your contacts to your iPod, although those utilities work solely with Microsoft Outlook, the email client and personal information manager included with Microsoft Office. Among those utilities, you'll find:

- Mike Matheson's $14 iPodSync (http://iccnet.50megs.com/iPodSync)
- iPodSoft's free iPod Agent (www.ipodsoft.com/ipodagent.aspx)
- PocketMac's $23.41PocketMac iPod Edition (www.pocketmac.net)
- Conrad Hagemans' free iAppoint (www.xs4all.nl/~hagemans)
- Oliver Stoer's free Outpod (www.stoer.de/ipod/ipod_en.htm)
- Joe Masters' free EphPod (www.ephpod.com)
- Red Chair Software's $25 Anapod Explorer (www.redchairsoftware.com)

## iPodSync

iPodSync is Mike Matheson's attempt to re-create the Mac's iSync application on Windows. For the most part, he succeeds quite well. Within the iPodSync window, you can choose to synchronize your Outlook contacts, calendars, to-do items, and notes to your iPod. To move your contacts to the iPod, follow these steps:

**1.** Mount your iPod as a removable drive on your PC.

**2.** Launch iPodSync, and click the Contacts button.

**3.** In the expanded window that appears, select the Synchronize Contacts option (**Figure 7.13**).

**Figure 7.13**

iPodSync's contact-synchronization options.

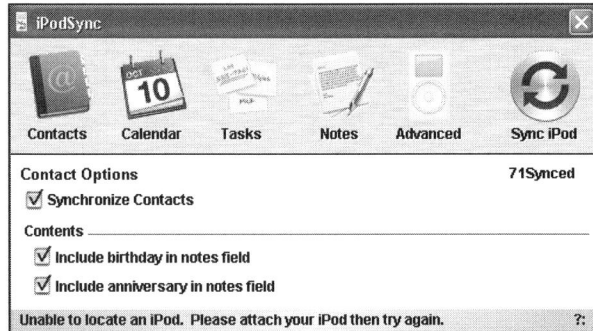

4. Choose whether to include birthday and anniversary events in the Notes field.

5. Click the Sync iPod button to copy your contacts to the iPod.

   Your Outlook contacts are copied as a single vCard file (called contacts) to your iPod's Contacts folder.

## iPod Agent

It's tough to argue with free, particularly when the free utility is as capable as iPodSoft's iPod Agent. To synchronize your contacts, just follow these steps:

1. Mount your iPod as a removable drive on your PC.

2. Launch iPod Agent, and click the Synchronize button.

3. Click the Options button, and in the resulting Sync Options window, select the items you want to synchronize with your iPod (**Figure 7.14**).

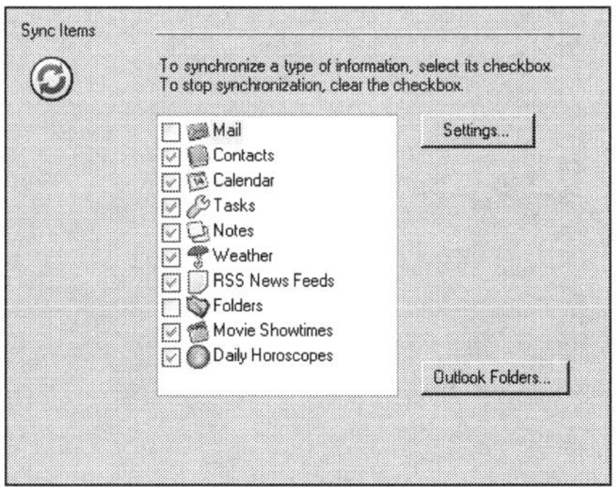

**Figure 7.14**

iPod Agent's Sync Options window.

4. Click the Outlook Folders button in this window, and choose which Outlook folders you want to synchronize your iPod with—Personal Folders and Archived Folders, for example.

5. Click OK to dismiss the Outlook Folders window, and click OK again to close the Sync Options window.

6. Click the Sync button in the iPod Agent window.

    The selected Outlook items will be synced with your iPod.

 When you're using some of these utilities, Windows may toss up a warning that an outside application is attempting to access data from Outlook. That warning is for your protection. Some viruses, for example, attempt to grab Outlook contact information in the same way. To allow these tools to do their job, click the Allow Access For option, and choose 1 Minute from the pop-up menu. These settings give utilities such as iPod Agent plenty of time to transfer your contacts before shutting the door on this kind of activity.

## PocketMac iPod Edition

PocketMac makes two versions of the PocketMac iPod Edition: one for the Macintosh that acts as a conduit within iSync for synchronizing Microsoft Entourage data, and another for Windows that copies Outlook data to the iPod. It's a breeze to use:

1. Mount your iPod as a removable drive on your PC.

2. Launch PocketMac iPod Edition, and click the Gear icon.

3. Choose those items that you want to synchronize with your iPod (**Figure 7.15**).

    You can synchronize contacts, calendars, email, Word documents, tasks, and notes.

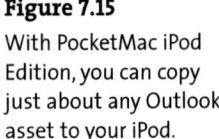

**Figure 7.15**
With PocketMac iPod Edition, you can copy just about any Outlook asset to your iPod.

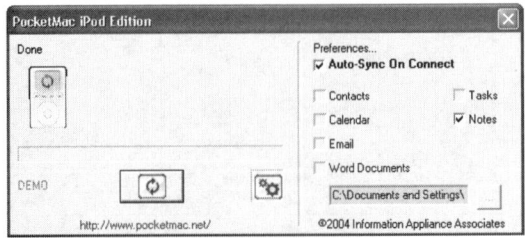

4. If you want your iPod to be synchronized whenever it's attached to your PC, enable the Auto-Sync on Connect option.

5. Click the Sync button, and the selected items will be copied to your iPod.

## iAppoint

iAppoint can also move both Outlook calendar and contact information to the iPod. To use it for this purpose, follow along:

1. Mount your iPod as a removable drive on your PC.

2. Launch iAppoint, and click the Contacts button.

3. In the resulting window, enter a path to your iPod's Contacts folder in the Save Path field—e:\Contacts\contacts.vcf, for example, if your iPod appears as the E drive on your PC (**Figure 7.16**).

**Figure 7.16**
Enter the path to your iPod in iAppoint.

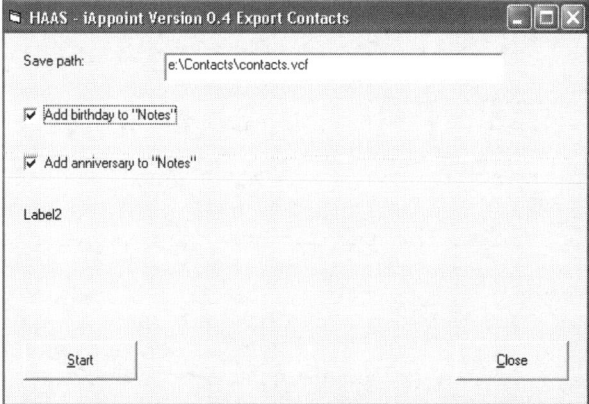

4. Disable the options to save birthday and anniversary data to each contact if you don't want that information displayed on your iPod.

5. Click the Start button to copy your Outlook contacts to the iPod.

Your contacts are copied as a single vCard file (called contacts) to your iPod's Contacts folder.

 Unlike iPodSync, iAppoint copies only your default contacts to your iPod.

## Outpod

Yes, Outpod can transfer calendar and contact information, too. Here's how:

1. Mount your iPod as a removable drive on your PC.

2. Launch Outpod, and click the Contacts entry on the left side of the Outpod window.

   Your Outlook contacts appear on the right side of the window (**Figure 7.17**).

**Figure 7.17**
Outpod's contact-list view.

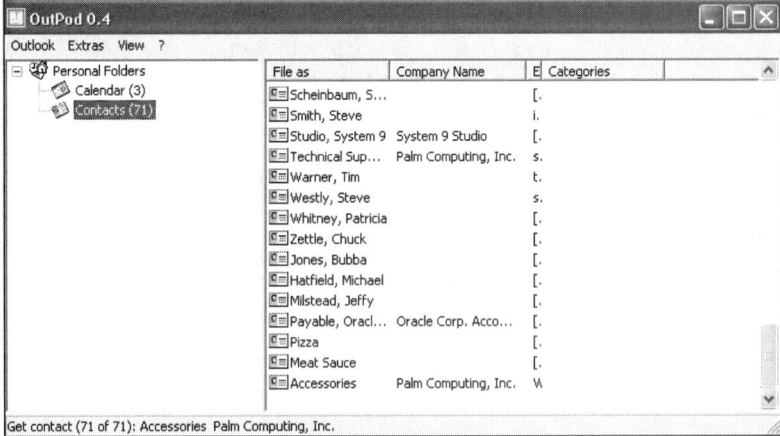

3. Select the contacts that you want to copy to your iPod.

4. From the Outlook menu, choose Save Selected Items (if you want to save each contact as a separate vCard file) or Save Selected Items in One File (if you want to save your contacts in a single file).

   If you choose the first command, you'll get the Browse for Folder window. In this window, navigate to your iPod's Contacts folder, and click OK to copy your contacts to the iPod.

   If you choose the second command, a Save As dialog box appears. In this dialog box, name the contact file, navigate to the iPod's Contacts folder, and click Save to copy your contacts to the iPod.

## EphPod

EphPod is an ever-changing beast. In the past, it could display Outlook contacts and synchronize them on your iPod while it also synchronized your iPod's music library. As I write these words, this capability is broken. But because I expect it to be fixed by the time you read this book (or shortly thereafter), I'll include not only the steps for synchronizing your contacts from within EphPod, but also those for creating new contacts.

1. Mount your iPod as a removable drive on your PC.

2. Launch EphPod, and click Get Outlook Contacts in the toolbar.

   Outlook may toss up the warning I mentioned earlier.

3. Click Yes to proceed.

4. In the Microsoft Outlook warning dialog box that appears, click the Allow Access For option, choose 1 Minute from the pop-up menu, and click Yes.

5. When the hourglass icon disappears, click the Contacts entry in the iPod View portion of the EphPod window.

   Your contacts appear in a column to the right of the Column entry (**Figure 7.18**).

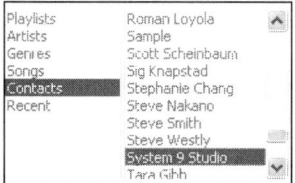

**Figure 7.18**
Contacts displayed in EphPod.

6. Click the Sync Folders button in the toolbar.

   Your contacts are transferred to your iPod.

EphPod has a couple of other contacts-related tricks up its sleeve. If you double-click a contact, for example, you can edit the information in it. This trick is useful if you want to add a note at the last minute before moving your contacts to the iPod.

You can also create a new contact by choosing New Contact from the File menu. You'll be asked to enter a name for your contact; then the Contact Information window appears. In that window, you can enter such information as your contact's email address, phone number, and work and home addresses (**Figure 7.19**).

**Figure 7.19**
You can edit and create contacts within EphPod.

In addition, you can create memos and move those memos to your iPod. One way to do this is to choose New Memo (as Contact) from the File menu and then enter text in the resulting Edit Memo window. Or you can choose Import Memo from File to create a memo from an existing text file. After the transfer, both types of memos appear as contacts on your iPod.

## Anapod Explorer

Sheesh, is there nothing this utility can't do? No wait, don't answer, I'll tell you: No, not really. Along with its musical talents, Anapod Explorer can also synchronize your contacts and, like EphPod, let you create new contacts. Here's how:

**1.** At the risk of repeating myself, mount your iPod as a removable drive on your PC.

**2.** Choose Connect iPod from the Anapod Explorer menu in the System Tray, and once Anapod Explorer recognizes the iPod, choose Open Anapod Explorer from this same menu.

3. Click the Contacts entry on the left side of the Anapod Explorer window.

4. Depending on what you want to do with your contacts, you have the following options:

- Click New Contact to create a new contact.

- Click Sync with Outlook (Default Folder) to synchronize contacts between the contacts in Outlook's default folder to the iPod.

- Click Sync with Outlook (Choose Folder) to navigate to a different Outlook folder and synchronize those contacts with the iPod (**Figure 7.20**).

**Figure 7.20**
Anapod Explorer lets you copy contacts from Outlook, as well as create your own.

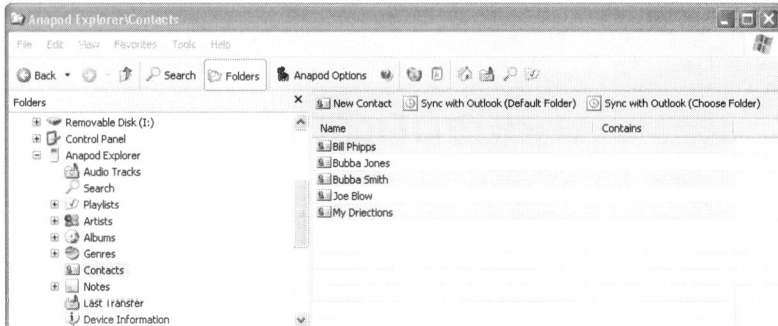

# Removing Contacts from Your iPod

So you've broken up with your boyfriend, your favorite dry cleaner has gone out of business, or you can't recall who this "Jane" person is? There's no need to pack your iPod with contacts you don't need; you can remove them easily. Here's how:

1. If your iPod's not connected to your computer, make the connection, and wait for its icon to appear on the Mac's Desktop or in Windows' My Computer window.

2. Configure your iPod so that it mounts on the computer as an external hard drive.

**3.** Double-click the iPod icon to open the iPod's hard drive.

**4.** Locate and open the Contacts folder on this hard drive.

**5.** Select the contacts you'd like to remove, and drag them to the Trash on the Mac or the Recycle Bin on the PC.

**6.** Disconnect your iPod by dragging its icon to the Trash on the Mac or by unmounting it in Windows' System Tray.

If the contact you want to remove is part of a single vCard file that contains multiple names, you can edit the contact out in a text editor. Just open the vCard file in a text editor, delete the BEGIN:vCard and END:vCard entries (and everything in between), and the contact will be gone. (See "Hacking a .vcf file" later in this chapter for more information.)

# Beyond Addresses

Sure, Apple made its intentions pretty clear when it added the Contacts heading to the iPod's main screen, but there's no reason on earth why you have to use the Contacts area as a location for storing names and addresses. Think outside the stainless-steel-and-Lucite box, and you can come up with countless ways to move the information you need to your iPod.

For instance? Well, how about:

- Notes for your important business meeting
- Your grocery list
- Favorite recipes
- Your master birding list
- Your to-do list for that day
- Car-rental and hotel-reservation confirmation numbers
- For your next overseas vacation, translations of the phrases "Where can I exchange money?", "Where is the bathroom, please?", and "No, honestly, I'm Canadian; please stop sneering at me."

In short, any information that you keep on a small piece of paper and jam into your pocket or purse, you can easily store on your iPod.

Placing the information on your iPod is a simple matter. You can do so by editing an existing .vcf file or by using a contact manager or Address Book program. The following section shows you how to use both methods to create a file that contains the Spanish translation of the phrase "Meatballs, didn't I tell you?"

## Hacking a .vcf File

To edit an existing .vcf file, follow these steps:

1. With your iPod mounted, make a copy of a .vcf file, and open that file in a text editor such as Mac OS X's TextEdit, Mac OS 9's SimpleText, or Windows' Notepad.

   You'll see something like this:

   ```
   BEGIN:vCard
   VERSION:2.1
   FN:Elvis Costello
   N:Costello;Elvis
   EMAIL;INTERNET:thebestelvis@mcmanus.com
   END:vCard
   ```

2. Delete `EMAIL;INTERNET:thebestelvis@mcmanus.com`.

3. Remove the words following `FN:` and `N:`, and enter the word **Meatballs**.

 Make sure that you don't allow any spaces between the colon and the first word.

4. In the line after `N:Meatballs`, enter **NOTE:**.

5. Following `NOTE:`, enter **¿Albóndigas, no te dije?**.

6. Save the file, and copy it to your iPod's Contact folder.

7. Unmount your iPod.

8. When the iPod reboots, choose Contacts from the main menu; scroll down to the Meatballs entry; and burst into happy tears, knowing that you'll never be at a loss for words when you spy meatballs in a Spanish-speaking country.

To add a carriage return so that a space appears between lines, enter **\n** at the end of the line. For your text to appear in this form:

```
Hola Isabel,
¿Cómo estás?
¿Albóndigas, no te dije?
Cristóbal
```

You'd type this:

```
Hola Isabel,\n¿Cómo estás?\n¿Albóndigas, no te dije?\nCristóbal
```

## Entering Data Via an Email Client or Contact Manager

If the manual method is more than you can bear, do the job with a program such as Palm Desktop, Microsoft Entourage or Outlook, or Mac OS X or Windows' own Address Book. Follow these steps:

1. With your iPod mounted, launch one of the applications listed in the preceding section.

2. Create a new contact.

3. In the First Name field, enter **Meatballs**.

4. In the Title field, enter **¿Albóndigas, no te dije?**.

5. Close and, if necessary, save the contact (**Figure 7.21**).

**Figure 7.21**
Roll your own vCard with Mac OS X's Address Book.

6. Drag the Meatballs contact from the application to the Mac's Desktop or the PC's desktop (**Figure 7.22**).

**Figure 7.22**
The results of your handiwork.

7. Drag the resulting Meatballs.vcf file into your iPod's Contacts folder.

8. Unmount your iPod.

9. When the iPod reboots, choose Contacts from the Extras menu; scroll down to the Meatballs entry; and do a little dance, knowing that this helpful phrase is just a couple of clicks away.

Why use the Title field rather than the Notes field? Your email client or contact manager may not offer a field for notes. Truth be told, it doesn't really matter what kind of field you use, because the vCard standard allows you to enter text in any supported field. The Title field, however, has several advantages: All email clients and contact managers use it, the applications rarely use it, and the iPod supports it.

## Additional Utilities of Interest

After Apple opened the door to accessing information on the iPod, it didn't take developers and hobbyists long to find ways to exploit that capability. Up to this point, most efforts had been directed toward moving the information intended for the iPod—names, addresses, and phone numbers—to the device. But some intrepid individuals strayed from this obvious goal and devised some unexpected uses for the iPod's contact capabilities.

### iPod It (Mac OS X only)

www.zapptek.com/ipod-it

Michael Zapp's $15 iPod It can move a wealth of information to the Contacts and Calendars portion of your iPod—including your Microsoft Entourage mail, calendars, notes, and to-do tasks; Apple's iCal calendars, Address Book contacts, Mail message, and Stickies notes; as well as driving directions and weather forecasts (**Figure 7.23**). iPod It is comprised of an application and AppleScript. You can also delete groups of items—weather forecasts, events, and mail, for example—from within the program. iPod It supercedes Zapp's previous iPod applications EntourageEvents, EntourageMail, and EntourageNotes.

**Figure 7.23**
iPod It's many synchronization options.

The latest version of iPod It (version 2.4) allows you to move data into the Notes area of third- and fourth-generation iPods, the iPod Photo, and iPod minis.

## iSpeak It (Mac OS X only)

www.zapptek.com/ispeak-it

Mr. Zapp has more iPod tricks up his sleeve than iPod It. His $13 iSpeak It will take any text, RTF, Word, AppleWorks, or HTML text copied into one of its documents; convert that text to spoken-word files (using the Mac's built-in speech capabilities and robotic voices); turn those spoken-word files into an AIFF file; and convert that AIFF file to the Import format you've selected in iTunes (**Figure 7.24**). When you next sync your iPod, the spoken-word files are added to your iPod.

**Figure 7.24**

If you can stand the robotic narrator, iSpeak It is a great way to listen to text files on your iPod.

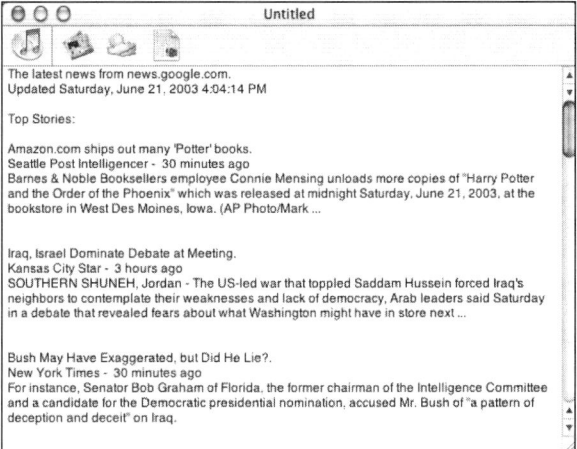

## Pod2Go (Mac OS X only)

www.kainjow.com/pod2go

Kevin Wojniak's $12 Pod2Go downloads headlines, weather, stock quotes, movie listings, driving directions, and text files to your iPod (**Figure 7.25**). Pod2Go includes several syncing options, including the option to auto-sync when you plug in your iPod. On first- and second-generation iPods, Pod2Go stores its data in the Contacts area. You'll find this data in the Notes section on third- and fourth-generation iPods, iPod Photo, and the iPod mini.

**Figure 7.25**

You want that Pod2Go?

## PodWriter (Mac OS X only)

http://steigerworld.com/doug/podwriter.php

The name pretty well describes the function. PodWriter is Doug Steigerwald's free Cocoa application for creating notes that you then copy to your iPod (**Figure 7.26**). Just enter a title, description, and text; save the note; and drop it into your iPod's Contacts folder. The note takes up residence on the iPod. You can also import text into PodWriter. The latest version allows you to spell-check your notes with Mac OS X's built-in spelling checker. Recent versions of the program allow you to view a list of the music files on your iPod and copy them to a destination of your choosing.

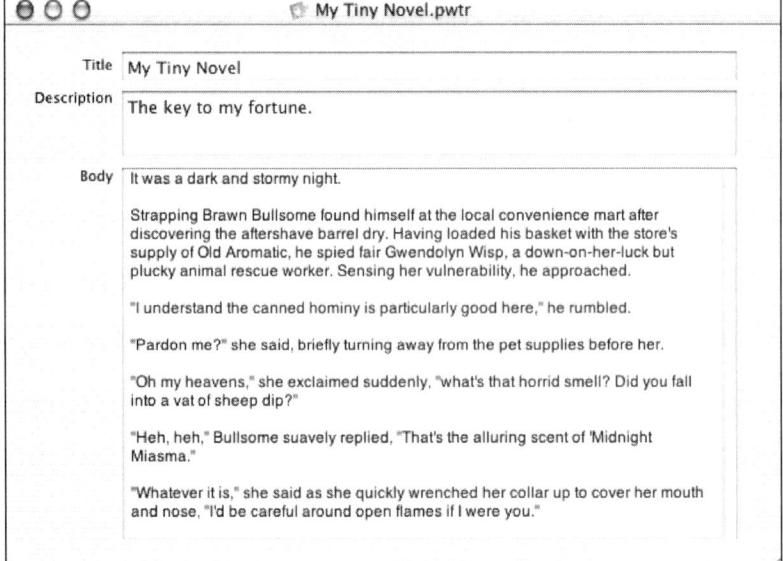

**Figure 7.26**
Take your novel-in-progress with you with PodWriter.

To seek out additional contact utilities, drop by VersionTracker (www.versiontracker.com), and enter **iPod** in the search field in the Macintosh and Windows sections. In next to no time, VersionTracker presents a rich list of utilities for your portable pal.

# Notes

Given that third-party developers and users were concocting new and interesting ways to store text files on their iPods, it's no surprise that Apple introduced a Notes function with third-generation iPods. This function becomes evident when you choose Extras from the iPod's main menu. There, you'll find Notes listed right behind Clock, Contacts, and Calendar. If you mount your iPod as a FireWire or USB 2.0 disk, you'll also spy a Notes folder nestled against the Contacts and Calendars folders when you double-click your iPod.

If you select Notes on your iPod and then select the Instructions entry in the Notes screen, you'll learn that you can view notes on your iPod by copying text files into the iPod's Notes folder. But there's more to know about Notes than that:

- **Notes are strictly limited to 4 kb (kilobits).** If a note exceeds 4 kb, the excess text is cut off.

- **The iPod can hold up to 1,000 notes.** If the iPod's Notes folder contains more than 1,000 notes, only the first 1,000 notes are displayed. (The first 1,000 are determined by alphabetical order rather than creation date.)

- **Notes are cached in memory.** After you've viewed a note, its contents are stored in a 64 Kb (kilobyte) memory cache. This cache is useful because it allows the iPod to display the note without spinning up the hard drive, thereby extending the battery charge. When the cache overflows (because you've read more than 64 Kb of data into it), the oldest notes are given the boot to make room for the information being copied into the cache.

- **Notes support a very basic set of HTML tags** (the Hypertext Markup Language codes used to create Web pages). These tags allow you to create notes that link to other notes or to songs on your iPod.

You may be thinking, "Well, ain't this ducky, Chris, but other than providing a place to store directions to Aunt Vilma's suburban manse or the French translation of 'I'm sorry, but this éclair appears to be stuffed with haddock,' what earthly use are these notes?"

Just this: The iPod can be thrown into something called NotesOnly (or Museum) mode, a mode that locks out everything on the iPod's interface *except* notes, forcing those who use the iPod to start there. This option holds potential for museum curators, tour guides, or real-estate agents who'd like to use the iPod as a guide for presenting facts about a painting, a historical center, or an overpriced property, respectively. It also allows you to turn an iPod into the perfect romantic gift. Because studies indicate that readers of this book are more interested in matters of the heart than most, let's explore this option further.

## The Truth about Tags

Before we do, I must touch upon the iPod's limited HTML support. When I say that it supports basic tags, I mean *basic*. The iPod can't display styled text, so you'll find no tags for creating italic or boldface type. Instead, the included tags are designed to help the iPod interpret Web pages and create links.

These tags are limited to line breaks (`<br>`), opening and closing paragraph marks (`<p>` and `</p>`, respectively), and a tag for creating titles (`<TITLE>The Title You Want</TITLE>`). Normal HTML rules *don't* apply: a `<p>` tag, for instance, doesn't create a line space after a paragraph. You need to use a `<p>` and a `<br>` tag, as I do here, or use two `<p>`s or two `<br>`s.

For example, if you want to produce the following text, enter this in your text editor in a note called Oooh, Baby, Baby:

```
Oooh, my little snookums!
I'll never forget the night we met. The moon, the smell
of your perfume, the drenching rain.
I'm so happy you're mine!
```

Then save the file as plain text, and mount your iPod as an external drive. (To do that, select the iPod in the iTunes Source window, click the Display iPod Options button in the right corner of the iTunes window, select Enable Disk Use, and click OK.) Copy the file to the iPod's Notes folder:

```
<TITLE> Oooh, Baby, Baby</TITLE>
Oooh, my little snookums!<br><p>I'll never forget the
night we met. The moon, the smell of your perfume, the
drenching rain.</p><br><p>I'm so happy you're mine!</p>
```

## The Missing Links

You've made a good start, but you may find it difficult to really bare your soul in a 4Kbits file. You might want to create additional notes and link to them from the original Oooh, Baby, Baby note.

To do so, enter `<a href="the note you refer to">the link text</a>`.

For example, you may want to include a link to an old love letter stored in a file called Letter1.txt, which you've placed in the iPod's Notes folder. Let's say you want that link to say Words of Love. You'd type `<a href="Letter1.txt">Words of Love</a>`.

On the iPod, the words *Words of Love* will be underlined. To travel to that note, simply scroll down until the link appears and then click the Select button. If two links appear on the screen, the active link will be displayed as a solid black line. Other links will be gray. Use the scroll wheel to activate links above or below the active link. Use the Menu button to return to the main text when you're done.

If you'd rather not clutter the top level of the Notes folder with hundreds of notes—and if you want to ensure that your little sweet pea starts in the right place—you can create subfolders within the Notes folder. To refer to files within one of these subfolders, your link must use this format:

```
<a href="folder name/note name">the link text</a>
```

If you have a file called Our First Smooch.txt inside a folder called Great Dates, you might create a Things I'll Never Forget link that reads `<a href="Great Dates/Our First Smooch.txt">Things I'll Never Forget</a>`.

File names in links are not case-sensitive, but you will need to spell out the full name of the note, including the .txt extension, if it has one. And you can't link to notes stored outside the iPod's Notes folder.

Keep in mind that a folder can be a destination, so you could create a link that takes you to the Great Dates folder (which, presumably, contains several notes) by typing `<a href="Great Dates">Unforgettable Moments</a>`.

# Say It with a Song

Unless you're romantically linked with someone who has an abnormal enthusiasm for geeks and loves gadgets, the object of your affection may wonder why you've put a mash note on an iPod. It is, after all, a music player, and you'll get far more bang for your buck if links in your notes play songs or sound effects that describe your feelings.

You might add an entry to Oooh, Baby, Baby that reads, "When I see you, my heart sings." To link the words *my heart sings* to the Ohio Players' "Love Rollercoaster" on the iPod, use this form: `<a href="song=Love Rollercoaster">my heart sings</a>`.

You could just as easily link to a stored recording of you reading a Shakespearean sonnet or of the sound of a gentle, lapping ocean to accompany a recounting of hours spent under the boardwalk.

Like other links, the phrase in the note will be underlined. When you highlight the link by scrolling down the page and then click the iPod's Select button, the linked song or sound will play. When it's done, the iPod returns to the note.

You can also use links to point to a particular playlist, genre, artist, composer, or album. If you wanted to link to the playlist Funky Love

Songs with the phrase "Select me to groove all night!", you'd create this link: `<a href="ipod:music?playlist=Funky Love Songs">Select me to groove all night!</a>`.

If your iPod has more than one version of a song—both the studio version and the live recording, for example—you can combine filters to zero in on a specific song. A link that reads "Select me to hear how I feel!" could play the studio version of James Brown's "Prisoner of Love" from the album *Can Your Heart Stand It!!* Just use this form: `<a href="ipod:music?album=Can Your Heart Stand It!!&song=Prisoner of Love">Select me to hear how I feel!</a>`.

## Locking It Down

Your present is nearly complete. But your gift will be far more effective if it launches directly to the Notes screen when your loved one first switches on the iPod.

For this to happen, you must configure the iPod to launch into NotesOnly mode. To do so, create a plain-text document, and enter this line of text: `<meta name="NotesOnly" content="true">`.

Save the file with the name Preferences, and copy it to the top level of the iPod's Notes folder. When the iPod next launches, it will display the Notes screen, and it won't let you navigate outside the Notes area. You can steer to notes with the scroll wheel and the Select button, but you can't access screens other than those in the Notes area unless you hook the iPod up to your computer and remove the Preferences file you placed in the Notes folder.

Your multimedia masterpiece is complete. Give the iPod a final charge, wrap it in a colorful case, and present it on bended knee to strike the perfect note.

For more information on the subject of creating notes, I strongly suggest that you download Apple's iPod Note Reader Users Guide, which you can find here: http://developer.apple.com/hardware/ipod/ipodnotereader.pdf.

# Notes Tools

I have nothing but sympathy for those who read the previous section and thought, "*Criminy*, isn't the iPod supposed to be *easy*? There must be a better way to create linked notes than this!"

As a matter of fact, if you're using a Mac, there are a couple of easier ways to get linked notes into your iPod: the iPod scripts collection and Flying Meat's VoodooPad.

## The iPod scripts collection (Mac OS X only)

www.apple.com/applescript/ipod

The AppleScript crew at Apple created a few useful scripts for moving text files into your iPod. In this collection, you'll find scripts that clear all the notes from your iPod, copy the contents of the Mac's Clipboard into a note, create a list of notes on your iPod, and download Web pages (with some links intact) to your iPod.

To activate these scripts, follow these steps:

**1.** Open the Applications folder at the root level of your Mac OS X volume and then the AppleScript folder within it.

**2.** In Mac OS X 10.2 (Jaguar), double-click the Script Menu.menu folder. In Mac OS X 10.3 (Panther), go to this same location, and double-click the Install Script Menu application.

This action places an AppleScript menu in the menu bar.

**3.** Travel to www.apple.com/applescript/ipod, and download the iPod scripts collection.

On this Web page, you'll find more details about exactly what these scripts do.

**4.** Choose Go to Folder from the Finder's Go menu, enter **~/Library**, and press the Return key.

This step opens the Library folder inside your users folder.

# Making iContact

5. Look for a Scripts folder in the open Library window.

   If you don't see a Scripts folder, create a new folder, and call it Scripts.

6. Move the iPod folder that you downloaded into the Scripts folder.

   An iPod folder appears in the AppleScript menu in the Mac's menu bar.

7. Launch iTunes, and make sure that the iPod is configured to mount as a removable drive.

   These scripts won't work unless your iPod is mounted on the Desktop. If you've forgotten how to configure your iPod to mount as a hard drive, see Chapter 2 for details.

8. Now it's simply a matter of picking the script you want to run from the iPod folder in the AppleScript menu (**Figure 7.27**).

**Figure 7.27**
The iPod scripts in the Finder's Script menu.

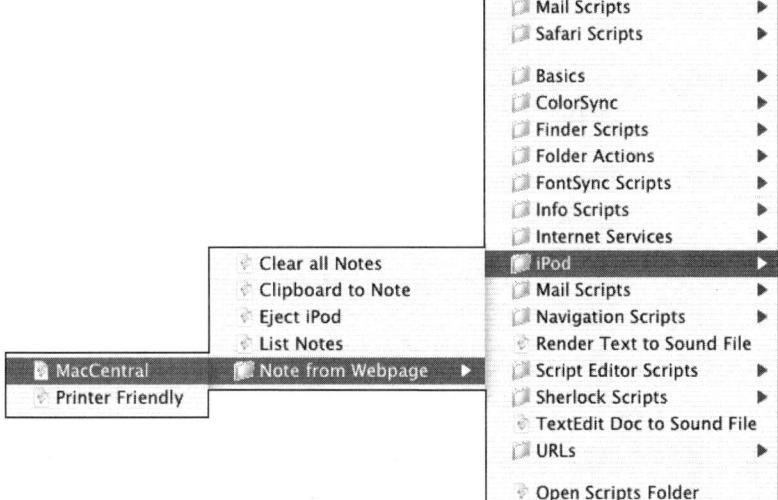

## VoodooPad

www.flyingmeat.com

Flying Meat's $20 VoodooPad is an application that allows you to create notepads with linked pages and then export these notepads to your iPod. How useful could this app be? Take a look by walking through the steps necessary to create a personal-organizer notepad:

1. Download the trial version of VoodooPad, launch it, and choose New Document from the File menu.

   You see a new Welcome to VoodooPad page.

2. Click one of the underlined portions of text.

   If you click the GroceryList text, for example, you open a new window that reads "Write about GroceryList here." This is how VoodooPad creates new pages.

3. Return to the Welcome to VoodooPad page, select all the text, and press the Mac's Delete key to remove all the text on the page.

   You're just clearing the page so that you can create a notepad without the default home page.

4. Enter the following:

   - ToDo
   - Memos
   - UnpleasantChores

   You'll notice that both the ToDo and UnpleasantChores items are underlined. VoodooPad automatically underlines words that contain an internal cap.

5. Click ToDo.

   A new page appears that reads "Write about ToDo here."

6. Type a few things that you need to do.

7. Return to the home page, and double-click Memos to select it.

8. Click the Link button.

   A new page appears that reads "Write about Memos here."

9. Enter any memos you like on this page.

10. Return to the home page, click UnpleasantChores, and list your least-favorite tasks on the resulting page (**Figure 7.28**).

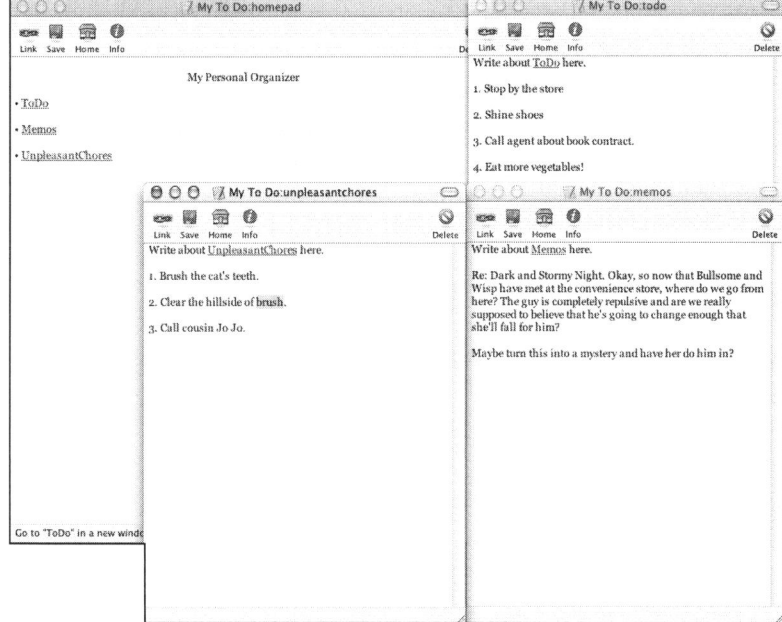

**Figure 7.28**
The voodoo that VoodooPad does so well.

11. When you've completed your notepad, choose Save from the File menu to name and save your notepad.

12. Mount your iPod on the Mac's Desktop.

    VoodooPad won't be able to save its notepads to your iPod unless the iPod is mounted as a removable drive.

13. Choose Export from the File menu, and from the submenu, choose either Export to iPod Notes or Export to iPod Contacts.

    If you have a third- or fourth generation iPod, iPod Photo, or iPod mini, you'll likely want to choose Export to iPod Notes. Because the first- and second-generation iPods don't support Notes, choose Export to iPod Contacts if you own one of these iPods.

If you have more than one iPod attached to your Mac, you'll see a message that reads "You've got more than one iPod!" You lucky dog. Well, for now, I'm just going to use the one named *NameofiPod* (where *NameofiPod* is the name of the iPod VoodooPad has chosen to use).

14. Unmount your iPod, and whisper "Oooohhh" when you find the notepad you just created on your iPod.

# 8

# Make a Date

After Apple sanctioned the iPod for use as a contact keeper, none of us should have slapped our foreheads and bellowed, *"Who woulda thunk it?"* when the diminutive device was later updated to display calendars. Contact and calendar management go hand in hand, and if the iPod was going to serve as a personal information manager, eventually, it also had to support calendars.

Since the release of version 1.2 of the iPod software, it does—in iPods formatted for either the Mac or Windows. Such support likely wouldn't exist were it not for standards that make it easy to move calendar information from one place to another—computer to computer, computer to the Web, and computer to iPod, for example. Fortunately, such standards live in the form of vCalendar and iCalendar: universal formats, similar to the vCard standard, that allow you to transport contact information easily from hither to yon (and beyond).

In this chapter, I'll give you the lowdown on these standards and show you how to best put them to use with your iPod and your computer's calendar application.

# Va-va-va-vCal

To understand how your iPod handles appointments and events, it helps to know what's going on behind the scenes.

## A Little History

Flip back a chapter, and you'll learn that during the 1990s, the Versit group created the vCard standard. Undoubtedly, as the members of this group clapped themselves on the backs for a job well done, one member interrupted with "Ahem, excuse me, but since the bus to the airport won't be here for another hour, what say we hammer together a standard for swapping calendar information as well?"

And thus were born the vCalendar and iCalendar standards.

vCal, as the vCalendar standard is affectionately known, is a format for exchanging calendar and scheduling information between vCal-aware applications and devices. (vCal-aware devices include Palm Computing devices and the iPod.) iCalendar, which lacks an affectionate nickname, is a format for exchanging calendars on the Internet. You can recognize iCalendar files by their .ics file extension (mycalendar.ics, for example). The iPod can read both vCal and iCalendar files.

These standards were written to be platform-independent, meaning that you can use them on a variety of computers running an assortment of operating systems (such as Windows, the Mac OS, and Linux).

## Anatomy of a vCal File

Were you to open a very basic vCal file in a text editor, you'd see that it contains such information as the application you used to create the file (Apple's iCal or Microsoft Outlook, for example); your time zone (U.S. Pacific, for example); and the date, time, and duration of your appointment. These files can also contain alarm information (whether to display an audible or visual alarm, or both), notes, and attendees (those whom you've invited to your appointment).

Here are the contents of a vCard file I created with Apple's iCal application:

```
BEGIN:VCALENDAR
CALSCALE:GREGORIAN
X-WR-TIMEZONE;VALUE=TEXT:US/Pacific
METHOD:PUBLISH
PRODID:-//Apple Computer\, Inc//iCal 1.0//EN
X-WR-CALNAME;VALUE=TEXT:Meeting
VERSION:2.0
BEGIN:VEVENT
SEQUENCE:10
DTSTAMP:20050109T223001Z
SUMMARY:My Appointment
UID:D26B4DF8-F432-11D6-82DE-00039366F0C4
ORGANIZER;CN=Bubba Jones:mailto:bubba@bubba.com
X-WR-ITIPSTATUSML;VALUE=TEXT:UNCLEAN
DTSTART;TZID=US/Pacific:20050109T160000
DURATION:PT1H30M
DESCRIPTION:Mention the goat?
END:VEVENT
END:VCALENDAR
```

The entries worth paying attention to are:

- **PRODID.** This entry is the name of the program you used to create the file.

- **DTSTAMP.** This entry is the date and time that you created the file. I created this file on January 9, 2005—thus, the 20050109 entry.

- **SUMMARY.** This entry is the name of my appointment.

- **ORGANIZER.** This event was created by my alter ego, Bubba Jones, so Bubba's name and email address are attached to the file.

- **DTSTART.** The event is scheduled for January 9, 2005, U.S. Pacific time at 4:00 p.m. (The T160000 entry indicates 4:00 p.m. on a 24-hour clock.)

- **DURATION.** This entry details how long the appointment lasts. In this case, my appointment is scheduled for an hour and a half.

- **DESCRIPTION.** Any notes you've created for the appointment follow the DESCRIPTION entry.

If you add an appointment to your iPod, this information will appear in the Event screen:

- **The date of the appointment.** Displayed in day/month/year format—11 Jan 2005, for example.

- **The time and duration of the appointment.** Displayed as 4:00–5:30 PM, for example.

- **The name of the appointment.** If you've named it My Appointment in your computer's calendar application, so shall it be named on your iPod.

- **The attendees.** If you've added attendees to the appointment in your computer's calendar application, those names will appear next in the Event screen.

- **Notes.** Any notes you've entered on your computer will appear last in the Event screen.

Visual and audible alarms are also transferred to your iPod. But you'll see no indication in the Event screen—or anywhere else, for that matter—that such alarms exist (though you'll have a pretty good idea when the alarm goes off).

# Working with Calendars

Now that you're more familiar with the underpinnings of calendars on your computer and iPod, you're all set to do something practical with them. In the following pages, I'll show you how to create calendars in common Macintosh and Windows applications and then move those calendars to your computer. I'll also reveal the steps for removing expired calendar events from your iPod.

# Creating Calendars

Apple would have looked mighty foolish adding calendaring capabilities to the iPod without also providing Mac users a calendar application. It did so by releasing iCal, a free, basic calendar application that runs under Mac OS X 10.2 and later (including Mac OS X 10.3, Panther).

If you have a Mac that's incapable of running the last couple of iterations of Mac OS X, fear not; iCal isn't the only Macintosh application that's compatible with the iPod. Both Microsoft Entourage (part of Microsoft Office X and Microsoft Office 2004 for Macintosh) and Palm's Palm Desktop 4.x can also export iPod-compatible vCal files.

Windows users can create iPod-friendly calendar files, too. Unfortunately, they can't do it with an Apple application. Although iCal and the Windows iPod were announced in nearly the same breath and iTunes has recently been brought to the Windows platform, Apple didn't feel compelled to release a version of iCal for Windows. Fortunately, Windows users who have a copy of Microsoft Office will discover that Outlook can export calendar files that are compatible with the iPod, as can Palm's Palm Desktop 4.x.

## iCal (Mac OS X 10.2 or later)

iCal allows you to import both vCal and iCalendar files. It exports only iCalendar files. (Its inability to export vCal files is no great loss to iPod owners, however, as the iPod can read both formats.)

I don't intend to give you a complete overview of iCal; I'll leave that to the author of *Secrets of iCal*. I will, however, offer you the basics, showing you how to create a calendar and make that calendar ready for transfer to your iPod. You'll start by creating an *event* (iCal's term for an appointment). Follow these steps:

1. If you're running Mac OS X 10.2 or later, download and install a copy of iCal, if you haven't already (www.apple.com/ical).

2. Launch iCal.

    You'll see that the iCal window is divided into three panes: Calendars (where your individual calendars are listed), the main view (where you view your calendar by month, week, or day), and the To Do pane. The program also includes an Event Info drawer where you enter information such as the name, time, and the interesting details about a particular event (**Figure 8.1**).

**Figure 8.1**

Apple's iCal.

3. Click the Home entry in the Calendars pane.

   iCal ships with two calendars: Home and Work. (You can create additional calendars by clicking the plus-sign [+] button at the bottom of the iCal window.) Right now, though, you're going to add an event to the Home calendar.

4. Click the Week button at the bottom of the iCal window to switch to Week view.

   You can use any view you like. I suggest using Week view because it illustrates one of the easiest ways to create an event.

5. Click and drag in a date column to create an event (**Figure 8.2**).

   When you let go of your mouse, highlighted lettering appears within the event box.

**Figure 8.2**

An iCal event.

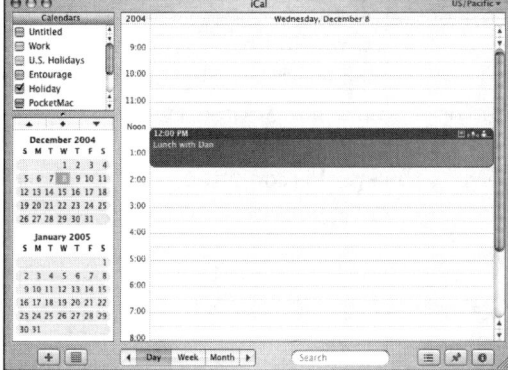

**6.** Begin typing to name your event.

**7.** Rearrange the event to your satisfaction.

To move the event earlier or later in the day, for example, drag it to a new location. To move it to a different day, drag it to the day you desire. To adjust the length of the appointment, drag the top or bottom border of the event box.

**8.** Double-click inside the dark area at the top of your event to open the Event Info drawer (**Figure 8.3**).

**Figure 8.3**

An iCal Event Info window.

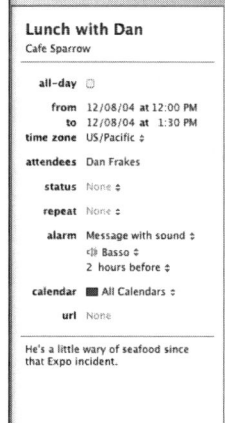

Within this window, you can adjust the date and time of your event, switch on audio and visual alarms, determine how often the event repeats (daily, weekly, monthly, or yearly), add invitees, and create notes.

**NOTE** Setting an iCal alarm to be visual-only has no bearing on how the iPod presents the alarm. When you configure the iPod to play an aural alarm (see the "Alarming Events" sidebar later in this chapter), the alarm will sound off even if you've created a visual-only alarm.

9. When the event is configured to your liking, feel free to create additional events.

10. To export your completed calendar, make sure that the Home calendar is still selected in the Calendars pane, and choose Export from the File menu.

11. In the resulting iCal: Export dialog box, select a destination for your calendar, give it a name, and click Export.

Your calendar is saved to the destination and ready to move to your iPod.

## What's the Big To Do?

One feature introduced with the third-generation iPod is support for To Do items—little reminders, such as "shampoo the llama" and "burnish the banister," that you enter in your calendar application.

Getting To Do items onto your iPod is a cinch if you're using iCal and the iPod Software 2.0.1 Updater or later. Just run iSync, as I outline in Chapter 7, and your To Do items will be copied to the iPod. You can find To Do items on your iPod by following this path: Main Menu > Extras > Calendars > To Do. All the To Do items that have been copied to your iPod are listed in the To Do screen.

To view a To Do item, simply choose an item in the To Do screen and press the Select button. While viewing a To Do item, you can view another such item by pressing the iPod's Forward or Back button. Regrettably, there's no way to "tick off" a To Do item. If you've indicated the successful completion of a To Do item by checking it in iCal, however, when you next sync your iPod with your iCal calendars the words "Status: Completed" appear below the item in the iPod's To Do screen.

In Outlook, To Do items are called Tasks. Currently, Outlook doesn't give you a way to move Tasks directly into the To Do area of the iPod. But Mike Matheson's iPodSync and iPodSoft's iPod Agent (programs I mention in Chapter 7) will place Tasks in the To Do area on third- and fourth-generation iPods, iPod Photo, and the iPod mini.

## Microsoft Entourage (Mac OS X)

Microsoft Entourage, the email client and personal information manager application included with Microsoft Office X and Microsoft Office 2004, offers less support for transportable calendar files than iCal does. Unlike iCal, Entourage doesn't allow you to export entire calendars; rather, you can export only single events (and not in a terribly intuitive fashion). Here's how it works:

1. Launch Entourage, and click the Calendar button.

2. Select Week view in the toolbar at the top of the window.

   You can use any view you like. I suggest using Week view because it illustrates one of the easiest ways to create an event.

3. Click and drag in a date column to create an event (**Figure 8.4**).

**Figure 8.4**
An Entourage event.

When you let go of your mouse, a range of time is selected.

4. Double-click within this range to produce an untitled window where you can adjust the date and time of your event, schedule alarms, add notes, determine how often the event repeats, and add invitees (**Figure 8.5**).

**Figure 8.5**
Inside an Entourage event.

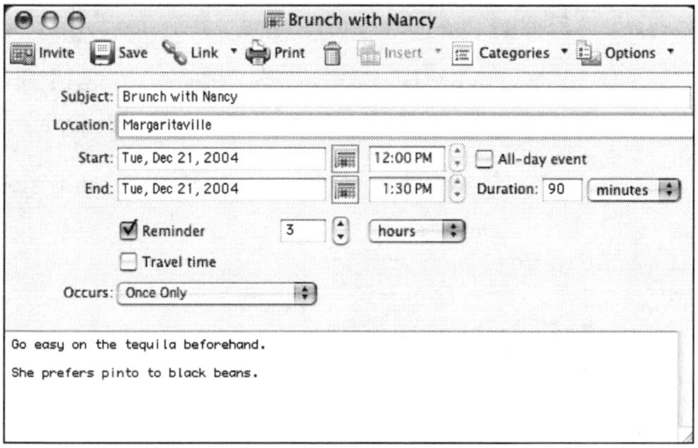

5. Click the Save button at the top of the window to save your event and close the window.

To move the event earlier or later in the day, drag it to a new location. To move it to a different day, drag it to the day you desire. To adjust the length of the appointment, drag the bottom border of the event box.

Entourage offers no command for exporting calendars or events. To create a file for your event, you must drag it from your calendar to the Mac's Desktop or into a Finder window, where it turns into a .ics file.

The version of Entourage included in Microsoft Office 2001 doesn't support vCal or iCalendar files.

## Palm Desktop 4.x (Mac OS 9, Mac OS X)

Palm's free Palm Desktop offers vCal support in both the Mac OS 9 and OS X versions of the application, giving those who are using Apple's older operating system a chance to create calendars for their iPods. Regrettably, vCal files created with Palm Desktop don't display Notes or Invitees information on the iPod.

Creating calendars with both the Mac OS 9 and Mac OS X versions works the same way. Here's how to do it:

1. Download and install a copy of Palm Desktop (www.palmone.com/us/software/desktop/mac.html).

2. Launch Palm Desktop, and select Date Book in the toolbar.

3. Click the Week tab in the Date Book window.

   You can use any view you like. I suggest using Week view because it illustrates one of the easiest ways to create an event.

4. Click and drag in a date column to create an event (**Figure 8.6**).

**Figure 8.6**
A Palm Desktop event.

5. In the resulting event window, name your event.

6. Double-click the event to open the Event window, where you can adjust the date and time of your event, schedule alarms, and determine how often the event repeats (**Figure 8.7**).

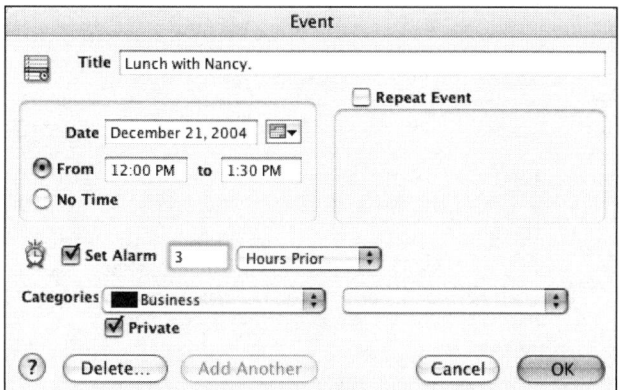

**Figure 8.7**
The makings of a Palm Desktop event.

Unlike its counterparts in iCal and Entourage, the Palm Desktop Event window doesn't allow you to designate invitees or add notes to your event. Although you can add contacts and memos to a Palm Desktop event, that information doesn't transfer to the iPod. For this reason, if you use Palm Desktop, you should type notes and contact information after the name of the event.

7. Click OK after you've configured the event to your liking.

   To move the event earlier or later in the day, drag it to a new location. To move it to a different day, drag it to the day you desire. To adjust the length of the appointment, drag the bottom border of the event box.

8. Move events, if you so desire.

You can move events out of Palm Desktop in two ways.

- Simply drag the event to the Mac's Desktop or a Finder window. When you do, the event is saved as a vCal (.vcs) file.

- Choose Export from Palm Desktop's File menu. In the Export: Palm Desktop dialog box, you'll have the opportunity to save your entire

Date Book as a single vCal file. To do so, choose Date Book from the Module pop-up menu, All Datebook Items from the Items pop-up menu, and vCal from the Format pop-up menu (**Figure 8.8**). Then name your file and click the Export button.

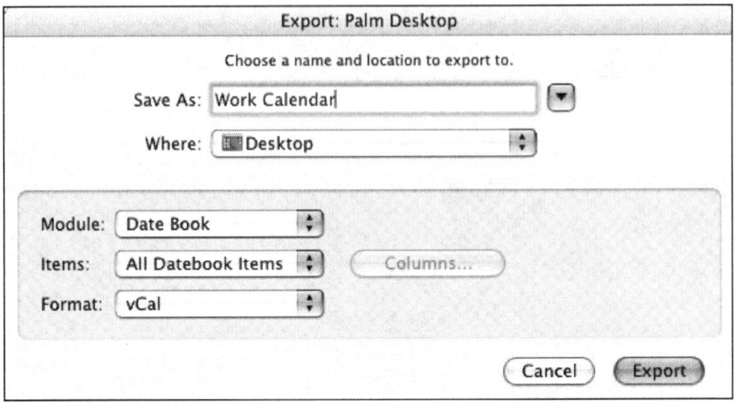

**Figure 8.8**
Use these settings to export a Palm Desktop Date Book as a vCal file.

## iCal: The Easier Way

Given that iCal is a snap to use and that you can use it to export entire calendars to your iPod, why shouldn't Mac users abandon these other applications and use iCal exclusively?

You may be reluctant to do so because all your appointments are already in Entourage or Palm Desktop. Or you may prefer the additional features of these other applications.

Far be it for me to muck with the way you organize your life, but may I suggest that if you intend to use your iPod extensively as your mobile calendar-keeper, you consider switching to iCal—even if only as a conduit for moving data from the other applications to your iPod? If you employ iCal (and Apple's device-synchronization application, iSync), you will find it much easier to move both your contacts and calendars on and off your iPod.

## iCal: The Easier Way *(continued)*

Moving appointments from Entourage and Palm Desktop to iCal is not difficult. Here's how:

**Entourage.** To import calendar events into iCal from Entourage, choose Import from iCal's File menu. In the resulting Import dialog box, you'll see the Import Entourage Data option. Select this option, and click Import (**Figure 8.9**).

**Figure 8.9**
Importing Entourage calendars in iCal.

If it isn't already open, Entourage will launch, appearing as the frontmost application. A progress window appears as events and *tasks*—Entourage's term for To Do items—are brought into iCal. When iCal is finished, you'll find your imported data in the Entourage calendar that's now listed in iCal's Calendars pane.

**Palm Desktop.** Now you know that you can export events in Palm Desktop's Date Book as a single vCal file. Do so. When you have the exported file in hand, launch iCal, and choose Import from the File menu. Select the Import a vCal File option, and in the resulting dialog box, navigate to the vCal file you exported from Palm Desktop. The data in the vCal file will be imported into the currently selected calendar.

## Outlook (Windows)

Microsoft's ubiquitous Outlook supports both vCal and iCalendar files, though not all the information you enter in an Outlook appointment will appear on your iPod. Here's the Windows way:

**1.** Launch Outlook, and click the Calendar button.

**2.** Choose any view you like, right-click the date you want to add an event to, and choose Add Appointment from the contextual menu.

3. In the resulting Untitled-Appointment window (**Figure 8.10**), adjust the day and time of your appointment, schedule alarms, and determine how often the event repeats (by clicking the Recurrence button).

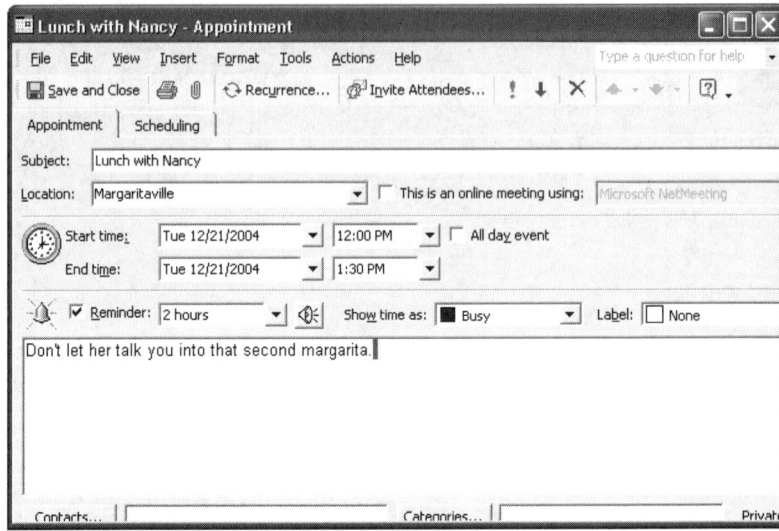

**Figure 8.10**
An Outlook Appointment window.

Although Outlook has a couple of places where it appears that you can include invitees in your appointment, those invitees will not appear in the calendar item on your iPod.

4. When the appointment is configured to your satisfaction, save and close the appointment.

   In Day and Work Week view, you can alter the date and time of your event by dragging the event. To move the event earlier or later in the day, drag it to a new location. To move it to a different day, drag it to the day you desire. To adjust the length of the appointment, drag the top or bottom border of the event box.

5. Click an appointment, and choose Save As from the File menu.

6. In the resulting Save As dialog box, choose iCalendar Format from the Save As Type pop-up menu, name your file, and click Save (**Figure 8.11**).

**Figure 8.11**

Use these settings to save an Outlook appointment as an iCalendar file.

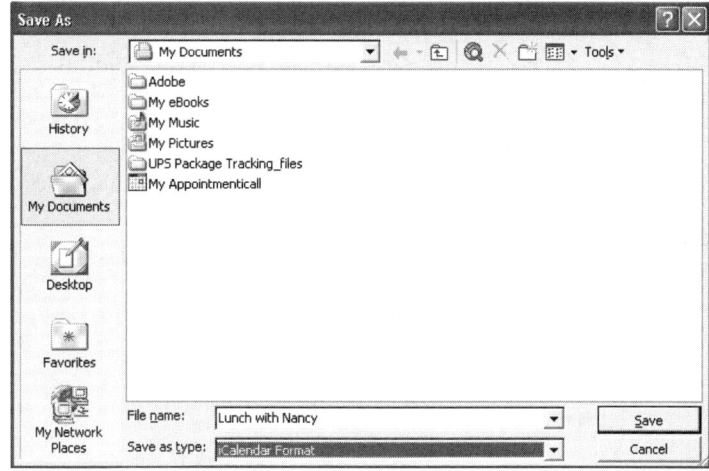

Why not save your file in the vCalendar format that's also offered in this pop-up menu? For good reason. If you save your Outlook appointment as a vCal file, the alarms don't work on the iPod. Appointments saved in the iCalendar format broadcast their iPod alarms as they should.

And as tempting as it may be to pretend that you're using a Mac and drag an Outlook appointment to the Desktop, don't bother. If you do, you'll create an Outlook file that your iPod can't read.

## Palm Desktop 4.x (Windows)

Palm Desktop 4.x for Windows works much the same way as the Macintosh version. Where it differs is in its capability to include notes that the iPod can read and in its incapability to transfer working alarms to the iPod. Here's how to set it up:

1. Download and install Palm Desktop (www.palm.com/software/desktop).

2. Launch Palm Desktop, and click the Calendar button.

3. Click the Week tab in the Date Book window.

   You can use any view you like. I suggest using Week view because it illustrates one of the easiest ways to create an event.

4. Click and drag in a date column to create an event.

**5.** In the resulting event window, name your event.

**6.** Double-click the event to open the Edit Event window.

In the General tab, you can adjust the date and time of your event and schedule alarms (**Figure 8.12**).

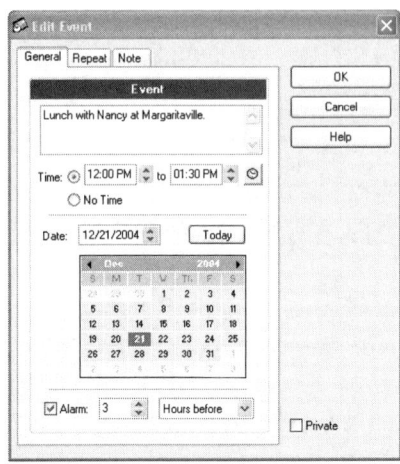

**Figure 8.12**
Editing a Palm Desktop event.

To schedule repeating events, click the Repeat tab, and specify how often you want the event to repeat. To add a note to your event, click the Note tab, and type your text (**Figure 8.13**).

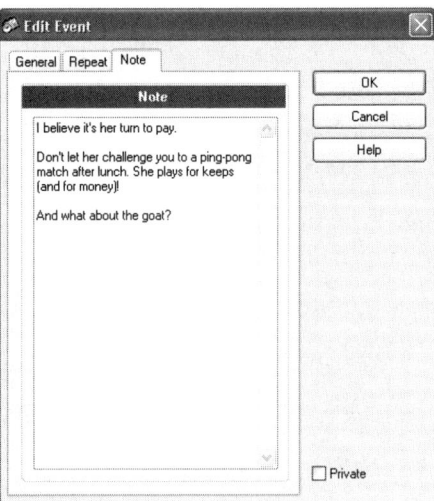

**Figure 8.13**
Why doesn't the Mac version of Palm Desktop offer a Note window?

As in the Macintosh version of the program, you can't attach invitees to events and expect them to appear within a calendar event on your iPod.

**7.** When you've finished editing your event, click OK.

To move the event earlier or later in the day, drag it to a new location. To move it to a different day, drag it to the day you desire. To adjust the length of the appointment, drag the triangle that appears at the bottom of the event.

**8.** To export your event, select it and choose Export vCal from the File menu.

**9.** In the resulting Export As dialog box, name your file, and click Export.

As I hinted earlier, the vCal files exported from Palm Desktop for Windows don't create alarms that work on the iPod. Regrettably, unlike Outlook, Palm Desktop can't save events as .ics files (which play alarms correctly).

## Alarming Events

With all this talk of alarms, you may wonder exactly how event alarms work on your iPod. (Alarms associated with the iPod's alarm-clock function are a completely separate kettle of carp; we're discussing strictly alarms associated with calendar events.) Allow me to reveal all.

To begin with, if you expect your iPod to play or display alarms, you have to tell it to do so. The means for communicating your desire is the Alarms entry. On iPods running iPod Software 2.0 Updater or later, you'll find this entry in the iPod's Calendars area (which you find by following this path: Main Menu > Extras > Calendars > Alarms). If you have a first- or second-generation iPod, you'll find Alarms in the Settings screen.

The Alarms entry has three settings: Off, Silent, and On/Beep (it's called On on the earlier iPods and Beep on third- and fourth-generation iPods, iPod Photo, and the iPod mini). You cycle through these settings by selecting Alarms and repeatedly pressing the Select button. By default, Alarms are set to On/Beep. This means that your alarm will beep and display an alarm message. (This message won't disappear until you press the Select button.) Note, however, that this beep emerges from inside the iPod and is *not* played through the iPod's sound port.

*continues on next page*

> ### Alarming Events (continued)
>
> That's why the displayed alarm message doesn't go away until you press Select. Should you miss the aural alert, a single glance at the iPod's active display will tell you that an alarm has gone off. (Don't worry—alert messages won't keep your iPod awake and, thus, deplete your battery. If you haven't dismissed the alarm message when the iPod goes to sleep, it will appear onscreen when you next awaken your iPod.)
>
> When you select Silent in the Alarms screen, your iPod won't emit its little beep to alert you when an alarm event occurs. Instead, the iPod displays the alert message only. This is a good option to choose if you take your iPod to places where a shrillish alarm would be unappreciated (movie theaters, restaurants, and church services, for example).
>
> And the Off alarm setting tells the iPod to pay no mind to alarms attached to your calendar events.
>
> Note that the iPod mini's alarm sound is pretty quiet in comparison to the alarm on the white iPods. Unless the mini is close by, you're likely to miss the sound.

## Manually Transferring Calendars to the iPod

Now that you have all these calendar files, you should do something useful with them. To add them to your iPod manually, follow these steps:

1. Plug your iPod into your computer, and wait for it to mount.

    The iPod icon will appear on the Mac's Desktop or in Windows' My Computer window.

2. Double-click the iPod icon, and keep an eye peeled for the Calendars folder (**Figure 8.14**).

**Figure 8.14**

The iPod's Calendars folder.

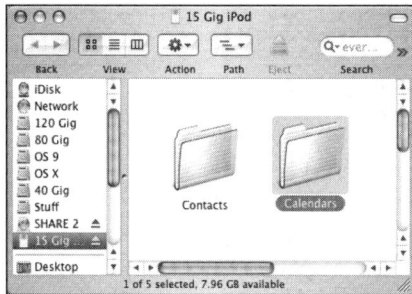

3. Drag your calendar files to this Calendars folder.

4. Unmount your iPod, and unplug it.

5. When the main screen appears, scroll down to Extras, press Select, scroll to the Calendar entry, and press Select again.

   If you've moved multiple iCal calendars to your iPod, the screen you see will contain a list of those calendars (Home, Work, and Billy's Aussie Rules Football Schedule, for example). Scroll to the calendar you want to view, and press Select. In the next window, you'll see an overview of the current month. Those days that include events will be marked with a single black dot. (Days that contain multiple events don't display multiple dots.)

   If your iPod doesn't contain multiple calendars, when you press Select with the Calendars item highlighted, you'll be taken directly to the screen that displays the overview of the current month.

6. To view the appointments on a particular day, scroll to the date of the appointment, and press Select.

   In the next window, a list of appointments for that day appears.

7. Scroll to the appointment you want to view, and press Select again.

   The details of that appointment are displayed in the iPod's Event screen.

 If you want to dash from month to month, it's easy to do if you're running the iPod Software 1.3 Updater on a first- or second-generation iPod or using a third- or fourth-generation iPod, iPod Photo, or iPod mini. Just select a calendar and press the Forward or Back button to move ahead or back a month, respectively.

# Manually Removing Calendars from the iPod

Unless you make a habit of alienating your business associates, friends, and family members, you probably don't need to remove contacts from your iPod routinely. Calendar items, on the other hand, are a different story. That lunch you had with your cousin last March 28th is now a dim memory (except for the fact that he stuck you with the check *again*) and could easily be expunged from your iPod's memory.

To do so, follow these steps:

1. Plug your iPod into your computer, and wait for it to mount.

    The iPod icon will appear on the Mac's Desktop or in Windows' My Computer window.

2. Double-click the iPod icon, and keep an eye peeled for the Calendars folder.

3. Open the Calendars folder, and drag the appropriate vCal or .ics file out of the folder (and into the Trash or Recycle Bin, if you like; **Figure 8.15**).

    The events associated with that file no longer appear on your iPod.

**Figure 8.15**
Drag calendar files out of the iPod's Calendars folder to remove events from your iPod.

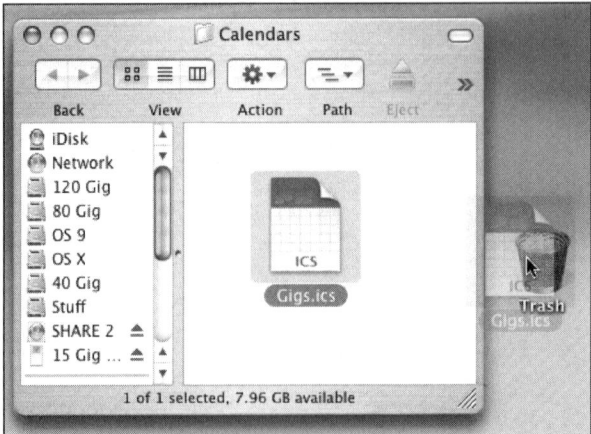

Before you remove one of these files, bear in mind that if a vCal or .ics file contains multiple events, trashing that file might obliterate both past and future appointments. It's always a good idea to know exactly what a file contains before trashing it. One way to avoid doing The Bad Thing is to update your calendar on your computer and then replace the calendar file on your iPod with an updated version. (Apple's iSync and some Windows utilities I discuss later can do this for you.)

You needn't worry that a load of calendars is going to overburden your iPod. Even if you're very busy, a year full of appointments and notes will create a calendar file far smaller than a single four-minute AAC file. For this reason, you may choose to keep your old appointments on your iPod, which can come in handy at tax time, when you're tallying the past year's entertainment and travel expenses.

# Automatically Transferring Calendars to the iPod

The manual methods for moving calendars on and off your iPod are hardly backbreaking, but why bother dragging files out of applications and into folders when a utility can do the job for you? Such utilities are available for users of both Mac and Windows iPods.

## iSync (Mac OS X 10.2 and later)

As much as I'd love to offer you a thicker book by reprinting the iSync material from Chapter 7, I'd feel guilty knowing that a few more trees met a pulpy end because of it. On the other hand, I hate to force you to flip back and forth from chapter to chapter, should you have read Chapter 7 when you were particularly sleepy. With that in mind, allow me to refresh your memory by providing these short-and-sweet instructions for using iSync to move iCal calendar events to your iPod:

1. Launch iSync.

2. If your calendars aren't in iCal, import them, using the methods I described earlier.

3. Mount your iPod.

4. If the iPod doesn't appear in iSync, add it by choosing the Add Device command from iSync's File menu.

5. Click the iPod's icon in the iSync window.

6. Make sure that the Contacts check box is checked and that you've selected the calendars you want to place on your iPod (**Figure 8.16**).

**Figure 8.16**
Select the calendars you want to synchronize with iSync.

7. Click the Sync Now button.

## Other and iCal

iCal provides a unique advantage for iPod owners who use a Mac—the iPod can display your calendars in individual screens. It's like this:

If you're using a dockable iPod, an iCal file appears as a separate entry in the Calendars screen and bears that calendar's name—Home, for example. These iPod models also let you view all your information in one calendar called All, accessible from the Calendars screen. Earlier iPod models consolidate all calendars, regardless of the originating application, into a single calendar.

On dockable iPods, vCal files and iCalendar files created in an application other than iCal are jammed into a single calendar named Other. A note for Mac users: If you have an iPod with a dock connector, and you want to display your individual calendars separately, you can import your calendars into iCal and then save them to your iPod. (Windows users don't have this option; they'll find all their calendars under the Other heading.)

### Windows utilities

Yes, I gave away the plot for these utilities in Chapter 7 as well. Most of the Windows utilities I mention that allow you to move your Outlook contacts to the iPod easily—iPodSync, iPod Agent, iAppoint, Outpod, and EphPod—can also transfer Outlook calendar events to your iPod. Try 'em and see!

# 9

# Accessories

*Accessories.* What accessories? Everything you need to operate the iPod comes in the box, right?

*iPod*...Check.

*Headphones*...Check.

*Foam covers for those headphones*...Check.

*Software*...Check.

*Power adapter*...Check.

*FireWire cable*...Check.

*USB 2.0 cable for fourth-generation iPod, iPod Photo, and iPod mini*...Check.

*Plastic belt clip for iPod mini...Check.*

*Dock with 40 GB fourth-generation iPod and iPod Photo models...Check.*

*Case with iPod Photo...Check.*

*A/V cable with iPod Photo...Check.*

*Instructions...Check.*

*Other paperwork...Check.*

What else could you possibly need?

In all likelihood, it won't be until you prepare to exploit the portable portion of the iPod's personality that you'll consider this question seriously. And then, consider it you shall.

"Hmm. I suppose I could put this 20 GB iPod in my front pocket with my keys and loose coins, but I'll bet the shiny back scratches pretty easily."

*or*

"In one hand, I have my white iPod, capable of storing many gigabytes of data. In hand number two, I have my digital camera, capable of storing only so many pictures and movies on its CompactFlash card. There must be an easy way to get data from that camera to my iPod."

*or*

"My new original iPod is supposed to record my voice, but where on earth is the microphone?"

*or*

"Man, I'd love to play these tunes in my car and on my home stereo, but how am I supposed to make the connection?"

*or*

"Whoa! I've got a long road trip ahead of me, and I'm not sure I can afford to stop for an hour at a gas station every time I want to recharge the iPod's battery."

*or*

"Ouch! The size of my ear canals must fall outside the norm. These earbuds don't fit at all!"

So although Apple does include everything you need to get started with the iPod, what is included is *only* a start. To incorporate the iPod into your active life completely, you need more. And more is exactly what I'll discuss in this chapter.

## The Clip-on iPod

It didn't take long after the first iPods shipped for iPod owners to notice the effect gravity can have on objects dropped from an inverted shirt pocket. These same owners undoubtedly noticed that when an unprotected original iPod shared accommodations with a pants-pocketful of loose change and keys, the iPod's shiny metal back came out worse for the wear.

Having paid careful attention to these concerns, Apple issued cases with its third-generation 20 and 40 GB iPods. (By default, 15 GB third-generation iPods remained unprotected, though you could purchase the case separately for $39. The iPod mini is protected only by an included belt clip, which prevents it from falling from your person, but offers no scratch or ding protection.) Although the case was stylish and provided some protection, it required that you remove the iPod to access the front-panel controls (not a terrible burden, considering that the 20 and 40 GB models also shipped with the remote control), and the case bore a clip that was too easy to break.

So all in all, an unsatisfactory case—though a free one.

When Apple released the fourth-generation iPod, it cut some costs by leaving this case and the formerly bundled remote control out of the box. Given that many people soon replaced Apple's case with one that was more robust (or simply more fun), this isn't a terrible loss. Likewise, not everyone appreciated the charms of Apple's Remote Control, so its absence is hardly a deal-breaker.

Apple's case reappeared as a bundled item with the iPod Photo. The remote control, however, remains an optional add-on for those who want it.

So if Apple's iPod case doesn't measure up, and the iPod mini is vulnerable to having its face scratched, what should one look for in a case?

# What to Look For

A good case should offer the following features (**Figures 9.1** and **9.2**):

**Figure 9.1**
Waterfield Designs' iPod Case has all the features you'd look for in an iPod case: padding, easy access to controls and ports, a belt clip, and stylish design.

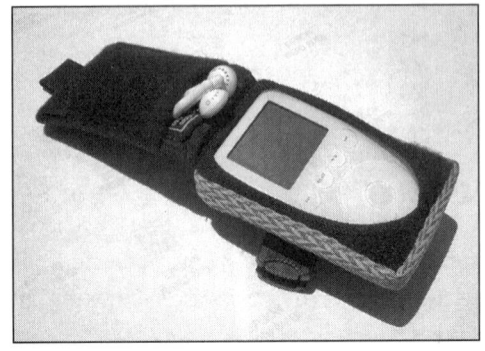

**Figure 9.2**
Detachable belt clips are mighty convenient.

- A system for attaching the iPod to your body (a belt clip or strap, for example)
- Construction sturdy enough to protect the iPod from scratches
- A place to store the iPod's earbuds (a roomy case will also hold the remote control)

These features are the bare minimum you should expect from your case. Frankly, with a piece of bubble wrap, a clothespin, and a couple of pieces of duct tape, you could construct a case that meets these requirements. Looking beyond the essentials, what else might you look for?

- A way to detach the iPod from your body easily

  At times, you'll want to fiddle with the iPod—adjust the volume, flick on the Hold switch, or use the controls to skip a song. You'll find it more convenient to do so if you don't have to detach some elaborate harness or use a pair of pliers to pry apart a belt clip. Look for the kind of quick-release clip you find on many of today's cellular-phone cases.

- A way to access the controls easily

  Although the remote control has made access to the controls less necessary than it was during the pre-remote-control days, at times you'll still need to punch and scroll around the face of the iPod—particularly when you're searching for contact or calendar information. A case that opens in the front will make these kinds of operations far more convenient. You should also be able to access the audio jack—and, ideally, the data/power port and Hold switch—without having to disassemble the case.

- Design sturdy enough to provide your iPod a reasonable chance of survival, should you drop it

  Although an unscratched iPod has its aesthetic benefits, little good it does you if it won't play because you've dropped the poor thing and broken it. The iPod is fairly resilient, but it won't hurt to give it a helping hand by swaddling it in a well-padded case.

- Design that makes a statement

  Let's face it—you dropped a lot of cash on your iPod. There are far cheaper (and less elegant) music players on the market. Do you really want to encase this jewel in a shoddy-looking case? The iPod is cool. It deserves a cool case.

# On the Cases

Realizing that there was a crying need for iPod cases, several companies produced some worthwhile products. When Apple rearranged the design of the iPod and issued the iPod mini, case manufacturers had to modify their designs as well. The move to the fourth-generation design initiated yet another case change. Most case manufacturers now sell cases for the first three generations of the white iPod, and iPod mini cases are more common. As we go to press, the fourth-generation iPod is new on the market, and few cases are available for it (though a case designed for a first- or second-generation iPod will do in a pinch). By the time you read this, the case manufacturers listed below are likely to offer cases for the fourth-generation iPod and iPod Photo as well.

Now let's get down to some of my favorite cases.

## Cases by Waterfield Designs

www.sfbags.com

Waterfield Designs' $40 iPod Case meets all the aforementioned criteria. It features a quick-release clip that releases only if you turn the case to the side (to prevent accidental unclipping), a padded front panel that flips up to give you complete access to the iPod's front controls, and a slit top and bottom that allow you to reach the iPod's ports and switches. It's a stylish, mostly-black case that comes with red, white, gray, or blue highlights (refer to Figures 8.1 and 8.2).

Waterfield offers cases for all white iPod designs but doesn't currently make a case for the iPod mini.

Waterfield has two other carriers for your iPod. The first is the $35 iPod Gear Pouch. Men who are the tiniest bit insecure about their masculinity may shun the iPGP because it resembles a clutch purse. But those who aren't bothered by carrying the pouch will find it a stylish way to store not only their iPods, but also their earbuds, Dock, power adapter, and any other extraneous iPod gear that they typically shove into a spare pocket. The iPod Gear Pouch is mostly black with blue, white, red, and gray highlights.

Proving that Waterfield is more than a little enthusiastic about the iPod, it has even more recently released the $49 iPod inMotion Case (**Figure 9.3**). About the size of a case designed for medium-strength binoculars, this case is intended for those who wish to truck not only their iPod with them, but also a set of Altec Lansing's $150 inMotion portable speakers (discussed below). The iPod inMotion Case is predominantly black with blue, red, gray, or yellow piping.

**Figure 9.3**
Waterfield Designs' roomy iPod inMotion Case.

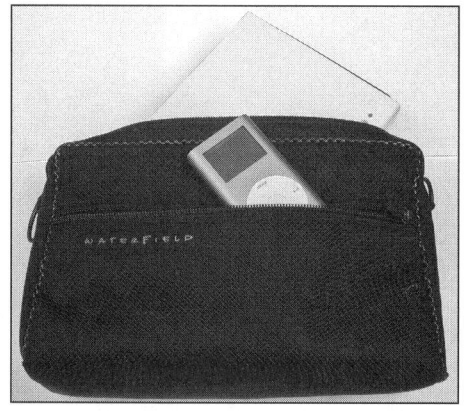

## iPod mini Arm Band

www.apple.com

Although Apple's $29 iPod mini Arm Band provides no protection for the face of the iPod mini, active mini users may find it to their liking. Much like with the iPod mini's included clip, the Arm Band holds the mini securely in place with the assistance of a U-shaped clip (**Figure 9.4**). "Arm Band" is an apt description for this device. The band is long enough to fit around the bicep of most people. The current governor of California would find it a little snug, however.

**Figure 9.4**
Serving as both a storage place for the active iPod mini owner and a tourniquet is Apple's iPod mini Arm Band.

## Cases by Marware

www.marware.com

Marware makes three models of the SportSuit case for the white iPods and three cases and a wrist band for the mini.

The $40 SportSuit Convertible Case (**Figure 9.5**) includes a shaped lid suitable for storing your earbuds; you can flip up this lid to access the iPod's controls. You can also get to the Headphone jack and Remote jack at the top of the iPod without lifting the lid (though you must remove the cover to access the Hold switch). The case includes a flexible belt-clip system that allows you to remove the clip and attach an armband, belt, bike holder, car holder, or lanyard. (The basic package includes a nonrotating belt clip and armband.) The design features a reinforced back and sides, and the lid is sturdy enough to protect the face of the iPod. It's a good-looking case that comes in black, navy (dark blue), blue (wetsuit blue), gray, red, and yellow. This case is available for all white iPods. Marware also offers a similarly configured case for the mini—the Mini SportSuit Convertible, priced at $35.

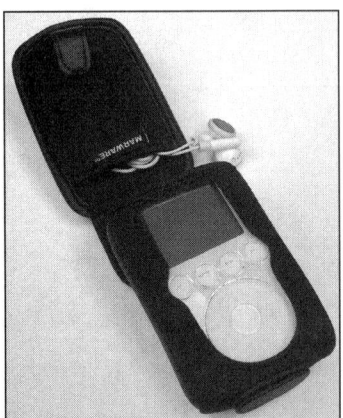

**Figure 9.5**

Marware's versatile SportSuit Convertible Case.

The 4G SportSuit Basic is a $25 neoprene case designed specifically for the fourth-generation iPod and iPod Photo. It lacks storage for your headphones but does come with a flexible clip system, and it provides access to all the iPod's ports and front controls. Marware also sells the Mini SportSuit Basic for $25.

The $20 SportSuit Sleeve is a much more basic case. It includes a nondetachable rotating belt clip, a pouch for your earbuds, a neoprene exterior (with vulcanized neoprene sides), and a top flap that provides a single hole for access to the audio jack. To access the controls, you have to remove the iPod from the case. It comes in the same colors as the SportSuit Convertible Case. The company offers a similar $20 case for the mini, called the SportSuit Safari. Why Safari? These cases feature a fuzzy exterior in animal prints.

The $35 C.E.O. Classic case (which comes in two styles—one for the first- and second-generation iPods, and another for the third-generation iPod) has everything you'd want in a case: easy access to the front controls and top ports, adequate padding, a plastic screen protector, storage on the lid, and a flexible clip system. (You can put a variety of clips on the thing.) The one drawback is that it comes in a single style: black leather. If you're a vegan or looking for a more colorful case, you'll need to look elsewhere.

Marware also makes a wrist-mounted case for the iPod mini: the $30 Mini SportSuit Runabout. The $35 Mini SportSuit Convertible, which includes an armband, clip, and protective cover, looks like a better deal than Apple's armband.

## XtremeMac cases

www.xtrememac.com

XtremeMac makes a couple of interesting iPod cases. The first, the $30 Xtremity iPod Accessory System, is designed for third- and fourth-generation iPods and will likely fit the iPod Photo. It features a plastic holster design that can be used with or without a clear plastic cover. This cover has no holes, so you must unsnap it to access the iPod's wheel and navigation controls. The back of the case includes the SecureSlide system for attaching such accessories as a belt clip, battery pack, or lanyard. If you prefer a more traditional look, check out the company's $30 Deluxe iPod Case, which is available in black leather only.

If you have a first- or second-generation iPod, check out XtremeMac's Designer iPod Case—a solid case for only $13. Such a deal!

## Contour Design cases

www.contourdesign.com

If you'd like to show off your first- or second-generation iPod (5, 10, and 20 GB models only) even when it's tucked snugly into its case, check out Contour Design's completely clear, $30 iSee case. The case provides access to the ports and controls; it features a low-profile clip and four small plastic feet on the back (a nice idea if you don't want your iPod skittering across an airplane tray table). Accompanying the iSee is a small white plastic case for the earbuds.

If you have a third- or fourth-generation iPod or an iPod Photo, take a look at Contour's $40 Showcase case. Much like the iSee, the Showcase attempts to show you as much of the iPod as possible while also protecting the device. The Showcase's rubber edges make it easy to grip, and the clear front includes holes for accessing the iPod's controls.

## Lilipod hardshell case

www.lilipods.com

If you seek the ultimate in iPod protection, check out Erock Studios' $40 Lilipod. Resembling an oversize cigarette lighter, the Lilipod encases your iPod in a 2mm-thick, watertight hard plastic shell (**Figure 9.6**). If you routinely take your iPod skiing or rock climbing, or if you fall way over to the extreme end of the clumsiness bell curve, the Lilipod is the case for you. Once the case is closed, you have no access to the controls or ports. Then again, if you did, it wouldn't be nearly so protective.

**Figure 9.6**
For the ultimate iPod protection, try the waterproof Lilipod.

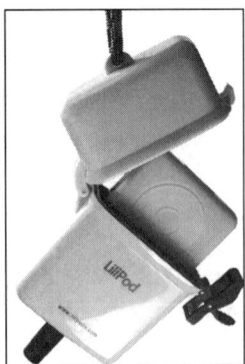

## iPod Armor

http://matias.ca/ipodarmor

Matias' $50 iPod Armor case has slightly less chance than the Lilipod case does of surviving a nuclear winter. Unlike the Lilipod case, this one lets you access the top and bottom ports of your iPod—though not the front controls—once it's closed. It cushions your iPod with a layer of dense foam.

Matias also makes the iPod Armor mini and Clear iPod Armor mini. These $50 cases look great and offer serious protection to your mini.

## Incase Belt for iPod

www.goincase.com

Suppose that you want to take your white iPod jogging, to the gym, or on a bike ride. An iPod clipped to your belt may just get in the way. What you might find more suitable is a fanny-pack arrangement such as the one provided by the Incase Belt for iPod (**Figure 9.7**). As the name implies, this $25 nylon-and-neoprene carrier belt was designed to hold any iPod. Just press the iPod's Play button, shove the iPod into the pouch, belt on the carrier, and start working that cardiovascular system.

**Figure 9.7**
Bicycle-bound iPod users might be interested in the clip-on Incase Belt for iPod.

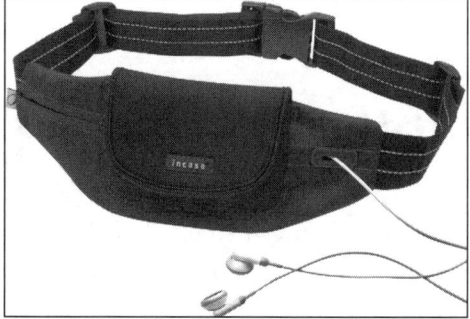

No, you won't have easy access to the front controls (though there are special holes cut into the thing for earbud access), but when you're on a cross-country bike ride, you really shouldn't be taking your hands off the handlebars to fiddle with the iPod's controls anyway.

### The "anything's better than nothing" solution

A quick crawl through the local electronics mart will reveal lots of other ways to protect your iPod. That padded PDA case will do in a pinch, or perhaps the generic $12 MP3 and MiniDisc player case would work. And if you just want something to keep your iPod from being scratched when you throw it into your backpack, how about that cheap camera case?

The fact is, if you don't care about access or style, you can put your iPod in anything more robust than a paper bag that will accommodate a standard deck of playing cards. Only you know how much abuse you're going to direct at your iPod and the level of protection you need.

---

### Skin Game

*Skins*—the thin plastic or rubbery sheaths designed to protect your iPod from scratches—are very popular among iPod owners, and for good reason. Because skins aren't designed to protect your iPod from serious bumps and bruises, they're quite sleek and pleasing to the eye.

That said, I recommend that you purchase a skin only if you promise to buy a real case, too. Skins offer scratch protection only. Should you drop your iPod when it's encased in a skin, you'll get no more protection than if you dropped a naked iPod. To help ensure your iPod's long and productive life, padding is paramount.

---

## Adaptive Technology

Although the iPod's audio jack is labeled with the headphones symbol, that jack can accommodate more than the iPod's earbuds. Unlike the headphone jack on some other electronic devices, the iPod's audio jack can send out perfectly clean audio from this port to your computer's sound input port or to a home or car stereo. All you need to perform this feat is the right cable. The same goes for the third-generation iPod and iPod mini Dock. Its Audio Out port is comfortable with a variety of audio cables. In this section, I'll show you exactly which cables to use and how to string them properly from the iPod or Dock to the device of your choice (**Figure 9.8**).

**Figure 9.8**

Make connections with your iPod with these common audio connectors, which include (from left to right) RCA connectors, a female miniplug jack, and a male miniplug.

## iPod to Computer

You already know that if you want to swap data between your iPod and Mac or PC, you use the FireWire or USB 2.0 cable. But in some instances—when one of your computers doesn't have a FireWire or USB 2.0 port, for example—you may want to record directly from your iPod to your computer. To do so, you need an adapter cable that carries stereo Walkman-style miniplugs on both ends. (You can distinguish a stereo miniplug from the mono variety by the two black bands on the plug. A mono miniplug has just one black band.)

Just plug one end of the cable into the iPod's or Dock's audio jack and the other into your computer's audio input port. (Note: Audio input ports are missing from some Mac models. For these Macs, you need a USB audio adapter, such as Griffin Technology's $35 iMic audio adapter.) To record audio from the iPod on your computer, you'll need some variety of audio-editing application. When you have that application installed properly, click the Record button in that program and then press the iPod's Play button. The iPod's audio will be recorded on the computer.

You can find such cables at your local electronics boutique for less than $5 for a 6-foot cable. Higher-quality cables that include better shielding, thicker cable, and gold connectors can cost significantly more.

## iPod to Home Stereo

Take the *personal* out of *personal music player* by attaching your iPod or Dock to your home stereo and subjecting the rest of the household to your musical whims. You need nothing more than a cable that features a stereo miniplug on one end and two mono RCA plugs on the other.

Plug the miniplug into the iPod's or Dock's audio jack and the two RCA plugs into an input on your stereo receiver (the AUX input, for example). With this arrangement, you can control the volume not only with your stereo's volume control, but with the iPod's scroll wheel as well.

A cheap version of this cable also costs less than $5. Griffin Technology (www.griffintechnology.com) offers the $15 iPod Home Connect Kit, which includes a high-quality version of this cable—a 4-foot miniplug-to-male RCA adapter cable—along with a cable that features a pair of female RCA plugs and a stereo miniplug. The cables are iPod-color-coordinated and carry gold-plated connectors. With the first cable, you can connect your iPod to your stereo. Using the cables in tandem, you can connect your iPod to your computer or to computer speakers that carry female miniplug connectors for input.

## iPod to Hard-wired Computer Speakers

Some computer speakers are *hard-wired*, meaning that the manufacturer, in its cheapskate wisdom, decided to save a couple of pennies by attaching the speaker cable permanently to the speaker. To connect your iPod to such speakers, you need a cable that features a male stereo miniplug on one end and a female miniplug on the other. To make the connection, plug the adapter cable's male miniplug into the iPod's or Dock's audio port and the speaker's male miniplug into the female miniplug connector on the other end of the adapter cable.

Inexpensive versions of these cables also cost less than $5 and are available at your local electronics boutique.

## iPod to Two Headphones

There may (and I hope there *will*) come a time when you'll want to snuggle up with your snookums and listen to your Special Song played on an iPod. A touch of romance goes out of this ritual, however, when you have to split a pair of earbuds between your li'l sweet potato and you.

To bring the intimacy back to your musical relationship, purchase a stereo line splitter. Such an adapter bears a single stereo male miniplug connector on one end (the end you plug into the iPod) and two stereo female miniplug connectors on the other. Plug a pair of headphones into each female connector, and you're set. (Well, you're *almost* set; you still get to argue about who controls the volume.)

XtremeMac (www.xtrememac.com) sells such a connector, called the iShare Earbud Splitter, for $13. Belkin (www.belkin.com) offers a Headphone Splitter Cable for $5. You'll find similar adapters at your local electronics bazaar.

## iPod to Car Stereo

This one's a bit trickier. A few car stereos include a miniplug jack labeled *CD*. If you have such a jack, you're in luck. Just use a stereo miniplug-to-miniplug cable (like the one I recommend for the iPod-to-computer connection), and you're ready to rock. If you don't have a connector, a technician at a Ye Olde Auto Stereo Shoppe may be able to provide one by tapping into a hidden connector on the back of the car stereo. If taking your car to such a tech sounds like a bother, though, you might try one of these adapters.

### A new BMW

www.ipodyourbmw.com

Apple and BMW have teamed up to create an integrated iPod adapter that works with dock-connector iPods and 3 Series, X3 and X5 SAVs, and Z4 Roadsters made in 2002 and later. This adapter basically makes your iPod work like a CD changer, allowing you to access tracks in up to five specially created playlists (you must name them BMW1 through BMW5) from the audio controls on the car's steering wheel.

This sounds cool, but I was taken aback by how primitive the system is. When you pay your BMW authorized service provider the $250 necessary to purchase and install the adapter, you'll find a single cable rattling around in the glove compartment—no mounting unit or decorative iPod holder. And the car's stereo can't display title or album information. Instead, you'll see something like CD 4-32. Unless you've memorized the order of the songs in each playlist—or have created playlists that you know you'll desire while driving—navigating the playlists will be a chore.

Then again, as the owner of a broken-down VW, maybe I'm just envious.

### Alpine KCA-420i (iPod Interface)

www.alpine-usa.com

Alpine offers a solution for those who don't care to purchase a BMW simply to control their iPod from a car stereo. That solution is the $100 KCA-420i (iPod Interface). This plain-ish white box acts as an interface between the iPod and an Alpine Ai-NET head unit (a car stereo manufactured by Alpine). Like the BMW doohickey, the Alpine unit moves music from the iPod to the car stereo, as well as powers the iPod. Unlike BMW's scheme, Alpine's system allows you to view title, artist, and album information on the front of the car stereo. Although you're welcome to store your iPod in the glove compartment, installation doesn't require that the iPod connector cable be routed to it. If you prefer to keep your iPod in a handy cup holder or overhead storage bin, just tell your installer to pull the cable to the location of your choosing.

### Cassette-player adapter

If your car has a cassette player, you can use a cassette adapter (**Figure 9.9**). This thing looks exactly like an audiocassette, save for the thin cable that trails from the back edge of the adapter. To use one of these adapters, shove the adapter into your car's cassette player, plug its cable into your iPod, and press the Play buttons on both the iPod and the cassette player. Music should issue from your car's speakers.

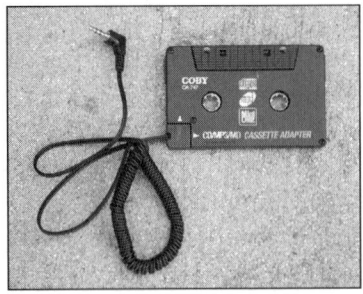

**Figure 9.9**
A cassette adapter allows you to play your iPod through a cassette player.

These adapters cost less than $20.

Although you can use these adapters in any cassette player—a boom box or home stereo, for example—you may have some difficulty ejecting the adapter from players that feature snap-down doors. The adapter's cable may wedge between the door and the inside of the player, making it difficult to open the door.

## Wireless music adapter

Cassette adapters are fine as long as your car has a working cassette player and you don't mind having a cable trailing from your player to wherever you place your iPod. But if you lack such a player (or just can't stand the untidiness inherent with such adapters), consider a wireless music adapter.

This small device works like a tiny radio station, broadcasting whatever is plugged into it to a nearby FM radio. Some of these devices offer you the choice to switch among a few frequencies in the college-radio and National Public Radio range (88.1, 88.3, 88.5, and 88.7 MHz, for example); others provide buttons or a dial so that you can fine-tune reception; yet one other allows you to pick the station on which you'd like to broadcast right from within one of the iPod's playlists.

Most wireless music adapters work in a very limited range. Move them more than a couple of feet from the radio's antenna, and you'll pick up interference. For this reason, most are not ideal for use with a home stereo. Their effectiveness in an automobile depends on how heavily populated the airwaves around you are and how sensitive your car's antenna is. A strong radio signal will overpower these devices, rendering them ineffective. If you live in an urban area with a plethora of active radio stations (or plan to travel in one routinely), you may want to explore a hard-wired connection or a cassette adapter.

## PodFreq

www.sonnettech.com

The most effective of the bunch that I've tried is Sonnet Technologies' $100 PodFreq (**Figure 9.10**, next page). No, it's not cheap, and yes, it works only with third- and fourth-generation iPods. But it does what it's supposed to do: puts out a signal strong enough to overpower weaker stations and broadcast effectively up to around 30 feet (making it useful around the house). I've attempted to put a 60 GB iPod Photo into a PodFreq and I'm afraid it's too big. Hopefully Sonnet will have an iPod Photo-compatible model by the time you read this.

**Figure 9.10**
Gettin' mighty freq-y with the PodFreq.

This device draws its power from the iPod, so there are no batteries to fool with. And it carries both a mini USB 2.0 connector and a 6-pin FireWire connector. With an automobile power adapter, you can charge the iPod while driving.

The PodFreq is bulky. But part of that bulk is comprised of a rectangular unit on the bottom of the device that includes a clear LCD display, a power button, and two buttons that make it easy to change the device's frequency.

## iTrip and iTrip mini

www.griffintechnology.com

The coolest of the bunch are Griffin Technology's $35 iTrip and $40 iTrip mini (**Figure 9.11**). These sleek doodads fit snugly atop the iPod and plug into the Headphone jack on early iPods and into the Headphone jack and Remote port on third- and fourth-generation iPods, iPod Photos, and iPod minis. This is the adapter that allows you to pick a frequency from a playlist for the iPod to broadcast on. It works this way:

**Figure 9.11**
Play your iPod through your car's FM radio with a wireless music adapter, such as Griffin Technology's iTrip.

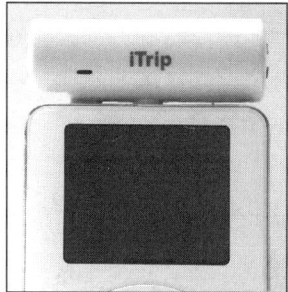

1. Install the software from the iTrip CD-ROM.

   A passel of short MP3 files representing the various FM radio frequencies is loaded into iTunes or, if you've not moved to iTunes on your PC, Musicmatch Jukebox.

2. Update your iPod so that the iTrip files are downloaded to it.

3. Attach the iTrip to your iPod.

4. Navigate to the Playlists screen, where you'll see an entry labeled iTrip Stations.

5. Highlight this entry, and press Select.

6. Use the scroll wheel to move to the frequency you'd like to broadcast on (107.5 MHz, for example).

7. Press the iPod's Play button (*not* the Select button).

8. When the iTrip's blue LED begins to blink rapidly, press Play again.

 So what happened here? Griffin created different tones to instruct the iTrip to broadcast to particular stations. When you select a frequency in the iTrip Stations playlist, your iPod plays the tone associated with that station, and the iTrip programs itself to broadcast on that frequency.

Unlike some wireless adapters, the iTrip doesn't require batteries; it's powered from the iPod's internal battery.

 Although this is an intriguing scheme, it's also potentially dangerous if you're trying to dial in a new frequency while driving. If you use an iTrip and feel the need to fiddle with its frequencies, please pull over.

## And others

iRock (www.myirock.com) makes the $30 iRock 300W Wireless Music Adapter, which features a cool design, requires two AAA batteries (should last for about 20 hours of use), and includes a selector switch that lets you choose among four frequencies—88.1, 88.3, 88.5, and 88.7 MHz. The iRock works with all iPods—albeit sometimes not very well. If these four frequencies are occupied by strong radio stations, you're out of luck. Also, the iRock doesn't put out a very strong signal, so you may still hear static even when these frequencies are unoccupied.

Belkin (www.belkin.com) offers the $40 TuneCast Mobile FM Transmitter and the $60 TuneCast II Mobile FM Transmitter. Like the iRock, the less expensive TuneCast requires two AAA batteries and allows you to choose among the same four frequencies as the iRock. With the TuneCast II, you can choose any station on the FM dial by selecting a frequency with a couple of tuning buttons. Better yet, it preserves battery power by switching itself off when it detects no signal after 60 seconds. I've found that the TuneCasts have better range than the iRock.

Arkon Resources (www.arkon.com) makes the diminutive $25 SoundFeeder SF121 FM Stereo Transmitter. This device also requires two AAA batteries and includes a dial that allows you to select any frequency between 88 and 95 MHz. This unit is also plagued by poor range.

## TransPod

www.everythingipod.com

Digital Lifestyle Outfitters' $100 TransPod, available from Netalog, is the automotive all-in-one solution. The device is comprised of a power adapter, an FM transmitter, and a mounting bracket that you attach to a convenient location on your car's dashboard. When you slide your original iPod into the bracket, the TransPod pulls power from the car's cigarette-lighter receptacle (now labeled a power receptacle in many cars) and is ready to broadcast to a user-designated FM radio station (**Figure 9.12**).

**Figure 9.12**
Take an iPod on your next road trip with Digital Lifestyle Outfitters' TransPod.

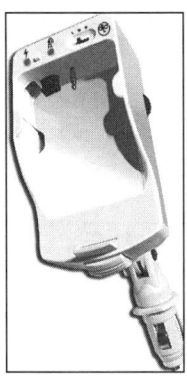

## Having It All

Given the number of ways you can accessorize your iPod, you may think that you'll spend a fair amount of time ordering online or hopping from shop to shop to get everything you need. Relax—there's an easier way.

Dr. Bott LLC (www.drbott.com) provides just about everything you require in its iPod Connection Kits. The company's $50 iPod Universal Connection Kit with FM Transmitter includes the SoundFeeder FM stereo transmitter (with two AAA batteries), the PocketDock mini-dock connector (see the next section of this chapter), an auto-charger adapter for charging your iPod from your car's cigarette lighter, a carrying pouch, and the three cables I list earlier in this chapter. The $48 iPod Universal Connection Kit with Tape Adapter substitutes a cassette-tape adapter for the FM transmitter. These connection kits are compatible with all iPods, thanks to the inclusion of the PocketDock.

XtremeMac.com offers its $50 Get Connected Bundle. This bundle includes a variety of adapter cables (including the iShare Earbud Splitter), an auto charger, and an audio cassette adapter. XtremeMac offers two Get Connected Bundles—one for first- and second-generation iPods, and another for iPods with dock connectors.

Apple has released its $79 iPod Stereo Connection Kit with Monster Cable, which includes an iPod Dock, iPod Power Adapter, iPod Dock Connector to FireWire Cable (the standard data/power cable that comes with all iPods with a dock connector), and a Monster Cable Mini-Stereo to RCA Cable. Although this kit is designed so you can attach your iPod to your home stereo easily, you may find that the pieces it contains are useful in other situations—when you need a backup set of iPod gear for your office or when you take your iPod on the road, for example.

# Power to the People

Like the heads of government, your iPod needs power to do its job. To bring power to your iPod, consider these accessories.

## iPod Power Adapter

Apple included one of these (**Figure 9.13**) with the iPod, correct? Correct. But the iPod is a portable music player, and if you routinely truck it between a couple of locations—your home and office, for example—it might be convenient to have a power adapter at each end of your journey. Also, if you've purchased an additional Dock to use with your home stereo, you'll want an additional power adapter to provide juice to your iPod while it sits in that Dock. You can purchase an additional iPod Power Adapter at the online Apple Store (http://store.apple.com) for $49.

**Figure 9.13**
It's twice as nice to have an extra Apple iPod Power Adapter.

## PocketDock

If you've upgraded from an older iPod to an iPod with a dock connector, you may be a bit dismayed to discover that some of your old accessories—specifically, the gear that has a FireWire connector—doesn't work with your new iPod (because of that iPod's proprietary data/power port). Send Station (www.sendstation.com) comes to the rescue with its $19 PocketDock (**Figure 9.14**). This just-a-bit-larger-than-a-quarter doohickey bears a standard female six-pin FireWire connector on one end and Apple's proprietary male data/power connector on the other. When you want to use your old stuff with your new iPod—an auto charger, for example—just plug the PocketDock into the bottom of the iPod and string a standard FireWire cable between the PocketDock and a device that bears a standard FireWire port.

**Figure 9.14**
Just about every dock-connector-iPod owner should have a PocketDock.

Even if you don't have old gear, the PocketDock is a nice thing to carry. FireWire cables are common enough that they're easy to borrow from a buddy or pick up in just about any store that carries computer equipment. Finding Apple's iPod Dock Connector to FireWire Cable in a pinch can be difficult.

Send Station recently released two additional versions of the PocketDock. The $23 PocketDock Combo includes both a FireWire and a USB 2.0 port, and the $30 PocketDock with Line Out includes—you guessed it—an audio line out port along with the FireWire port.

## World Travel Adapter Kit

The iPod can automatically accommodate the world's two major power standards: 115 and 230 volts. The power adapter, however, is designed to accommodate only the kind of plug used in the country in which the iPod was sold. If you plan to take your iPod globetrotting, you'll need the proper plug adapter. Apple's $39 World Travel Adapter Kit contains adapters that support outlets in North America, Japan, China, the United Kingdom, continental Europe, Korea, Australia, and Hong Kong.

## FireJuice

SiK's FireJuice (www.sik.com) is a very adaptable power adapter that comes in three refreshing flavors (**Figure 9.15**). The basics of each are similar. Each adapter features a switch that lets you use external power (an iPod AC adapter or auto adapter, for example), no power, or power from the computer's FireWire port. The FireWire data connection is always on. The difference among the models—the FireJuice 6, FireJuice 4, and FireJuice 6 for iPod w/Dock Connector—is the computer connector. These adapters include a 6-pin FireWire connector, a 4-pin FireWire connector, and Apple's proprietary data/power connector for dock-connecting iPods, respectively. The first two models are priced at $21, and the FireJuice 6 for iPod w/Dock Connector costs $40.

**Figure 9.15**
The iPod's most adaptable adapter, FireJuice.

Why would you want such a feature? As you may recall, you can't charge an iPod from an unpowered FireWire port—a port on a FireWire PC card or a four-pin FireWire PCI card, for example. The FireJuice adapter makes it possible to charge your iPod when it's connected to such an unpowered port. Those who are using their iPods with a PowerBook or iBook running on battery power would set the FireJuice to the "no power" position so that the iPod won't attempt to charge from the laptop's battery during syncing (thus saving precious battery life on the laptop).

## Auto Charger

That extra iPod Power Adapter is so much useless metal and plastic when you're in a car miles from the nearest electrical outlet. To keep your iPod topped off on the road, you need an auto charger. The device plugs into your car's cigarette lighter or 12-volt receptacle, and power is delivered to your iPod through a plug that fits in the iPod's data/power port (**Figure 9.16**). Dr. Bott (www.drbott.com), Griffin Technology (www.griffintechnology.com), SiK (www.sik.com), XtremeMac (www.xtrememac.com), and Belkin (www.belkin.com) make auto chargers.

**Figure 9.16**
Keep your iPod charged on the road with an auto charger.

Dr. Bott's Auto Charger for iPod costs $30; it includes a power indicator and a replaceable fuse to protect the iPod should too much juice slip through the adapter. It also includes a PocketDock, so it can be used with all iPods.

Griffin Technology's PowerPod Auto Adapter costs $25 and also includes a power indicator and replaceable fuse. Unlike the charger from Dr. Bott, this charger comes in two pieces: the body and the cable. The body bears a female 6-pin FireWire connector, to which you attach a FireWire cable. This design is particularly useful because it means that you can use the PowerPod with *any* iPod. Griffin includes a cable with a FireWire connector on one end (for plugging into the adapter) and a dock connector on the other (for plugging into a third- or fourth-generation iPod, iPod Photo, or iPod mini). Owners of first- and second-generation iPods can use a standard FireWire cable to power their iPods.

XtremeMac offers two models of its iPod Car Charger: one for first- and second-generation iPods, and another for iPods with a dock connector. Both models cost $20 and include coiled cords and fuses.

Belkin's $50 Auto Kit power adapter is designed specifically for the iPods with dock connectors. The Auto Kit does more than power your iPod; it also includes a built-in amplifier (with volume control) and audio out port for playing your iPod through the car stereo. (Your car stereo must have an available input jack for the audio out port to be useful.)

SiK's $30 Imp is close to the do-it-all auto charger. Included in the package is a standard fused auto charger to 6-pin FireWire cable adapter suitable for charging a first- or second-generation iPod. With Imp, you also receive a Y-cable that bears Apple's proprietary power/data cable connector (the one that plugs into the bottom of third- and fourth-generation iPods and the iPod mini) on one end (**Figure 9.17**). The cable splits out to a female miniplug connector and a female FireWire connector.

**Figure 9.17**
SiK's Imp. Impish, it's not. Multitalented, it is.

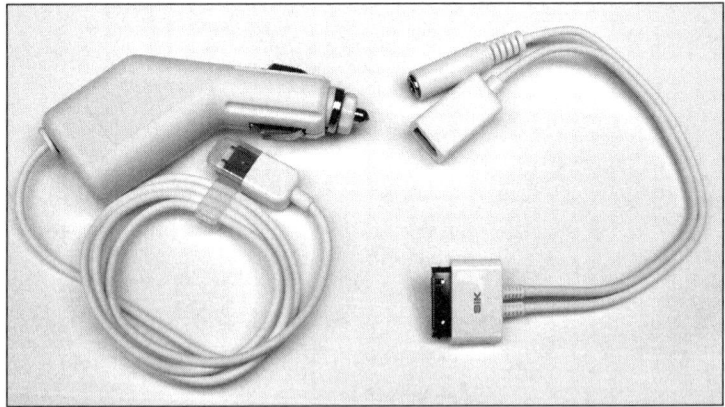

It takes a second or two to wrap your brain around how you'd put Imp to best use. You could, for example, plug the auto charger into your car's cigarette lighter, plug the adapter's FireWire plug into the Y-cable's female FireWire connector, and then plug the power/data connector into your iPod mini to power the mini in the car. Or you could string a standard FireWire cable between the Y-cable's FireWire connector and your iPod's power adapter, and connect your home stereo to the Y-cable's miniplug jack. See what I mean? A little confusing at first, but once you get the hang of it, you realize that Imp is a very versatile adapter.

Note that with all of these adapters, you can play your iPod while it's charging.

# Backup Batteries

Fat lot of good an extra power adapter and auto charger do you if you're flying halfway around the world or traipsing through one of the less welcoming Costa Rican jungles during the latest Eco-Challenge. If you plan to be removed from a ready source of power for a period longer than the typical life of an iPod charge, you need some extra help. Currently, two companies offer that help.

Belkin's (www.belkin.com) Backup Battery Pack (**Figure 9.18**) holds four AA batteries and piggybacks onto a third- or fourth generation iPod or iPod Photo with the help of two clear suction cups. The device provides between 15 and 20 hours of additional playing time. Although it wasn't designated for the iPod mini, it will charge this iPod, and its suction cups are narrow enough to grip the mini. It's not a pretty sight, however, as the Backup Battery Pack dwarfs the poor iPod.

The Backup Battery Pack doesn't charge the iPod's battery. Rather, after you plug the device's power connector into the bottom of the iPod and switch on the battery pack, the iPod draws its power from the pack.

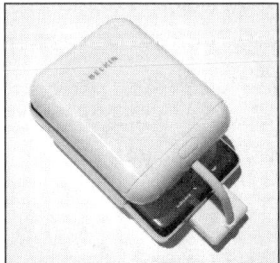

**Figure 9.18**
Give your iPod a power boost with Belkin's Backup Battery Pack for iPod.

Battery Technology (www.batterytech.com) does the Backup Battery Pack at least two times better with its $100 iPod Battery. Advertised to power the iPod for up to 40 hours of music play time (though I have reliable reports of up to 45 hours of play time from this battery), this rechargeable lithium-ion battery ships with three cradles: one for the iPod mini, another for a lower-capacity third-generation iPod (a 15 GB model, for example), and another for a higher-capacity third-generation iPod (the 40 GB model). By the time you read this, Battery Technology will likely also offer cradles for fourth-generation iPods and the iPod Photo.

> ### Building Your Own Battery Charger
>
> The Belkin Backup Battery Pack is a very nice device—solidly built, with some particularly attractive green LED lights that indicate just how much power is left in your batteries—but it doesn't work with first- and second-generation iPods.
>
> If you have one of these earlier iPods, are handy with electrical tape and heat-shrink tubing, and desire such a charger, you might consider building your own. Allen Evans shows you how at http://users.adelphia.net/~evansa/iPodCharger.html.
>
> To adapt Mr. Evans' charger to an iPod with a dock connector, you'd need to find a female-to-female FireWire adapter, and plug the charger into one side of the adapter and the FireWire end of the iPod docking cable into the other. The extra effort you may have to expend to track down one of these connectors and wire it into your adapter may persuade you to forgo the cost savings and simply purchase the Belkin charger instead.

## HotWire

Have you ever been frustrated that you can't listen to your iPod when it's being recharged via your Mac or PC? End that frustration with SiK's $11 HotWire cable. This power-only cable, which is compatible with first- and second-generation iPods (or a dock-connector iPod with a PocketDock connector), allows you to have full access to your iPod's controls while the iPod charges, so you can play your iPod during the process.

## The Ears Have It

The iPod's earbuds are perfectly serviceable. But this style of headphone is inherently problematic, because (a) not all ear canals are the same size, so a one-size-fits-all set of earbuds may not fit all and (b) some people get the heebie-jeebies when items are lodged inside their ears. For these reasons, your list of accessories may include an additional set of headphones. Headphones come in a variety of styles—including earbuds, neckband, open-air, and closed—from such companies as Etymotic, Shure, Sony, Koss, Aiwa, Panasonic, Philips, and Sennheiser.

# Earbuds

If you like earbud-style headphones but find those included with the iPod (**Figure 9.19**) to be uncomfortable (particularly if you have the original earbuds, which many users thought were too big), earbuds are available from a variety of manufacturers. Look for earbuds that fit well, don't require a lot of fiddling to focus (meaning that you don't have to move them around continually to make them sound good), and offer reasonably well-balanced sound.

**Figure 9.19**
The iPod includes a set of earbud-style headphones.

Apple recently began offering in-ear headphones priced at $39, called, aptly enough, Apple In-Ear Headphones. Although they produce decent sound, they're not for everyone. Their shape can cause them to slip out of some people's ears, which defeats the purpose of having a pair of in-ear headphones. These aren't the kind of headphones that you can try before you buy, so see if a friend has a pair that she'd be willing to let you borrow.

High-quality in-ear headphones include those made by Etymotic (www.etymotic.com), Shure (www.shure.com), and Future Sonics (www.futuresonics.com). If sound quality is of paramount importance to you—and you have a fair chunk of disposable income—check out Etymotic's $330 ER-4P earphones. These earphones—and others such as Shure's $180 E3c and $500 E5c headphones and Future Sonics' $160 EM3 headphones—were designed specifically for portable players such as the iPod.

If money really is no object, Future Sonics and Ultimate Ears (www.ultimateears.com) offer custom-fitted earpieces—headphones that are shaped to match the exact dimensions of your ear canals. To obtain such headphones, you must visit an audiologist to have a silicon mold taken of the inside of your ears. You ship this mold to the headphone company, where your custom earpieces are created. Such headphones cost between $300 and $600. For between $100 and $200, Westone Laboratories (www.westone.com) will make custom earpieces that fit headphones such as Shure's E5c and Etymotic's ER-4P models.

## Neckband Headphones

These popular headphones are secured to your head with wires that drape over the tops of your ears. Imagine putting on a pair of tight glasses backward, so that the lenses are on the back of your head, and you'll get the idea (**Figure 9.20**). Neckband headphones are comfortable but easy to dislodge if you tug on the cable. Also, they don't provide a lot of sound isolation, which means that sounds from outside tend to filter through. (This isn't necessarily a bad thing if someone's trying to get your attention or your smoke alarm goes off.)

**Figure 9.20**
Neckband headphones are easy to store and produce reasonable sound.

## Open-air Headphones

Open-air headphones sit over the ears without enclosing them completely (**Figure 9.21**). When you bought your portable CD or cassette player, open-air headphones likely were included in the box. These headphones are comfortable, but the less-expensive models can sound thin. Like neckband headphones, they don't provide much isolation.

**Figure 9.21**
Open-air headphones such as these are lightweight and comfortable.

## Closed Headphones

Closed headphones cover your ears completely and provide a lot of isolation, leaving you undistracted by outside sounds and those around you undisturbed by a lot of sound bleeding out of your headphones (**Figure 9.22**). Some closed headphones can be a bit bulky and uncomfortable, particularly if you wear glasses, so be sure to try before you buy. And because of their size, these headphones aren't terribly portable.

**Figure 9.22**
Closed headphones, such as this Sony MDR-V6 model, sound great but are bulky.

## Shopping for Headphones

You wouldn't purchase a pair of stereo speakers without listening to them, would you? Of course not. It's just as important to audition a set of headphones that you intend to spend a lot of time with. When you're auditioning those headphones, keep the following factors in mind:

- **Sound quality.** A good set of headphones provides a nice balance of highs and lows without emphasizing one band of frequencies over another. Listen for a natural sound. If the headphones lack brightness—or if you can't clearly discern low-frequency instruments (such as bass guitar, cello, or a kick drum), and hearing your music clearly matters to you—move on. These aren't the headphones for you.

- **Comfort and fit.** If you're an enthusiastic listener, you may wear those headphones for long stretches of time. If they pinch your ears or head, slip out of your ears, or fall off your head, you'll grow tired of them quickly.

- **Size.** If you plan to take your headphones with you, look for a pair that fits easily into a pocket or iPod case.

It's also a good idea to seek the opinions of others before purchasing a set of headphones. The HeadWize (www.headwize.com) Web site is a wonderful repository of information for headphone enthusiasts. Check HeadWize's forums for user reviews of popular (and more-obscure) headphones.

# Miscellanea

And then there are the iPod accessories that defy categorization. If you've done the rest, try these accessories on for size.

## Belkin Voice Recorder and Universal Microphone Adapter

This $60 microphone/speaker (**Figure 9.23**) from Belkin allows you to record hundreds of hours of audio on your third- or fourth-generation iPod or iPod Photo (iPod Software 2.1 Updater or later required). The iPod supports recording voice memos as mono, 16-bit audio, 8 kHz .wav files.

**Figure 9.23**
The Belkin Audio Recorder.

As I said earlier in the book, audio at this resolution is hardly pristine. 8 kHz is termed voice-quality because although it's perfectly fine for recording lectures or meetings, it's not the kind of device you'll want to use to bootleg the next concert you attend. And even if the iPod didn't limit your iPod to recording such lo-fi files, the microphone built into this device doesn't handle the low and high ends of the audio spectrum. It offers a frequency response of 500 Hz to 12 kHz. Compare this with the 20 Hz-to-20 kHz range provided by your typical home stereo, and you get the idea.

The $39 Universal Microphone Adapter allows you to plug the microphone of your choosing (as long as it can connect to the device's miniplug input jack) into your iPod.

## iTalk

Griffin's $40 iTalk voice recorder does everything the Belkin Voice Recorder does—and more. The iTalk features a more robust speaker than the one on the Belkin recorder, producing louder, brighter sound than the Belkin device does. The iTalk also includes a pass-through miniplug jack that allows you to plug in your headphones while the iTalk is attached. You're also welcome to plug a microphone into this jack.

 Neither the iTalk nor Belkin's Voice Recorder currently works with the iPod mini, as the mini's software doesn't support this feature.

### Recording voice memos

To begin recording, plug the Voice Recorder, Universal Microphone Adapter, or iTalk into your iPod; select Record on the Voice Memo screen that appears; and press the Select button. The screen immediately displays two commands: Pause, and Stop and Save. After a delay of a couple of seconds, you'll see the word *Recording* flashing on the screen. As you might assume, your iPod is now recording.

Should you wish to take a moment to collect your thoughts without recording yourself muttering, "Um…er…well, dang, what was I gonna say?", press Select to pause your recording. When you're finished recording for good and all, use the Scroll wheel to select Stop and Save; then press Select. The iPod saves your recording. You can access the file from the Voice Memos screen, where it's labeled by date and time of recording (4/5 2:12 PM, for example).

## iPod playback

To locate your voice memos, select Extras in the Main screen and then Voice Memos in the Extras screen. To play a voice memo, select the memo in the Voice Memos screen and then press Select. In the next screen (titled with the day and time of the recording), select Play and then press Select. The iPod's standard Now Playing screen appears, and your memo begins playing.

And yes, because this is just any old recording as far as your iPod is concerned, you can navigate through it just as you can any other audio file on your iPod. Not only that, but you can also assign a rating to the thing, if you like.

If the Voice Recorder is attached to your iPod, the recording plays through its built-in speaker. Otherwise, the iPod plays the memo through whatever device (headphones or speakers) you've plugged into the iPod's Headphone jack.

Should you care to delete your memo, just return to the memo screen and select Delete. In the resulting Delete Memo screen, select Delete Memo and then press Select. The memo is deleted, and you return to the Voice Memos screen, where you can choose to record a new memo or listen to another memo you have stored on your iPod.

## Transferring memos

iTunes is on the job when it comes to transferring memos. When your iPod contains new memos, and you plug it into your Mac or PC equipped with iTunes, the memos are copied into iTunes—if you've configured the iPod to be updated automatically. If you've configured the iPod for manual updating and plug an iPod into your computer, iTunes pops up a message that reads: "The iPod *youriPodname* contains new voice memos. Would you like to copy these voice memos to your Music Library?" Click Yes or No as the mood strikes.

When you move voice memos to your computer, either automatically or manually, iTunes creates a new Voice Memos playlist that contains all the memos you've transferred to iTunes. After each transfer, you'll discover that your voice memos have disappeared from the iPod's Voice Memos screen. Don't fret—they're not gone. iTunes and the iPod have simply moved them to the Voice Memos playlist at the bottom of the iPod's Playlist screen. Should you want to copy voice memos to your computer without going through iTunes, you'll find them stored in the Recordings folder on your iPod.

# Media Reader for iPod and Digital Camera Link for iPod w/ Dock Connector

Belkin and Apple put their heads together for these as well—a $100 device (**Figure 9.24**) that allows you to download photos and movies from removable media, and a similar $80 device that connects directly to your digital camera via its USB connector. The Media Reader for iPod supports CompactFlash (Type 1 and 2), SmartMedia, Secure Digital (SD), Memory Stick, and MultiMedia Card (MMC) media. The device works with third- and fourth-generation iPods or iPod Photos running iPod Software 2.1 Updater or later. (The Media Reader isn't supported by the iPod mini.) The Media Reader for iPod is powered by four AAA batteries and plugs into the data/power port on the bottom of the iPod.

**Figure 9.24**
Belkin's Media Reader for iPod.

The Digital Camera Link requires two AA batteries, uses a USB-A to 5-pin Mini-B USB cable to transfer images between the camera and iPod (cable not included), and works with third-generation iPods as we go to press. Belkin expects that by the time you read this, the device will also be compatible with fourth-generation iPods and iPod Photos (though it's not supported by the iPod mini).

Although I've mentioned the following in chapter 3, it warrants repeating here: The iPod Photo won't display pictures that you've imported with one of these readers. Before your iPod can display these pictures, they must be transferred to your computer, converted to a form acceptable to the iPod by iTunes, and then transferred to the iPod via iTunes.

## Importing pictures and movies

When you plug the Media Reader or Digital Camera Link into the iPod, the iPod displays the Import screen. If there's no media plugged into the device or camera, the iPod displays a message that tells you so: "No card inserted."

When you insert a hunk of media, the screen changes to read something like this:

```
Type: Media card
Photos: 41
Free: 81.8 MB of 91.4 MB
```

At the bottom of the screen, you'll see the Import and Cancel commands. If you press the Import button, the iPod shifts to the Importing screen, begins pulling data from the media card, and places that data on the iPod.

As the data transfers, the LED on the top of the Media Reader blinks, and the iPod's Importing screen displays the Stop and Save or Cancel command. If you click Stop and Save, the pictures and movies already copied to your iPod will be saved. Cancel does just that.

The Media Reader works wonderfully with media 128 MB and smaller. Transfer rates for larger media—256 MB and more—are painfully slow.

When the transfer is complete, you'll see the Done and Erase Card commands. Clicking Done takes you back to the Import screen, where your photos are labeled as rolls, along with the number of pictures each roll contains—Roll #1 (41) and Roll #2 (165), for example. Erase Card performs that very action.

When you select a roll and press the Select button, you go to the Roll screen, where you'll see the date the roll was saved, the number of photos it contains, and the size of the roll. From this screen, you can delete the roll or select Cancel to move to the Photos screen.

## Downloading pictures to a Macintosh

When you plug an iPod that contains photos into a Mac and fire up iPhoto, iPhoto switches to the Import screen and recognizes the iPod as a device that contains pictures. Click the Import button, and the pictures on the iPod are downloaded to your Mac and into iPhoto. When you dump photos into your Mac, the photos aren't shifted from their original locations on the iPod (unlike voice memos). If you want to access these rolls again—to delete them, for example—just select Extras in the Main iPod screen, Photo Import in the Extras screen, and then a particular roll in the Photos screen.

Speaking of deleting rolls, a nifty way to do this in one shot is to select the Erase Camera Contents After Transfer option in the Import portion of the iPhoto window. When you enable this option, every time you download photos to your Mac, they'll be automatically deleted from the iPod.

## Downloading pictures to a PC

At the risk of disappointing those of you who use your iPods with Windows, I have to report that because there is no iPhoto for Windows, you can't move the photos from your iPods to your PC quite as elegantly as Mac users can. However, Mike Matheson's iPodSync (a utility I discuss in some depth in chapter 7), can copy pictures and voice memos from the iPod and place them wherever you like on your PC.

You can also copy pictures to your PC manually by following these simple steps:

**1.** Mount your iPod, and when iTunes opens, click the iPod in the Source list.

2. Click the iPod icon in the bottom-right corner to open the iPod Preferences window.

3. Check the Enable Disk Use check box.

   This option allows you to view the iPod's hard drive from the My Computer window.

4. Open the My Computer window and then double-click the icon that represents your iPod.

5. Open the DCIM folder you find within; then open one of the picture folders inside that DCIM folder.

   The name of the picture folder on your iPod (or folders, if you've downloaded more than one roll to your iPod or if your media card contained pictures from multiple cameras) depends on the kind of camera you used the card with. My Nikon camera, for example, produces folders named 100APPLE, 101APPLE, and so on. A Canon camera may produce a folder called CANONMSC. Regardless of what the folder is called, this is where your pictures are stored. In Windows XP you should see your photos as thumbnails in the picture folder (whatever it may be called). If you don't, choose Thumbnails from the window's View menu.

6. Select the files that you'd like to transfer to your PC, and choose the Copy the Selected Items command from the File and Folder Tasks portion of the window.

7. In the resulting Copy Items window, choose a destination on your hard drive for the photos, and click Copy.

   The photos are copied to the destination you specified.

Alternatively, you can select the files, right-click, choose Send To from the resulting contextual menu, and copy the files to one of the destinations in this Send To submenu. Or you can choose the Open With command from the contextual menu and open the files in the Windows Picture and Fax Viewer program, Paint, or another graphics application of your choosing.

To delete the photos from your Windows iPod, simply drag the picture folder(s) to the Recycle Bin.

## Movies from the Media Reader?

Eagle-eyed readers noticed my claim that movies can also be pulled from a camera's media card, placed on a third- or fourth-generation iPod, and then transferred to your computer. Before you get all het up with the idea that the iPod can import movies from a camcorder, let me explain that I'm talking about the short .avi movies recorded by digital cameras such as Canon's PowerShot models. These movies are stored on the camera's media card and transferred, along with the camera's still pictures, to the iPod via the Media Reader. From there, you can transfer these movies to your computer for playback. But there's a trick to it.

Regrettably, the trick for Windows users is to move them manually. Follow the same instructions I issued for copying pictures from the iPod to Windows.

You can transfer them automatically if you're using a Macintosh, however. The means for doing so is an application other than iPhoto, which recognizes only still-photo files. That application is Apple's Image Capture. Here's how it works:

1. Connect your iPod to your Mac, and ensure that it's configured to mount in FireWire Disk Mode (an option in the iPod Preferences window).

2. Launch Image Capture.

    An iPod window opens.

3. Click the Download All button.

    All your still pictures are copied to the Pictures folder inside your user folder, and the movies are copied to your Movies folder. When the copy operation is complete, these folders open in the Finder so that you can access the new items within.

    Alternatively, you can click the Download Some button and, in the resulting window, choose just the items you want to download to your Mac.

4. Double-click the movie file to open it in QuickTime Player.

    Before leaving Image Capture, be sure to check out the options in the Automatic Tasks pull-down menu. After downloading your pictures, Jaguar's version of Image Capture can turn the pictures into a slide show or open them in Preview. In addition to performing both these tricks, the Panther version of Image Capture can build a Web page from your pictures, as well as crop them. Too cool!

## iPod Remote

If you have a 10 or 20 GB second-generation iPod or an original 15, 20, 30, or 40 GB third-generation iPod (not the $299 15 GB third-generation iPod), you already have Apple's iPod Remote (**Figure 9.25**)—the company's wired remote control. If you have a 5 GB iPod, an earlier iPod model, the $299 third-generation 15 GB iPod, the iPod mini, a fourth-generation iPod, or an iPod Photo, the $39 iPod Remote is worth considering. It allows you to access the iPod's play controls without removing the device from a case or pocket. Very handy. The iPod Remote includes a set of Apple's earbuds.

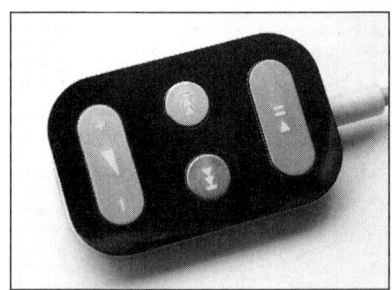

**Figure 9.25**
Tired of flipping open your case every time you want to change tunes? Try Apple's Remote Control.

 Apple changed the design of the iPod Remote with the third-generation iPods. The new remote won't work with old iPods; neither will the old remote work with current iPods.

 The iPod Remote works only with music; its Forward and Back buttons have no effect on an iPod Photo's slideshows. To move through a slideshow you must use the iPod Photo's click wheel.

## iPod Dock/iPod mini Dock

If you have a 15 GB third-generation iPod, an iPod mini, or a 20 GB fourth-generation iPod, and you routinely plant it next to your computer or home stereo, the $39 Dock is for you. (I describe the Dock at length in Chapter 1.) Even if you already have a Dock, getting an extra one is worthwhile if you often plug your iPod into your home stereo.

If you already have a Dock and have purchased an iPod mini, there's no need to purchase a mini Dock also. The original Dock will work perfectly well with the mini, though those who are finicky about aesthetics may be displeased by the empty space on either side of the mini as it sits in the Dock.

## NaviPod Wireless Remote

TEN Technology's (www.tentechnology.com) $50 NaviPod is perfect for the iPodding couch potato whose iPod is tethered to a home entertainment system. Just plug the NaviPod into the data/power port on the iPod, and you can control such functions as Play/Pause, Next Track, Previous Track, Volume Up, and Volume Down with the included wireless remote control (**Figure 9.26**).

**Figure 9.26**
You have complete control of your iPod with the NaviPod wireless remote.

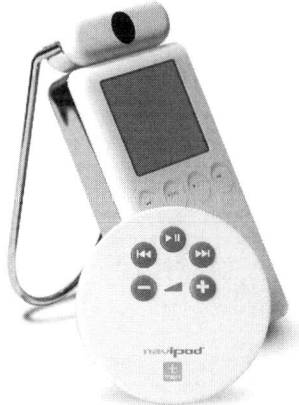

The NaviPod comes in two models: one for first- and second-generation iPods, and the other for the new models. The NaviPod for third- and fourth-generation iPods and the iPod Photo also works with the iPod mini but, like Griffin Technology's iTrip, it extends off to one side due to the petite nature of the mini and the placement of its headphone and remote ports.

 Like Apple's Remote Control, the NaviPod won't control the slideshows on an iPod Photo, though it controls the music functions perfectly well.

# Altec Lansing inMotion Speakers

If you doubt the inspirational power of the iPod, you no longer will once you set eyes on Altec Lansing's (www.alteclansing.com) series of inMotion portable speakers. The $180 inMotion iM3 (**Figure 9.27**), $130 inMotion iMmini, and original $150 inMotion speakers are works of art. The original inMotion and iM3 speakers are about the size of a quality paperback book and serve as both a dock for your third- or fourth-generation iPod and as perfectly reasonable-sounding-given-their-size powered stereo speakers. (As we go to press, the iPod Photo doesn't fit in the dock slot of these speakers.)

**Figure 9.27**

Altec Lansing's ultra-slick inMotion iM3 portable speakers.

The design of the original inMotion speakers gives you a notion of how these things work. To start, you flip the speaker unit up and over the top of the unit and then place your third- or fourth-generation iPod between the two speakers, connecting its data/power port to the connector on the speaker base. (If you own these speakers and have adopted an iPod mini, Altec-Lansing will send you an adapter that allows the mini to work with the speakers.) Turn on the inMotion's power switch, and start playing your iPod. The music on your iPod plays through the speakers.

The iPod's volume control has no effect on the inMotion's speakers when the iPod is connected to it. Instead, you control the speakers' volume with the up and down volume buttons on the front of the unit. You can, however, attach headphones to the iPod's Headphone jack and control the headphone volume via the iPod's volume control. The inMotion bears a headphone jack of its own. Plugging headphones into this port turns off the speakers.

The inMotion also carries an auxiliary input jack on the back of the unit, allowing you to play another device through the inMotion speakers—your laptop or a first- or second-generation iPod, for example. To accommodate these earlier iPods, the inMotion includes a cover for its iPod connector, allowing you to rest an older iPod between the speakers. A short stereo cable is included to make the connection between the older iPod's Headphone jack and the inMotion's auxiliary jack.

The inMotion also carries Apple's data/power connector on the back. When you string Apple's cable between this jack and your computer and then connect the inMotion to the iPod, the iPod behaves much as it would if you attached the iPod to Apple's Dock. It mounts on your computer, and you can't play audio through the inMotion speakers. When you unmount the iPod from your computer, the speakers work with the iPod.

The inMotion runs on either AC power (an adapter is included) or four AA batteries. When the inMotion is running on AC power or plugged into a computer's powered FireWire port, you can charge a dock-connector iPod by placing it in the inMotion's dock. The iPod won't charge if the inMotion is running on battery power.

## JBL On Stage

Resembling nothing so much as a 1950s flying saucer, JBL's (www.jbl.com) $200 On Stage portable speaker carries four small speakers, includes a dock-connector slot, and is powered by the included AC adapter (**Figure 9.28**). Like the inMotion speakers, it features an auxiliary input port so you can use it with a first- or second-generation iPod (by stringing an audio cable between the iPod's headphone port and the On Stage's audio input port). As I write this, it's possible to fit an iPod Photo into the On Stage but that fit is pretty tight. Frankly, if you want to use your iPod Photo with the On Stage, see if JBL has reengineered it to accommodate Apple's most colorful iPod.

**Figure 9.28**
No, it's not an ashtray or an extraterrestrial vehicle. It's JBL's On Stage speakers.

## Bose SoundDock

Yet another hint that the iPod inspires creative design is Bose's (www.bose.com) SoundDock. This $300 system places the iPod in a dock slot with a full-face metal grill behind (**Figure 9.29**). This grill hides two speakers a bit larger than what you find in the inMotion and On Stage. These larger speakers allow the SoundDock to deliver a richer bass than these other portable systems. Regrettably, it doesn't include a pass-through dock connector that allows you to connect the iPod to your computer while it's sitting in the SoundDock. Also, unlike the inMotion and On Stage speakers, there's no auxiliary audio input jack, so you can't attach a different audio device to the unit. That said, the SoundDock, though more expensive than the competition, delivers better sound. It also includes a credit-card-sized remote control that lets you play, pause, skip forward or back, adjust the volume, and turn the iPod on or off. Though it was made prior to the release of the iPod Photo, the SoundDock can accommodate an iPod Photo, using the included fourth-generation iPod adapter (but it's a tight fit).

**Figure 9.29**

Bose's $300 SoundDock delivers better sound than the competition.

## Tivoli Audio iPAL

Purists will fight over this one. Tivoli Audio's (www.tivoliaudio.com) $130 iPAL is a great-sounding monophonic AM/FM radio that happens to include an audio input port that you can use to connect the iPAL to your iPod's headphone port. Those aforementioned purists will scoff at the idea of using a stereo iPod with a device that broadcasts in mono. Yet these same folks will reluctantly admit that to get the best listening experience from a stereo system, you must plant your ears equidistant from the left and right speakers—this triangulation scheme provides optimal separation between the two stereo speakers. Essentially, this means placing your nose on the front of the inMotion and On Stage speakers.

Mono though it may be, the iPAL sounds great.

## FMXtra

A feature lacking on the iPod that's included on a couple of lesser digital music players is an FM tuner. Digisette (www.digisette.com) offers a way to incorporate such a tuner into your personal listening experience with its $25 FMXtra (**Figure 9.30**). This radio-on-a-lanyard sports a pendant that looks a bit like a slightly garish bolo tie. The pendant is actually an FM tuner that features two buttons for auto-scanning up and down the FM band, a set of earbuds attached to the lanyard, and a pass-thru stereo miniplug that you can plug into your iPod.

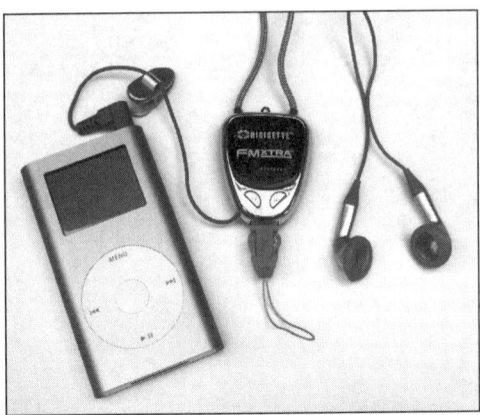

**Figure 9.30**
Would you like an order of FM with that iPod? Digisette's FMXtra will do the job.

When you want to listen to the radio, switch on the FMXtra and, if it's connected to the FMXtra, turn off your iPod. Press either of the two scan buttons. When the device encounters a station with a signal strong enough to be listenable, it stops at that station. The FMXtra offers a two-stage volume control—loud and louder (yes, I wish there were one setting a bit quieter than loud).

# Groove Bag Triplet and Tote Speaker Purses

I'm aware that a fair number of iPod owners buy the device not only because it's the finest portable music player on the planet, but also because it's fashionable to own one. If you're seeking the almost-ultimate fashion accessory for your iPod (see the next item for the ultimate accessory), check out the Groove Bag Triplet (**Figure 9.31**) and Groove Bag Tote Speaker purses, sold by Dr. Bott at www.drbott.com. That's right—these $145 white synthetic-leather purses double as boom boxes, including two speakers and a clear plastic compartment for your iPod. Compatible with all iPods, the Groove Bag Triplet and Tote Speaker purses make a statement.

**Figure 9.31**
The world's most fashionable boombox.

## PowerMate

Griffin Technology's $40 programmable USB audio and media controller, PowerMate (**Figure 9.32**), isn't exactly an iPod accessory, in the sense that you can't attach it directly to the iPod. You can, however, attach this jog-wheel controller to your Mac and use it to adjust your iPod's volume within iTunes.

**Figure 9.32**
Griffin Technology's PowerMate audio controller.

Just attach the PowerMate to a free USB port, install the driver, and restart your Mac. Upon restart, launch iTunes; click your iPod in the Source list; open the iPod Preferences window; and select the Manually Manage Songs and Playlists option, which allows you to play your iPod through your Mac's speakers.

Then press down on the PowerMate to start playback, and turn the wheel up or down to adjust volume. Bonus: The PowerMate will perform these iTunes chores even when iTunes is not the active application.

# AirPort Express

Apple helped put wireless networking on the map way back in The Day with its AirPort Base Station and AirPort wireless cards—two devices, uncommon in their day, that allow you to connect computers to each other (and to the Internet) without the benefit of wires. In the summer of 2004, Apple released the smaller second cousin to these devices: the $129 AirPort Express Base Station (**Figure 9.33**).

**Figure 9.33**
The musically expressive AirPort Express.

There are surely some of you who will be elated to learn that the AirPort Express is a smallish 802.11g wireless hub that plugs into a power socket and offers wireless printing to compatible USB printers and an Ethernet port for attaching a broadband modem. But given the subject matter of this book, you're more interested in the fact that with the help of the AirPort Express, you can stream music wirelessly from one end of your abode to another. It works this way:

1. Plug the AirPort Express into an electrical socket near a stereo receiver somewhere within 150 feet of a computer that bears a compatible wireless networking card.

   Obviously, Apple's AirPort Extreme cards are going to be the most compatible cards for this purpose.

2. String an appropriate adapter cable (likely one with a stereo mini-plug on one end and two RCA connectors on the other) between the AirPort Express' audio out port and an auxiliary input port on your receiver.

3. Run the AirPort Express Setup Assistant, and somewhere along the way, you'll be asked if you'd like to stream your music. Of course you do, so you respond in the affirmative.

4. Once you've run through the Setup Assistant, fire up iTunes 4.6 or later on the computer that contains the wireless card.

   Shimmy with delight when you gaze down at the bottom of the iTunes window and spy a pop-up menu you've never seen before (**Figure 9.34**).

5. From this AirTunes pop-up menu, select the wireless network you've created with the AirPort Express Setup Assistant.

**Figure 9.34**
Select locally, play globally.

The selected song is converted to the Apple Lossless Codec format, encrypted, and streamed wirelessly to the AirPort Express and the audio device attached to it. Although this may sound like a complicated process (and it is), it doesn't take long. There are a few seconds' delay to start the first tune, and from them on, the music plays back without interruption (because the device caches music as it can).

## The Personalized iPod

What could personalize your personal music player more than having your name and favorite quote etched across the shiny back of your iPod or aluminized rear of your iPod mini (**Figure 9.35**)? As we go to press, Apple offers engraving for free when you purchase your iPod from the online Apple Store. This offer may end by the time you read this—check the Apple Store (http://store.apple.com) for details. Although I can't predict prices, I can tell you that whatever the cost, Apple will engrave the back of an original iPod with two lines of text, comprised of 27 characters per line (and yes, spaces and punctuation count as characters). If you wish to engrave your iPod mini, you're allowed 23 characters per line.

**Figure 9.35**
Make your personal player even more personal.

Should you already own an iPod and desire this kind of personalization, try taking your iPod to a local jewelry store. For the right price, a jeweler should be able to do the job for you.

# 10

# Troubleshooting Your iPod

I regret to report that—except for you, dear reader, and me—nothing is perfect. No, not even the iPod. Whereas it may tick happily along one day, the next day, its menu structure is a mess; it refuses to start up when you're sure it has a full battery; or when it does start up, it displays an icon indicating that it is feeling far from well.

In this chapter, I'll look at the common maladies that afflict the iPod and what, if anything, you can do about them. I'll also examine the hidden diagnostic screen on the original iPod, the iPod Photo, and the iPod mini. Finally, I'll take you on a tour of the inside of the first- and third-generation iPods and the iPod mini and offer suggestions about when it might be a good idea to crack yours open.

# Problems and Solutions

Unlike a computer, which can fail in seemingly countless and creative ways, the iPod exhibits only a few behaviors when it's feeling poorly. Following are the most common problems and (when available) their solutions.

## The Missing iPod

When you plug your iPod into your Mac or PC, it should make its presence known in short order—appearing in iTunes or some third-party software on your Windows PC (Anapod Explorer or, if you're using older Windows software, Musicmatch Jukebox). If you've configured your iPod to mount as a disk drive, it will instead materialize on the Mac's Desktop or within Windows' My Computer window.

If your iPod formatted for Macintosh refuses to mount, restart your Mac while holding down the Shift key. This boots your Mac running Mac OS X into Safe Mode. iPods that do not mount otherwise have been known to do so on a Mac running in Safe Mode.

If that doesn't do the trick (or if this trick isn't applicable because you're using your iPod with a Windows PC), first reset the first-, second-, or third-generation iPod by plugging it into a power outlet and holding down the Play and Menu buttons for 6 seconds. If you have a fourth-generation iPod, iPod Photo or an iPod mini, press and hold Select and Menu for 6 seconds. When you see the Apple logo, hold down the Previous and Next buttons on the first three generations of the white iPod, or hold down Select and Play on the fourth-generation iPod, iPod Photo or iPod mini. This forces the iPod into Disk Mode—a mode that may allow your iPod to mount.

Obviously, neither technique is a good long-term solution, as you don't want to restart your Mac in Safe Mode every time you try to access your iPod or have to force your Mac or Windows iPod into Disk Mode whenever you plug it in. An iPod that won't mount is one that should be restored with the latest iPod Software Updater. On the Mac, boot into Safe Mode; restore the iPod with the Updater (it erases all data on the iPod, so be sure that your data and music are backed up); and restart your computer normally, without holding down the Shift key. With luck, the iPod will appear as expected.

If an iPod formatted for Windows refuses to mount on your Windows PC, and you're using a FireWire card, make sure that the FireWire (IEEE 1394) card is certified by Windows Hardware Quality Labs (WHQL). The literature that came with the card should indicate whether it's compliant; if not, check the vendor's Web site for compatibility information.

## The Confused iPod

Clues that your iPod is confused are the absence of playlists, artists, and songs that used to be there; a capacity that appears to be 5 GB on a 10 GB iPod; the failure of the iPod to boot beyond the Apple logo; or the appearance of a folder icon with an exclamation point. I'll look at each scenario in the following sections.

### Absence of items

While I was attempting to use an original iPod formatted for the Macintosh with Windows, my PC crashed, and when I unplugged the iPod, its playlists were missing. I could still play music from the iPod through the Songs screen, but things were not right.

In an attempt to restore a sense of sanity to my iPod, I tried these remedies:

1. **Reset the iPod** (again, plug the first three generations of iPod into a power source and then press and hold Play and Menu for 6 seconds; for the fourth-generation iPod, iPod Photo and mini, press and hold Select and Menu).

    Resetting the iPod is similar to pushing the Reset switch on your computer. It forces the iPod to restart and (ideally) get its little house in order. In this case, the iPod remained confused.

2. **Restore the iPod** (run the latest iPod Software Updater).

    If reset doesn't work or your iPod can't seem to find its operating system (it displays a folder icon with an exclamation point), there's nothing else for it than to restore the iPod to its original factory state—meaning that all the data on it is removed and the iPod's firmware is updated. To restore the iPod on the Macintosh, launch the most recent copy of iPod Software Updater. (As we go to press, this is iPod Updater 2004-10-20, which contains the latest updaters for each version of the iPod: iPod Software 1.4 Updater for first- and second-generation iPods, iPod Software 2.2 Updater for third-generation iPods, iPod mini 1.1 Updater for the iPod mini, iPod Software 3.0.1 Updater for the fourth-generation iPod, iPod Software 1.0 Updater for the iPod Photo). Then click the Restore button in the resulting window (**Figure 10.1**). Confirm that you want to restore by clicking Restore in the warning sheet (Mac OS X) or dialog box (Mac OS 9) that appears (**Figure 10.2**).

**Figure 10.1**
Click the Restore button in the iPod Software Updater window to begin the restore process.

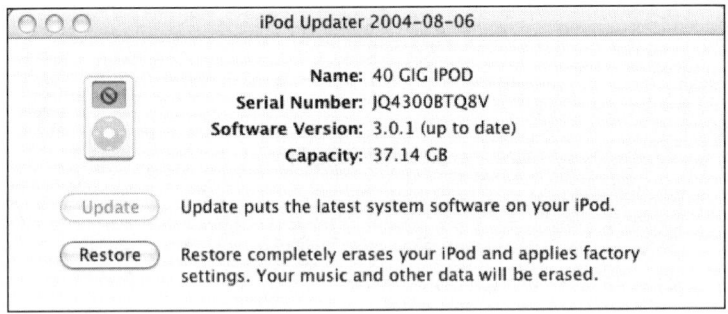

**Figure 10.2**
Are you sure?

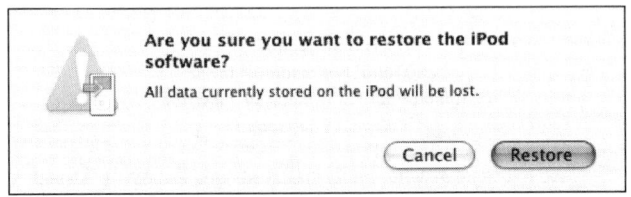

To restore the iPod on a Windows PC, use the Start menu to navigate to the iPod folder inside the Program Files folder (**Figure 10.3**). Launch the Updater application, located inside the iPod folder. Then click the Restore button to begin the restoration process. If your iPod is connected to the PC via a 6-pin FireWire connection, it will reboot, and the firmware will be updated. If the iPod is connected to the PC via an unpowered connection (a 4-pin FireWire or USB 2.0 port), you'll be asked to plug the iPod into a power source: a powered

FireWire connection or your iPod's power adapter. This is for your iPod's safety. When the iPod's firmware is being updated—basically, a fresh set of instructions are programmed into a chip inside the iPod—you don't want the iPod to run out of power. If it does, the information written to that chip may be corrupted, making it difficult (perhaps even impossible) to restore your iPod properly.

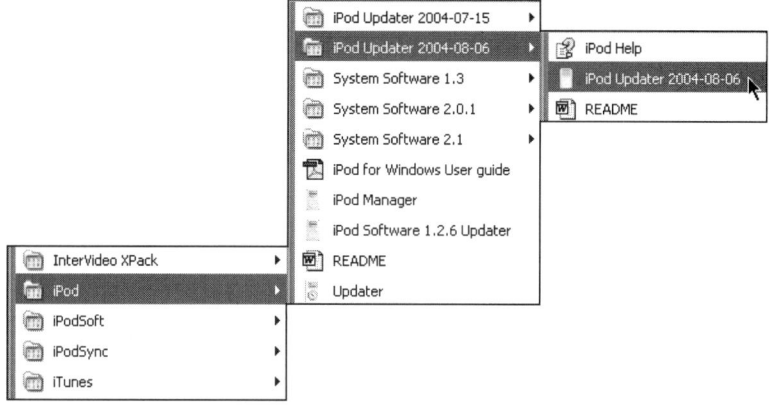

**Figure 10.3**
Navigate to the iPod Updater with Windows' Start menu.

Note that the Windows version of the Updater doesn't ask you to confirm your decision to restore the iPod. Be sure that you really want to restore the iPod before clicking the Restore button.

If you're using a version of the iPod Software Updater before version 1.3 for the Mac (for the first- and second-generation iPods) or 2.0 for both Windows and Mac (for the third-generation iPod), you must unplug and replug the iPod for the restore process to complete. After you replug the iPod, it will appear to restart several times. When the process is complete, the Updater window will return to its initial state, offering you the option to restore your iPod.

If you're working with iPod Software 1.3 or 2.0.x Updater, a first-, second-, or third-generation iPod should restart and complete the restore without your having to unplug it. But a fourth-generation iPod, iPod Photo, or an iPod mini, when connected to a PC with a USB 2.0 connection, will ask you to unplug it and then plug it into a power adapter before it can be fully restored.

In past editions of this book, I said that if the iPod doesn't want to restart after a couple of minutes, you should feel free to unplug it. Recently, though, I tried this very thing on an original iPod formatted for the Macintosh and met with disastrous results. The iPod didn't seem to be doing anything, so I disconnected it—fully expecting that it would finish updating the firmware, as it had in the past. Wrong. The iPod locked up and refused to boot. Even after I used every technique I outline in this chapter, the iPod remained uncooperative. I wound up taking it into an Apple Store, where the Genius confirmed that it was deader than a dodo.

Given my experience, I urge you to allow the iPod plenty of time to update itself—an hour or more, if need be (though it normally updates in about a minute). If, after a very long time, the iPod doesn't appear to respond, you can try unplugging it with the understanding that if it breaks, you'll blame no one but yourself.

> When you double-click your iPod's icon on the Mac's Desktop or in Windows' My Computer window after the restore, you'll see that the device contains only the Calendars, Contacts, and (on third- and fourth-generation iPods, iPod Photos, and the iPod mini) Notes folders, with the sample contacts and Notes instructions supplied by Apple.
>
> To put your songs back on the iPod, just launch iTunes or the iPod software you use with your Windows PC and sync the iPod.
>
> Those Windows users who've elected to use Musicmatch Jukebox will find that after they restore their iPods, Musicmatch launches and presents the Device Setup dialog box (**Figure 10.4**). You've undoubtedly seen this dialog box in the past, but as a reminder, this is where you can name your iPod, choose whether it will update all playlists or selected playlists when the iPod is synchronized with Musicmatch Jukebox, choose to synchronize the iPod and Musicmatch Jukebox when the iPod is plugged into the PC, and enable the iPod for disk use. Mediafour's XPlay presents its own setup dialog box when it encounters a newly restored iPod.

**Figure 10.4**

The Device Setup dialog box.

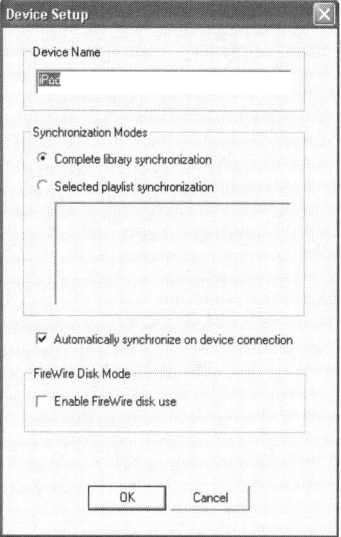

## Mixing Generations

The iPod is a popular-enough item that many people have more than one. Given that the current iPod can't be successfully updated or restored with versions of the iPod Software Updater earlier than version 2.0, and given that first- and second-generation iPods and the iPod mini can't be properly updated or restored with the iPod Software 2.0.x Updater and later, is it possible for old and new iPods to coexist on the same computer?

Yes.

If you have a first- or second-generation iPod, a third-generation white iPod, a fourth-generation iPod, an iPod Photo, and an iPod mini, you must update and restore the five of them with different versions of the iPod Software Updater.

Apple recently placed all five updaters within a single package (called iPod Updater 2004-10-20 as we go to press, but there's likely to be a newer version by the time you read this). This single package contains all five of the iPod Updaters. To restore your iPod, just launch this utility. The utility should pick the correct iPod model. If it doesn't, you'll see a screen that asks you to pick your iPod model. Select the appropriate model, and restore your iPod. Should you attempt to restore your iPod with the wrong updater, you'll see a message that says the updater is incompatible with your iPod.

*continues on next page*

> **Mixing Generations** *(continued)*
>
> If you're a Windows user with a third-generation iPod and iPod Software 2.0.x Updater, you should upgrade to iPod Software 2.1 Updater or later. I suggest this not just so you'll get the added features that accompany the 2.1 release, but also because the 2.0.x updater makes it difficult to install updaters for new and old iPods on the same PC.
>
> The problem stems from the fact that when you install the iPod Software 2.0.x Updater on your PC, it erases previous versions of the iPod software.
>
> Because it does, if you want to use an older and a newer iPod on your Windows PC, you must install the iPod Software 2.0x Updater (and resign yourself to erasing the older updater). Then download and install the latest updater for your first- or second-generation iPod (version 1.4 as this book goes to press).

## Incorrect capacity

Speaking of incorrect software updaters, a problem with capacity can occur when you've restored a Macintosh iPod with a software updater that's not intended for that device. The original 10 GB iPod, for example, should be restored only with iPod Software 1.1 Updater or later. If you restore with the version 1.0.4 updater, for example, your 10 GB iPod will be confused and display a capacity akin to that of a 5 GB iPod (though it will still hold as much data as a 10 GB iPod). Apple no longer offers this updater online, so if the original 10 GB iPod is your first iPod, you're highly unlikely to have this problem.

You'll also get an incorrect capacity reading if you use the iPod Software 1.3 Updater and place a 15 GB hard drive from a new iPod into a first- or second-generation iPod. In this case, however, the iPod's confusion appears to work in your favor. When you restore the iPod with the iPod Software 1.3 Updater, your iPod will appear to hold as much data as a 20 GB iPod—iTunes, the Mac's Finder, and the iPod itself tell you that it can hold over 18 GB of data. It can't, of course, but it's a pleasing illusion. Current iPod Software Updaters are smart enough to recognize the true capacity of the drive.

## Failure to boot

There are a few possible reasons why an iPod might not boot beyond the Apple logo—some benign and others not so.

**The Hold switch is on.** Go ahead and smack yourself in the head (and then breathe a sigh of relief) if your iPod won't start up because the Hold switch is engaged.

**Drained battery.** Among the most benign problems is an iPod battery that's drained (though not dead; I'll discuss dead iPod batteries later in this chapter). If the iPod is functioning normally otherwise, when you attempt to switch on an iPod with a very nearly drained battery, you see a low-battery icon. If the battery is completely drained, the iPod is incapable of mustering the energy even to display this icon; the screen remains black, and the drive refuses to spin up. Plug your iPod into the power adapter or your computer, and let it charge. If everything's hunky-dory after that, pat yourself on the back for a job well done.

If you find that your iPod's battery can't seem to hold a charge for more than a day—say, you switch it off with a full charge on Monday, but its battery is drained when you try to use it on Wednesday—see whether a more recent version of the iPod Software Updater is available. iPod Software 1.2.4 Updater, for example, was notorious for causing iPods to lose their charge quickly, but the iPod Software 1.2.6 update fixed that problem.

If you've plugged the iPod's data/power cable into a computer that isn't currently charging it, unplug it. Some people have reported that when the iPod isn't being charged—it's attached to a sleeping computer, for example—the charge can dissipate quickly.

In some rare cases, the battery may not be drained enough for the iPod to be reset. If you've tried other solutions and failed, unplug the iPod from a power supply for 24 hours; then plug it into a power source and attempt to reset it by holding down the Play and Menu buttons for 6 seconds on the first three generations of the iPod, or by pressing Select and Menu for those same 6 seconds on a fourth-generation iPod, iPod Photo, or iPod mini.

**Confused iPod.** If the iPod still refuses to boot, attempt to reset it by pressing and holding the Play and Menu buttons for 10 seconds.

**Incorrect formatting.** At some point, you might have thought it would be a nifty idea to reformat your iPod's hard drive—partitioned it on a Macintosh to install Mac OS 9 on one partition and Mac OS X on the other, for example. Or you used a Windows utility other than the iPod Software Updater to format the drive. Bad idea. You should format the iPod only with the iPod Software Updater—and, as I mention at some length in the "Mixing Generations" sidebar earlier in this chapter, only with the updater appropriate for your iPod. To put things right, you must restore your iPod (see the "Restore the iPod" step in "Absence of items" earlier in this chapter).

There's nothing to keep you from formatting your Mac iPod as a Windows iPod (as I said in Chapter 6), or vice versa. Just be sure that if you're subjecting your iPod to a platform change, you use the appropriate iPod Software Updater to do the job.

## Songs skip

Songs played on the iPod may skip for several reasons, which include:

**Large song file.** Large song files ("Mountain Jam" from the Allman Brothers' classic *Eat a Peach*, for example) don't play particularly well with the iPod's 32 MB RAM buffer. Such large files race through the RAM buffer, requiring the iPod to access the hard drive more often. This situation can lead to skipping if the iPod is pulling the song almost directly from the hard drive. If possible, reduce the size of files by employing greater compression, or chop really long files (such as audio books) into pieces.

**Damaged file.** A damaged song file may skip. If you find that the same song skips every time you play it—and other songs seem to play back with no problem—go back to the source of the song (an audio CD, for example), rip the song again, and replace the copy on the iPod with the newly ripped version.

**iPod that needs to be reset.** Yes, an iPod that needs to be reset may cause songs to skip. (Refer to "The confused iPod" earlier in this chapter for instruction.)

**iPod that needs to be restored.** If a reset won't do the trick, make sure that all the data on your iPod is backed up, and restore the iPod with the latest appropriate version of iPod Software Updater. (Instructions are also in "The confused iPod" earlier in this chapter.)

## Unpleasant sound as the hard drive spins up

This symptom appeared in some early releases of the fourth-generation iPod and a very few iPod Photos. Typically, iPods with this problem will make noise through the headphone port whenever the iPod's hard drive spins up. Static accompanies the first couple of seconds of songs played after the iPod spins up.

This appears to be a grounding issue that makes itself known only when you've plugged in headphones whose audio connector bears a metal base that comes in contact with the iPod's case. This metal-to-metal contact transmits this sound through your headphones. To troubleshoot the issue, place a small plastic washer on the post of any affected headphones.

Note that not all iPods exhibit this problem. Apple has been known to replace iPods that are thus afflicted. If you have a real problem with it, try taking it into Apple for an exchange. When you do so, find a display model iPod that matches yours and plug your headphones into it. If the display iPod doesn't have the problem, you can make a reasonably strong case that your iPod is out of the norm—the Store's iPod doesn't buzz, why should yours?

## Remote control doesn't work

On first- and second-generation iPods, the connection between the iPod and the remote control needs to be *very* snug. If your remote control isn't working, give the plug a good, hard push (and a twist) into the Sound Output port.

Don't twist the plug on the newest remote controls. These remotes plug into both the Sound Output port and a special Remote Control port on third- and fourth-generation iPods, iPod Photos, and iPod minis. If you twist the plug, you'll likely break the remote control (and may damage the iPod as well).

# The Really Confused iPod

Your iPod may be so confused that it won't mount on your Mac's Desktop or in Windows' My Computer window and can't be restored. Follow these steps to mount the iPod:

1. Connect a first-, second-, or third-generation iPod to a built-in FireWire port on your computer (rather than an unpowered FireWire port on a PC Card or a USB 2.0 port, for example). Because the fourth-generation iPod, iPod Photo, and iPod mini can be powered via a USB 2.0 connection, feel free to use such a connection with your Mac or Windows PC.

2. Reset the first-, second-, or third-generation iPod by pressing the Play and Menu buttons for 6 seconds. Reset the fourth-generation iPod, iPod Photo, and iPod mini by holding down Select and Menu for 6 seconds.

3. When you see the Apple logo, press and hold the Previous and Next buttons on the first three generations of the iPod until you see a message that reads "Do not disconnect." On the fourth-generation iPod, iPod Photo, or iPod mini, press Select and Play.

The click-wheel iPods (fourth-generation iPod, iPod Photo, and iPod mini) can be very finicky about these multibutton presses; half the time they don't work. Keep trying. You'll get the timing right eventually.

The key combination outlined in step 2 resets the iPod much like pressing the Reset switch on a PC or Mac resets the computer. The second key combination forces the iPod into Disk Mode—a mode that will help your computer recognize and mount the iPod.

With luck, your iPod should appear on the Mac's Desktop or in Windows' My Computer window. Then you should be able to restore it with the iPod Software Updater.

If you're using a version of the iPod Software Updater before version 1.2 (and this version would be for Macs only, because 1.2 was the first version to ship with the Windows models), don't be alarmed if you see a FireWire symbol instead of the "Do not disconnect" message in the iPod's display. The operation (and effect) are the same; only the display is different.

## Kelly's Sidebar: "Do not disconnect"

Shortly after Apple released the second generation of iPods, my friend Kelly contacted me in what can be politely described as a state of concern. Our conversation went something like this:

She: "I can't disconnect my iPod from my computer! I thought this was supposed to be a *portable* music player!"

Me: "What do you mean, you can't disconnect it? Is the cable stuck?"

She: "I don't think so."

Me: "You don't think so? Have you tried?"

She: "No. I'm afraid to!"

Me: "Why?"

She: "Because my iPod is flashing this warning sign and says, 'Do not disconnect.' I'm afraid I'll break something if I pull the cable out!"

Me: "Ohhh...."

And that, dear reader, is why this is Kelly's sidebar.

There's a shortish explanation for why you see this message (or its more-positive partner, the "OK to disconnect" message): Versions of the iPod that bore software before version 1.2 didn't make it particularly clear when it was and wasn't a good idea to break the FireWire connection between the iPod and computer. More often than not, you'd pull the FireWire cable from the iPod's FireWire port, only to be greeted by a message on your computer screen indicating that you'd severed a vital FireWire connection and that you'd be well advised to shove the cable back in at your earliest convenience. (There might have been an "And I mean right *now*, buster!" in there somewhere, too.)

To address this issue, Apple created a warning that makes it abundantly clear that you should not feel at liberty to unplug your iPod whenever the mood strikes. Instead, you should take care to unmount your iPod before unplugging it.

In iTunes, you can do this by selecting the iPod's icon in the Source list and then clicking the Eject iPod button in the bottom-right corner of the iTunes window. Or, on the Mac's Desktop, you can drag the iPod's icon to the Trash.

*continues on next page*

### Kelly's Sidebar: "Do not disconnect" *(continued)*

In Windows, you can click the Safely Remove Hardware icon in the System Tray and select your iPod from the resulting contextual menu. Or, if you're using Musicmatch Jukebox, you can click the iPod in the Device window, select the iPod in the Source list, and click the Eject button in the bottom-left corner of the Device window (or right-click the iPod in the Device window and choose Eject Device from the contextual menu).

After you've unmounted the iPod, the "Do not disconnect" message will change to "OK to disconnect," signaling that you're welcome to unplug the data/power cable whenever you like.

But the unspoken question remains: Will your iPod explode (or quietly whimper and die) if you unplug the data/power cable when the "Do not disconnect" message is displayed?

Probably not. You shouldn't break the connection when the computer is transferring data to the iPod; that could corrupt the hard drive, requiring you to restore the device. If the iPod is just sitting around, merrily charging its battery, it's not likely to suffer terribly if you unplug it. But why take the chance? After all the pleasure your iPod has given you, treat it with respect, and honor its one simple request.

## The Ultra-really Confused iPod

If your iPod won't start up no matter what you've tried, you might be able to make it work again by disassembling the unit (see "It's what's inside that counts: disassembling the first-generation iPod" later in this chapter), unplugging the battery and hard drive, plugging the battery and hard drive in again, and reassembling the iPod.

 If your iPod is still under warranty, take advantage of that warranty and have your iPod looked at rather than pulling it apart yourself. As you'll learn later in this chapter, disassembling late-model iPods can be devilishly difficult, and you could destroy your iPod in the process. Also, if Apple learns that you've opened an iPod, there's a distinct possibility that the company won't honor your warranty.

## Secret Button Combinations

By pressing the proper combination of buttons on the iPod's face, you can force the device to reset, enter Disk Mode, scan its hard disk for damage, and perform a series of diagnostic tests. Here are those combinations and the wonders they perform:

- **Reset.**

  *First three generations of the white iPod:* Plug the iPod into a powered FireWire device (the Apple iPod Power Adapter, an auto adapter, or a built-in FireWire port), and press and hold Play and Menu for 6 seconds.

  *Fourth-generation iPod, iPod Photo, and iPod mini:* Plug the mini into a powered device (the Apple iPod Power Adapter, an auto adapter, or a built-in FireWire port) or a high-powered USB 2.0 port; then press and hold Select and Menu for 6 seconds.

  When you reset your iPod, your data remains intact, but the iPod restores the factory settings. This technique reboots the iPod and is helpful when your iPod is locked up.

- **Disk mode.**

  *First three generations of the white iPod:* Reset the iPod. At the Apple logo, press and hold the Previous and Next buttons.

  *Fourth-generation iPod, iPod Photo, and iPod mini:* Reset the iPod. At the Apple logo, press and hold the Select and Play buttons.

  Use this technique when you need to mount your iPod on a Mac with an unpowered FireWire card (a FireWire PC Card in your older PowerBook, for example) or on a PC with a similarly unpowered FireWire or USB 2.0 connection.

- **Disk scan.**

  *First three generations of the white iPod:* Reset the iPod. At the Apple logo, press and hold Previous, Next, Select, and Menu. An animated icon of a disk and magnifying glass with a progress bar below it appears.

  *Fourth-generation iPod, iPod Photo, and iPod mini:* Click-wheel iPods don't offer a button combination to scan the hard drive. Rather, you must access this function through the iPod's Diagnostic screen (which I explain at great length later in this chapter).

*continues on next page*

> ### Secret Button Combinations *(continued)*
>
> Use this combination when you want to check the integrity of the iPod's hard drive. This test can take 15 to 20 minutes, so be patient. Be sure to plug your iPod into the power adapter when you perform this test so that the iPod doesn't run out of juice before the scan is complete. If the scan shows no problems, a check mark appears over the disk icon. To return your iPod to regular use, press Play.
>
> - **Diagnostic mode.**
>
>   *First three generations of the white iPod:* Reset the iPod. At the Apple logo, press and hold Previous, Next, and Select.
>
>   *Fourth-generation iPod, iPod Photo, and iPod mini:* Reset the iPod. At the Apple logo, press and hold Select and Previous.
>
>   Diagnostic mode includes 16 tests for the first three generations of the white iPod, 19 tests for the iPod mini, 21 tests for the fourth-generation iPod, and a mess o' tests for the iPod Photo that may help you determine what's wrong. See the "Doing Diagnostics" sidebar later in this chapter for more details.

# The Far-too-quiet European iPod

My American readers may be unaware of the fact that The Powers That Be across the Atlantic are concerned about hearing loss. I'm quite serious. Some European countries are so concerned about the dangerous mix of excessive volume and unprotected eardrums that they've barred personal listening devices such as the iPod from blasting sound beyond 100 decibels (dB). To accommodate the desires—and laws—of these countries, Apple placed a volume cap of 100 dB on the iPods it sells in Europe. (The American iPod can play up to a theoretical limit of 104 dB, which is 2.5 times louder than 100 dB.)

Some European iPod owners are disappointed that they can't put their hearing at risk, as their American counterparts can. If you count yourself among that number, relief is at hand in the form of a couple of free utilities that adjust the iPod's database file to allow audio to play at a higher volumes.

Macintosh users can accelerate the onset of tinnitus with Hans-Peter Dusel's iPod VolumeBooster utility, which you can find at http://volumebooster.tangerine-soft.de. Windows users who'd like to experience similar ear-ringing goodness should download iMod from www.pochoirs.de/software_es.htm or give Espen Ringom's euPOD VolumeBoost (www.espen.se) a try.

## The Broken iPod

It's a machine, and regrettably, machines break. If none of these solutions brings your iPod back from the dead, it may need to be repaired. Contact Apple at http://depot.info.apple.com/ipod/index.html for instructions on how to have your iPod serviced.

### My One Bad iPod

I've mucked with a fair number of iPods, and every one of them performed like a champ—save one. That one was a new, third-generation 15 GB iPod that was funky from the get-go (and I don't mean the funky-in-a-good-way-like-James-Brown sense). It routinely locked up when I attempted to download my iTunes library, and until I toggled its Hold switch a few times, the controls refused to work. Repeated attempts to restore it did no good.

Interestingly enough, after whirring away for no more than 15 minutes, the iPod performed a very convincing imitation of an overly efficient hand-warmer: It ran excessively hot. This heat affected the iPod's display, turning it so dark that I could read it only by turning the contrast setting all the way down.

Owning such an iPod is unlikely to brighten your day—unless you're writing a book about the iPod. To me, this funky iPod was exactly the opportunity I needed to test-drive Apple's support for the device.

I repacked the iPod, dug out the receipt, and trundled over to the Apple Store in Palo Alto, California, where I presented the device to Ian, the Genius behind the Store's Genius Bar. He politely asked me what was bothering my little digital buddy, listened patiently while I described its symptoms, ran a couple of tests, and concluded that the iPod was indeed ill. Although I purchased the iPod from Apple's online store, he explained that he could authorize an exchange for a new iPod from the Store's stock.

This he did, and I was on my way out the door with a brand-new iPod in a matter of minutes. That iPod hasn't given me a lick of trouble.

# The Frozen iPod

Just like a computer, the iPod can freeze from time to time. To thaw it, attach your iPod to a power source—the power adapter, a powered FireWire port, or a Mac or PC's high-powered USB 2.0 port—and, on the first three generations of the iPod, press and hold the Play and Menu buttons for 6 seconds. For the fourth-generation iPod, iPod Photo, and iPod mini, press and hold Select and Menu for these same 6 seconds.

## Failure to charge

There are several reasons why an iPod might not charge. They include all of the following.

**A sleeping computer.** The iPod won't charge when it's attached to a sleeping computer. Wake up your computer if you want the iPod to charge.

**The wrong cable.** Remember, a USB 2.0 connection carries no power to a third-generation iPod (though it does to a fourth-generation iPod, iPod Photo, and iPod mini). To charge your first-, second-, or third-generation iPod on a Windows PC, you must plug your iPod into a powered FireWire port or the iPod's power adapter.

**More than one FireWire device on the chain.** Although you can chain multiple FireWire devices together, doing so with an iPod isn't such a good idea. To begin with, a FireWire device on the chain before the iPod (a hard drive, for example) may be hogging all the power. Second, there have been reports of iPods that got corrupted when they were left on a chain with other FireWire devices. To be safe rather than sorry, don't put the iPod on a chain. If you must use multiple FireWire devices, purchase a powered FireWire hub (which costs between $45 and $65).

**A frozen iPod.** An iPod that's frozen won't charge. While a first-, second-, or third-generation iPod is attached to a power supply, press and hold the Play and Menu buttons for 6 seconds. For the fourth-generation iPod, iPod Photo, and iPod mini, press and hold Select and Menu for the same length of time.

**A faulty cable.** Cables break. Try a different data/power cable, just in case yours has gone the way of the dodo.

**A faulty computer port.** It's possible that the FireWire or USB 2.0 port on your computer has given up the ghost. Try charging the iPod from the Apple iPod Power Adapter.

**A funky power adapter.** The Apple iPod Power Adapter could also be bad. Attempt to charge your iPod from your computer.

**A faulty data/power port on the iPod.** This problem is more common on first- and second-generation iPods than it is on current iPods. As you plug and unplug the FireWire cable from the iPod's FireWire port, it's possible to put too much stress on the internal connectors that deliver power to your iPod's FireWire port, breaking the bond between those connectors and your iPod's motherboard.

If your iPod is out of warranty, and you're handy with a soldering iron, you could open your iPod (see "It's What's Inside That Counts: Disassembling the First-generation iPod" later in this chapter), check for broken connections, and resolder those connections. This kind of repair is one that only the truly skilled should attempt, however.

**A dead battery.** Like all lithium-ion batteries, the iPod's battery is good for 300 to 500 full charges. When you've exhausted those charges, your iPod needs a new battery. See the sidebar "Assault on Batteries" for more details.

**Broken iPod.** I've mentioned this before: iPods occasionally break. In this case, the battery may be dead. If none of these solutions brings your iPod back from its never-ending slumber, it may need to be replaced. Contact Apple at http://depot.info.apple.com/ipod/index.html.

 There's no harm in keeping the iPod plugged into a power source after it's charged. It won't stress the battery in any way.

## Assault on Batteries

There's been a great deal of hoopla surrounding the iPod's battery—specifically, how long it should last and why it's so darned difficult (and expensive) to replace. Let's set the record straight.

All iPods carry a lithium-ion (Li-ion) battery. Theoretically, lithium-ion batteries, by their very nature, can be fully charged up to 500 times. In actual practice, your iPod's battery will put up with between 300 and 450 complete charges before it gives up the ghost.

This is all well and good if you charge your iPod once a week or so. However, if you use your iPod constantly—and, thus, fully charge it four or five times a week—you'll discover that after about a year and a half, it's kaput.

As you might imagine, those who've seen their iPods kick the bucket after a year and a half have been less than joyous about it. After all, a device you paid several hundred dollars for should have a longer shelf life than a Twinkie. Adding to this unhappiness was Apple's policy of charging $255 to replace the iPod.

Apple and some third-party battery vendors got hip to the situation as the first couple of revisions of the iPod began to go south due to dead batteries. In late 2003, Apple instituted a battery-replacement service, which works like this: If your iPod is more than a year old, and it fails to hold a charge, Apple will replace it with another "functionally equivalent new, used, or refurbished iPod" for $99 (plus shipping and sales tax). That "functionally equivalent" stuff means that you won't get back the same iPod that you send in. If you send in an engraved iPod, Apple will take the back plate off your iPod and put it on the replacement iPod. For more details, visit http://depot.info.apple.com/ipod.

iPodResQ (www.ipodresq.com) offers a similar service for $79. You contact the company, it ships you a postage-paid box for your iPod, you ship it to iPodResQ HQ, and your iPod is returned in a few days with a brand-new battery. PDASmart (www.pdasmart.com) will do the job for $68, and Small Dog Electronics (www.smalldog.com) will tackle battery replacement on third-generation iPods for $50.

If you're a do-it-yourselfer (and you may want to become one after you read my instructions later in this chapter for replacing your iPod's battery), you can procure a battery and service the iPod on your own. iPodResQ, Newer Technology (http://eshop.macsales.com/Catalog_Item.cfm?ID=7157&Item=NWTIPOD210012), PDASmart, Small Dog Electronics, Laptops for Less (www.ipodbattery.com), and Unity Electronics (www.unityelectronics.com) offer battery-replacement kits. Along with the battery, these companies include tools for opening the iPod and instructions for doing so.

If you have a first- or second-generation iPod and would like greater playtime from your iPod, I urge you to check out Newer Technology's high-capacity iPod Replacement battery (http://eshop.macsales.com/Catalog_Item.cfm?ID=7157&Item=NWTIPOD210012). I flung one of these $40 suckers into my first-generation 5 GB iPod, which then played continuously for 21 hours and 25 minutes. Yow!

## Disk-scan icons at startup

There may come a time when you start up your iPod, and a disk-scan icon appears. This situation occurs when the iPod senses a problem with the hard drive. When the disk scan is complete (a 15- to 20-minute process), you'll see one of four icons. These icons indicate the following conditions:

- The disk scan failed and will be repeated when you next restart or reset your iPod.

- Everything's cool. Your iPod's hard drive passed with flying colors.

- The scan found some problems but was able to fix them. If you see this icon, you should restore your iPod.

- This is bad. The Sad iPod icon indicates that the iPod can't retrieve data from the hard drive. If you see this icon, it's time to send your iPod to the shop.

*There's actually one more disk-scan icon, which indicates that you canceled the disk scan by holding down the Select button for 3 seconds. The next time you switch on your iPod, the disk scan will be repeated.*

## Doing Diagnostics

Ever wonder what Apple technicians do when they want to test an iPod? Just as you can, they reset the iPod, and when they see the Apple logo, they press Previous, Next, and Select on the first three generations of white iPods, and Select and Previous on an iPod mini or fourth-generation iPod.

When you do this, you'll hear a chirp. Release the buttons. You'll see (very briefly) a reversed Apple logo and a splash screen that displays the version of the diagnostic test; then, finally, you'll see a list of tests.

**First-, second-, and third-generation iPods**

On the first three white iPods, you'll find these tests:

**5 IN 1.** This test causes the iPod to run a series of these tests. On first- and second-generation iPods using iPod Software 1.3 Updater, the iPod runs LCM, RTC, SDRAM, FIREWIRE, and FLASH.

*continues on next page*

## Doing Diagnostics (continued)

On a third-generation iPod, wait for the tests to complete; then press Select to hear a long beep, Rewind to hear the iPod's scroll-wheel clicking sound, Menu to hear a long beep pitched lower than the Select beep, and Fast Forward to hear a chirp reminiscent of Atari video games.

**RESET.** This test resets the iPod.

**KEY.** When you activate this test, you have 5 seconds to press all the buttons on the iPod. As you do so, the name of each button appears on the display. Press all the buttons in that 5-second time limit, and the words KEY PASS appear.

**AUDIO.** This test checks the iPod's audio subsystem. If everything's OK on a first- or second-generation iPod, you'll see 0X00000001 DONE in the display. The third-generation iPod doesn't display anything—and it doesn't need to. Plug in a set of headphones, and you'll hear a repeated drumbeat when you activate this test. (You'll hear this drumbeat on all iPods, but interestingly enough, it's faster on third-generation iPods.)

**REMOTE.** This screen is for testing the remote control. As you press each button on the Apple remote control plugged into your iPod, a white bar appears. When you push all buttons successfully, you see the message RMT PASS. If no remote control is plugged into the iPod, you'll see a single white bar across the top of the display, and the only way to regain control of your iPod is to reset the device by pressing Menu and Play for 10 seconds.

**FW ID.** This test checks the iPod's FireWire port. If everything's OK, you'll see FW PASS in the display. (This test is labeled FIREWIRE on first- and second-generation iPods.) If you press Select on a third-generation iPod, you'll see the words DISK MODE; then the iPod reboots in Disk Mode.

**SLEEP.** This test puts the iPod to sleep. When you attempt to wake it, you'll see a low-battery icon. To regain control of an iPod running a version of the updater earlier than 2.0.x, you must reset the iPod. To reboot an iPod running iPod Software 2.0.x Updater, press the Menu button and then the Play/Pause button.

**A2D.** This test checks the iPod's power system. When my 20 GB iPod running iPod Software 1.3 Updater passed this test, the display read CHG OK FW 1 BAT 1. A third-generation iPod that passed the test read ADC TEST ID 004A, BAT 001AE ACC 003FF ACC2 000FF. I assume that these results are good.

**OTPO CNT.** When you turn the scroll wheel, its value is displayed in hexadecimal code.

**LCM.** This display test scrolls through a different pattern when you press Select (two patterns total; the second pattern is displayed with backlighting turned on).

## Doing Diagnostics *(continued)*

**CHG STUS (third-generation iPods only).** This test appears to report how the iPod is being charged. When the iPod is operating on battery power, the test screen reads STATUSTEST USB 0 FW 1 HP 0 BAT CHR 1 CHGR 00000. If the iPod is plugged into the Dock, the FW value changes to 0, and the CHGR value changes to a different hexadecimal value. Although this test doesn't appear among the list of tests on the third-generation iPod, it is run as part of the 5 IN 1 test on these newer iPods.

**USB DISK (third-generation iPods only).** The display reads USB DISK when you activate this test. Press the Fast Forward button, and the words FW DISK appear. A few seconds later, the iPod reboots in Disk Mode.

**RTC (first- and second-generation iPods only).** This test displays a different hexadecimal code each time you press Select. iPoding.com (www.ipoding.com) suggests that the test measures the iPod's real-time clock.

**SDRAM (first- and second-generation iPods only).** This test checks the iPod's onboard RAM. If the iPod passes, you'll see SDRAM PASS in the display. Although this test doesn't appear among the list of tests on the third-generation iPod, it is run as part of the 5 IN 1 test on these newer iPods.

**FLASH (first- and second-generation iPods only).** iPoding.com believes that the hexadecimal number that results from this test represents the iPod's ROM version.

**CHK SUM (third-generation iPods only).** This test appears to be the same as FLASH.

**CONTRAST (third-generation iPods only).** Spin the scroll wheel during this test to increase or decrease the iPod's contrast. The iPod's current contrast settings are not affected by this test.

If you discover that you can't see the screen when you invoke Diagnostic Mode (as I couldn't on one of my 15 GB iPods), you can make it visible with the Contrast test. Regrettably, because you can't see the screen, you'll have to do it blind. To do so, enter Diagnostic Mode, press the Back button three times, press Select, and start spinning the scroll wheel until the contrast is adjusted to the point where you can read the screen.

**WHEELA2D (first- and second-generation iPods only).** This test seems to check for scroll-wheel movement. In versions of the iPod software before 1.2, this test is labeled OTPO.

**HDD SCAN.** This test initiates the disk-scan test (which can take 15 to 20 minutes).

**RUN IN.** This test runs a series of internal diagnostic tests until you press and hold the Play button to return to the diagnostic screen.

*continues on next page*

## Doing Diagnostics *(continued)*

**The missing tests.** The iPod Software 2.0 Updater—the software that shipped with the very first third-generation iPods—included two tests that are no longer listed in the Diagnostic screen: RECORD and LIN REC. These tests demonstrated that the audio chip in the third-generation iPods was capable of both playing and recording audio. When you install the iPod Software 2.0.1 (or later) Updater, these tests disappear from the Diagnostic screen.

**Fourth-generation iPod and iPod mini**

The fourth-generation iPod and iPod mini's tests are a bit different from those on the original iPods. They include:

**Initial test (fourth-generation iPod only).** When you first throw the fourth-generation iPod into Diagnostic Mode, it displays the diagnostic version (version AC0728A is displayed on both my 20 and 40 GB fourth-generation iPods) and performs a quick test of the internal RAM. To move to the main diagnostic screen, press Play. The iPod briefly displays one of the video test screens, and its internal alarm beeps once.

**5 IN 1.** This test performs a series of exams, including checking the backlight, memory, internal clock, and USB ports.

**RESET.** This test resets the iPod and is one way to exit the Diagnostic screen.

**KEY.** Press the keys; this test tells you whether they work.

**CHGRCUR (called CHGR CURR on the fourth-generation iPod).** This test seems to allow you to turn charging methods on and off.

**REMOTE.** This test allows you to test the buttons on the remote control.

**HP STAT (called HP STATUS on the fourth-generation iPod).** This test indicates whether something is plugged into the headphone jack and shows the state of the Hold switch.

**SLEEP.** This test puts the iPod to sleep.

**BATT A2D.** This test checks the mini's power supply and may indicates the amount of charge in the battery.

**A2D STAT.** This test relates to the battery and power supply.

**FIREWIRE.** This test checks the FireWire chip.

## Doing Diagnostics *(continued)*

**HARD R/W.** This test checks the read and write functions of the hard drive and displays HDD PASS if all goes well.

**SMRT DAT.** Another hard drive test, this one reads RETRACTS 4 REALLOCS 0 PENDING 0.

**SMRT SCAN (iPod mini only).** This test appears to be akin to a first-, second-, or third generation iPod's Disk Scan test. The test takes several minutes, so don't perform it unless the mini is plugged into a power source.

**HDD SCAN (fourth-generation iPod only).** This test appears to be akin to a first-, second-, or third generation iPod's Disk Scan test. The test takes several minutes, so don't perform it unless the iPod is plugged into a power source.

**READ SN (fourth-generation iPod only).** This test displays the iPod's serial and model numbers.

**DRV TEMP.** This test displays the drive temperature and is the next-to-last test on the fourth-generation iPod.

**DISKMODE.** This test throws the iPod into Disk Mode.

**WHEEL.** Run your thumb around the wheel, and watch the values change.

**CONTRAST.** This test initiates the contrast test. My mini's Diagnostic screen was really light; running this test made the screen much darker and more legible. Proceed through the screens by pressing the Play button.

**AUDIO.** This test displays audio gain. You can move up as high as 127 by pressing the Forward button. The default is 120.

**STATUS.** This test tells you what's plugged into your iPod—whether it's being charged via FireWire and has something plugged into the headphone jack, for example.

**IRAM TEST (fourth-generation iPod only).** This appears to test the internal RAM more extensively than the test performed when you first enter Diagnostic Mode.

To advance from one test to the next, press the Next button. To move back through the tests, press the Previous button. To activate a test, press the Select button. To return to the Diagnostic screen at the end of a test, press the Play button.

To exit Diagnostic Mode, you must reset your iPod by pressing and holding the Play and Menu buttons for approximately 10 seconds or by running the RESET test.

*continues on next page*

## Doing Diagnostics (continued)

**iPod Photo**

With the iPod Photo, Apple completely reorganized Diagnostic Mode to include commands and submenus to some of those commands. You access Diagnostic Mode, just as you would with a fourth-generation iPod or iPod mini, reset the iPod, and then hold Select and Back when you see the Apple logo. Here's how the iPod Photo does diagnostics:

The main screen reads iPod Diagnostics and displays SRV followed by a date below (I assume this is the date of the firmware). Below is a list of these test suites:

   **Memory**
   **IO**
   **Power**
   **Status**
   **SysCfg**
   **Diskmode**
   **Reset**

You can use the scroll wheel or Forward and Back buttons to move from one suite to another. To invoke a suite or test, press Select. The suites contain these tests:

**Memory**

**SDRAM.** Clicking SDRAM takes you to a screen that lists a single SDRAMFullTest. Click Select in this screen and the iPod tests the internal memory chip. The screen displays SDRAM OK if the SDRAM is indeed, okay.

**Flash.** The iPod displays Checksum=0xE937 on my iPod when I run this test. This test checks the device's flash memory.

**IRAM.** Another, more extensive, memory test. When complete the iPod resets.

**IO**

**Comms.** Three tests appear when you click Comms—USBTest, FirewireTest, and Remote. Their names describe them aptly. In order to run the first two tests successfully, you must make the appropriate connection—the iPod's data cable must be connected to a USB port or FireWire port for the first two tests and the iPod's Remote Control must be attached for the Remote test.

## Doing Diagnostics *(continued)*

**Wheel.** When you click Wheel, two tests appear—KeyTest and WheelTest. KeyTest asks you to engage the click wheel's five buttons. To pass the WheelTest, just scroll your thumb around the wheel.

**LCD.** Two tests here: Backlight and Color. Engaging Backlight allows you to run through the iPod's varying degrees of brightness. The setting you leave the test with does not affect the iPod's brightness after you reset it. The Color test requires that you press Select to see each of these colors/patterns: blue, red, green, black, white, red to black gradient, green to black gradient, blue to black gradient, gray to black gradient, checkerboard pattern, black, and gray to black gradient again.

**Headphone.** detect Indicates whether something is plugged into the headphone port and whether the Hold switch is on or off.

**HardDrive.** This screen includes four tests—HDSpecs, HDScan, HDSMARTData, and HDRW. The HDSpecs test provides you with the hard drive's specs (its model number and firmware revision, for example). This test is akin to a first-, second-, or third-generation iPod's Disk Scan test. The test takes several minutes, so don't perform it unless the iPod is plugged into a power source. The HDSMARTData test provides a summary of the drive's S.M.A.R.T. (Self-Monitoring, Analysis, and Reporting Technology) information—the drive's self-diagnostic data. Finally, HDRW is the drive's read/write test.

The **HDScan** test is one of the few useful-for-end-user tests. The first three generations of iPod had a Disk Scan test that could be invoked by resetting the iPod and holding down Back, Forward, Select, and Menu. This key combination isn't possible on click wheel iPods and no other secret key combo has been introduced for recent iPods. Accessing the test through Diagnostic Mode is the only way to do it.

**Audio.** This screen leads you to two tests, Playback and Mic. Pressing Select in the Playback test screen causes the iPod to blast a short burst of audio. Plug a microphone with a mini-plug connector into the iPod and invoke the Mic test to record a few seconds of audio.

**Power**

**A2Dtests.** This test leads to a host of power tests that check the battery as well as input charging.

**Sleep.** This screen takes you to two sleep tests—SleepShort and SleepForever. Invoking SleepShort puts the iPod to sleep for a few seconds. SleepForever shuts down the iPod.

*continues on next page*

> **Doing Diagnostics** *(continued)*
>
> **Status**
>
> No submenus on this one. This simply tells you the LCD setting (it should read "Sharp"), whether something's plugged into the headphone port, and whether the iPod is getting power from a FireWire or USB connection.
>
> **SysCfg**
>
> Another command with no submenus. This displays the iPod's serial number, hardware version number, and Apple part number.
>
> **Diskmode**
>
> If, for some very odd reason, you can't remember the button combination for throwing your iPod into Disk Mode, you can use this command instead.
>
> Bit of trivia: When you access Disk Mode this way, the iPod Photo won't display Disk Mode at the top of the screen.
>
> **Reset**
>
> Another safety-net command. If you'd rather not press Select and Menu to get out of Diagnostic Mode, you can invoke this command.

# Inside the First- and Second-generation iPods

Come on, admit it—you've always wondered what the inside of your iPod looks like. Please allow me to save you the trouble of finding out on your own. The following pictures and descriptions illustrate how the first-generation iPod is put together and what makes it tick.

## Beneath the Cover

If you were to perform surgery on your iPod, here's what you'd find.

## The battery

The first thing you see when you remove the back plate of a first- or second-generation iPod is the Sony Fukushima 4.15 lithium polymer battery. This battery, which is about 0.11 inch thick, plugs into the iPod's main circuit board. The battery on a third-generation iPod is about one-third the size of the original iPod's battery.

## The hard drive

The first-generation iPods carried 5 and 10 GB Toshiba hard drives. The second-generation carried Toshiba drives that held 5, 10, or 20 GB of data. The drive's detachable data connector is at the bottom of the iPod.

## The circuit board

The iPod's circuit board hosts the components necessary for the iPod to do its job. Here, on a first- or second-generation iPod, you'll find the following items (**Figure 10.5**):

**Figure 10.5**
The innards of the original iPod and resident chips.

- **The FireWire controller chip.** As the name implies, this Texas Instruments TSB43AA82 chip controls the iPod's FireWire functions.

- **The SDRAM chip.** This 32 MB Samsung K4S561632C chip serves as the iPod's 20-minute music buffer. Music is read from the hard drive and moved into this chip, allowing the hard drive to spin down (thus saving battery power). When the buffer is nearly empty, the hard drive spins back up and loads additional music into the chip.

  The third-generation iPod's SDRAM chip is much smaller and made by Sharp.

- **The Central Processing Unit (CPU).** The PortalPlayer PP5002B chip takes care of processing music on the iPod, including encoding and decoding MP3 and AAC files and producing effects such as EQ and bass boost.

- **The Digital Audio Converter (DAC) chip.** On the flip side of the circuit board is the DAC chip, which is responsible for delivering sound through the headphone and data/power ports.

# It's What's Inside That Counts: Disassembling the First-generation iPod

 These instructions are for first-generation iPod models only. The second-generation iPod is similarly configured on the inside, except for the inclusion of some shock-absorbing material; it's more difficult to open because the back plate overlaps the top ports.

My greatest desire is that you'll never feel compelled to open your iPod. But there are occasions when pulling it apart makes sense—when your iPod apparently has given up the ghost; its warranty has expired; you want to salvage parts from it; or other troubleshooting techniques have failed, and before pungling up more than $255 plus tax for Apple to repair or replace it, you'd like to try one more thing. Here's how to accomplish that one more thing:

1. Turn off the iPod, and engage its Hold switch so that it doesn't turn on while you're working on it.

2. Find a thin piece of smooth plastic a little thinner than a credit card (my library card did the trick).

   You'll use this plastic as a wedge to remove the back plate. Don't use a screwdriver, as it can bend and score the case.

3. Hold the iPod upright, facing you; insert an edge of the plastic between the FireWire port and the symbol for that port; and push forward toward the corner of the iPod.

If you're left-handed, you'll probably want to start below the Hold switch and push toward the corner nearest to it.

The corner of the back plate should pull slightly away from the front.

4. With the plastic wedged between the back case and the front, continue pushing around the corner and down the side of the iPod, working the back case away from the front.

Work slowly; the 12 plastic clips that hold the back plate in place can break if you wrench the back plate away too violently.

5. Work the plastic all the way around the back plate, and when the back plate is free, pull it off (**Figure 10.6**).

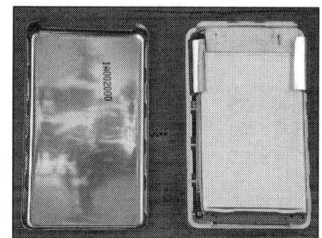

**Figure 10.6**
The backless iPod.

6. Pull out the battery.

The battery is held in place by a couple of thin sticky rubber pads that are *really* sticky. To dislodge the battery from the hard drive, you must use a fair amount of force. Before applying the force, hold the hard drive in place. If you don't, the hard drive is likely to pull up along with the battery, and you could damage the hard drive's data connector (**Figure 10.7**).

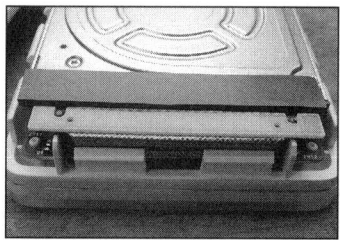

**Figure 10.7**
The hard-drive connector.

7. Fold the battery away from the iPod so that you can access the hard drive without pulling on the thin battery cables (**Figure 10.8**).

**Figure 10.8**
The battery laid aside.

8. Gently pull the hard drive away from the iPod's circuit board, pulling from the top first (**Figure 10.9**).

**Figure 10.9**
Pull the hard drive away from the top of the iPod.

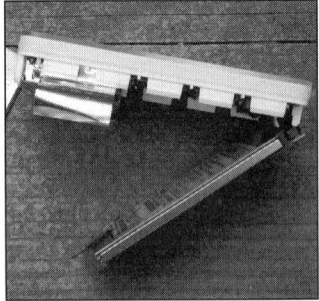

9. When the top and bottom pads are free, detach the hard drive's data connector by grasping it and gently pulling the drive away from the connector (**Figure 10.10**).

**Figure 10.10**
The hard drive removed.

10. To detach the battery from the circuit board, grasp the top of the white plastic connector with a pair of needle-nosed pliers, and gently pull straight up (**Figure 10.11**).

**Figure 10.11**
The battery connector.

11. To reassemble the iPod, reattach the battery connector, replace the hard drive and data connector, place the battery back on top of the hard drive, and press the back plate into place.

Be sure that the battery wires are out of the way so that the back plate doesn't pinch (or break) them.

## Can You Upgrade the Hard Drive?

I've made it a habit to disassemble the very first iPod—a 5 GB model—whenever I'm called upon to speak to an audience about this little digital wonder. Because the folks I address have a strong desire to know what the iPod looks like under the hood (and are more than willing to see someone else risk his iPod to satisfy their curiosity), I do my best to oblige.

Invariably, once the iPod is apart, someone shouts, "Can I put a higher-capacity hard drive into my iPod?"

*continues on next page*

## Can You Upgrade the Hard Drive? *(continued)*

Yes, you can—depending on the iPod you intend to upgrade. I have successfully transplanted the hard drive from a first-generation 10 GB iPod into the body of a first-generation 5 GB iPod. After the operation, I checked this FrankenPod's About screen, and sure enough, it thought that it was a 10 GB iPod. As you would expect, all the data—music, playlists, calendars, and contacts—worked perfectly.

You won't have this kind of luck moving the drive from a second-generation 20 GB iPod to a first- or second-generation iPod of lesser capacity unless you also use that 20 GB iPod's back case. Because the hard drive in the first 20 GB iPod is physically larger; it won't fit in the original case of an earlier iPod.

The third-generation iPod bears an entirely different form factor from the previous two generations of iPods—both inside and outside. The hard drive in the 15 and 20 GB third-generation iPods, however, is the same dimension and weight as the 5 and 10 GB hard drives used in earlier models and is indeed swappable—but not without a degree of preparation.

The difficulty is that the drive from a third-generation iPod includes software that the earlier iPods can't comprehend—the software that allows the On-The-Go menu feature to work, for example. When you plug one of these drives into an older iPod, the older iPod displays an icon indicating that it can't find the software necessary to boot the iPod. To make the drive compatible with your old iPod, you must restore it with the iPod Software Updater appropriate for that iPod model. After you do, the iPod boots from the higher-capacity drive. Should you want to return the drive to a third-generation iPod, you must restore it with the iPod Software Updater designed for that kind of iPod.

Plunking a 30 or 40 GB drive from a third-generation iPod into an early iPod is impossible. The drive is too large to fit in the iPod's case.

PDASmart is the only company I'm aware of that sells replacement iPod hard drives and as this book goes to press, it sells only 5 and 10 GB drives for first- and second-generation iPods. Its 5 and 10 GB drives are priced at $100 and $140, respectively. (Add $10 to have PDASmart install the hard drive for you.)

# Opening the Third-generation iPod

The second- and third-generation iPods are tougher to crack (and easier to damage) because the metal back wraps around the ports. If you wrench away the back plate improperly on a third-generation iPod, you could break the internal connections to the data/power and audio ports, thus turning your iPod into a very expensive paperweight.

But being the kind of person who, seconds after unwrapping the latest digital gewgaw, wonders what makes it tick, I understand that some of you won't be satisfied until you know what the inside of a new iPod looks like. Fine. Allow me to save you the trouble (and risk) of opening your musical pal by taking you on a tour of the third-generation iPod.

## The Hard Drive

When you open a third-generation iPod, you'll find the hard drive, rather than the battery, on top. As I mention in the sidebar "Can You Upgrade the Hard Drive and Battery?" earlier in this chapter, this iPod carries a Toshiba hard drive that's the same dimensions and weight as the drives in the earlier iPods. (The 15 and 20 GB hard drives are the same size and weight as the earlier 5 and 10 GB drives, and the 30 and 40 GB drives are approximately the same size and weight as the hard drive in the earlier 20 GB model.)

The hard drive is surrounded by a blue plastic grommet that acts as a shock absorber. It's plugged into a data connector that's attached to a flexible polymer EMI shield assembly (made of this same shock-absorbent material). The shield assembly bears a data connector on the bottom that plugs into the iPod's circuit board.

## The Battery

The lithium polymer battery is far smaller than the battery used in the first- and second-generation iPods. About the size of an after-dinner mint, the battery rests against the front of the iPod's case in the bottom-left corner (as you're looking at the iPod's front).

# The Circuit Board

The iPod's circuit board (**Figure 10.12**), which is cut out in such a way that it surrounds the battery on three sides, hosts the components necessary for the iPod to do its job. Here, you'll find the following items:

**Figure 10.12**
The circuit board and battery of the third-generation iPod.

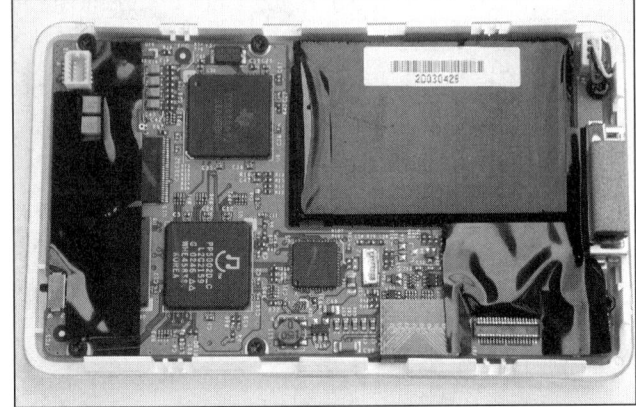

- **The FireWire controller chip.** As the name implies, this Texas Instruments TSB43AA82 chip controls the iPod's FireWire functions. This chip is the same FireWire controller chip used in earlier iPod models.

- **The USB 2.0 controller chip.** The third-generation iPod supports USB 2.0, and Cyprus Semiconductor's CY7C68013 is the chip behind that magic.

- **The SDRAM chip.** This chip is much smaller than its predecessor in first- and second-generation iPods. The 32 MB Samsung K4S561633C-RL75 chip serves as the iPod's 25-minute music buffer. Music is read from the hard drive and moved into this chip, allowing the hard drive to spin down (thus saving battery power). When the buffer is nearly empty, the hard drive spins back up and loads additional music into the chip.

- **The Central Processing Unit (CPU).** The PortalPlayer PP5002D_C chip takes care of processing music on the iPod, including encoding and decoding MP3 and AAC files and producing effects such as EQ and bass boost.

- **The Digital Audio Converter (DAC) chip.** On the flip side of the circuit board is the DAC chip, which is responsible for delivering sound through the headphone and data/power ports.

The choice of DAC chip used in third-generation iPods is important because, unlike the DAC chips in the first- and second-generation iPods, the new iPod's Wolfson Microelectronics WM8731L supports both audio out and audio in—meaning that you can record audio with this chip. This chip is what allows the Belkin Voice Recorder attachment to do its job.

## It's What's Inside That Counts: Disassembling the Third-generation iPod

These iPods are very difficult to get into. Please read the sidebar "It's What's Inside (That You're Likely to Break) That Counts: Disassembling the Third- and Fourth-generation iPod, iPod Photo, and iPod mini" before undertaking this operation.

1. Turn off the iPod, and engage its Hold switch so that it doesn't turn on while you're working on it.

2. Place the iPod face down, and insert a very small, thin flat-head screwdriver between the metal back and acrylic lip of the iPod six centimeters from the top-left side of the iPod, creating a space large enough to insert the corner of a credit card.

3. Carefully run that credit card around the edge of the iPod, moving up toward the top-left corner first.

4. When the back plate is loose, turn the iPod over so that the metal plate is facing you and the iPod's headphone port is pointing up.

5. Push the back plate up slightly to clear the external Hold switch from the internal hold toggle switch.

   Failing to do this could cause the internal toggle switch to break.

6. Carefully lift the iPod's back plate to the right, as though you were turning back a page in this book.

   Don't pull the back plate directly away from the front case; an internal audio connector attached to the back plate is connected to the case.

7. Detach the back plate's audio connector from the connector on the circuit board (**Figure 10.13**).

**Figure 10.13**
What's immediately under the hood of the third-generation iPod.

8. To detach the hard drive, carefully lift up the EMI shield assembly, and detach the data connector that sits beneath the copper tape on the left side of the iPod's circuit board (**Figure 10.14**).

**Figure 10.14**
The internal data connector.

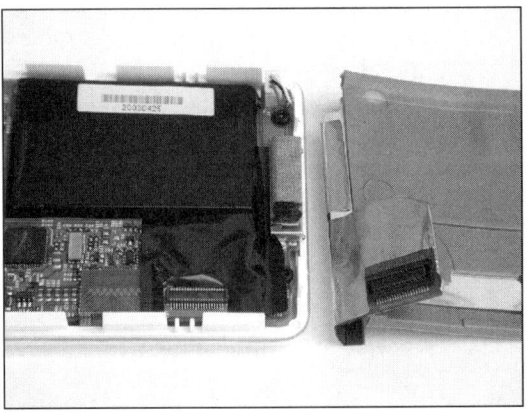

9. To remove the battery, detach the power connector in the bottom-right corner of the circuit board with a pair of needle-nosed pliers, untangle the power cable, and lift out the battery.

10. To reassemble the iPod, reverse these steps.

Make sure that the external Hold switch is in the same position it was in when you disassembled the iPod (in the Hold position). If it's in the "unheld" position, you could snap off the internal hold toggle switch.

## Monkeying with the Fourth-generation iPod and the iPod Photo

If, like me, you've developed the bad habit of opening (and usually destroying) every new iPod model that graces your workbench, you'll be happy to know that you needn't learn any new skills to crack open a fourth-generation iPod or iPod Photo. Apple used the same headphone-assembly-attached-to-back-plate scheme it used with the third-generation iPods. If you follow the instructions for carefully folding the back plate away from the front of the iPod that I outlined in my third-generation disassembly instructions, you and your iPod will be fine.

Because the procedure for pulling the fourth-generation iPod and iPod Photo apart is so similar to the third-generation iPod, I've determined to not waste your time by pointing out the finer points of the motherboard and hard drive. Suffice it to say that the hard drive sits atop the motherboard and that the important chips attached to the motherboard are similar to what you find in the iPod mini. (In terms of technology, the fourth-generation iPod, iPod Photo, and mini have more in common than the fourth-generation and previous white iPods.)

I will mention, however, that removing the battery from a fourth-generation iPod and iPod Photo is a little more difficult than pulling the battery from a third-generation model. Apple attaches the fourth-generation iPod's battery to the back of the click-wheel assembly with a bit of adhesive. If you want to remove the battery one day, you should direct the output of a warmish hair dryer to the battery to loosen this adhesive.

Once you've loosened the battery, don't jerk it away from the click wheel. The click wheel's ribbon connector is under the battery, and if this ribbon connector is stuck to the battery as you pull it away, you could damage it and ruin your iPod. If you must remove your iPod's battery, do so slowly and carefully (or, better yet, have a trained professional perform the job).

# Opening the iPod mini

In the past, I believed that nothing could be more difficult to open than the third-generation iPod. I was wrong. Working with the innards of a third-generation iPod is child's play compared with performing a similar operation on an iPod mini. The truth is, most people will have more luck removing their own kidney than they will with opening and closing an iPod mini effectively.

Fortunately, you don't have to when I'm willing to risk the health of my mini for the sake of my loyal readers. Here's how it looks.

## The Hard Drive

When you finally manage to slide the guts of the mini out of its aluminum sheath, you'll find the hard drive on the back of the mini below the battery (not underneath, but "south" of the battery). Although the drive resembles a compact flash card, it's actually a 4 GB microdrive manufactured by Hitachi (model number HMS360404D5CF00, if you must know) inside the shell of a compact flash card (**Figure 10.15**). It's wrapped in black tape and held in place by friction and the small connector at the top that attaches to the mini's circuit board.

**Figure 10.15**
The mini's hard drive.

## The Battery

The mini's battery is above the hard drive. The battery is manufactured by Sanyo (model number EC003) and is a little larger than a quarter (**Figure 10.16**). It's held in place by friction and a small sticky pad on the battery's bottom-right underside. The battery is connected to the circuit board with a connector similar to the kind used in the original iPods.

**Figure 10.16**

The mini's mini lithium-ion battery.

## Lose mini, Gain Microdrive

It should come as no surprise to those who are familiar with my mechanical skills that when I disassembled my iPod mini for this book, I managed to destroy it. Determined to salvage what I could from my former music player, I disconnected its 4 GB Hitachi microdrive, unwrapped the black plastic tape from around it, removed its three blue bumpers, and—because I understood that the drive was encased in a Compact Flash case—plugged it into my USB LaCie Hexa Media Drive.

Lo (and, may I add, behold), the microdrive mounted on my Mac's Desktop, just as a good removable drive should. Because the drive had been formatted with the iPod mini 1.0 Updater, it displayed the icon of the mini and contained all the items you'd normally find on an iPod's hard drive: the Contacts, Calendars, and Notes folders, along with the invisible folder that holds the iPod's music.

Despite its mini icon, the drive could not be formatted with the iPod mini 1.0 Updater when mounted by my card reader, but I had no trouble formatting it as an HFS+ volume with Mac OS X 10.3's Disk Utility.

As we go to press, these drives cost upward of $500 when sold separately. Some digital-camera owners have purchased the iPod mini and Creative's Nomad MuVo2 (which uses the same Hitachi drive) to pluck the drives from the music players and use them with their cameras.

Those who tried this trick with early models of the MuVo2 were rewarded with a drive that worked in some digital cameras. If you attempted the same feat with an iPod mini, you met with less success. Apple mucked with the drive's firmware in such a way that it wouldn't work in another device. My understanding is that since Hitachi had a stern talk with Creative—and Creative made a few adjustments at the factory—the drives in newer MuVo2's follow the mini's proprietary example and no longer work in digital cameras.

## The Circuit Board

The mini's circuit board (**Figures 10.17** and **10.18**) sports a host of very tiny chips. Among them, you'll find:

**Figure 10.17**
The front of the mini's circuit board and accompanying display.

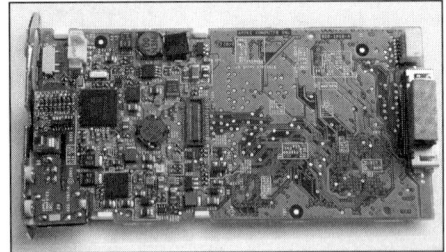

**Figure 10.18**
The back of the mini's circuit board, minus the hard drive and battery.

- **The FireWire controller chip.** Apple also uses a Texas Instruments FireWire controller chip in the mini. The TSB41AB1 on this iPod, however, is much smaller than the chip used in the original iPods.

- **The SDRAM chip.** This is the same Samsung K4S561633C-RL75 32 MB SDRAM chip used in third-generation iPods.

- **The Central Processing Unit (CPU).** Apple uses a very interesting chip for the mini's CPU. The PortalPlayer PP5020 chip supports encoding and decoding of not only MP3, AAC, and ACELP.NET (format used by Audible.com) files, but also files in the Windows Media audio format, (.wma). Additionally, the chip can decode JPEG and MJPEG graphics files. And yes, the inclusion of this chip hints that the iPod will one day support displaying graphics.

- **The Digital Audio Converter (DAC) chip.** The mini uses the same DAC chip as the third-generation iPods: the Wolfson Microelectronics WM8731.

# It's What's Inside That Counts: Disassembling the iPod mini

These iPods are incredibly difficult to crack. Without the able assistance of Greg Koenig, who described his experiences on iPodLounge.com (www.ipodlounge.com/articles_more.php?id=3059_0_8_0_C), and a hint or two posted on iPoding.com (www.ipoding.com), my mini would not have lived to play another day.

Given my experience, I can't imagine how anyone could open a mini without leaving obvious traces behind. Not only did I break my mini during the operation, but I left obvious evidence of my endeavors in the form of a badly scarred case. Please read the sidebar "It's What's Inside (That You're Likely to Break) That Counts: Disassembling the Third- and Fourth-generation iPod, iPod Photo, and iPod mini" before undertaking this procedure.

## Tools you'll need

1.5mm flat-head screwdriver

Philips #000 screwdriver

Needle-nose pliers

Internal snap-ring pliers

Hair dryer

## The operation

1. Turn off the iPod, and engage its Hold switch so that it doesn't turn on while you're working on it.

2. Switch the hair dryer to low, point it at the top of the iPod mini, and allow the case to get hot to the touch.

   The top and bottom plates of the mini are held in place not only by friction, but also by glue. You're heating the mini in the hope of melting that glue to the point where it's more pliable. If you fail to loosen the glue's grip, you'll scar these plates badly.

3. Squeeze the sides of the mini's case in the hope of exposing a small gap between the plastic plate and the side; then insert the flat-head

screwdriver into this gap and carefully run it around the edge, prying up gently as you go.

You may hear a faint snapping sound, which means that the plastic tabs that hold the plate in place are coming away from the case.

4. When the plate is loose all the way around, pry *straight up* to remove it.

If you pry the plate away at an angle, you'll break the internal Hold switch.

5. Repeat this procedure—hair dryer, prying, straight up—for the bottom plate.

At the bottom of the mini, you'll find a sheet-metal plate that fits into a groove carved on the inside of the mini (**Figure 10.19**).

**Figure 10.19**
The interior sheet-metal plate at the bottom of the mini.

6. To remove this plate, insert the points of the snap-ring pliers into the two holes on one side of the metal plate; squeeze the pliers; and gently pull up to dislodge the plate. Repeat for the other side of the plate and then remove it.

You can find internal snap-ring pliers at an auto-supply shop for less than $10.

7. Use the flat-head screwdriver to pry up (gently) and detach the orange ribbon connector that's marked Molex (**Figure 10.20**).

**Figure 10.20**
The detached scroll-wheel connector at the bottom of the mini.

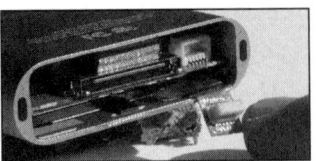

This ribbon cable connects the scroll wheel to the mini's motherboard. If you fail to disconnect this ribbon cable, you'll destroy your mini when you remove the guts from the outer shell.

8. Move to the top of the mini, and use the Philips screwdriver to remove the two minuscule screws on each end of the top plate (**Figure 10.21**).

**Figure 10.21**
The interior top plate, with tiny screws on each side.

Put these screws in a safe place. They're so tiny that if you drop them, they're gone for good.

9. Go back to the bottom of the mini, and gently push forward on the bottom of the connector you see to propel the mini's innards out the top of the case (**Figure 10.22**).

**Figure 10.22**
The back of the mini's circuit board, with battery and hard drive in place.

If you meet with any resistance, double-check that the scroll-wheel ribbon cable is completely disconnected.

10. To remove the battery, flip the inside assembly over so that the display is facing down; grip the battery connector on the top-right corner of the mini (as the mini's top is facing away from you) with the needle-nose pliers; and pull up gently.

Pull up on the left side of the battery until it pulls away from the sticky pad beneath it.

11. To remove the hard drive, disconnect the orange ribbon cable that's attached to the motherboard.

12. To reassemble the mini, reverse these steps.

## Additional notes and warnings

- When you slide the innards back into the mini's case, you'll meet with slight resistance—but *only* slight. When I put mine back together, the bottom of a rubber grommet that surrounds the display caught on the scroll-wheel assembly and peeled up. I was unable to reattach it, so I had to cut that section away. In hindsight, I should have backed out and tried again the moment I felt more than that slight resistance.

- Unless you plan to tear your mini apart on a regular basis, you should be prepared to reglue the top and bottom plates. I haven't a clue what sort of adhesive Apple uses in these things, but it grips like the devil. A good electronics shop can recommend a brand of goo that's likely to do the job.

- Before pushing the top plate back into position, be sure that its Hold switch is in the Hold position. The tabs on the bottom of the plate must line up with the internal Hold switch; if they don't, you could break the switch.

### It's What's Inside (That You're Likely to Break) That Counts: Disassembling the Third- and Fourth-generation iPod, iPod Photo, and iPod mini

After taking a long look at the instructions for pulling apart the white iPods and iPod mini, you may be tempted to try it yourself.

Unless you have a really good reason for doing so, please don't.

While I was disassembling my first third-generation iPod to take the pictures you see in these pages, I broke both the internal hold toggle switch and the audio connector cable. Although I can still play audio through the iPod via the Dock's Line Out port, with a dead headphone port, remote port, and Hold switch, my iPod can no longer be termed a portable music player.

## It's What's Inside (That You're Likely to Break) That Counts: Disassembling the Third- and Fourth-generation iPod, iPod Photo, and iPod mini *(continued)*

Initially, I had better luck with my mini, but its top and bottom are pretty well trashed. (Apple's reps will do little more than laugh uproariously if I attempt to take this mini in for service.) When I performed the operation a second time, I completely trashed it.

So given my misfortune, why do I present these peeks inside the iPod?

- To satisfy your curiosity (and keep you from doing it yourself).
- To benefit those of you who really need to open your iPods.

And what conditions should be met before you have a real need to open an iPod?

- The iPod is out of warranty.
- It's dead.

To illustrate my point, allow me to relate yet another personal story.

It just so happens that this book's publisher, Nancy Ruenzel, had an iPod that met both these conditions. Her 20 GB, second-generation iPod had recently celebrated its first birthday (and, thus, outlived its warranty). A dinner companion accidentally spilled red wine on the device while it was playing. It immediately stopped playing.

After she related her tale of woe, I did my best to get in good with the boss by offering every troubleshooting technique I could think of. Nothing worked. This was one dead iPod.

My final message to her consisted of one word:

"eBay."

Apple's claim that there are no user-*serviceable* parts inside an iPod is correct. There are, however, user-*salvageable* parts inside your iPod, and that, dear reader, is why I sent Nancy to eBay. Salvaging a perfectly good battery and hard drive from an otherwise-dead iPod to sell them to another iPod owner who needs such components is a darned good reason for opening your iPod. Apple charges a premium for "repairing" iPods (in fact, Apple doesn't repair them, but replaces them with new or refurbished models), and you may find that you do better by selling your iPod for parts and using the money you earn to help pay for a new iPod.

And, of course, there will come a day when your iPod's battery expires, and you'd like to replace it with a battery from one of the outfits I mention earlier in the chapter.

## How Much Abuse Can the iPod Take?

A final personal story:

In my duties as a contributing editor for *Macworld* magazine, I was tasked with the job of stress-testing one of the original 5 GB iPods. Because these early iPods didn't ship with a belt clip, case, or armband, my editor felt that it was *Macworld*'s duty to see how much abuse an iPod could take before it finally played its last MP3. Heartbreaking as it was to subject such a beautiful gadget to such treatment, I accepted the assignment.

I devised four tests, each of which involved dropping the iPod onto a hard surface. To replicate real-world situations, I determined to drop the iPod onto a slab of cement from waist-high, drop the iPod while jogging on a paved road, drop the iPod from a bicycle traveling approximately 25 mph, and drop that iPod from that same bicycle at 30 mph. The iPod was playing during all these tests.

Because I didn't have four iPods to sacrifice, I performed the tests on a single iPod—which, of course, calls the results into question due to the factor of accumulated damage. For this reason, I didn't send the results to the Pulitzer committee.

The results were:

- **Dropped from waist-high, with bottom plate facing down.** The iPod continued to play. But the front plastic was dinged, and the back was scratched.

- **Dropped while jogging, with the iPod held with ports facing skyward.** The iPod continued to play. The side of the back case was dented and pulled slightly away from the front. The back plate did not fit snugly after being pushed back into place.

- **Dropped from a bicycle at 25 mph, with the bottom plate facing down.** The iPod continued to play. The back plate was severely scratched and dented. The back plate pulled even farther away from the front. The back plate did not fit snugly after being pushed back into place.

- **Dropped from a bicycle at 30 mph, with the ports facing skyward.** The iPod stopped playing—and flew apart in spectacular fashion. The back plate fell off, as did the front scroll wheel and Select button. When it was reassembled, the iPod displayed the Sad iPod icon and could not be revived.

Depending on whether yours is a glass-half-empty or glass-half-full personality, you can view these results in two ways: You can be disappointed that the iPod eventually died, or you can be impressed that it suffered four separate instances of violent abuse before it finally met its maker.

Personally, I was pleased that the iPod took such a licking and kept on ticking. That doesn't mean, however, that I'd transport my iPod without a padded case equipped with a belt clip.

# Thank You

As thanks for purchasing this book, I'd like to give you a little something to put on your iPod. That little something is *Of Eve*, a solo piano album I recorded some years ago.

The music on *Of Eve* belongs to me, but you're welcome to download and place it on your computer and iPod for your personal listening pleasure. You may not, however, use this music in a public broadcast or for any commercial purposes without my permission.

You can find your copy here: www.peachpit.com/ipodsecrets.

I hope you enjoy it.

# Index

## A

A/V cables (iPod Photo), 13
.aa file extension (Audible.com), 37
AAC (Advanced Audio Coding) format
    converting to Windows Media Player format, 195
    *versus* other formats, 65–67
    supported audio formats, 17–18
About iPod screen, 29, 43
About settings, 47–48
accessories
    batteries
        Backup Battery Pack, 377, 378
        battery-replacement services, 420
        iPod Battery, 377
        self-built chargers (Allen Evans), 378
        self-service with purchased batteries, 420
    car chargers, 374–375
        Auto Charger for iPod, 375
        Auto Kit, 375–376
        Imp, 375–376
        iPod Car Charger, 375
        PowerPod Auto Adapter, 375
    car music adapters, 365, 371
        Alpine DCA-420i and Alpine Ai-NET head units, 366
        BMW iPod adapters, 365–366
        cassette players, 366–367
        iRock! 300W Wireless Music Adapter, 370
        iTrip and iTrip mini, 368–369
        PodFreq, 367–368
        SoundFeeder SF121 FM Stereo Transmitter, 370
        TransPod, 370–371
        TuneCast/TuneCast II Mobile FM Transmitters, 370
        wireless adapters, 367
    carrying cases
        alternate practical solutions, 362
        Apple, 10, 12
        belt clips, iPod mini, 12, 354
        CEO Classic case, 359
        Clear iPod Armor mini, 361
        Deluxe iPod Case, 359
        Designer iPod Case, 359
        Groove Bag Triplet and Groove Bag Tote Speaker purses, 396–397
        Incase Belt for iPod, 361
        included with some iPods, 353
        iPod Armor, 361
        iPod Armor mini, 361
        iPod Case, 356
        iPod Gear Pouch, 356
        iPod inMotion Case, 356–357
        iPod mini Arm Band, 357
        iSee case, 360
        Lilipod case, 360
        Mini SportSuit Basic (4G), 358
        Mini SportSuit Convertible, 358–359
        Mini SportSuit Runabout, 359
        purchasing guidelines, 354–355
        Showcase, 360
        skins, 362
        SportSuit Basic (4G), 358
        SportSuit Convertible Case, 358
        SportSuit Sleeve, 359
    connectors/adapters
        cables for hard wiring, 364
        Get Connected Bundle, 371
        Headphone Splitter Cable, 365
        HotWire cable, 378
        iMic, 363
        iPod Connection Kits, 371
        iPod Dock Connector to FireWire Cable, 371
        iPod Home Connect Kit, 364
        iPod Stereo Connection Kit, 371
        iPod Universal Connection Kit with FM Transmitter, 371
        iPod Universal Connection Kit with Tape Adapter, 371
        iShare Earbud Splitter, 365
        mono RCA plugs, 363–364
        Monster Cable Mini-Stereo to RCA Cable, 371
        PocketDock mini-dock connector, 371
        stereo miniplugs, 363–364
        Walkman-style miniplugs, 363

accessories *(continued)*
  earbuds/headphones
    Apple In-Ear Headphones, 379
    closed models, 381
    custom earpieces, 380
    E3c and E5c headphones, 379
    EM3 headphones, 379
    ER-4P earphones, 379
    HeadWize Web site, forums and reviews, 382
    in-ear models, 378–379
    iShare Earbud Splitter, 371
    neckband models, 378, 380
    open-air models, 381
    shopping guidelines, 382
    Sony MDR-V6, 381
  miscellaneous
    AirPort Express Base Station, 398–399
    Digital Camera Link, 386
    FMXtra tuner, 395–396
    Groove Bag Triplet and Tote Speaker purses, 396–397
    inMotion portable speakers, 391–393
    iPAL AM/FM radio, 395
    iPod Dock, 371, 390–391
    iPod Remote Control, 10, 12, 364, 390
    iTalk voice recorder, 383
    Media Reader for iPod, 385–389
    name engraving at Apple Store, 399–400
    NaviPod wireless remote control, 391
    PowerMate, 397
    SoundDock (Bose), 394–395
    On Stage portable speakers, 393–394
    Universal Microphone Adapter, 27, 39, 43, 383
    Voice Recorder for iPod with Dock Connector, 27, 39, 43, 96–97, 382–383
    Xtremity iPod Accessory System, 359
  power adapters
    FireJuice and FireJuice 6 for iPod w/Dock Connector, 374
    FireWire cables, 25
    iPod Power Adapter, 371, 372
    PowerDock, 372–373
    PowerPod Auto Adapters, 375
    World Travel Adapter Kit, 7, 347
adapters. *See* accessories, connectors/adapters; accessories, power adapters
Address Book, Contacts
  Macintosh, 287, 290, 312–313
  Windows, 289, 312–313

Advanced Audio Coding. *See* AAC
AIFF (Audio Interchange File Format)
  converting from .m4p, 174
  managing file formats, 70
  *versus* other formats, 65
  supported audio formats, 17–18
AirPort Express Base Station (Apple), 398–399
  supported by iTunes 4.6, 60
Akron Resources' SoundFeeder SF121 FM Stereo Transmitter, 370
alarms
  Alarm Clock screen, 39
  Calendar's event alarms, 343–344
album art
  displaying on iPod Photo, 31, 108
  transferring to iPod from iTunes Music Store, 180
Albums screen, 35
All Recorder (1st Benison Software), 71
  downloading/playing radio shows, 143
allowances for iTunes Music Store purchases, 149–151
Alpine DCA-420i and Alpine Ai-NET head units, 366
Altec Lansing's inMotion portable speakers, 391–393
Amazon.com, 69
Ambrosia Software's WireTap, 71
  downloading/playing radio shows, 143
Anapod Explorer (Red Chair Software)
  moving music using iPod as removable drive, 275
  playlists, 30
  Windows iPod
    Anapod Xtreamer, 230–231
    AudioMorph feature, 229
    basics, 223–224
    contacts, 232, 308
    loading Apple Lossless Codec or ACC files, 18
    playing music, 230
    playlists, 232
    Recover Missing Tracks feature, 232
    similarity to Windows Explorer, 224–227
    transferring music to iPod, 227–229
    volume adjustments, 232
Anapod Xtreamer feature (Anapod Explorer), 230–231

Apple
  AirPort Express Base Station, 398–399
    supported by iTunes 4.6, 60
  Apple Records *versus* Apple Computer, 128
  battery-replacement service, 420
  iCal application. *See* Calendar
  Image Capture, 389
  In-Ear Headphones, 379
  iPod Dock, 371, 390–391
  iPod Dock Connector to FireWire Cable, 371
  iPod mini Arm Band, 357
  iPod Power Adapter, 371–372
  iPod Remote Control, 10, 12, 364
    connectors, 26–27
    convenience, 390
  iPod Stereo Connection Kit, 371
  iSync
    Calendar, 338–339, 347–348
    Contacts, 293–295
  Media Reader for iPod, 385–389
  Monster Cable Mini-Stereo to RCA Cable, 371
  name engraving at Apple Store, 399–400
  OpenTalk, 72–74
  ResEdit, 263
  USB 2.0 + FireWire cables, 190
  World Travel Adapter Kit, 7, 373
Apple Lossless Encoder
  introduction with iTunes 4.5, 59–60
  managing file formats, 70
  *versus* other formats, 65–67
  supported audio formats, 17–18
AppleCare extended warranty plan, 3
AppleScripts
  Apple Web site for scripts, 104
  iPod Library Summary script, 104
  iPod Tracks -> Desktop, 270–271
  Notes collection, 322–323
  Open Pod, 273
appointments. *See* Calendar
Artists screen, 34–35
Atrac format (Sony), 70
Audible.com, audio books
  advertisements on audio books, 145
  Audiobooks screen, 37
  downloading/playing files
    guidelines, 177–178
    Macintosh, 175–176
    Windows, 176–177

audio books
  Audiobooks link, 141–142, 144
  Audiobooks screen, 37
  Audiobooks settings, 50
  sources, 37
Audio Hijack/Audio Hijack Pro (Rogue Amoeba), 71
Audio Interchange File Format. *See* AIFF
audio resolution
  Kbps (kilobytes per second), 65–68
  Preferences, Importing settings, 65–68
audio scrubbing, 24, 32
Audiobooks Browse category, 33
Audiobooks link, 141–142, 144
Audiobooks screen, 37
Audiobooks settings, 50
AudioMorph feature (Anapod Explorer), 229
AudioX, voice recordings, 280–281
authorizations (iTunes Music Store), 130
  lost authorizations, 172–173
  purchasing music, 170–171
  streaming songs over networks, 73
Auto Charger for iPod (Dr. Bott LLC), 375
Auto Kit auto chargers (Belkin), 375–376
AutoDJ (Musicmatch Jukebox), 213–214
.avi movies, Image Capture (Apple), 389
Azuma, Daniel; FileTyper, 263–264

# B

backlit display, 22
  Backlight command, 28, 29
  Backlight Timer, 49–50
  power conservation, 7–8
Backup Battery Pack (Belkin), 377, 378
Balestra, Marco; iPod Tracks -> Desktop AppleScript, 270–271
batteries. *See also* accessories, batteries
  battery life, 7–8
  power conservation, 7–8
    Backlight Timer, 49–50
    iPod Photo TV Out, Off setting, 119
    major drains, 46
    Sleep Timer, 39
Battery Technology's iPod Battery, 377
beat matching, 98
beats-per-minute (bpm) tags, 98

Belkin
- Auto Kit auto chargers, 375–376
- Backup Battery Pack, 377, 378
- Digital Camera Link, 386
- Digital Camera Link for iPod, 43
- Headphone Splitter Cable, 365
- Media Reader for iPod, 42, 385–389
- TuneCast/TuneCast II Mobile FM Transmitters, 370
- Universal Microphone Adapter, 27, 39, 43, 383
- Voice Recorder for iPod with Dock Connector, 27, 39, 43, 382–383
  - using with iTunes, 96

belt clips, iPod mini, 12, 354
best-selling books. *See* Audiobooks link
Billboard
- Billboard Charts link, iTunes Music Store, 147–148
- Billboard.com, 69

Bit Cartel's RadioLover, 71
bit rate settings
- Anapod Explorer, 229
- basics, 65–68
- Musicmatch Jukebox, 203

Blondeau, Bruno; PodManager, 269–270
BMW iPod adapters, 365–366
Bombich, Mike; Carbon Copy Cloner, 253–256
books. *See* audio books
Books and Spoken link. *See* Audiobooks link
bootable drive. *See* removable drive
Bose SoundDock, 394–395
bpm (beats-per-minute) tags, 98
Breakout game. *See* Brick game
Bresink, Marcel; TinkerTool, 265–267
Brick game, 44–45
Browse command
- categories
  - Albums, 35
  - Artists, 34–35
  - Audiobooks, 37
  - Composers, 36
  - Genres, 36
  - Songs, 36
- *versus* Music command, 29

# C

cables and adapters. *See* accessories, connectors/adapters; accessories, power adapters

Calendar, 41–42
- To Do items, 334
- EphPod's Calendar Editor, 239
- event alarms, 343–344
- exporting data
  - from Microsoft Entourage (Macintosh), 335–336
  - from Microsoft Outlook (Windows), 339–341
  - from Palm Desktop (Macintosh), 336–338
  - from Palm Desktop (Windows), 341–343
- history, 328
- iCal application, 331–334, 338–339
  - individual screen displays, Macintosh, 349
- iCalendar standard/files, 328
- iSync, 338–339, 347–348
- removing data, 346–347
- transferring data
  - automatically, 347–348
  - manually, 344–345
- vCal (vCalendar) standard/files, 328–330

car chargers. *See* accessories, car chargers
car music adapters. *See* accessories, car music adapters
Carbon Copy Cloner (Mike Bombich), 253–256
carrying cases. *See* accessories, carrying cases
Casady & Greene's SoundJam, 58
CD package
- iPod, 2–4
- iPod mini, 11
- iPod Photo, 13–14
- iPod Special Edition: U2, 2–4

CEO Classic case (Marware), 359
charging all iPod models, 6–7
Clear iPod Armor mini (Matias), 361
click wheels, 20
Clicker settings, 53
Clock, 38–40
CompactFlash media type, 385
Composers screen, 36
compressed files
- managing file formats, 70
- *versus* uncompressed, 65–67

connectors/adapters. *See* accessories, connectors/adapters
Contacts, 282–283
- Anapod Explorer, 232
- EphPod, 239
- Extras screen, 40–41
- iPod Organizer, 278–279

iTunes, 282–283
Macintosh, automatic processes
    data entry with email client or contact manager, 312–313
    Eudora 6.1, 297–298
    iSync, 293–295
    NETsettings NowPod, 300–301
    Now Contact, 299
Macintosh, manual processes, 286–289
moving contacts
    from Entourage, 296
    from older contact managers, 297
    from Palm Desktop, 296–297
removing contacts, 309–311
Settings screen, 54
sorting, 286
uses other than contacts, 310–311
    with iPod It, 313–314
    with iSpeak It, 314–315
    with Pod2Go, 315
    with PodWriter, 316
vCard standard, 284–285
    PIMs and email applications supported, 285
.vcf files, hacking, 311–312
Windows, automatic processes
    Anapod Explorer, 308
    data entry with email client or contact manager, 312–313
    EphPod, 307–308
    iAppoint, 305
    iPod Agent, 303–304
    iPodSync, 302–303
    Outpod, 306
    PocketMac iPod Edition, 304–305
Windows, manual processes, 289–291
Contour Design
    iSee case, 360
    Showcase, 360
Contrast display settings, 53
Creative's Nomad MuVo2 drives, 441

# D

DataViz's MacOpener, 233
Date & Time screen
    Extras screen, 39
    Settings screen, 53
Date Book (Palm Desktop), 339
DCIM folder (iPod Photo), 114
Dekorte, Steve; SoundConverter, 70–71
Deluxe iPod Case (XtremeMac), 359
Designer iPod Case (XtremeMac), 359

Digisette's FMXtra tuner, 395–396
Digital Camera Link for iPod (Belkin), 43, 386
Digital Lifestyle Outfitters' TransPod, 370–371
display controls, 19–22
Dock. *See* iPod Dock
Dolby Laboratories' Advanced Audio Coding. *See* AAC
Dr. Bott LLC
    Auto Charger for iPod, 375
    Groove Bag Triplet and Groove Bag Tote Speaker purses, 396–397
    iPod Connection Kits, 371
    iPod Universal Connection Kit with FM Transmitter, 371
    iPod Universal Connection Kit with Tape Adapter, 371
    PocketDock mini-dock connector, 371
Dusel, Hans-Peter; VolumeBooster, 416–417

# E

earbuds/headphones. *See also* accessories, earbuds/headphones
    European volume restrictions, 25–26
    iPod, 5–6
    iPod mini, 12
elapsed time display, 27
EM3 headphones (Future Sonics), 379
Entourage (Microsoft)
    compatible with iCal application, 331
    Contacts, 312–313
    Macintosh, 287, 296
EphPod (Joe Masters)
    moving music using iPod as removable drive, 275
    playlists, 30
    Windows iPod
        alternative to iTunes, 232–233
        basics, 234–237
        Calendar Editor, 239
        contacts, 239, 307–308
        loading Apple Lossless Codec or ACC files, 18
        memos, 239
        music piracy issues, 240
        news services, 240–241
        playlists, 239
        rippling files, 236
        setup, 233
        transferring music on/off iPod, 238–239
EQ (equalization) settings, 52
    batter power conservation, 7–8
    iTunes, 99

Erock Studios' Lilipod case, 360
Etymotic's ER-4P earphones, 379
Eudora, Contacts, 287–288, 297–298
European iPod volume restrictions, headphone jacks, 25–26
Evans, Allen; self-built battery charger, 378
events. *See* Calendar
Extras command, 28, 29, 34
    Calendar, 41–42
    Clock, 38–40
    Contacts, 40–41
    games, 44–47
    iPod, 25, 34
    Notes, 42
    Photo Import, 42–43
    Voice Memos, 43–44

## F

file sharing. *See* music sharing
FileTyper (Daniel Azuma), 263–264
FireJuice adapter (SiK), 190
FireJuice and FireJuice 6 for iPod w/Dock Connector (SiK), 374
FireWire cable connectors/adapters, 6–7, 25
    Dock Connector ports, 27
    iPod mini, 11–12
    removable drive, 244–246
    USB 2.0 + FireWire cables, 190
    Windows iPod, 187–192
1st Benison Software's All Recorder, 71
    downloading/playing radio shows, 143
Flying Meat's VoodooPad, 323–326
Flying Mouse Software's PodMaster, 271
FMXtra tuner (Digisette), 395–396
Fogware's Internet Radio Recorder, 71
Frakes, Dan; video flip books, 116
Franke, Norman; SoundApp, 70
FurthurNET, 69
Future Sonics
    custom-fitted earpieces, 380
    EM3 headphones, 379

## G

games
    Brick, 44–45
    Music Quiz, 44–45
    Parachute, 44, 46
    Solitaire, 44, 46–47
GarageBand, 68–69
    importing .m4p files and exporting as AIFF, 174

Genres screen, 36
Get Connected Bundle (XtremeMac), 371
Getting Started guide, 2
gift certificates for iTunes Music Store, 152–154
GoInCase's Incase Belt for iPod, 361
Griffin Technology
    iMic, 363
    iPod Home Connect Kit, 364
    iTalk, 27, 43, 383
        using with iTunes, 96
    iTrip and iTrip mini, 368–369
    PowerMate, 397
    PowerPod Auto Adapter, 375
    Walkman-style miniplugs, 363
Groove Bag Triplet and Groove Bag Tote Speaker purses (Dr. Bott LLC), 396–397

## H

Hageman, Carl; iAppoint, 305
hard drives. *See also* removable drive
    hot swapping, 244
    image storage (iPod Photo), 114
Headphone Splitter Cable (Belkin), 365
headphones. *See also* accessories, earbuds/headphones
    European iPod volume restrictions, 25–26
HeadWize Web site, 382
Help menu (iTunes), 104
High-Capacity iPod Replacement Battery (Newer Technology), 420
Hold switch, headphones, 26–27
hot swapping, 244
HotWire cable (SiK), 378

## I

iAppoint (Carl Hageman), 305
iCal application. *See* Calendar
iCalendar standard/files, 328
ID3 tags, 97
    definition, 37
If Then Software; Pod 2 iPod, 272
Image Capture (Apple), 389
iMic (Griffin Technology), 363
Imp auto charger (SiK), 375–376
In-Ear Headphones (Apple), 379
Incase Belt for iPod, 361
inMotion portable speakers (Altec Lansing), 391–393
Internet Radio Recorder (Fogware), 71
Internet Underground Music Archives Web site, 68–69

**Index** 457

Intervideo's XPack for Windows XP, 223
invisible music folder, 260–261
iPAL AM/FM radio (Tivoli Audio), 395
iPod. *See also* iPod mini; iPod Photo; Windows iPod
    battery power conservation, 7–8
    CD package, 2–4
    charging all models, 6–7
    cleaning, 9–10
    Dock, 8–9
    earbuds, 5–6
    exterior features, 9–10
    FireWire connectors/adapters, 6–7
    Getting Started guide, 2
    hard-drive capacity, 14–15
    Help menu, 104
    iPod Help (iTunes), 104
    iPod Special Edition: U2, $50 coupon offer, 10
    light-show feature, 103
    Musicmatch Jukebox incompatibility, 196
    name engraving at Apple Store, 399–400
    printing contents, 103
    renaming, 102
    restocking fee, 11
    software license agreement, 2–3
    Software Updater, 2
    tutorials, 2
    warnings, 4
    warranties, 3
    Windows FAT32 *versus* Mac OS Extended (HFS+) volumes, 16–17
iPod Agent, 303–304, 334
iPod Armor and iPod Armor mini (Matias), 361
iPod Battery (Battery Technology), 377
iPod Car Charger (XtremeMac), 375
iPod Case (Waterfield Design), 356
iPod Connection Kit (Dr. Bott LLC), 371
iPod Dock (Apple), 371, 390–391
    connector ports, 27
    iPod, 8–9
    iPod mini, 12
    iPod Photo, 14
iPod Dock Connector to FireWire Cable (Apple), 371
iPod for Windows. *See* Windows iPod
iPod Gear Pouch (Waterfield Design), 359
iPod Home Connect Kit (Griffin Technology), 364
iPod inMotion Case (Waterfield Design), 356–357
iPod It (Michael Zapp), 313–314
iPod mini. *See also* iPod; iPod Photo; Windows iPod
    battery power conservation, 7–8
    belt clips, 12
    charging, 6–7
    Dock, 12

Dock Connector ports, 27
earbuds, 12
FireWire connectors/adapters, 11–12
hard-drive capacity, 13
removable drive, 245–246
restocking fee, 11
User's Guide, 11
Windows FAT32 *versus* Mac OS Extended (HFS+) volumes, 16–17
iPod mini Arm Band (Apple), 357
iPod Organizer (ProVue Development), 278–279
iPod Photo
    A/V cables, 13
    album art, 108
    battery life, 7
    cables, 13
    carrying cases, 10, 14
    color use, 107–108
    Dock, 14
    earbuds, 13
    features, 106–107
    *versus* fourth-generation iPods, 106
    graphics formats supported, 111
    image storage, 114
    iTunes Photo tab, 89
        Include Full-Resolution Photos option, 113
        Synchronize Photos From option, 109–113
    iTunes version 4.7 requirement, 106
    Photos command, 28
    portable PowerPoint presenter, 122
    power adapters, 6–7
    Ratings screen, 107
    S-Video ports, 14, 109
        viewing photos, 120, 121
    shortcomings, 106–107
    slideshows on TV, 108–109
        no remote controls available, 391
        projecting photos, 120–122
        settings, 117–120
    Thumbs folder, Photo Database file, 114
    viewing photos, 115
        other S-Video or composite video connections, 120
        video flip books, 116
iPod Power Adapter (Apple), 371–372
iPod Remote Control (Apple), 10, 12, 364
    connectors, 26–27
    convenience, 390
iPod Soft's iPod Agent, 303–304, 334
iPod Special Edition: U2. *See* iPod
iPod Stereo Connection Kit (Apple), 371
iPod Tracks -> Desktop AppleScript (Marco Balestra), 270–271

iPod Universal Connection Kit with FM
    Transmitter (Dr. Bott LLC), 371
iPod Universal Connection Kit with Tape Adapter
    (Dr. Bott LLC), 371
iPod Voice Recorder. *See* Voice Recorder for iPod
    with Dock Connector (Belkin)
iPodResQ's battery services, 420
iPodSync (Mike Matheson), 302–303, 334,
    387–388
iRock! 300W Wireless Music Adapter, 370
iSee case (Contour Design), 360
iShare Earbud Splitter (XtremeMac), 365, 371
iSpeak It (Michael Zapp), 314–315
iSync (Apple)
    Calendar, 338–339, 347–348
    Contacts, 293–295
iTalk voice recorder (Griffin Technology), 27, 43,
    383
    using with iTunes, 96
.ithmb file extension (iPod Photo), 114
iTrip and iTrip mini (Griffin Technology), 368–369
iTunes
    AppleScripts
        Apple Web site for scripts, 104
        iPod Library Summary script, 104
    audio files
        bpm (beats-per-minute) tags, 99
        copy restrictions, 94–95
        downloading, file formats, 70–71
        downloading, Web site sources, 68–69
        ID3 tags, 97
        Multiple Song Information dialog box, 98
        Song Information dialog box, 96–97, 99
        streaming across networks, 72–74
        transferring into iTunes, 75–76
        transferring to iPod, 87–94
    Contacts, 282–283
    Get Info command, 96–98
    Help menu, 104
    iPod
        alternate music-management applications,
            61
        light-show feature, 103
        printing contents, 103
        renaming, 102
        Show Duplicate Songs command, 101–102
        View Options command, 102
    iPod Photo, 106
    iTunes Music Store
        advantages of using, 125–127
        improvements with version 4.5, 59–60
        iTunes Essentials link, 155–156

    *versus* Musicmatch Jukebox, 18
    operating system and processors
        requirements, 60–61
    playlists
        creating from selected items, 78–79
        creating standard lists, 77–78
        Party Shuffle feature, 102–103
        play count, 86–87
        printing jewel-case inserts, 103
        ratings, 86
        recently played songs, 87
        Shuffle feature, 102
        updating manually, 90–93
    Preferences, General tab (version 4.7)
        Enable Disk Use, 93, 95–96
        Open iTunes When This iPod Is Attached,
            93–94
    Preferences, Music tab (version 4.7)
        Automatically Update All Songs and
            Playlists, 89
        Automatically Update Selected Playlists
            Only, 90
        Display Album Artwork on Your iPod, 108
        Manually Manage Songs and Playlists,
            90–92
        Only Update Checked Songs, 93
    Preferences, Photo tab (version 4.7), 89
        Include Full-Resolution Photos option, 113
        Synchronize Photos From option, 109–113
    Preferences tab, 96
        audio resolution and bit rate settings,
            65–68
        Automatically Update All Songs and
            Playlists, 89
        Automatically Update Selected Playlists
            Only, 90
        Connect to Internet When Needed option,
            62
        Display Album Artwork on iPod, 31
        Enable Disk Use, 93, 95–96
        Load Complete Preview Before Playing
            option, 163
        Look for Shared Music option, 73
        Manually Manage Songs and Playlists,
            90–92
        Only Update Checked Songs, 93
        Open iTunes When This iPod Is Attached,
            93–94
        Show Links to Music Store option, 160
        two iPods connected to one computer, 89
        Use Error Corrections When Reading Audio
            CDs, 62

ripping CDs, 61–64
   unrippable discs, 64
Smart Playlists
   basics, 79–80, 85
   proposed lists, 81–84
   versions 4 and 4.5, 85
Sound Check, 99–100
   effectiveness debates, 100–101
Source list, 29
updating automatically
   all song/playlists, 89
   selected playlists, 90
version 2, 58
version 3, 58
version 4, 58–59
version 4.5, 59–60
version 4.6, 60
version 4.7, 60
versions, first release, 58
voice recordings, 96
iTunes for Windows
   audio formats
      converting Windows Media Player files to ACC format, 195
      supported, 18
   versions, 59
iTunes Music Store
   accounts
      AOL screen names and passwords, 132–133, 170–171
      Apple IDs and passwords, 132–133, 170–171
      creating, 131–134
      editing information, 166–167
   advantages of using, 125–127
   Apple Records *versus* Apple Computer, 128
   basic requirements for using, 128–130
   Customer Service, 172
   dearth of specific artists/genres, 127–128
   foreign country availability, 128
   improvements, iTunes version 4.5, 59–60
   iTunes
      advantages of using, 125–127
      iTunes Essentials link, 155–156
   iTunes and Music Store Help, 104
   iTunes Essentials link, 155–156
   music/books, previewing, 162–163
      alternate sites, 68–69, 105
      Artist Alert link, 164
      firewalls and proxies, 164
   music/books, purchasing
      allowances, 149–151
      alternate sites, 68–69, 105, 221
      authorizations, 130, 170–172
      authorizations, streaming songs over networks, 73
      burning to CDs, 144, 173–174
      burning to CDs, limitations, 131
      gift certificates, 152–154
      limitations in using, 130–131
      pick-and-pay method, 164–166
      playing purchased music, 170–171
      prepaid cards, 154–155
      shopping cart method, 167–170
      song compilations, 155
      wish lists, 170
   music/books, transferring to iPod, 179
      album art, 180
      requirements, 178
   music industry deals, 127
   origin, 124–125
   shopping/navigating
      Artist Alert link, 164
      Audiobooks link, 141–142, 144
      Billboard Charts link, 147–148
      Biography link, 138–139
      Browse button, 161
      Browse Music search link, 136–137
      Celebrity Playlists, 156
      Disney link, 145
      EXPLICIT/CLEAN labels, 162
      Genre pop-up menu, 157–158
      ID3 tags, 160
      iMix link, 145–147
      Influences & Contemporaries link, 138–139
      iTunes Essentials link, 155–156
      Music Trailers link, 149
      Music Videos link, 148–149
      Power Search, 140, 143
      Power Search, radio shows, 143
      primary links, 135–136
      Radio Charts link, 148
      Results area, 137
      returning to home page, 161–162
      Search field, 159
      Support link, 155
      Today's Top Songs/Albums, 157
   troubleshooting, 181–183
iVolume (Manfred Lippert), 100

## J

JBL's On Stage portable speakers, 393–394

## K

KaZaA, 124
Kbps (kilobytes per second)
    Anapod Explorer, 229
    basics, 65–68
    Musicmatch Jukebox, 203
Klondike card game. *See* Solitaire game

## L

Language settings, 54
Laptops for Less' battery services, 420
legal issues/settings, 54. *See also* music piracy
    copy restrictions, 94–95
Lifestyle Outfitters' TransPod, 370–371
Limewire, 124
Linux, Ogg Vorbis format, 70
Lippert, Manfred; iVolume, 100
lossy and lossless compression, 65

## M

.m4a AAC format, *versus* other formats, 65
MacDrive (Mediafour), 233
Macintosh
    downloading/playing audio books, 175–176
    iPod *versus* Windows iPod, 18
    iTunes, operating system and processor requirements, 60–61
    iTunes Music Store, basic requirements for using, 129
    OS Extended (HFS+) *versus* Windows FAT32 volumes, 16–17
    synchronizing photos, iPod Photo, 110–111
MacOpener (DataViz), 233
Main Menu settings, 47–48
main screen, 20
    Extras command
        Calendar, 41–42
        Clock, 38–40
        Contacts, 40–41
        games, 44–47
        Notes, 42
        Photo Import, 42–43
        Voice Memos, 43–44
    Music/Browse commands, 29
        On-The-Go playlist, 32–34
        playlists, 30–32
    overview, 28–29
    Settings screen
        About, 47–48
        Audiobooks, 50
        Backlight Timer, 49–50
        Clicker, 53
        Contacts, 54
        Contrast, 53
        Date & Time, 53
        EQ (equalization), 52
        Language, 54
        Legal, 54
        Main Menu, 48
        Repeat, 49
        Reset All Settings, 54
        Shuffle, 49
        Sound Check, 52–53
    Shuffle Songs command, 55
Marware
    CEO Classic case, 359
    Mini SportSuit Basic, 358
    Mini SportSuit Convertible, 358–359
    Mini SportSuit Runabout, 359
    SportSuit Basic (4G), 358
    SportSuit Convertible Case, 358
    SportSuit Sleeve, 359
Masters, Joe; Ephpod. *See* Ephpod
Matheson, Mike; iPodsync, 302–303, 334, 387–388
Matias
    Clear iPod Armor mini, 361
    iPod Armor and iPod Armor mini, 361
.m4b file extension (iTunes Music Store), 37
Media Reader for iPod (Belkin), 42, 363–367
Mediafour's XPlay. *See* XPlay
meetings. *See* Calendar
Memory Stick media type, 385
Menu button, 23
Microsoft
    Entourage
        compatible with iCal application, 331
        Contacts, 287, 296, 312–313
    iPod for Windows. *See* Windows iPod
    MSN Music Service, 125, 241
    Outlook
        Calendar, 339–341
        Contacts, 289–290, 312–313
Mini SportSuit Basic (Marware), 358
Mini SportSuit Convertible (Marware), 358–359
Mini SportSuit Runabout (Marware), 359
Monster Cable Mini-Stereo to RCA Cable (Apple), 371
movies, Image Capture (Apple), 389

.m4p AAC format
    converting to AIFF, 174
    *versus* other formats, 65
MP3 format
    converting from .m4p and AIFF, 173–174
    managing file formats, 70
    *versus* other formats, 65–68
    supported audio formats, 17–18
MSN Music Service (Microsoft), 125, 241
Multimedia Card media type, 385
Music command, 28
    *versus* Browse command, 29
    categories
        Albums, 35
        Artists, 34–35
        Audiobooks, 37
        Composers, 36
        Genres, 36
        Songs, 36
    playlists
        basics, 30–32
        On-The-Go, 32–34
music industry and iTunes Music Store
    history of development, 103–105
    origin, 127
music piracy. *See also* Legal issues/settings
    copy restrictions, 94–95
    EphPod, 240
    music sharing pros and cons, 261–262
Music Quiz game, 44–45
music sharing, history, 103–105
Music Store. *See* iTunes Music Store
Musicmatch Jukebox and Windows iPod, 186
    basics, 200–201
    editing track information, 210–211
    included in software package, 193
    installing/reinstalling, 197–198
    iPod Manager, 199–200
    Musicmatch Downloads, 125, 241
    playlists, 30, 205–207
        random lists, 213–214
    ripping CDs, 202–203
    shortcomings, 196
    supported audio formats, 18
    transferring music
        to iPod, 207–210
        into Jukebox, 203–205
    Volume Leveling feature, 212–213
My Top Rated Smart Playlist, 30

## N

name engraving at Apple Store, 399–400
Napster (commercial music service), 70, 104, 221
Napster (defunct free music sharing), 123–124
navigation controls, 19–21
NaviPod wireless remote control (TEN Technology), 391
NETsettings NowPod, Contacts, 300–301
Newer Technology's battery services, 420
Next/Fast Forward button, 22–23
Next Track button, battery power conservation, 7–8
Nomad MuVo2 drives (Creative), 441
Notes feature, 42, 295–296
    HTML links, 319–320
        notes to audio files, 320–321
    HTML tags, 318–319
    iPod AppleScripts collection, 322–323
    launching iPod in NotesOnly mode, 321
    VoodooPad, 323–326
Now Contact, 299
Now Playing screen, 30–32

## O

Ogg Vorbis format (Linux), 70
Omni Group's OmniWeb, 272–273
OmniWeb (Omni Group), 272–273
On Stage portable speakers (JBL), 393–394
On-The-Go playlists, 32–34
Open Pod AppleScript, 273
OpenTalk (Apple), 72–74
operating system and processors
    Macintosh, 60–61
    Windows, 61
Outlook (Microsoft)
    Calendar, 339–341
    Contacts, 289–290, 312–313
Outpod (Oliver Stoer), 306

## P

Palm Desktop
    Calendar
        compatible with iCal application, 331
        exporting data, 341–343
    compatible with iCal application, 331
    Contacts, 312–313
        Macintosh, 287–288, 296–297
        Windows, 290
    Date Book, 339

Parachute game, 44, 46
Party Shuffle feature, 102–103
PC and PCI cards, installing, 188–190
PDASmart
  battery services, 420
  replacement hard drives, 434
peer-to-peer file sharing, FurthurNET, 69
personal information managers (PIMs). *See* Calendar; Contacts
Photo Import, iPod and iPod Photo, 42–43
Photos command, 28
pick-and-pay method, iTunes Music Store shopping, 164–166
PIMs (personal information managers). *See* Calendar; Contacts
piracy of music. *See* music piracy
Play/Pause button, 19
playlists. *See also* Smart Playlists
  Anapod Explorer, 30, 206
  basics, 30–32
  creating
    from selected items, 78–79
    standard lists, 77–78
  EphPod, 30
  Musicmatch Jukebox, 30, 179–181
  On-The-Go, 32–34
  Party Shuffle feature, 102–103
  play count, 86–87
  Playlists command, 29
  printing jewel-case inserts, 103
  ratings, 24, 86
  recently played songs, 87
  Shuffle feature, 102
  updating automatically
    all songs and playlists, 89
    selected playlists, 90
  updating manually, 90–92
    checked songs only, 93
  XPlay, 30
Playlists command, 29
PocketDock mini-dock connector (Dr. Bott LLC), 371
PocketMac iPod Edition, 304–305
Pod 2 iPod (If Then Software), 272
PodFreq car adapters (Sonnet Technologies), 367–368
Pod2Go (Kevin Wojniak), 315
PodManager (Bruno Blondeau), 269–270
PodMaster 1000 (Flying Mouse Software), 271
PodWriter (Doug Steigerwald), 316
Portable Devices window (Musicmatch Jukebox), 207–210

power adapters. *See* accessories, connectors/adapters; accessories, power adapters
power conservation, batteries, 7–8
  Backlight Timer, 49–50
  iPod Photo TV Out, Off setting, 119
  major drains, 46
  Sleep Timer, 39
PowerDock adapters (Send Station), 372–373
PowerMate (Griffin Technology), 397
PowerPod Auto Adapter (Griffin Technology), 375
press*play* (defunct music subscription service), 124
Previous/Rewind buttons, 22
Previous Track button, battery power conservation, 7–8
ProVue Development's iPod Organizer, 278–279

# R

radio broadcast recordings, 71
  iTunes Music Store, 143
RadioLover (Bit Cartel), 71
ratings feature, 24
  iPod Photo, 107
Real Networks' RealPlayer format
  downloading/playing radio shows, 143
  purchasing music, 241
RealAudio files, 70
RealPlayer format (Real Networks)
  downloading/playing radio shows, 143
  purchasing music, 241
Recently Played Smart Playlist, 30
Red Chair Software's Anapod Explorer. *See* Anapod Explorer
The Red Ferret Journal, 68–69
remote controls. *See* iPod Remote Control
removable drive. *See also* iPod; iPod mini; iPod Photo; Windows iPod
  bootable iPods
    invisible music folder, 260–261
    limiting use, 259
    music sharing pros and cons, 261–262
    reasons for creating, 256–257
  data storage uses, 257–259
  FireWire technology, 244–246
  hot swapping, 244
  installing
    Mac OS 9, 247–249
    Mac OS X 10.1.x, 250–252
    Mac OS X 10.2.x, 253–256
    Mac OS X 10.3.x, 256
    minimum applications to low-capacity iPods, 246

## Index

iPod mini, 245–246
moving music
    Anapod Explorer, 275
    EphPod, 275
    file sharing pros and cons, 261–262
    iPod Tracks -> Desktop, 270–271
    manually with Mac OS 9, 263–265
    manually with Mac OS X, 265–267
    manually with Windows XP, 268–269
    OmniWeb, 272–273
    Open Pod, 273
    Pod 2 iPod, 272
    PodManager, 269–270
    PodMaster 1000, 271
    Senuti, 268–269
    XPlay 2, 274
Repeat settings, 49
ResEdit (Apple), 263
Reset All Settings, 54
resolution. *See* audio resolution
restocking fees, 11
ripping files
    from CDs (EphPod), 236
    iTunes, 61–64
    Musicmatch Jukebox, 202–203
    unrippable CDs, 28, 64
Rogue Amoeba's Audio Hijack/Audio Hijack Pro, 71, 123
RollingStone.com, 69

## S

S-Video ports (iPod Photo), 14, 109
    viewing photos, 120
scripts. *See* AppleScripts
scroll wheels, 20–21, 23–24
scrubbing audio, 24, 32
Secure Digital (SD) media type, 385
Select button, 24
Send Station's PowerDock, 372–373
Senuti (Whitney Young), 268–269
Sessions@AOL recordings, 132
Set Time Zone screen, 39
Settings screen, 28–29
    About, 47–48
    Audiobooks, 50
    Backlight Timer, 49–50
    Clicker, 53
    Contacts, 54
    Contrast, 53
    Date & Time, 53
    EQ (equalization), 52
    Language, 54

Legal, 54
Main Menu, 48
Repeat, 49
Reset All Settings, 54
Shuffle, 49
Sound Check, 52–53
shopping cart method, iTunes Music Store shopping, 167–170
Showcase (Contour Design), 360
Shuffle Photos command, 118
Shuffle Songs command, 28, 49, 55, 102
Shure's E3c and E5c headphones, 379
SiK
    FireJuice adapter, 190
    FireJuice and FireJuice 6 for iPod w/Dock Connector, 374
    HotWire cable, 378
    Imp auto charger, 375–376
SimpleSound voice recordings, 280
60's Music Smart Playlist, 30
skins, 362
skip protection, 15–16
Sleep Timer, 39
slideshows on TV (iPod Photo), 108–109
    no remote controls available, 391
    projecting photos, 120–122
    settings, 117–120
Small Dog Electronics' battery services, 420
Smart Playlists, 30. *See also* playlists
    AutoDJ, 213–214
    basics, 79–80, 85
    proposed lists, 81–84
    versions 4 and 4.5, 85
SmartMedia media type, 385
software license agreements, 2–3
Solitaire game, 44, 46–47
Songs screen, 36
Sonnet Technologies' PodFreq, 367–368
Sony MDR-V6 headphones, 381
Sony's Atrac format, 70
Sound Check, 52–53, 99–100
    battery power conservation, 7–8
    effectiveness debates, 100–101
    *versus* Musicmatch Jukebox's Volume Leveling feature, 212–213
Sound Recorder voice recordings, 282
SoundApp (Norman Franke), 70
SoundConverter (Steve Dekorte), 70–71
SoundDock (Bose), 394–395
SoundJam (Casady & Greene), 58
Source list, 29
SportSuit Basic, 4G (Marware), 358
SportSuit Convertible Case (Marware), 358

SportSuit Sleeve (Marware), 359
stealing music. *See* music piracy
Steigerwald, Doug; PodWriter, 316
stereo receivers
    European volume restrictions, 25–26
    plugging in iPod with Dock, 9
Stoer, Oliver; Outpod, 306
streaming audio
    across networks, 72–74
    Anapod Xtreamer feature, 230–231
    recording, 71

## T

TEN Technology's NaviPod wireless remote control, 391
Time setting
    12- or 24-hour clock, 40
    in Title screen, 40
TinkerTool (Marcel Bresink), 265–267
Tivoli Audio's iPAL AM/FM radio, 395
To Do items, 41–42, 312
Top 25 Most Played Smart Playlist, 30
TransPod car adapters (Lifestyle Outfitters), 370–371
troubleshooting all models of iPods
    absence of items, 403–407
    batteries
        battery-replacement services, 420
        battery self-repair, 420
    booting process
        failure to boot, 409–410
        unpleasant sounds, 411
    Diagnostic mode, 416
        iPod (first-, second-, and third-generation), 421–423
        iPod mini, 424–425
        iPods, fourth generation, 424–425
        iPod Photo, 426–428
    Disk Mode, 402
        forcing resets, 415
    "Do not disconnect" warning, 406, 413–414
    European volume controls, 416–417
    forcing resets, 415–416
    frozen iPods
        battery charging, 418–419
        Startup disk-scan icons, 421
    incorrect capacity, 408
    inside first- and second-generation iPods, 428–430
        disassembling, 430–433
    inside fourth-generation iPods and iPod Photo, 439, 446–447
    inside iPod mini, 440–442, 446–447
        alternate uses, 441
        disassembling, 443–446
    inside third-generation iPods, 435–437
        disassembling, 437–439, 446–447
    iPod Updater 2004-10-20, 407
    missing iPods, 402–403
    mixing generations, 407–408
    mounting iPods, 402–403
        click-wheel iPods, 412
    remote controls, 411
    Safe Mode, 402
    songs skipping, 15–16, 410–411
    tolerance level for abuse, 448
    upgrading hard drives, 433–434
    user-serviceable *versus* user-salvageable parts, 447
    warranties, 414
TuneCast/TuneCast II Mobile FM Transmitters (Belkin), 370
tutorials, 2
TV slideshows with iPod Photo, 108–109
    projecting photos, 120–122
    settings, 117–120

## U

Ultimate Ears' custom-fitted earpieces, 380
uncompressed
    *versus* compressed files, 65–67
    managing file formats, 70
Unity Electronics' battery services, 420
Universal Microphone Adapter (Belkin), 27, 39, 43, 383
USB 2.0 connectors/adapters, 6–7
    Dock Connector ports, 27
    iPod mini, 11–12
    USB 2.0 + FireWire cables, 190
    Windows iPod, 187–190

## V

vCal (vCalendar) standard/files, 328–330
vCard standard, 284–285
    PIMs and email applications supported, 285
.vcf files, hacking, 311–312
VersionTracker for listing of utilities, 269
video flip books with iPod Photo, 116
voice memos. *See* voice recordings

Voice Recorder for iPod with Dock Connector (Belkin), 27, 39, 382–383
  using with iTunes, 96
voice recordings
  AudioX, 280–281
  iTalk, 27, 43, 383
    using with iTunes, 96
  SimpleSound, 280
  Sound Recorder (Windows), 282
  third-party software, 27
    using with iTunes, 96
  Universal Microphone Adapter, 27, 39, 43, 383
  Voice Memos screen (iPod), 43–44, 360–363
  Voice Recorder for iPod with Dock Connector, 27, 39, 43, 382–383
    using with iTunes, 96
volume controls
  Anapod Explorer, 232
  European volume restrictions, 25–26
  iVolume, 100
  Musicmatch Jukebox, 212–213
  Sound Check, 52–53
    battery power conservation, 7–8
    effectiveness debates, 100–101
    iTunes, 99–100
    *versus* Musicmatch Jukebox's controls, 212–213
VoodooPad (Flying Meat), 323–326

# W

Walkman-style miniplugs (Griffin Technology), 363
warranties, 3
Waterfield Design
  iPod Case, 356
  iPod Gear Pouch, 359
  iPod inMotion Case, 356–357
WAV (Windows Audio Volume) format
  managing file formats, 70
  *versus* other formats, 65
  supported audio formats, 17–18
Westone Laboratories' custom earpieces fitting specific headphones, 380
WHQL (Windows hardware Quality Labs), 403
Windows
  downloading/playing audio books, 176–177
  iTunes for Windows, operating system and processor requirements, 61
  iTunes Music Store, basic requirements for using, 129
  synchronizing photos, iPod Photo, 112
  Windows hardware Quality Labs (WHQL), 403
Windows Audio Volume format. *See* WAV format
Windows iPod. *See also* iPod; iPod mini; iPod Photo
  Anapod Explorer
    Anapod Xtreamer, 230–231
    AudioMorph feature, 229
    basics, 223–224
    contacts, 232
    playing music, 230
    playlists, 232
    reasons for using, 234
    Recover Missing Tracks feature, 232
    similarity to Windows Explorer, 224–227
    transferring music to iPod, 227–229
    volume adjustments, 232
  EphPod
    alternative to iTunes, 232–233
    basics, 234–237
    Calendar Editor, 239
    contacts, 239
    memos, 239
    music piracy issues, 240
    news services, 240–241
    playlists, 239
    reasons for using, 234
    rippling files, 236
    setup, 233
    transferring music on/off iPod, 238–239
  history, 185–186
  *versus* iTunes, 18
  iTunes for Windows, converting Windows Media Player files to ACC format, 195
  iTunes Music Store, 186
    alternatives, 241
  Musicmatch Jukebox, 186
    basics, 200–201
    editing track information, 210–211
    installing/reinstalling, 197–198
    iPod Manager, 199–200
    playlists, 205–207
    playlists, AutoDJ, 213–214
    ripping CDs, 202–203
    shortcomings, 196
    transferring music into Jukebox, 203–204
    transferring music to iPod, 207–210
    Volume Leveling feature, 212–213
  OS Extended (HFS+) *versus* Windows FAT32 volumes, 16–17

Windows iPod *(continued)*
    PC installations/configurations
        basics, 187
        hardware connections, PC and PCI cards, 188–190
        registration, 194
        serial numbers, 194
        software, 190–195
    Windows Media Player (.wma) file conversion, 195
    XPlay
        basics, 214–215
        converting .wma files, 223
        copying music back to PCs, 220
        copying music with Windows Media Player, 220–223
        installing/configuring, 215–218
        reasons for using, 234
        transferring music to iPod, 218–220
Windows Media Player format. *See* WMA
WireTap (Ambrosia Software), 71
    downloading/playing radio shows, 143
WMA (Windows Media Player)
    converting to ACC format, 195
    converting to MP3, 223
    managing file types, 70
    not supported for iPods, 17–18
Wojniak, Kevin; Pod2Go, 315
World Travel Adapter Kit (Apple), 7, 373

# X

XPack for Windows XP (Intervideo), 223
XPlay (Mediafour)
    loading Apple Lossless Codec or ACC files on Window iPod, 18
    MacDrive, 233
    moving music using iPod as removable drive, 274
    playlists, 30
XtremeMac
    Deluxe iPod Case, 359
    Designer iPod Case, 359
    Get Connected Bundle, 371
    iPod Car Charger, 375
    iShare Earbud Splitter, 365, 371
    Xtremity iPod Accessory System, 359

# Y

Young, Whitney; Senuti, 268–269

# Z

Zapp, Michael
    iPod It, 313–314
    iSpeak It, 314–315